CLASSIC COUNTRY HOMES

Presenting 100 inspired country & farmhouse plans by Donald A. Gardner Architects, Inc.

A DESIGNS DIRECT PUBLISHING BOOK

Presented by

DONALD A. GARDNER
ARCHITECTS, INC.

Donald A. Gardner Architects, Inc.
150 Executive Center Drive, Suite 215
Greenville, SC 29615

Donald A. Gardner — CEO and Publisher
Angela Santerini — President
Kathleen Nalley — Editor
Bryan Polson — Graphic Artist
Paula Powers — Writer

Contributing Illustrators
Greg Havens
Barry Nathan
Architectural Art

Contributing Photographers
Matthew Scott Photographer, Inc.
Photographic Solutions
Riley & Riley Photography, Inc.
Stephen Stinson Photography
Windward Photography

Cover photo by Matthew Scott Photographer, Inc.
Interior accessories courtesy of Ruthie Millar, The Emporium, Greenville, SC
Printed by Toppan Printing Co., Hong Kong

First Printing, January 2004

10 9 8 7 6 5 4 3 2 1

 ISBN softcover: 1-932553-01-0.

Table of Contents

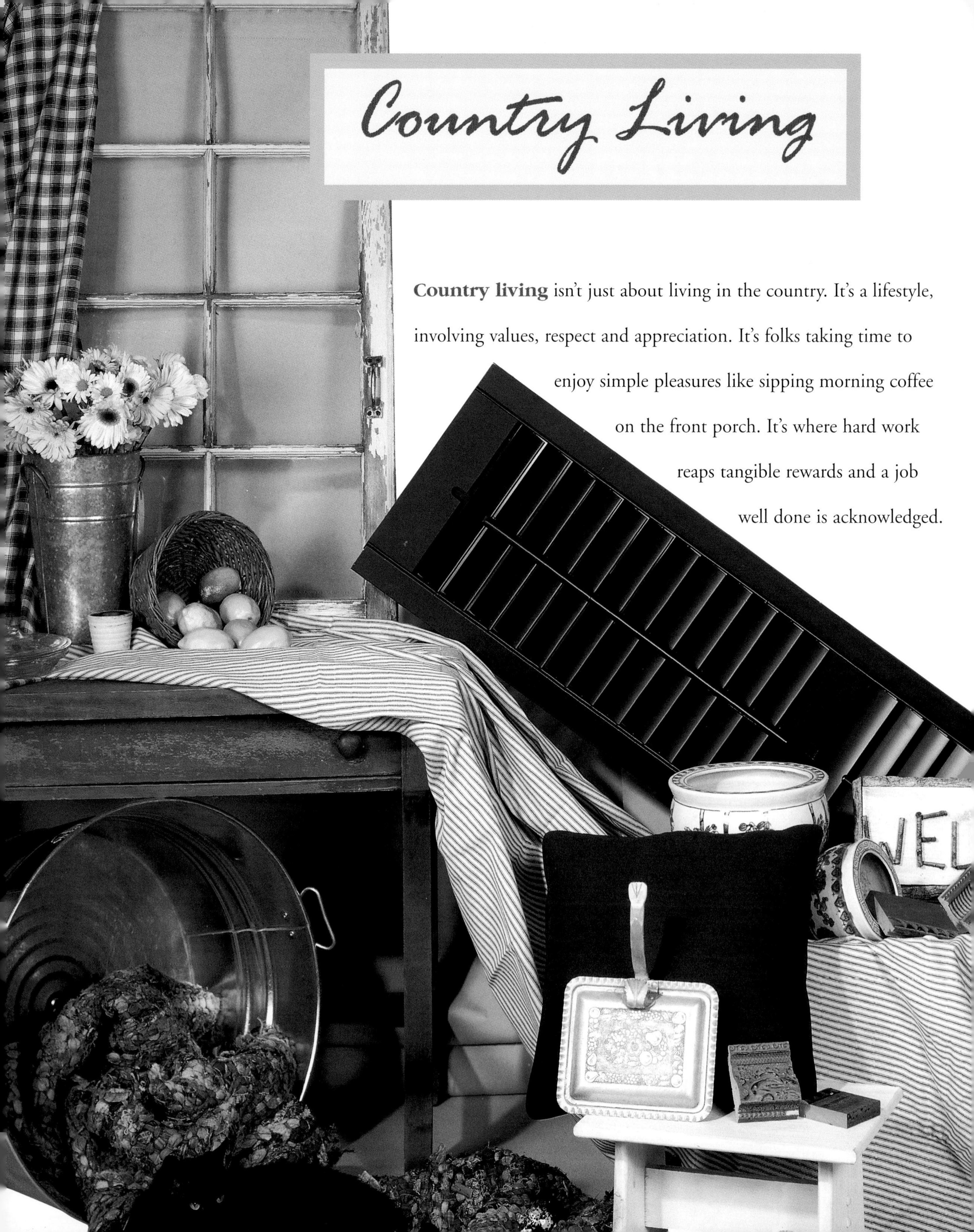

Country Living

Country living isn't just about living in the country. It's a lifestyle, involving values, respect and appreciation. It's folks taking time to enjoy simple pleasures like sipping morning coffee on the front porch. It's where hard work reaps tangible rewards and a job well done is acknowledged.

Country living allows people to get back to the basics — not just creeks and fields, but family, friends and community. It's where places and people balance multiple roles — a schoolhouse is a church house, a father is a son, a wife is a friend. It's where "thank you" and "you're welcome" are dished out like large portions of mashed potatoes around the dinner table and where neighbors make any excuse to have a gathering.

Country living doesn't rely on the stock ticker. It depends on the sun coming up, the rain watering the earth and the seasons changing. It trusts that roosters will crow, cows will give milk and fresh-cut roses placed on the dresser will smell sweet.

Country living is about making memories, never taking anything for granted and giving from the heart. It believes in a handshake and cherishes a smile. It knows nothing can replace late-night laughter with friends by the fireplace.

Country living embraces everyone — no matter who you are, who you've been or who you're going to be. It doesn't even matter where you came from or where you're going...Just be certain, regardless of whoever or wherever you are, if you've ever lived in the country, it leaves an impression you'll never forget and a longing that can't be filled by anything but living it.

Country style is different for every individual and region. It's personal — based on what you like and your surroundings. It's eclectic — a mixture of old and new — where you often find new uses for old things and distress new things to look old.

Country style borrows from nature. Generations of people have utilized their environment to build their homes. In the past, wood, stone and brick were staple elements both inside and out, while natural fabrics like cotton, wool and linen were popular for furniture coverings, bedding and window treatments. Consider how much of this is still true today.

Country style mimics the landscape. Colors once derived from berries, bark and flowers are now used, among other items, as inspiration for our palettes. A country home on the prairie might incorporate colors like wheat, clay or moss, while a country home on the coast might use sand, sky blue or jasmine. Think of the pale pinks and soft whites of wildflowers and the earthy colors of peat, cactus and rust. Look around for a color scheme that makes you comfortable and brings the outdoors inside.

Country style is about collecting and displaying. It's finding and pursuing your interests with objects. Antique fishing lures, tea sets and old cameras can be grouped together for impact or scattered throughout to continue a theme, but don't think you must pick one subject and only collect things within it.

The beauty of country collecting is randomness. Collect what makes you feel good.

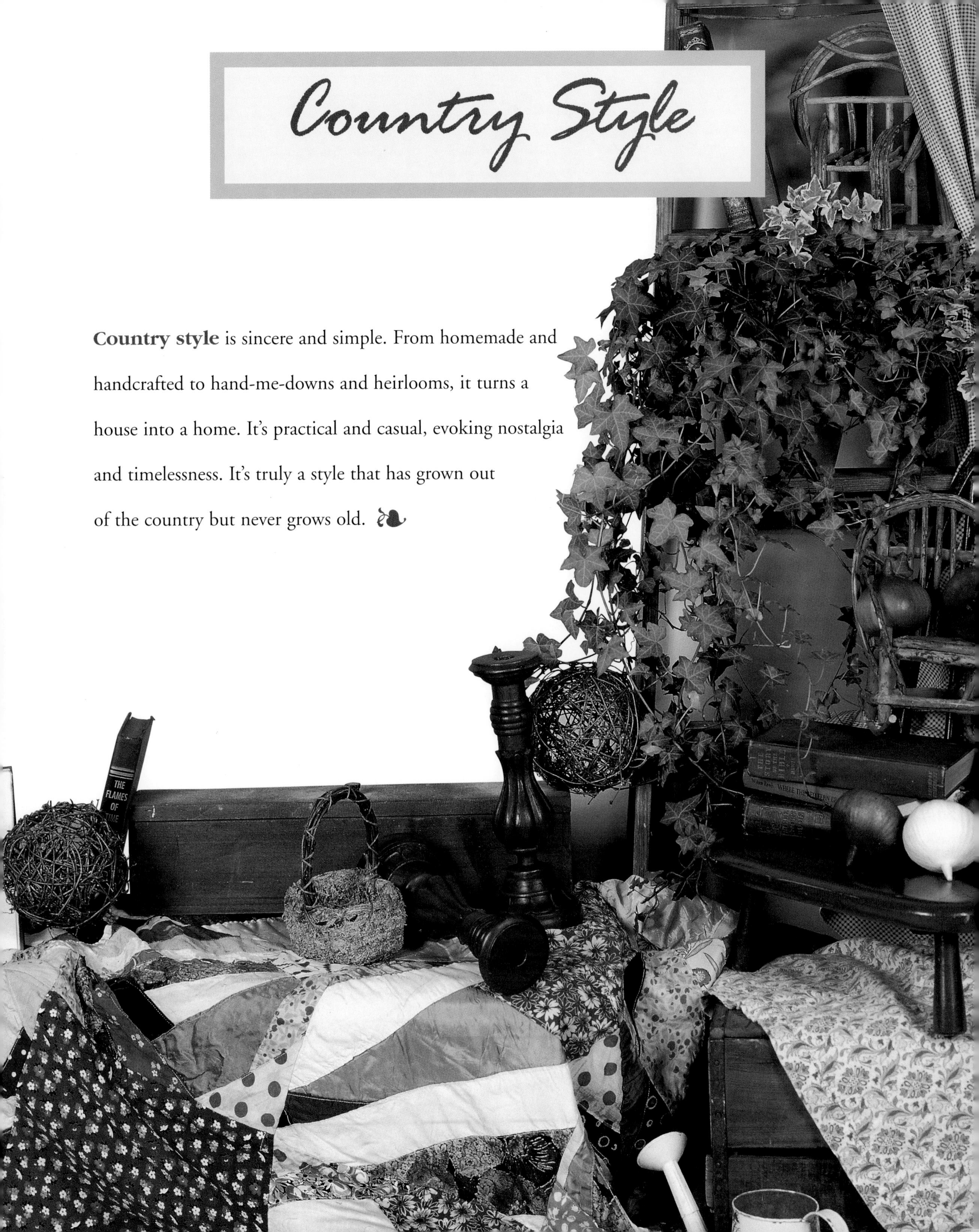
THE
FLAMES
OF
TIME

Country Style

Country style is sincere and simple. From homemade and handcrafted to hand-me-downs and heirlooms, it turns a house into a home. It's practical and casual, evoking nostalgia and timelessness. It's truly a style that has grown out of the country but never grows old.

Bringing the Country Home

Country living and **country style** revolve around one thing — the home. The country home is the one place that reflects you, your family and your land. It's more than a shelter; it's where dreams are harvested and memories stored. Whether you're looking for a classic country home or farmhouse, the purpose of this book is to provide you with the best of what country has to offer. Page after page is filled with homes that create a sense of place and purpose. And what sums up country better than Room To Roam, Hidden Spaces, Framing Views and Shady Spots?

Room To Roam • Featuring open floorplans and volume spaces, the *Room To Roam* section includes family-efficient homes that incorporate natural traffic flows, step-saving designs and architectural elements used to define rooms without enclosing space.

Hidden Spaces • Versatility is key to families and their changing needs, which is why the *Hidden Spaces* section provides homes with bonus rooms that can be transformed into family retreats, additional bedrooms or workspaces, among others.

Framing Views • The *Framing Views* section blurs the lines between indoor and outdoor living by integrating glasswork — such as dormers, transoms and French doors — that captures breath-taking scenery and invites natural light inside each home.

Shady Spots • Covered porches, screen porches and decks — no country home would be complete without at least one, and since much of the country life involves relaxation and entertainment, the *Shady Spots* section is dedicated to homes that promote outdoor living.

So please sit back, take your shoes off and make yourself at home. ❧

Neighborly Advice

Just because a floorplan is open and has volume spaces doesn't mean it's family-efficient. Family-efficiency requires a natural traffic flow, step-saving design and the incorporation of beautiful, functional architectural elements. In this section, you'll discover floorplans that meet these requirements. Here's what to look for:

Family-efficiency relates to grouping rooms for accessibility, complementing the way families live. A natural traffic flow doesn't force family members to go out of their way to reach gathering rooms nor do a lot of backtracking before going to another room. Step-saving promotes convenience by having rooms and appliances where needed, reducing the number of steps it takes to complete tasks. Step-saving also works with architectural elements like columns, allowing someone to cut corners by walking through rooms instead of around walls. Other elements include decorative ceilings that define rooms without enclosing space, bay windows that extend space and built-ins that provide organization and hide clutter.

ROOM TO ROAM

BLESS THIS HOUSE

ROOM TO ROAM

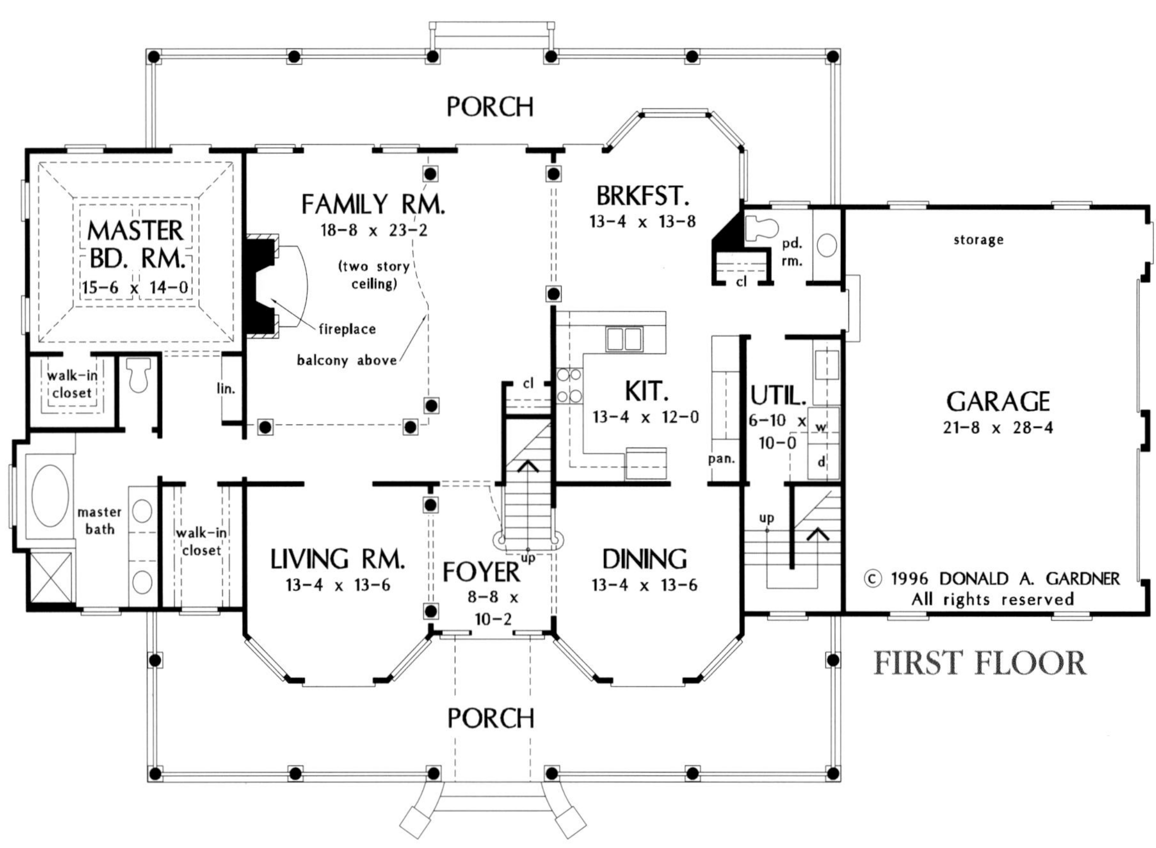
PORCH
MASTER BD. RM. 15–6 x 14–0
walk-in closet
lin.
master bath
walk-in closet
FAMILY RM. 18–8 x 23–2
(two story ceiling)
fireplace
balcony above
BRKFST. 13–4 x 13–8
pd. rm.
cl
storage
cl
KIT. 13–4 x 12–0
UTIL. 6–10 x 10–0
w
d
pan.
GARAGE 21–8 x 28–4
up
LIVING RM. 13–4 x 13–6
FOYER 8–8 x 10–2
up
DINING 13–4 x 13–6
© 1996 DONALD A. GARDNER All rights reserved
PORCH

FIRST FLOOR

DPCCH-452
The Arbordale

Total Living: 3163 sq. ft.

First Floor: 2086 sq. ft.

Second Floor: 1077 sq. ft.

Bonus Room: 403 sq. ft.

4 Bedrooms, 3-1/2 Baths

Foundation: Crawlspace

Width: 81'10"

Depth: 51'8"

Price Category: F

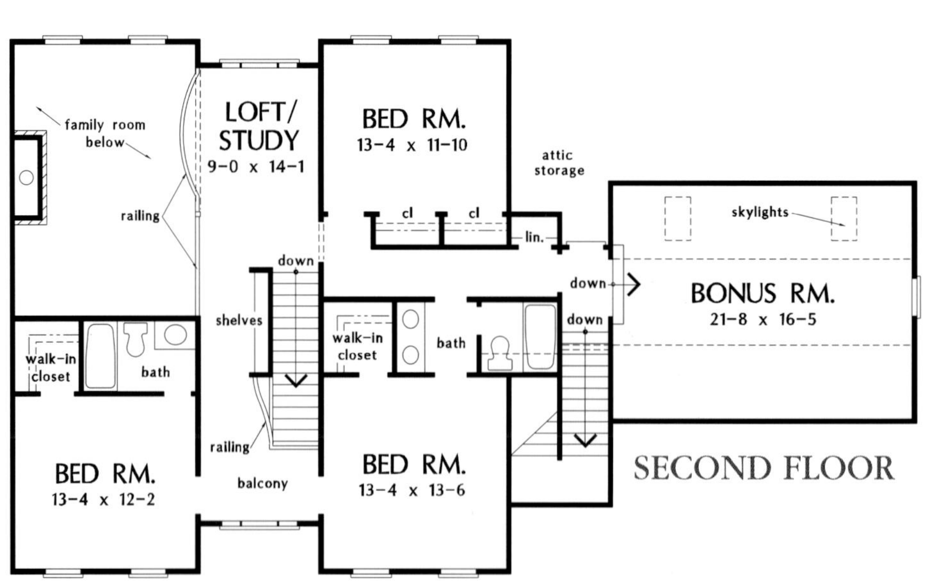
family room below
railing
LOFT/ STUDY 9–0 x 14–1
BED RM. 13–4 x 11–10
attic storage
cl
cl
lin.
skylights
down
down
BONUS RM. 21–8 x 16–5
shelves
walk-in closet
bath
walk-in closet
bath
railing
balcony
BED RM. 13–4 x 12–2
BED RM. 13–4 x 13–6

SECOND FLOOR

DESIGNER NOTE: *"We drew upon the traditional, grand farmhouse with its wide front porch and wrapped this exterior around contemporary, open, two-story spaces."*

My husband and I believe in supporting the local Feed & Seed store. They have everything from tiller replacement parts to baby chickens. They even have a "swap or sell" bulletin board for people who trade or sell antiques, livestock and other things. We purchased several antiques through that board, and we sell fresh honey through our own posting.

The Arbordale

REAR

Photographed home may have been modified from the original construction documents.

ROOM TO ROAM

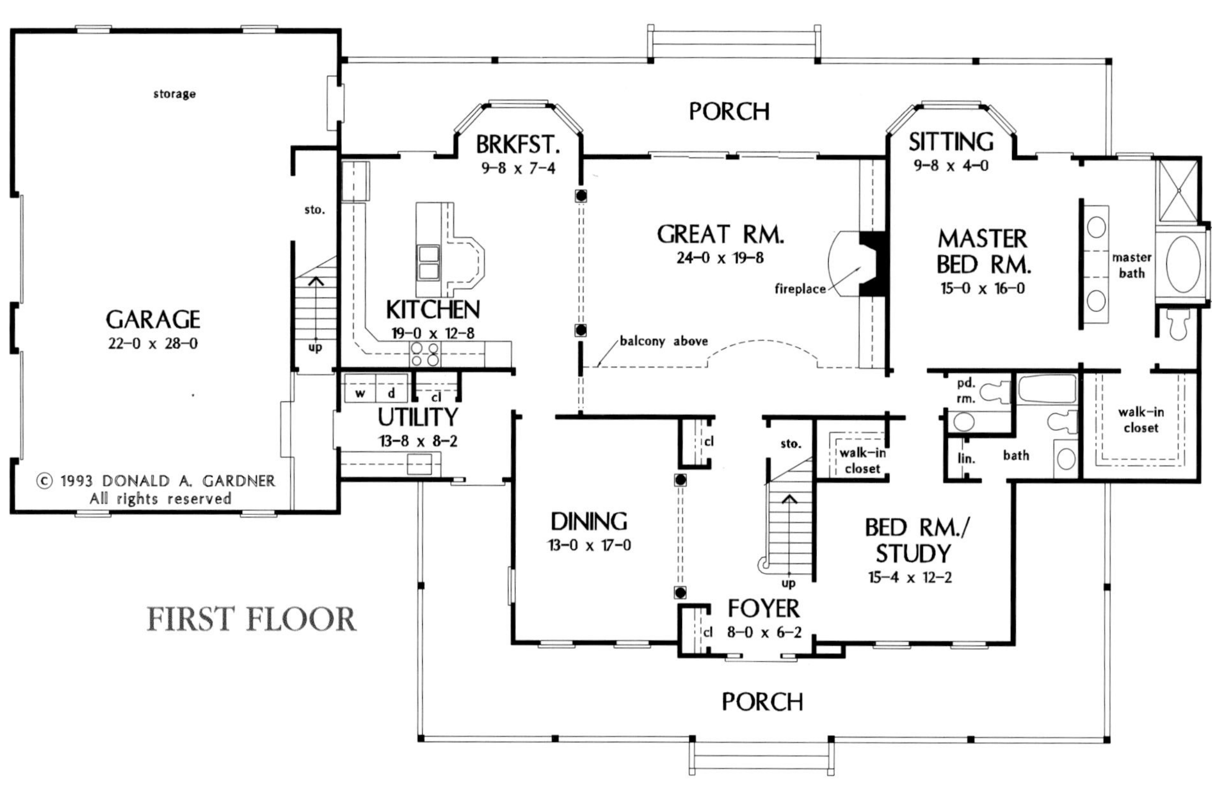

storage
GARAGE
22-0 x 28-0
sto.
up
BRKFST.
9-8 x 7-4
KITCHEN
19-0 x 12-8
w
d
cl
UTILITY
13-8 x 8-2
PORCH
GREAT RM.
24-0 x 19-8
fireplace
balcony above
SITTING
9-8 x 4-0
MASTER
BED RM.
15-0 x 16-0
master
bath
pd.
rm.
walk-in
closet
lin.
bath
cl
sto.
walk-in
closet
DINING
13-0 x 17-0
up
BED RM./
STUDY
15-4 x 12-2
FOYER
8-0 x 6-2
cl
PORCH
© 1993 DONALD A. GARDNER
All rights reserved

FIRST FLOOR

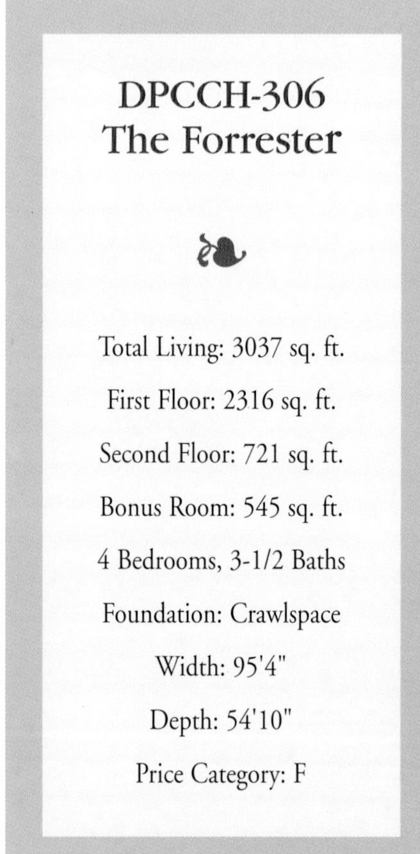

DPCCH-306
The Forrester

Total Living: 3037 sq. ft.

First Floor: 2316 sq. ft.

Second Floor: 721 sq. ft.

Bonus Room: 545 sq. ft.

4 Bedrooms, 3-1/2 Baths

Foundation: Crawlspace

Width: 95'4"

Depth: 54'10"

Price Category: F

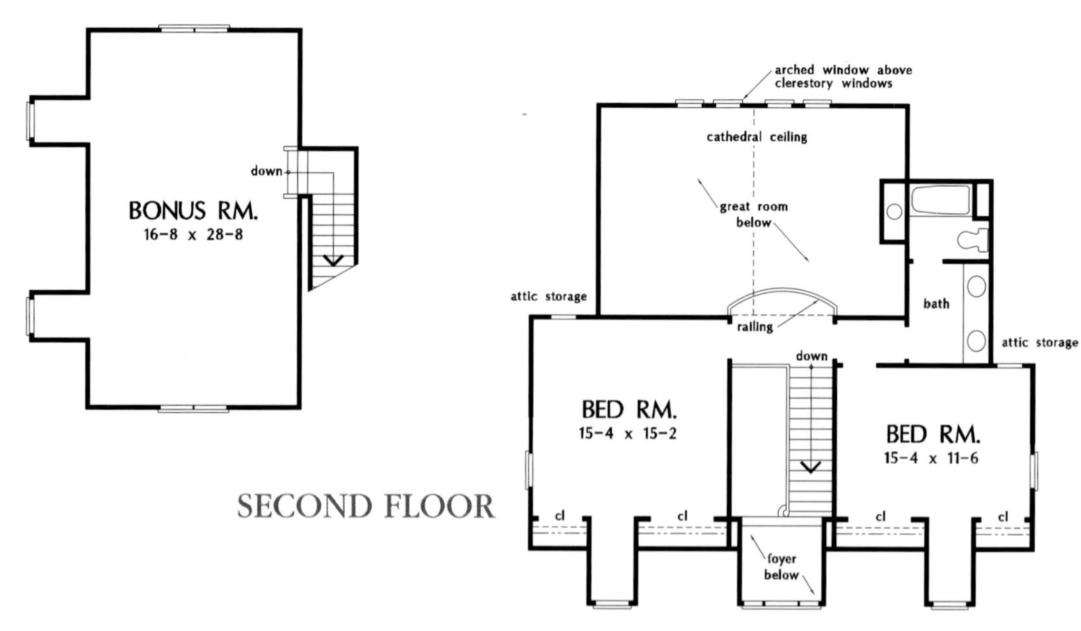

down
BONUS RM.
16-8 x 28-8
arched window above
clerestory windows
cathedral ceiling
great room
below
attic storage
railing
bath
attic storage
down
BED RM.
15-4 x 15-2
BED RM.
15-4 x 11-6
cl
cl
cl
cl
foyer
below

SECOND FLOOR

DESIGNER NOTE: *"This design focuses on the family's tendency to gather naturally in the oversized great room and spill into the kitchen/breakfast area or generous front and back porches."*

My husband used to comment that there weren't as many community get-togethers or socials as there were when he was a boy, so we've started our own. Every year we host a large neighborhood theme party. Next time he wants to throw a barn dance or hoedown. I'm not exactly sure what he's planning, but I know it will be lots of fun.

The Forrester

REAR

Photographed home may have been modified from the original construction documents.

ROOM TO ROAM

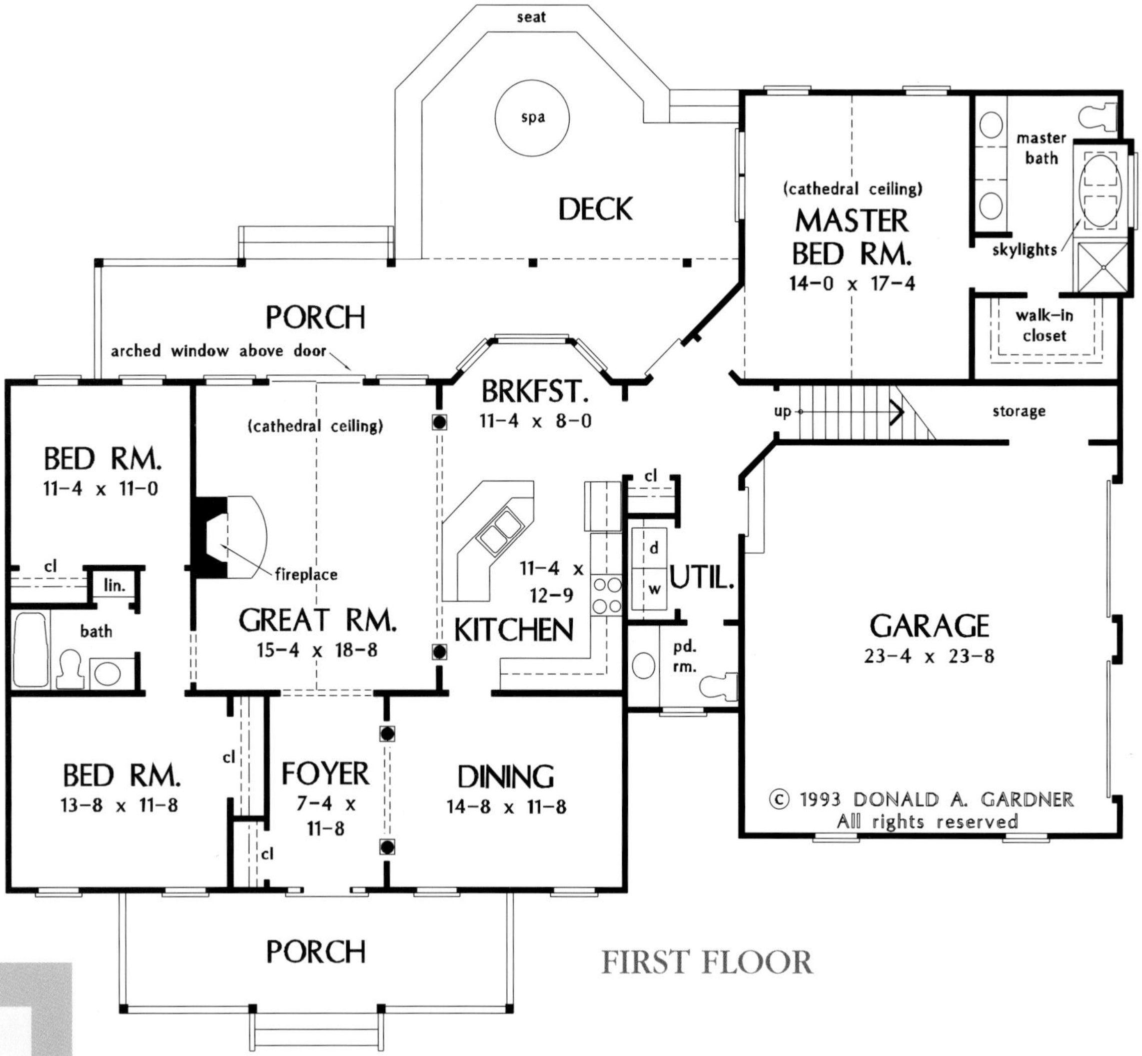

seat
spa
DECK
PORCH
arched window above door
(cathedral ceiling)
MASTER BED RM.
14-0 x 17-4
master bath
skylights
walk-in closet
BRKFST.
11-4 x 8-0
up
storage
BED RM.
11-4 x 11-0
(cathedral ceiling)
fireplace
cl
lin.
bath
GREAT RM.
15-4 x 18-8
cl
d
w
UTIL.
11-4 x 12-9
KITCHEN
pd. rm.
GARAGE
23-4 x 23-8
BED RM.
13-8 x 11-8
cl
FOYER
7-4 x 11-8
cl
DINING
14-8 x 11-8

PORCH

FIRST FLOOR

DPCCH-294
The Pennyhill

Total Living: 1864 sq. ft.

Bonus Room: 420 sq. ft.

3 Bedrooms, 2-1/2 Baths

Foundation: Crawlspace

Width: 71'

Depth: 56'4"

Price Category: C

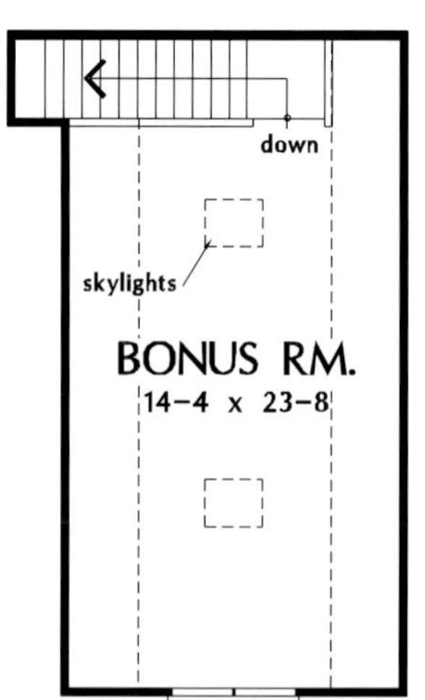
down
skylights
BONUS RM.
14-4 x 23-8

DESIGNER NOTE: *"We wanted to create an efficient, yet stately home that felt much bigger than it was and would complement any neighborhood."*

Call me biased, but country cooking is my favorite cuisine. It always has been. I remember coming home from school, and as soon as I neared the kitchen, I would walk into the aroma of hot peach cobbler, vegetable soup or something wonderful my mother had made.

The Pennyhill

REAR

Photographed home may have been modified from the original construction documents.

ROOM TO ROAM

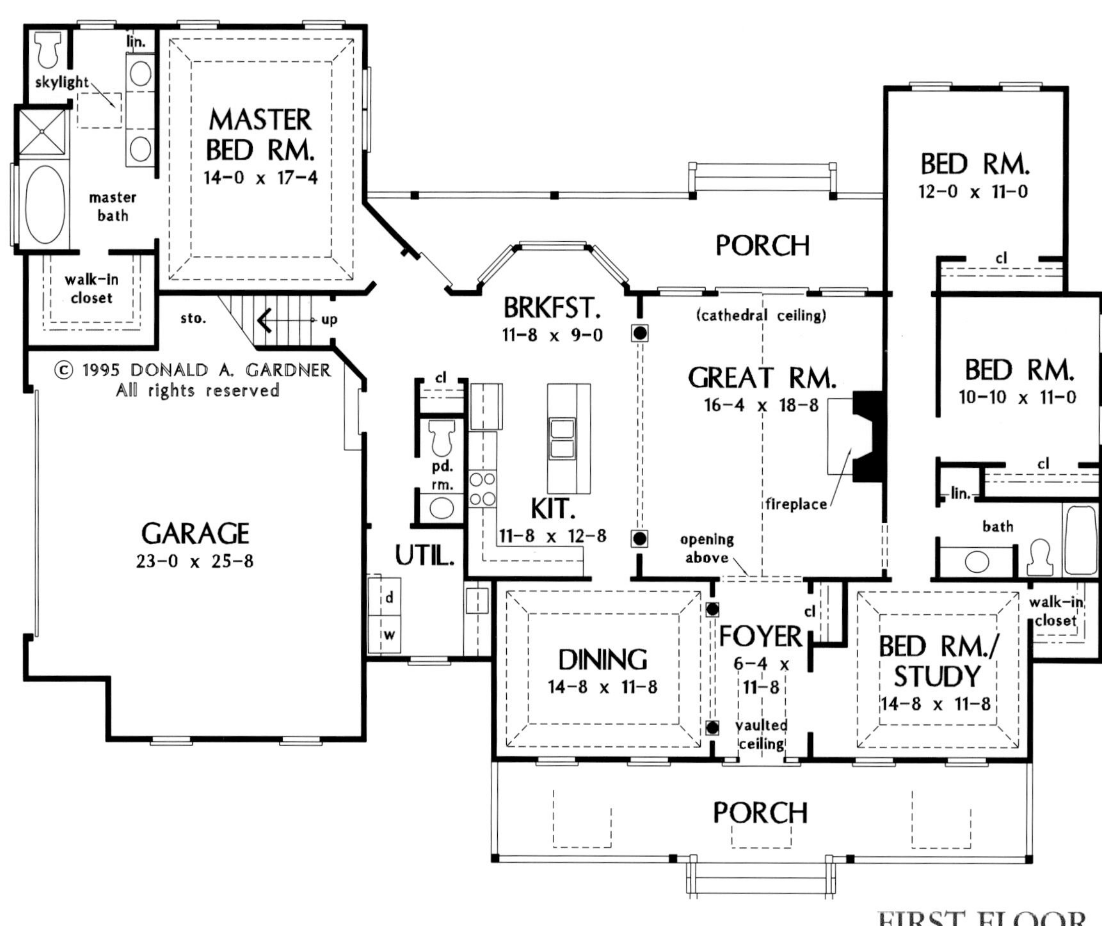
MASTER BED RM.
14-0 x 17-4
lin.
skylight
master bath
walk-in closet
sto.
up
© 1995 DONALD A. GARDNER
All rights reserved
GARAGE
23-0 x 25-8
PORCH
BRKFST.
11-8 x 9-0
(cathedral ceiling)
GREAT RM.
16-4 x 18-8
fireplace
opening above
cl
pd. rm.
KIT.
11-8 x 12-8
UTIL.
d
w
BED RM.
12-0 x 11-0
cl
BED RM.
10-10 x 11-0
cl
lin.
bath
walk-in closet
DINING
14-8 x 11-8
FOYER
6-4 x 11-8
vaulted ceiling
cl
BED RM./ STUDY
14-8 x 11-8
PORCH

FIRST FLOOR

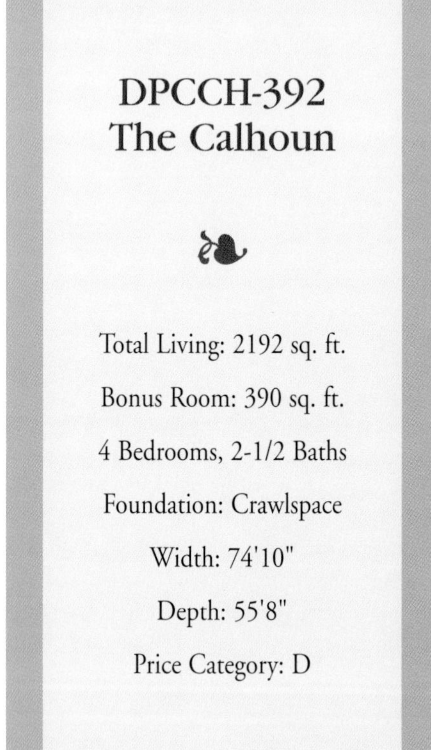

DPCCH-392
The Calhoun

Total Living: 2192 sq. ft.

Bonus Room: 390 sq. ft.

4 Bedrooms, 2-1/2 Baths

Foundation: Crawlspace

Width: 74'10"

Depth: 55'8"

Price Category: D

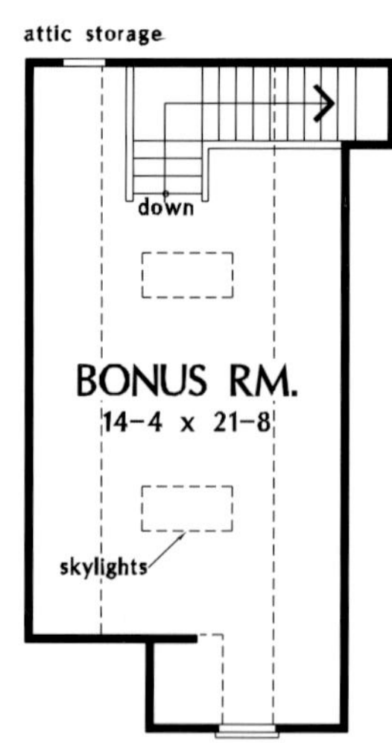
attic storage
down
BONUS RM.
14-4 x 21-8
skylights

DESIGNER NOTE: *"We took a successful design solution and made it more appealing by adding a flex space for the growing family."*

My son once caught a little bird, which he brought into the house to show me. He asked me to close my eyes and hold out my hands. When he placed the bird in my hands, it startled me. I let out a scream and up went the bird. We chased the little bird all over the house for quite a while until he flew out the door.

The Calhoun

REAR

ROOM TO ROAM

DESIGNER NOTE: *"Traditional neighborhood design inspired this plan with its rear garage and inviting front porch."*

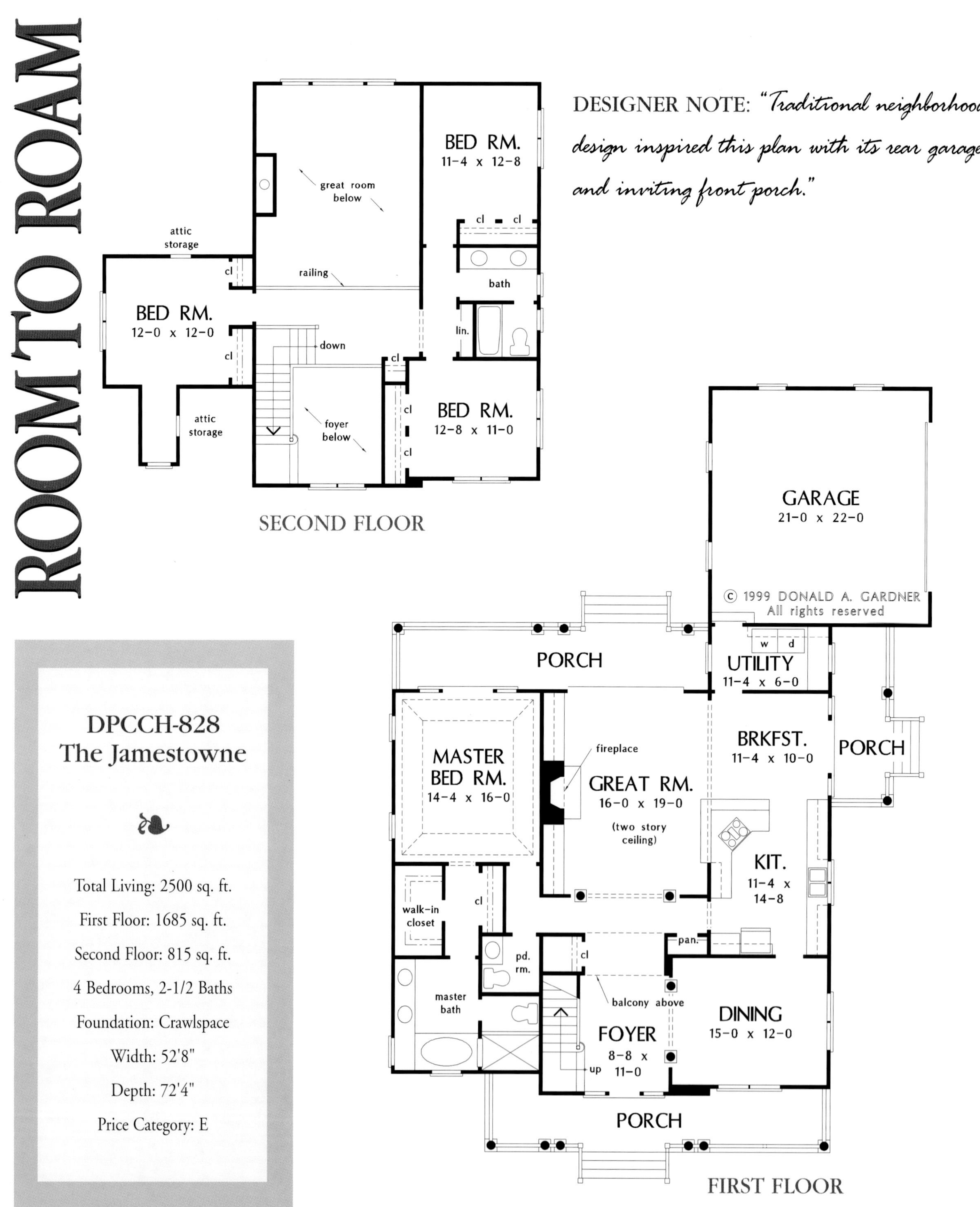

attic storage
BED RM.
12-0 x 12-0
cl
cl
attic storage
great room below
railing
down
foyer below
cl
BED RM.
11-4 x 12-8
cl
cl
bath
lin.
cl
cl
BED RM.
12-8 x 11-0
SECOND FLOOR
GARAGE
21-0 x 22-0
© 1999 DONALD A. GARDNER
All rights reserved
PORCH
w
d
UTILITY
11-4 x 6-0
MASTER BED RM.
14-4 x 16-0
fireplace
GREAT RM.
16-0 x 19-0
(two story ceiling)
BRKFST.
11-4 x 10-0
PORCH
KIT.
11-4 x 14-8
walk-in closet
cl
pd. rm.
cl
pan.
master bath
balcony above
FOYER
8-8 x 11-0
up
DINING
15-0 x 12-0
PORCH
FIRST FLOOR

DPCCH-828
The Jamestowne

Total Living: 2500 sq. ft.

First Floor: 1685 sq. ft.

Second Floor: 815 sq. ft.

4 Bedrooms, 2-1/2 Baths

Foundation: Crawlspace

Width: 52'8"

Depth: 72'4"

Price Category: E

When we bought our first house, we inherited the grandfather clock. It came from my husband's side of the family and is very special to us. As we were looking to build, we kept the clock in mind. Now that we're in our new house, our prized clock sits in a prominent place where you can see it from several rooms at a time.

The Jamestowne

REAR

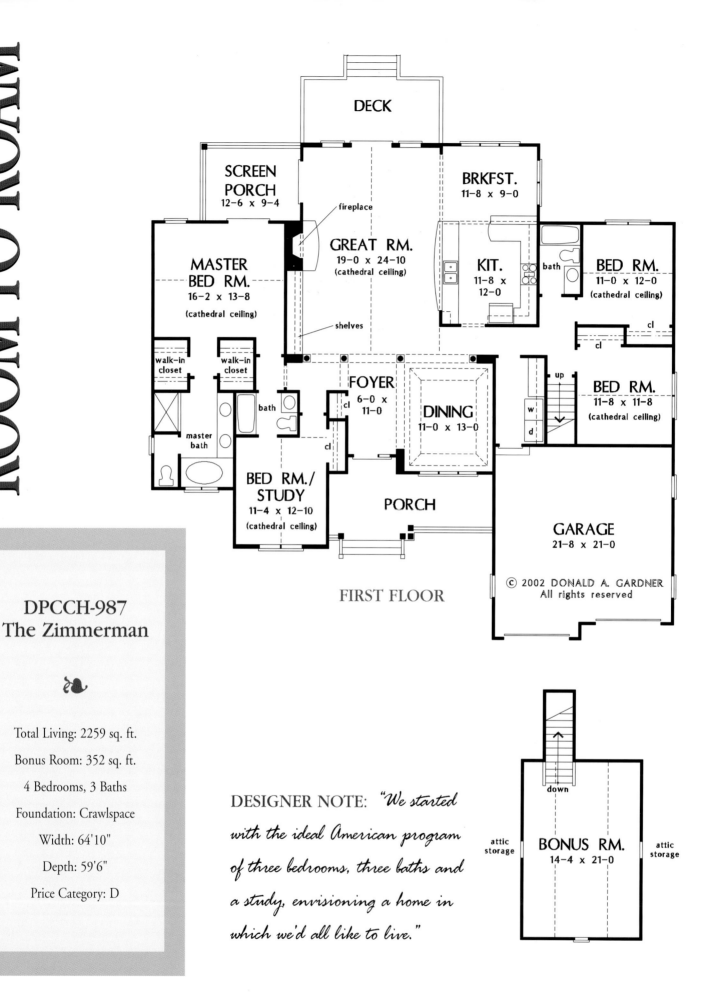

ROOM TO ROAM

DECK

SCREEN PORCH
12-6 x 9-4

BRKFST.
11-8 x 9-0

fireplace

GREAT RM.
19-0 x 24-10
(cathedral ceiling)

MASTER BED RM.
16-2 x 13-8
(cathedral ceiling)

KIT.
11-8 x 12-0

bath

BED RM.
11-0 x 12-0
(cathedral ceiling)

shelves

cl

walk-in closet

walk-in closet

FOYER
6-0 x 11-0

cl

DINING
11-0 x 13-0

up

BED RM.
11-8 x 11-8
(cathedral ceiling)

bath

w

d

master bath

cl

BED RM./ STUDY
11-4 x 12-10
(cathedral ceiling)

PORCH

GARAGE
21-8 x 21-0

FIRST FLOOR

DPCCH-987
The Zimmerman

Total Living: 2259 sq. ft.

Bonus Room: 352 sq. ft.

4 Bedrooms, 3 Baths

Foundation: Crawlspace

Width: 64'10"

Depth: 59'6"

Price Category: D

down

attic storage

BONUS RM.
14-4 x 21-0

attic storage

DESIGNER NOTE: *"We started with the ideal American program of three bedrooms, three baths and a study, envisioning a home in which we'd all like to live."*

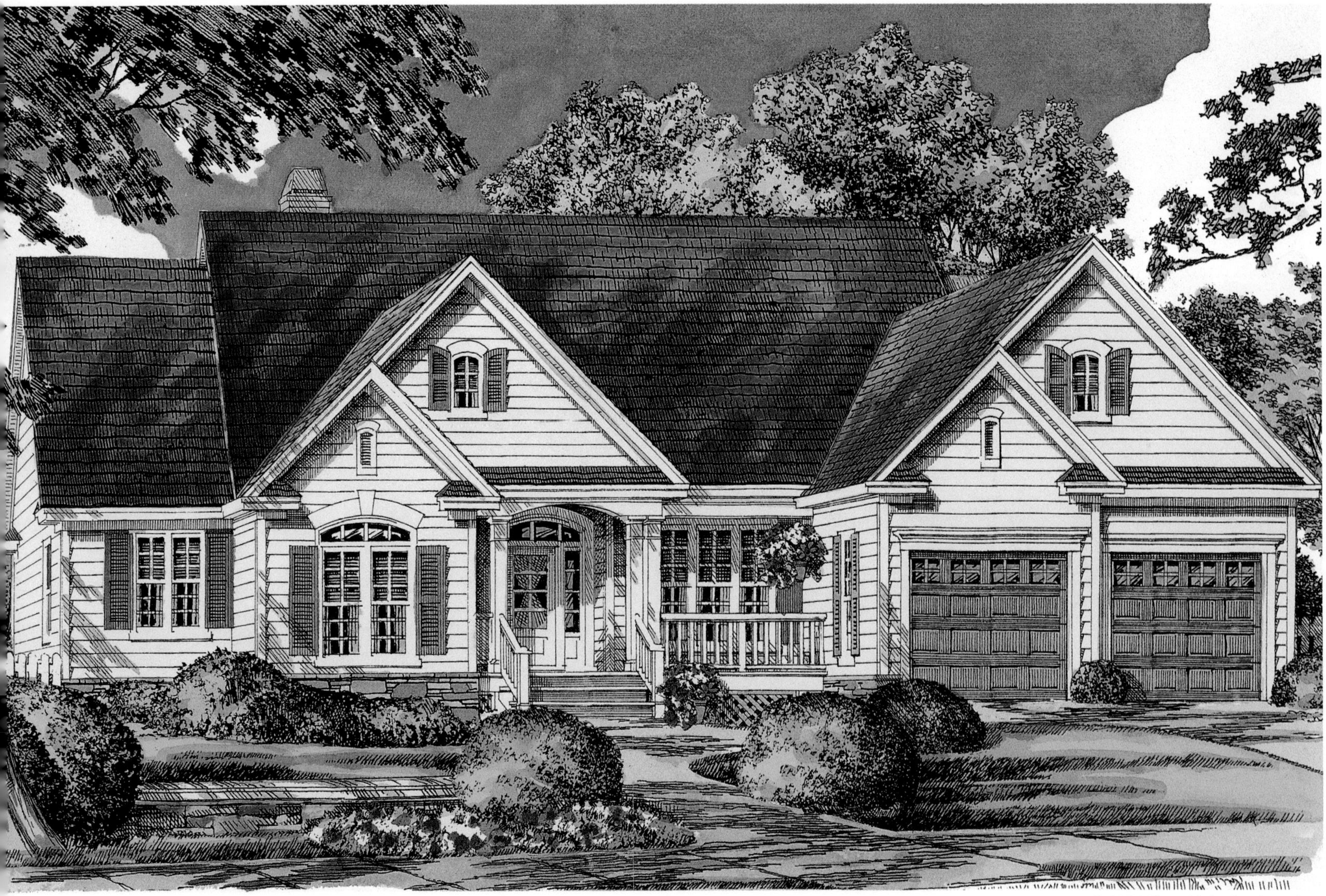

My wife loves fireplaces, and there's nothing quite as relaxing as sitting by the fire enjoying conversation or a good book. But what I like most about the fireplace is the way it adds a cozy feeling to all of the gathering rooms. You can enjoy it while having coffee in the breakfast area, cooking in the kitchen or eating in the dining room.

The Zimmerman

REAR

ROOM TO ROAM

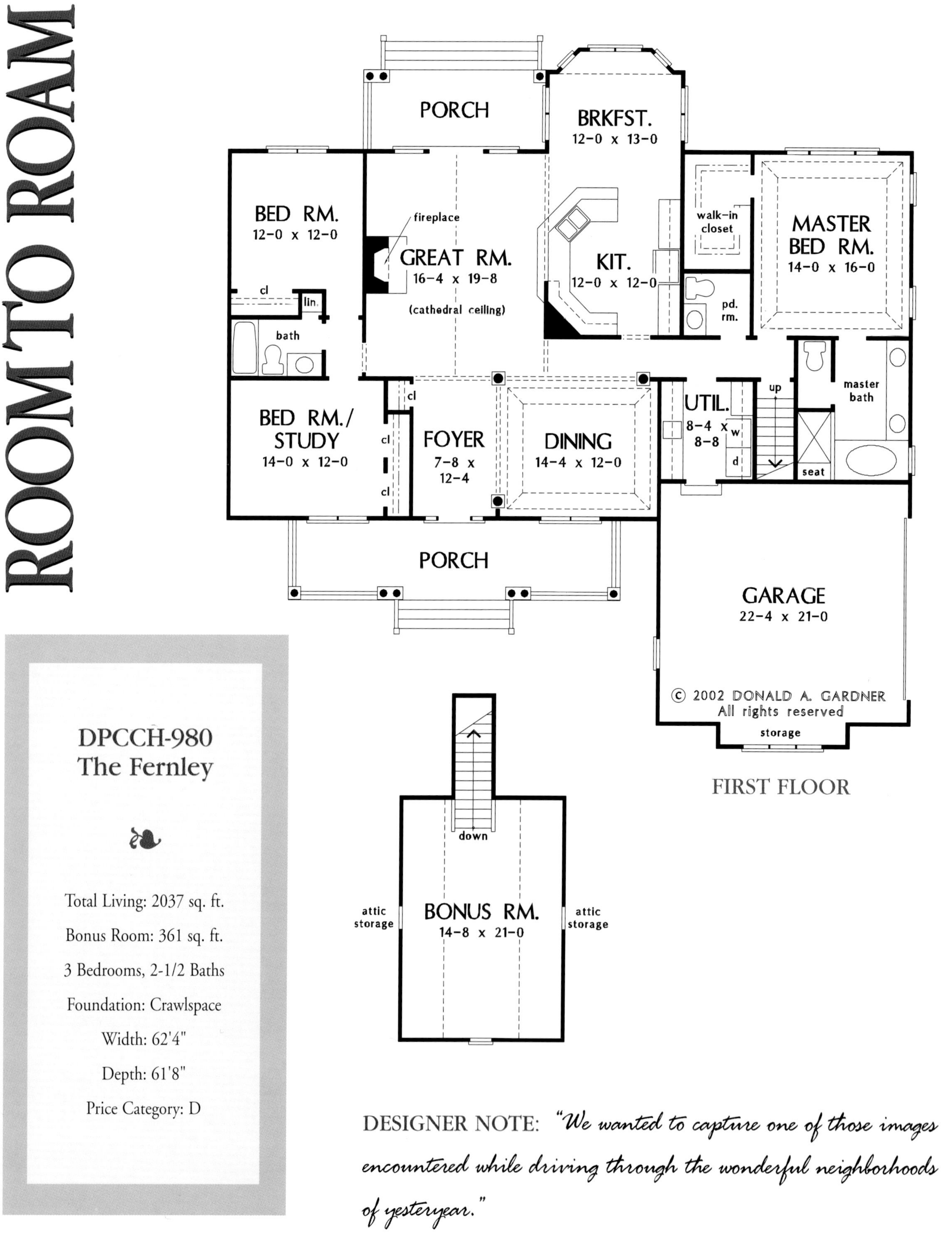
PORCH
BRKFST.
12-0 x 13-0
BED RM.
12-0 x 12-0
fireplace
GREAT RM.
16-4 x 19-8
(cathedral ceiling)
KIT.
12-0 x 12-0
walk-in
closet
MASTER
BED RM.
14-0 x 16-0
cl
lin.
bath
pd.
rm.
up
master
bath
cl
BED RM./
STUDY
14-0 x 12-0
cl
cl
FOYER
7-8 x
12-4
DINING
14-4 x 12-0
UTIL.
8-4 x
8-8
w
d
seat
PORCH
GARAGE
22-4 x 21-0
© 2002 DONALD A. GARDNER
All rights reserved
storage
FIRST FLOOR
down
attic
storage
BONUS RM.
14-8 x 21-0
attic
storage

DPCCH-980
The Fernley

Total Living: 2037 sq. ft.

Bonus Room: 361 sq. ft.

3 Bedrooms, 2-1/2 Baths

Foundation: Crawlspace

Width: 62'4"

Depth: 61'8"

Price Category: D

DESIGNER NOTE: *"We wanted to capture one of those images encountered while driving through the wonderful neighborhoods of yesteryear."*

Canning used to be a big event at our house. It would take days of preparation. Then a whole Saturday would be devoted to boiling the mason jars, filling them and sealing them properly. If we'd only had a breakfast nook connected to the kitchen back then, but at that time no one knew what a breakfast nook was.

The Fernley

REAR

ROOM TO ROAM

MASTER BED RM. 13-0 x 15-10 (cathedral ceiling)
seat
master bath
lin.
walk-in closet
UTILITY 7-4 x 6-0
d w
PORCH
seat
BRKFST. 12-0 x 9-4
GREAT RM. 16-0 x 19-0 (two story ceiling)
fireplace
KITCHEN 12-0 x 13-0
GARAGE 22-8 x 22-4
pd. rm.
up
DINING 12-0 x 13-4
FOYER 5-8 x 8-4
cl
PORCH

FIRST FLOOR

DESIGNER NOTE:

"When we designed this home we were thinking of an efficient, two-story floor plan that lived big and showed big from the outside."

DPCCH-1000
The Topeka

Total Living: 2064 sq. ft.

First Floor: 1562 sq. ft.

Second Floor: 502 sq. ft.

Bonus Room: 416 sq. ft.

3 Bedrooms, 2-1/2 Baths

Foundation: Crawlspace

Width: 54'

Depth: 55'10"

Price Category: D

BED RM. 12-0 x 11-0
attic storage
great room below
cl
lin.
bath
BONUS RM. 22-8 x 16-2
railing
down
down
shelf
cl cl
attic storage
foyer below
shelf
BED RM. 12-0 x 11-0

SECOND FLOOR

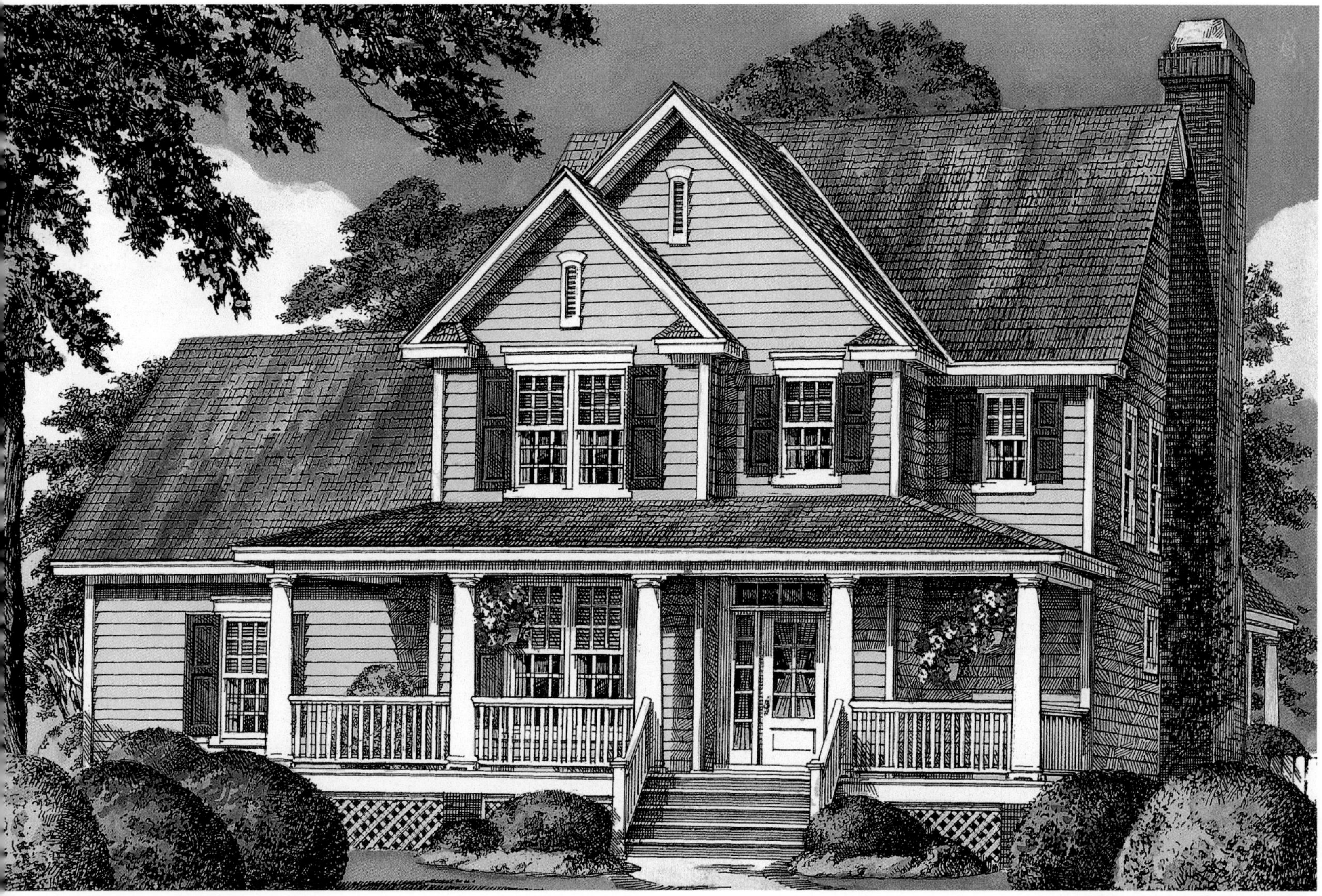

My dream had always been to live in the house I grew up in again, but when I moved back to my hometown, the house wasn't there anymore. I bought the property anyway and waited to build the perfect house. I was overjoyed when I found this one. It reminds me so much of my childhood home, but it's more open.

The Topeka

REAR

ROOM TO ROAM

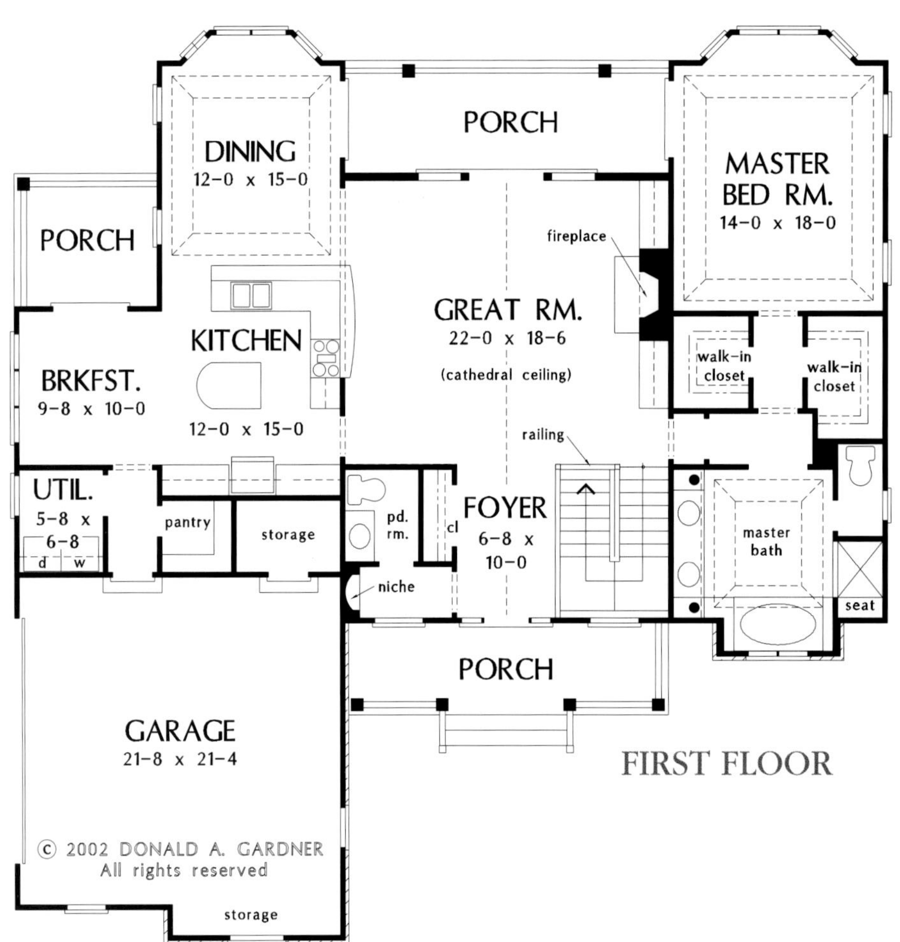
PORCH
DINING
12-0 x 15-0
MASTER
BED RM.
14-0 x 18-0
PORCH
fireplace
KITCHEN
GREAT RM.
22-0 x 18-6
(cathedral ceiling)
BRKFST.
9-8 x 10-0
12-0 x 15-0
walk-in
closet
walk-in
closet
railing
UTIL.
5-8 x
6-8
d
w
pantry
storage
pd.
rm.
cl
FOYER
6-8 x
10-0
master
bath
niche
seat
PORCH
GARAGE
21-8 x 21-4
FIRST FLOOR
© 2002 DONALD A. GARDNER
All rights reserved
storage

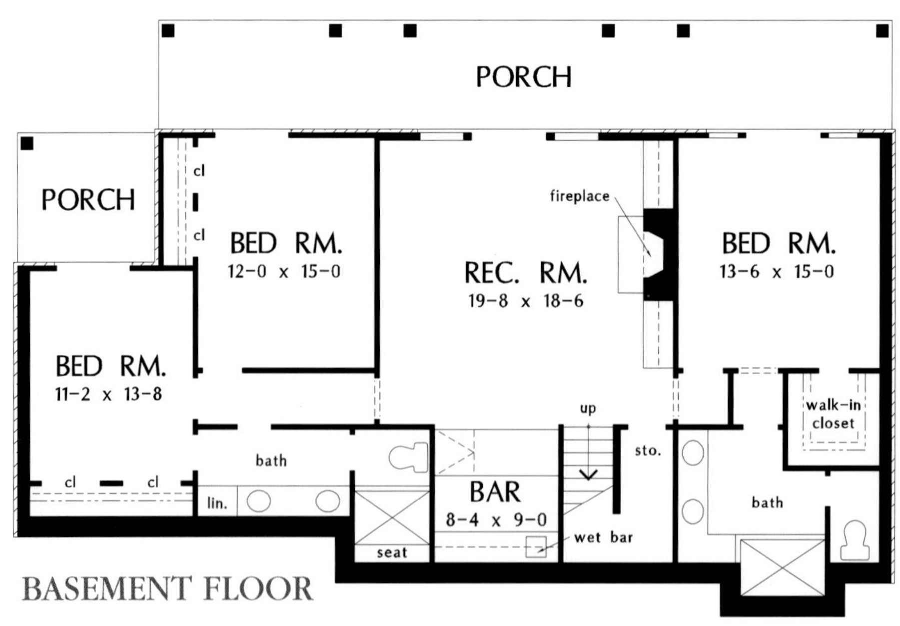
PORCH
PORCH
cl
cl
fireplace
BED RM.
12-0 x 15-0
REC. RM.
19-8 x 18-6
BED RM.
13-6 x 15-0
BED RM.
11-2 x 13-8
up
walk-in
closet
sto.
bath
cl
cl
lin.
BAR
8-4 x 9-0
bath
seat
wet bar
BASEMENT FLOOR

DPCCH-995
The Laycrest

Total Living: 3320 sq. ft.

First Floor: 1720 sq. ft.

Basement Floor: 1600 sq. ft.

4 Bedrooms, 3-1/2 Baths

Foundation: Hillside Walkout

Width: 59'

Depth: 59'4

Price Category: F

DESIGNER NOTE: *"We pictured this home on a gorgeous hillside lot, where multiple guest rooms would come in handy."*

Americana and Folk Art has grown from rural life. It's nostalgic, evoking sentiment and simplicity. Sometimes it's quirky — sometimes serious. From sculpture made from tractor parts to American Gothic paintings, it interprets and often recreates country life. We love collecting pieces and use our home as a gallery to showcase our passion.

The Laycrest

REAR

ROOM TO ROAM

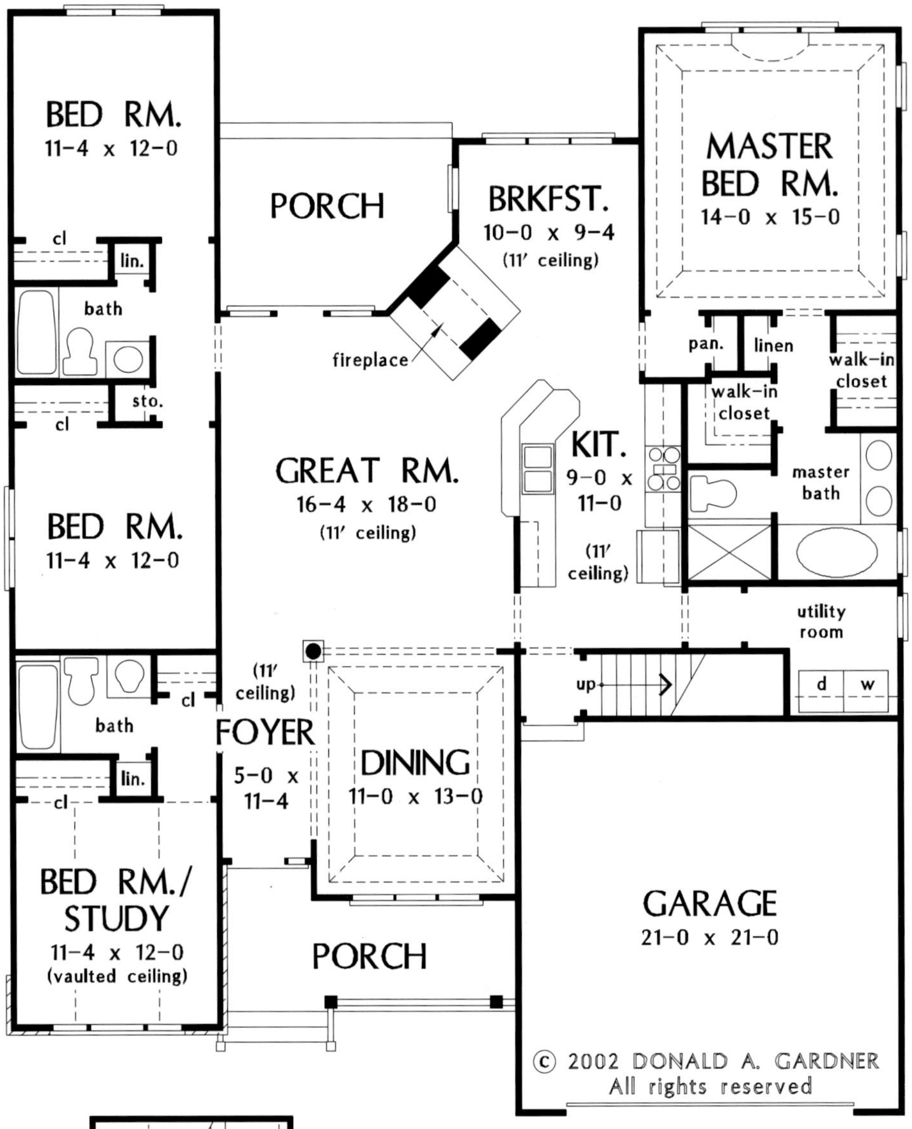

BED RM.
11-4 x 12-0
cl
lin.
bath
sto.
cl
BED RM.
11-4 x 12-0
bath
cl
lin.
cl
BED RM./
STUDY
11-4 x 12-0
(vaulted ceiling)
PORCH
fireplace
GREAT RM.
16-4 x 18-0
(11′ ceiling)
(11′
ceiling)
FOYER
5-0 x
11-4
DINING
11-0 x 13-0
PORCH
BRKFST.
10-0 x 9-4
(11′ ceiling)
KIT.
9-0 x
11-0
(11′
ceiling)
MASTER
BED RM.
14-0 x 15-0
pan.
linen
walk-in
closet
walk-in
closet
master
bath
utility
room
up
d
w
GARAGE
21-0 x 21-0

FIRST FLOOR

attic
storage
down
attic
storage
BONUS RM.
13-4 x 21-0

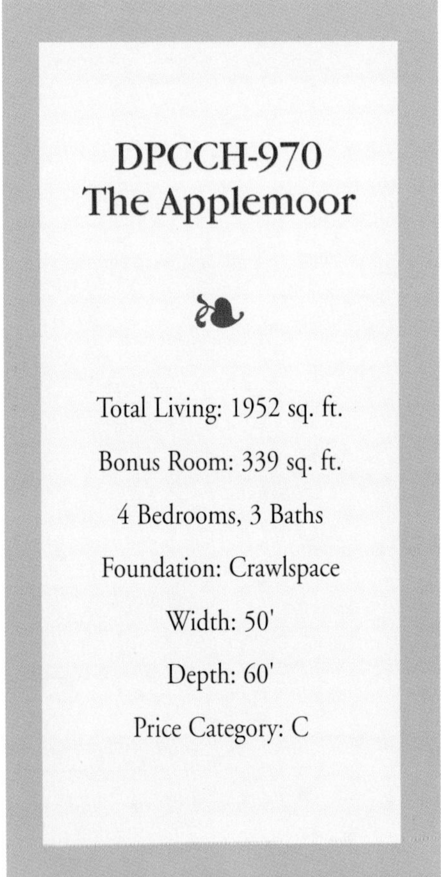

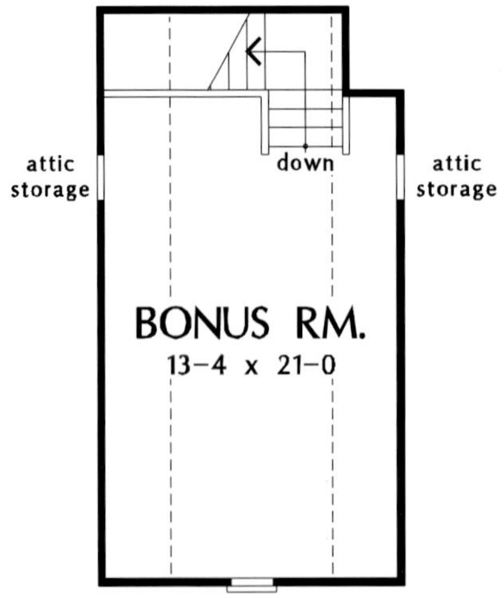

DPCCH-970
The Applemoor

Total Living: 1952 sq. ft.

Bonus Room: 339 sq. ft.

4 Bedrooms, 3 Baths

Foundation: Crawlspace

Width: 50'

Depth: 60'

Price Category: C

DESIGNER NOTE: *"A grand feel on a tight lot drove this design. We even wanted to throw in four bedrooms."*

We have an old apothecary chest we purchased at a barn auction that's proudly displayed in the great room.

Whenever we go to auctions, flea markets or antique shops, we look for old bottles of medicinal remedies.

Our favorites are snake oil, salve and anything with a doc or doctor in the title.

The Applemoor

REAR

ROOM TO ROAM

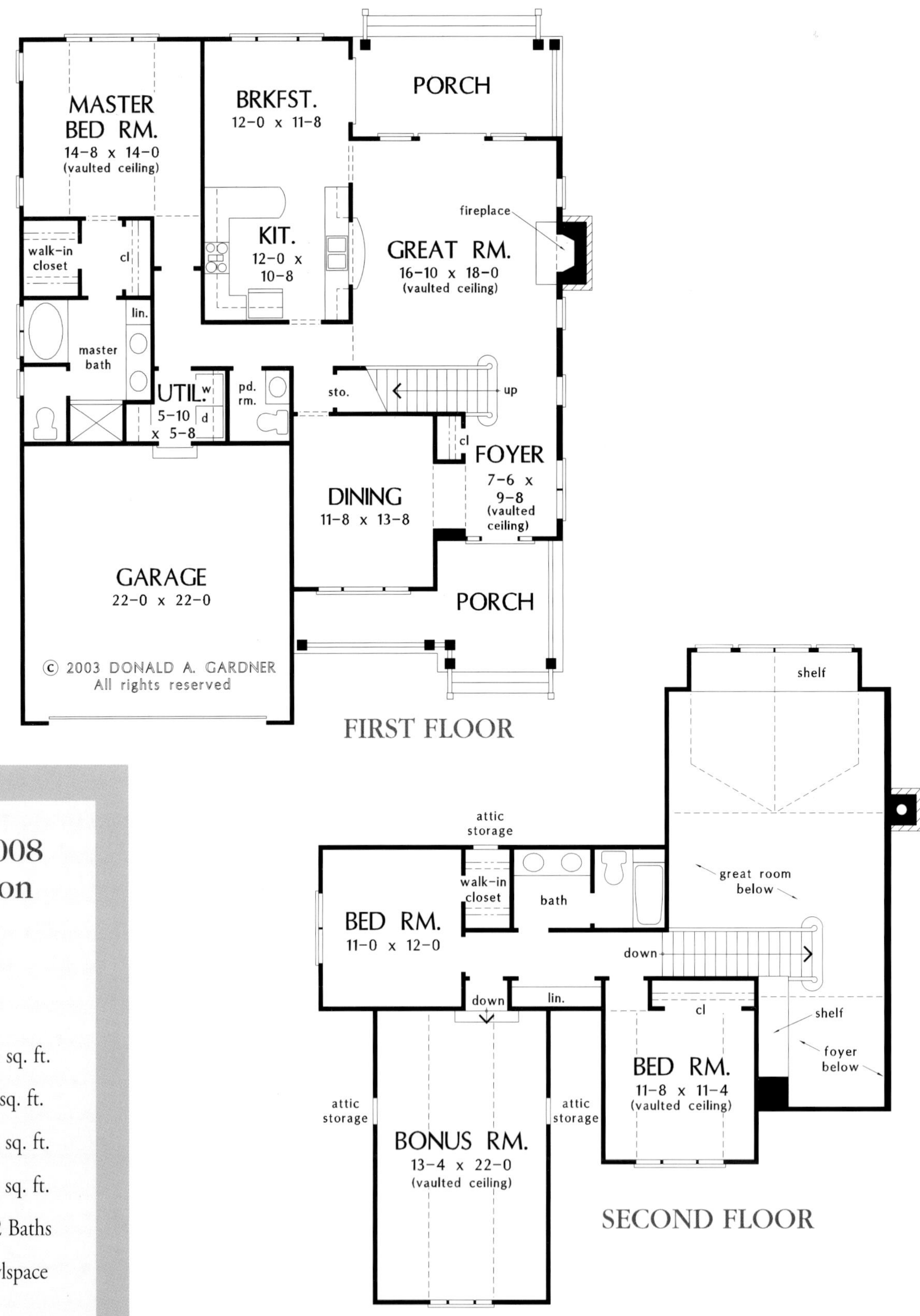
PORCH
MASTER BED RM. 14-8 x 14-0 (vaulted ceiling)
BRKFST. 12-0 x 11-8
KIT. 12-0 x 10-8
fireplace
GREAT RM. 16-10 x 18-0 (vaulted ceiling)
walk-in closet
cl
lin.
master bath
UTIL. 5-10 x 5-8
w
d
pd. rm.
sto.
up
cl
FOYER 7-6 x 9-8 (vaulted ceiling)
DINING 11-8 x 13-8
GARAGE 22-0 x 22-0
PORCH
© 2003 DONALD A. GARDNER All rights reserved
FIRST FLOOR
shelf
attic storage
walk-in closet
bath
great room below
BED RM. 11-0 x 12-0
down
down
lin.
cl
shelf
foyer below
BED RM. 11-8 x 11-4 (vaulted ceiling)
attic storage
attic storage
BONUS RM. 13-4 x 22-0 (vaulted ceiling)
SECOND FLOOR

DPCCH-1008
The Dayton

Total Living: 2073 sq. ft.

First Floor: 1569 sq. ft.

Second Floor: 504 sq. ft.

Bonus Room: 320 sq. ft.

3 Bedrooms, 2-1/2 Baths

Foundation: Crawlspace

Width: 47'

Depth: 55'

Price Category: D

DESIGNER NOTE: *"Thin is in, and we strove to keep this two-story tight while welcoming guests with a warm entry."*

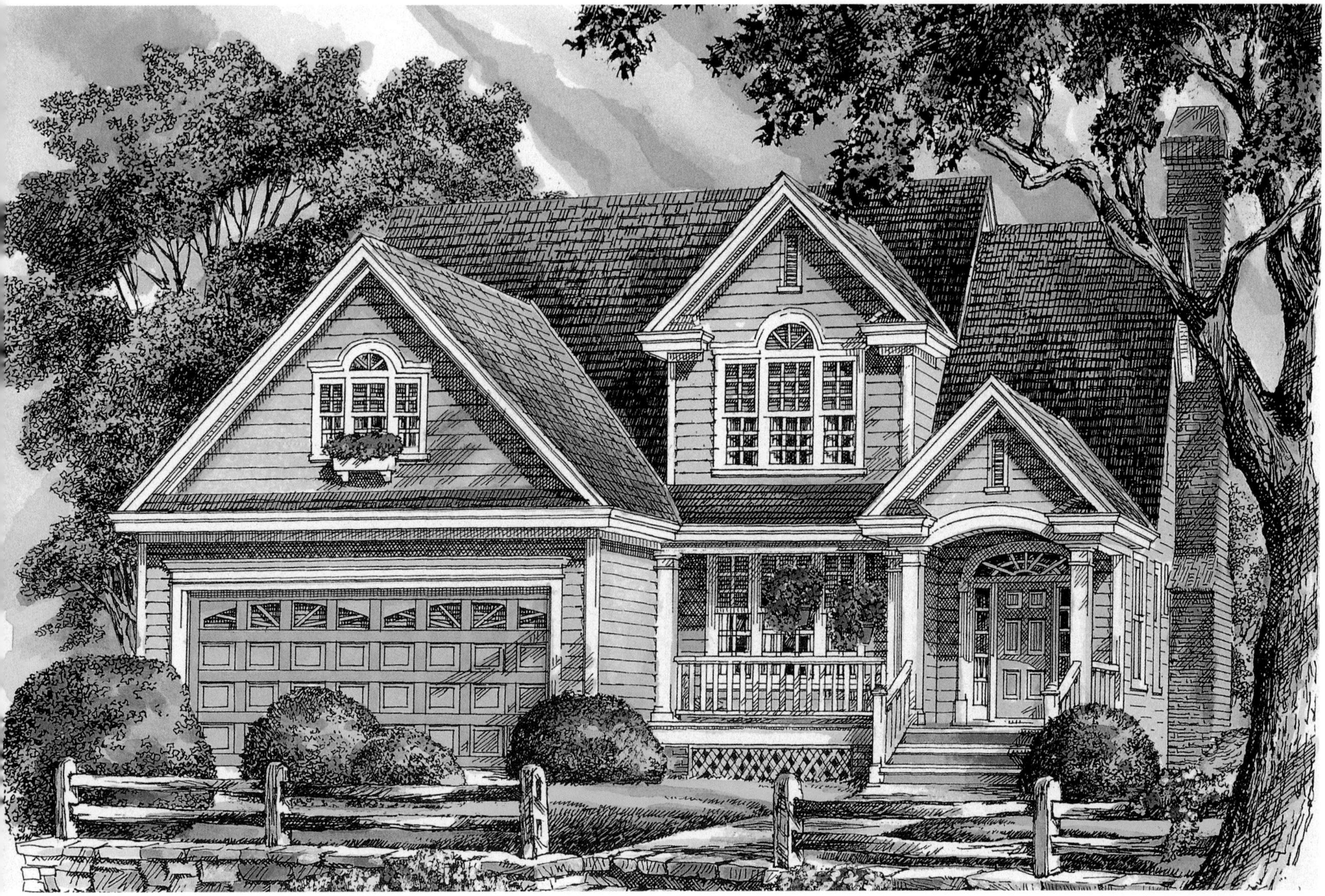

Every family should experience one good pillow fight — the kind that starts when you're watching a movie and no one expects it. I don't remember who started the last one but we all participated. It was great fun, and we were finding feathers weeks after the event. We laughed every time we found a feather in the most unlikely place.

REAR

The Dayton

ROOM TO ROAM

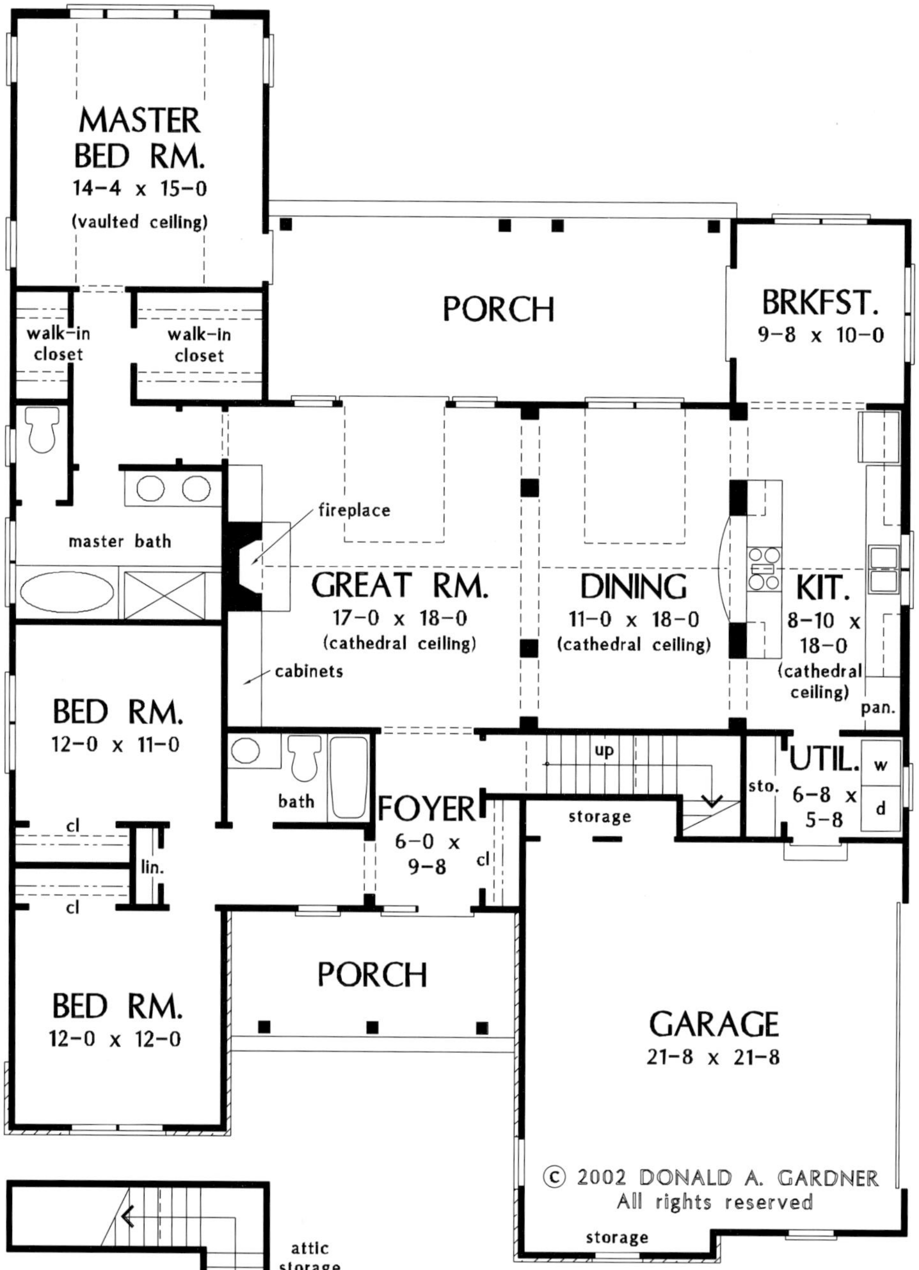

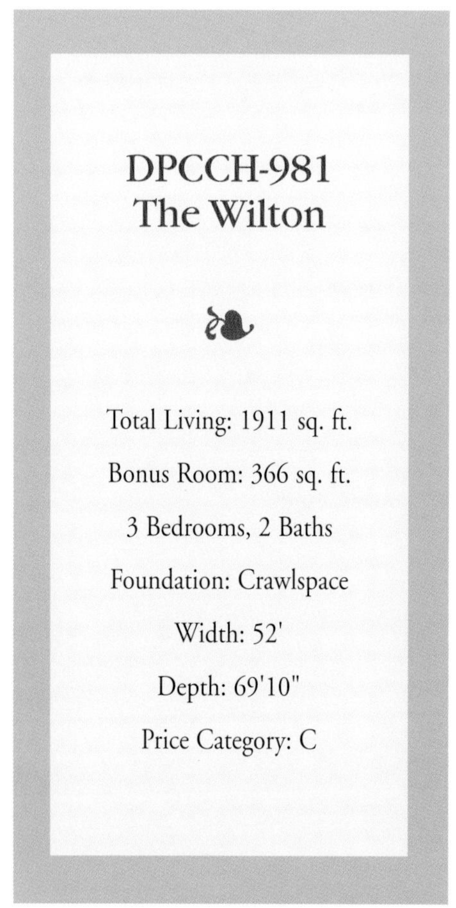

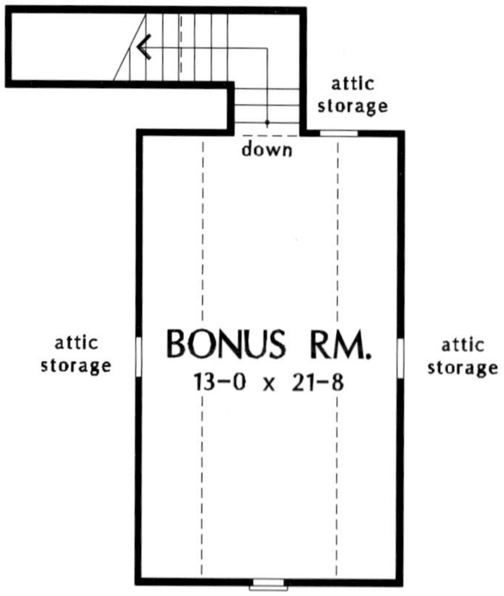

DPCCH-981
The Wilton

Total Living: 1911 sq. ft.

Bonus Room: 366 sq. ft.

3 Bedrooms, 2 Baths

Foundation: Crawlspace

Width: 52'

Depth: 69'10"

Price Category: C

MASTER BED RM. 14-4 x 15-0 (vaulted ceiling)
walk-in closet
walk-in closet
master bath
PORCH
BRKFST. 9-8 x 10-0
fireplace
GREAT RM. 17-0 x 18-0 (cathedral ceiling)
DINING 11-0 x 18-0 (cathedral ceiling)
KIT. 8-10 x 18-0 (cathedral ceiling)
pan.
cabinets
BED RM. 12-0 x 11-0
bath
FOYER 6-0 x 9-8
up
storage
sto.
UTIL. 6-8 x 5-8
w
d
cl
lin.
cl
cl
PORCH
BED RM. 12-0 x 12-0
GARAGE 21-8 x 21-8

storage

attic storage
down
attic storage
BONUS RM. 13-0 x 21-8
attic storage

FIRST FLOOR

DESIGNER NOTE: *"We looked back to the craftsman era for this design and incorporated a mix of materials and custom window patterns."*

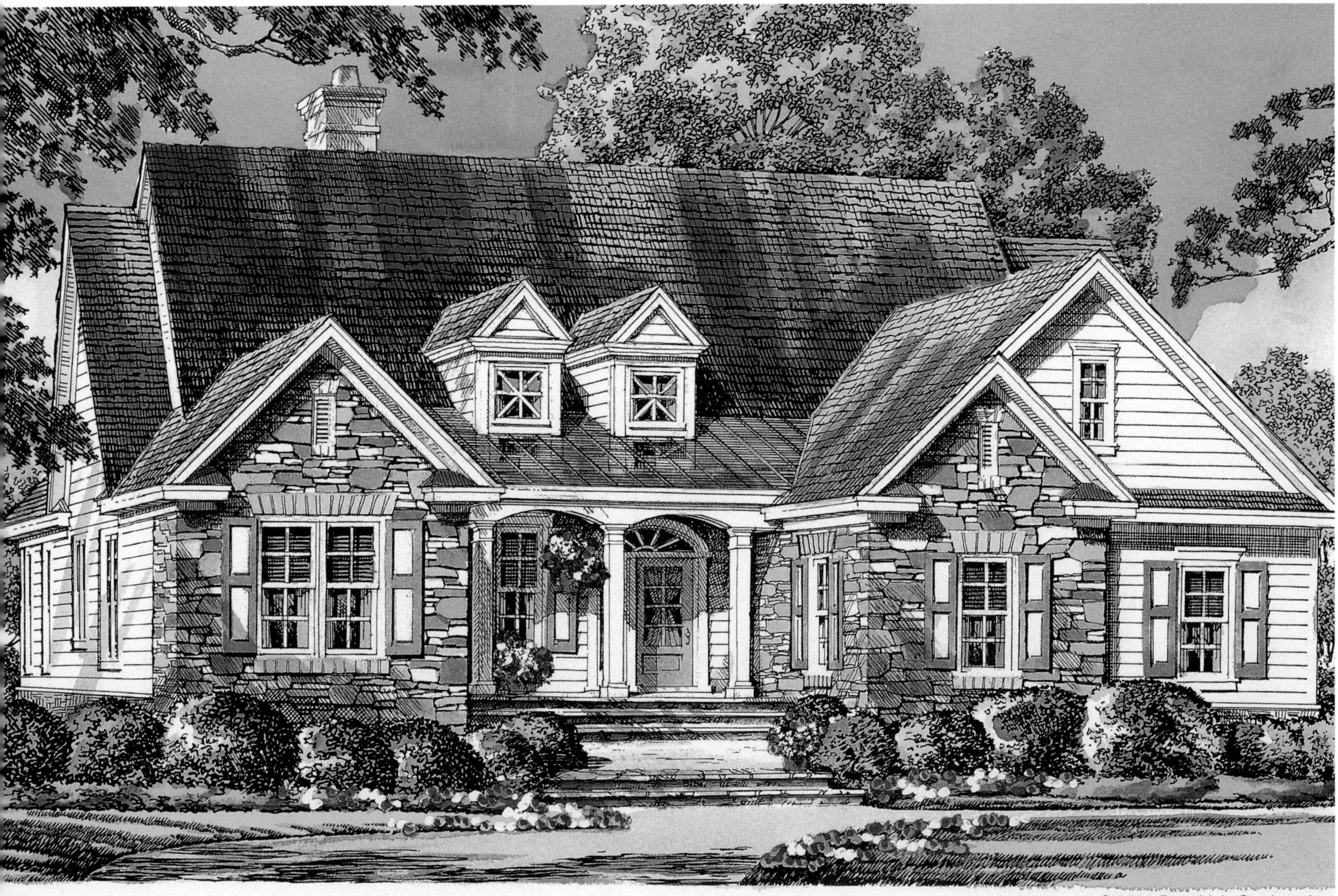

My daughter's young, and I love the fact that I can be cooking and pretty much keep an eye on her wherever she is. Of course when I make homemade biscuits, she's right there, begging to help. Flour gets everywhere, but we have a great time together. Her dad always brags that her biscuits are the best he's ever eaten.

The Wilton

REAR

ROOM TO ROAM

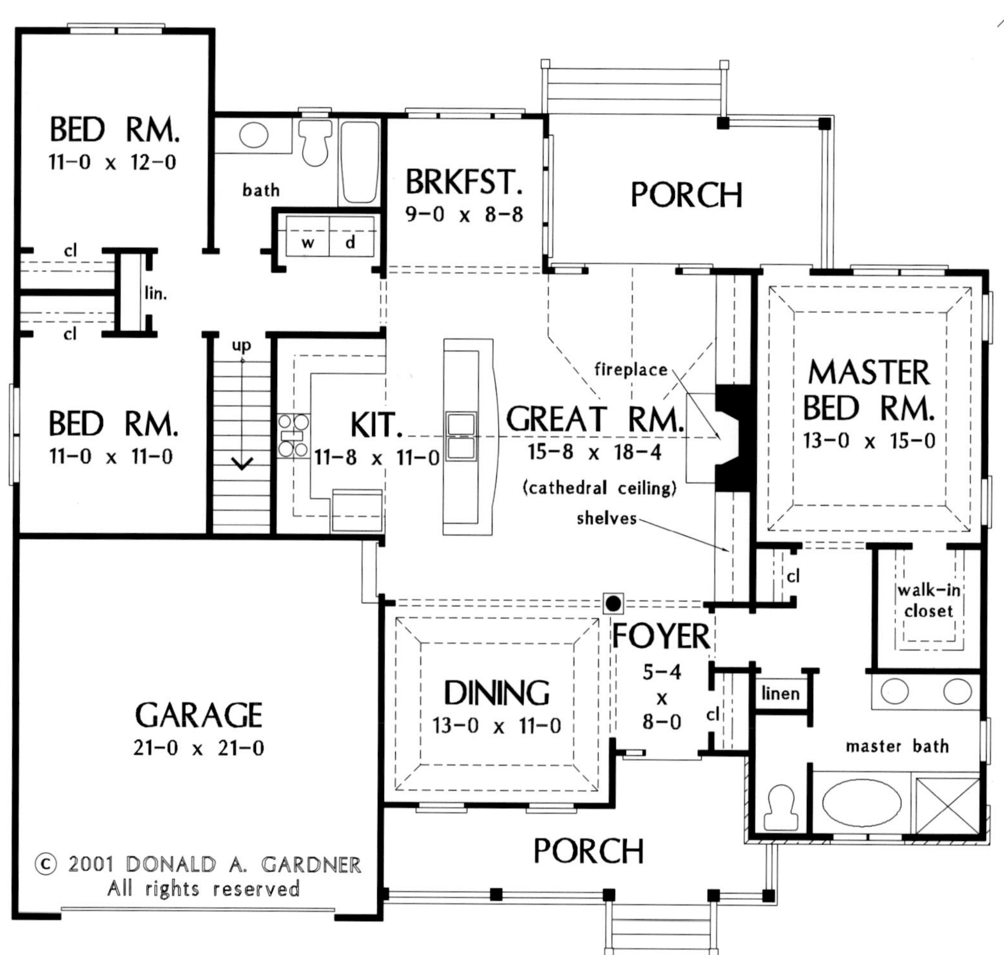

BED RM.
11-0 x 12-0
bath
w
d
BRKFST.
9-0 x 8-8
PORCH
cl
lin.
cl
up
fireplace
MASTER
BED RM.
13-0 x 15-0
BED RM.
11-0 x 11-0
KIT.
11-8 x 11-0
GREAT RM.
15-8 x 18-4
(cathedral ceiling)
shelves
cl
walk-in
closet
FOYER
5-4
x
8-0
linen
cl
GARAGE
21-0 x 21-0
DINING
13-0 x 11-0
master bath
PORCH
© 2001 DONALD A. GARDNER
All rights reserved

FIRST FLOOR

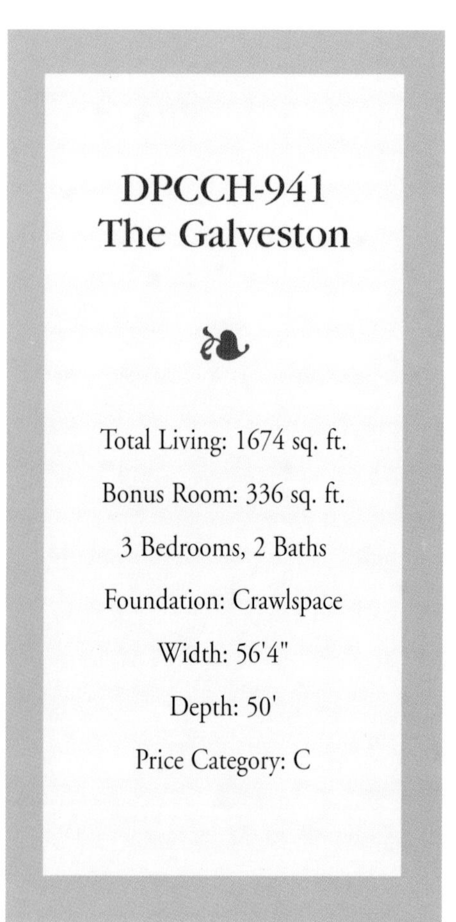

DPCCH-941
The Galveston

Total Living: 1674 sq. ft.

Bonus Room: 336 sq. ft.

3 Bedrooms, 2 Baths

Foundation: Crawlspace

Width: 56'4"

Depth: 50'

Price Category: C

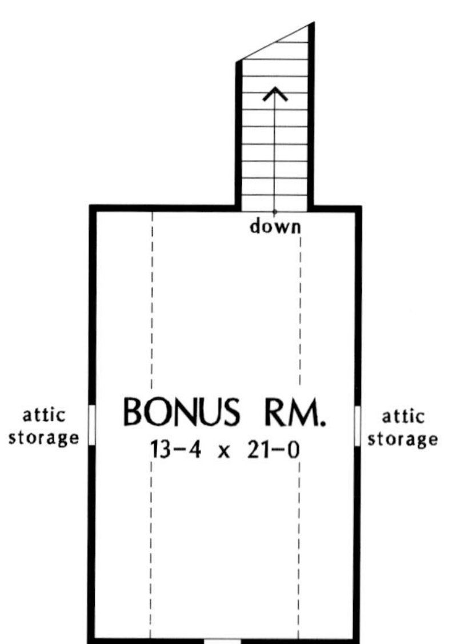

down
attic
storage
BONUS RM.
13-4 x 21-0
attic
storage

DESIGNER NOTE: *"When designing this house we thought of the homeowner who loves to entertain, whose kitchen is the heart of the home."*

Today I snipped flowers from the cutting garden and made a large, lovely arrangement. Old-fashion roses add a subtle fragrance and pink color to yellow irises, purple gladiola and blue hydrangeas. Ivy adds a ribbon effect to the finished bouquet. I placed it on my mantel where it could be seen and enjoyed from all of the gathering rooms.

The Galveston

REAR

ROOM TO ROAM

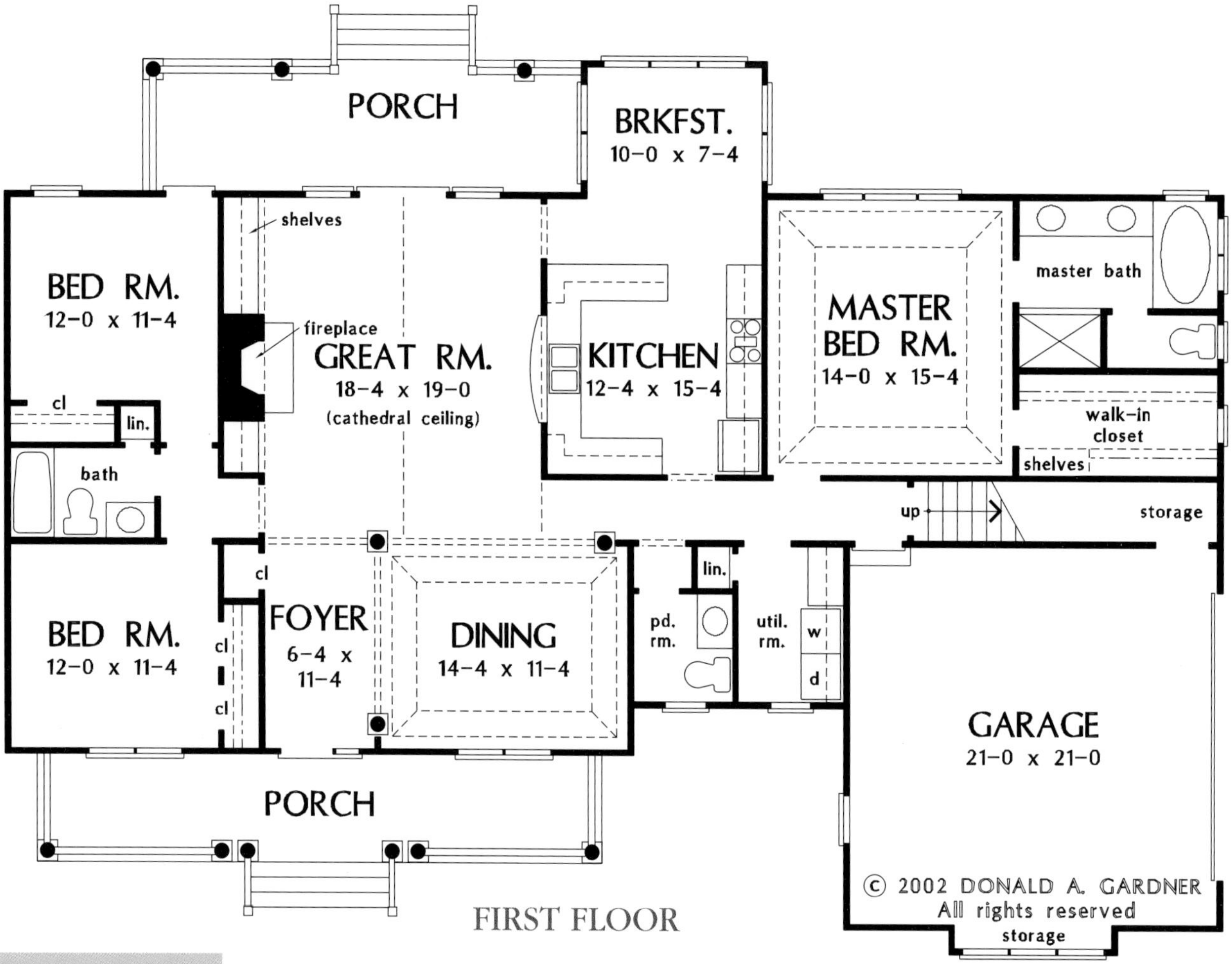

PORCH
BRKFST. 10-0 x 7-4
shelves
BED RM. 12-0 x 11-4
fireplace
GREAT RM. 18-4 x 19-0 (cathedral ceiling)
KITCHEN 12-4 x 15-4
MASTER BED RM. 14-0 x 15-4
master bath
walk-in closet
shelves
cl
lin.
bath
up
storage
cl
lin.
BED RM. 12-0 x 11-4
cl
cl
FOYER 6-4 x 11-4
DINING 14-4 x 11-4
pd. rm.
util. rm.
w
d
GARAGE 21-0 x 21-0
PORCH

storage

FIRST FLOOR

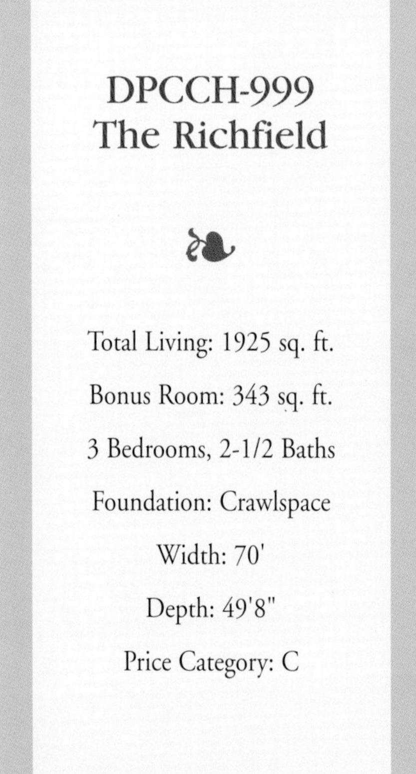

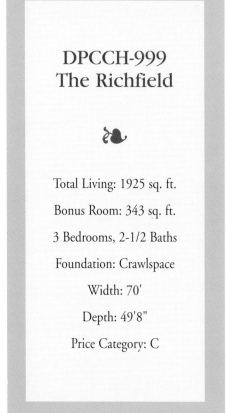

DPCCH-999
The Richfield

Total Living: 1925 sq. ft.

Bonus Room: 343 sq. ft.

3 Bedrooms, 2-1/2 Baths

Foundation: Crawlspace

Width: 70'

Depth: 49'8"

Price Category: C

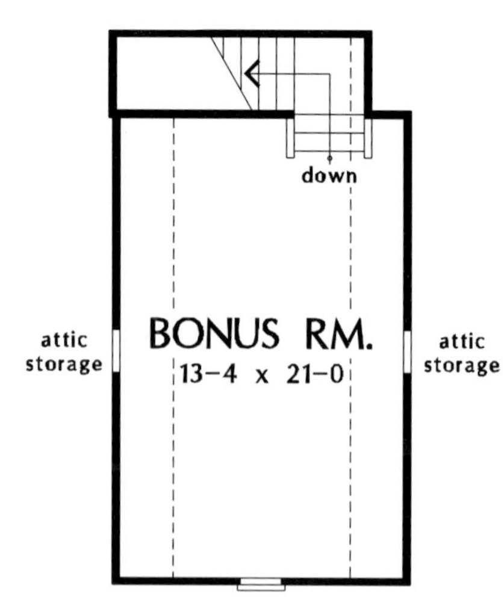
down
attic storage
BONUS RM.
13-4 x 21-0
attic storage

DESIGNER NOTE: *"Balance and symmetry are universally appealing, and we wanted this house to capture both with detail."*

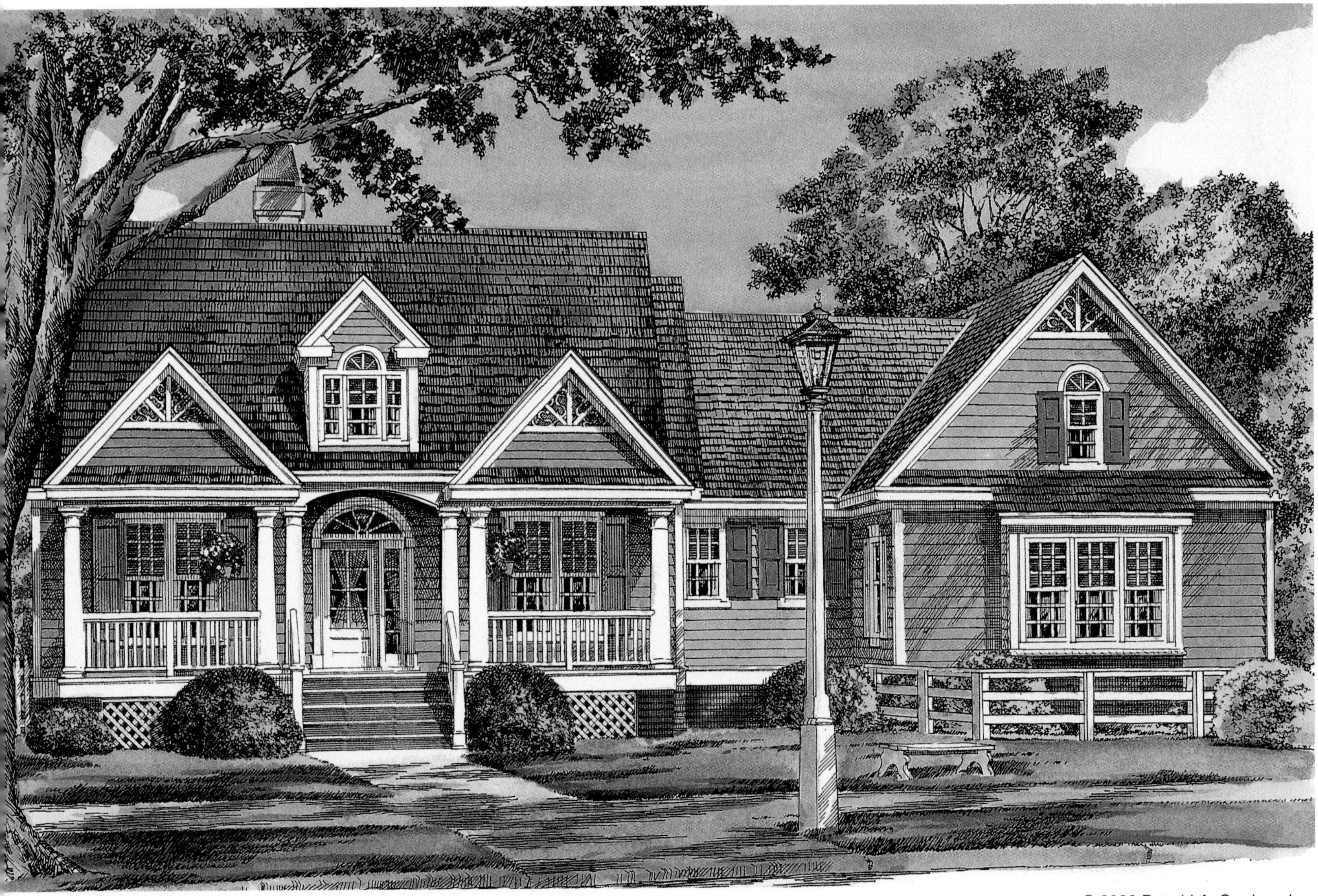

We took antique doorknobs and had them mounted on a wide plank of wood that was salvaged from an old barn floor. Now we have a coat and hat rack that greets visitors when they enter. It's really more for decoration than functionality. The rack adds so much country charm. Two straw hats are always on display.

The Richfield

REAR

ROOM TO ROAM

The kids used to play Cowboys and Indians when they were younger. The balcony was their mountain ridge.

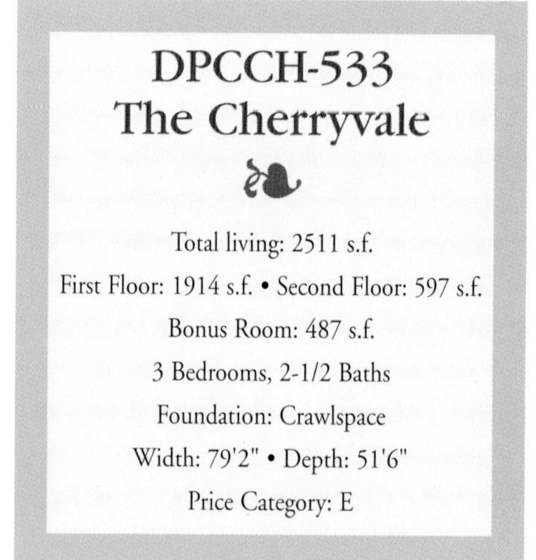

DPCCH-533
The Cherryvale

Total living: 2511 s.f.

First Floor: 1914 s.f. • Second Floor: 597 s.f.

Bonus Room: 487 s.f.

3 Bedrooms, 2-1/2 Baths

Foundation: Crawlspace

Width: 79'2" • Depth: 51'6"

Price Category: E

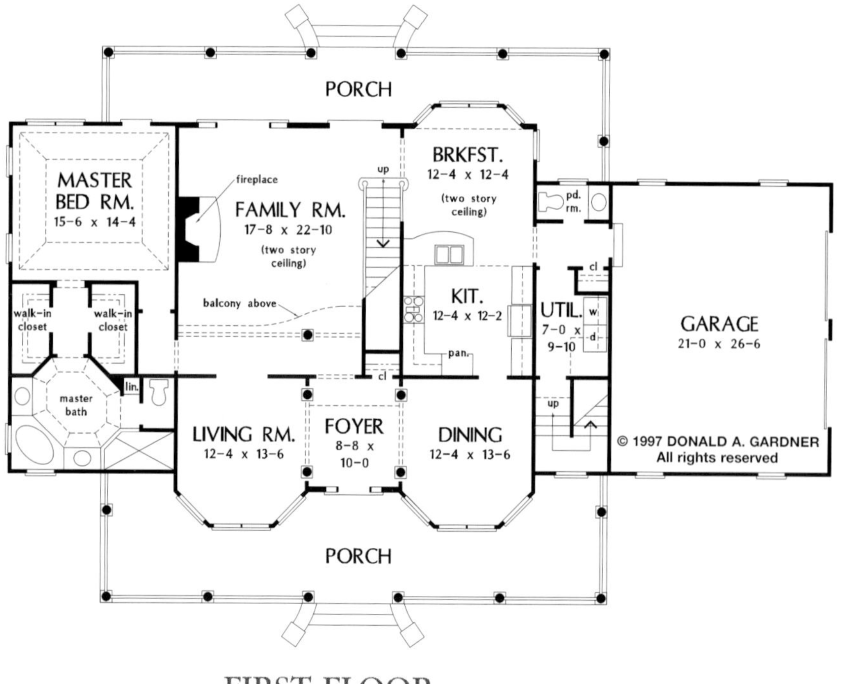
PORCH
MASTER BED RM. 15-6 x 14-4
fireplace
FAMILY RM. 17-8 x 22-10 (two story ceiling)
up
BRKFST. 12-4 x 12-4 (two story ceiling)
pd. rm.
cl
KIT. 12-4 x 12-2
pan.
UTIL. 7-0 x 9-10
w
d
GARAGE 21-0 x 26-6
walk-in closet
walk-in closet
balcony above
master bath
lin.
cl
LIVING RM. 12-4 x 13-6
FOYER 8-8 x 10-0
DINING 12-4 x 13-6
up
© 1997 DONALD A. GARDNER All rights reserved
PORCH

FIRST FLOOR

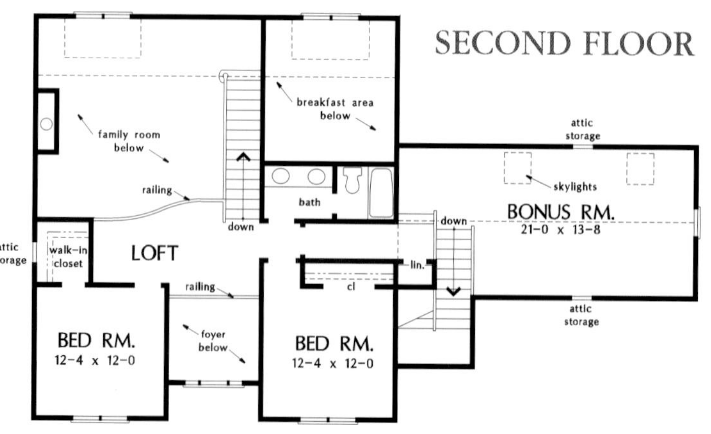
breakfast area below
family room below
attic storage
skylights
railing
bath
BONUS RM. 21-0 x 13-8
down
down
attic storage
walk-in closet
LOFT
lin.
railing
cl
attic storage
BED RM. 12-4 x 12-0
foyer below
BED RM. 12-4 x 12-0

SECOND FLOOR

© 2001 Donald A. Gardner, Inc.

ROOM TO ROAM

Hide-n-seek is the preferred rainy day game around here. The kids play all over the house, barely making a peep.

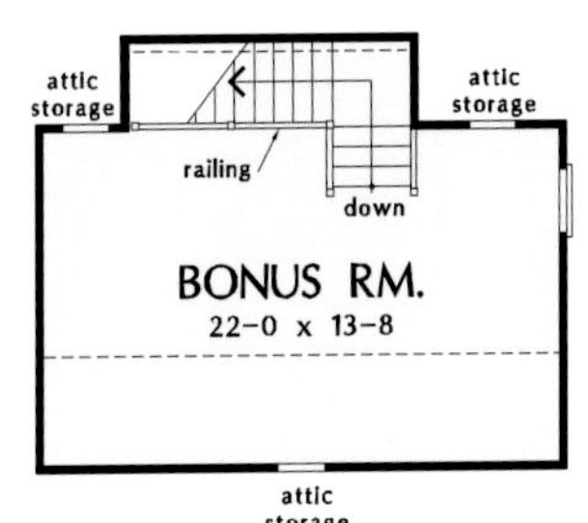

attic storage
attic storage
railing
down
BONUS RM.
22-0 x 13-8
attic storage

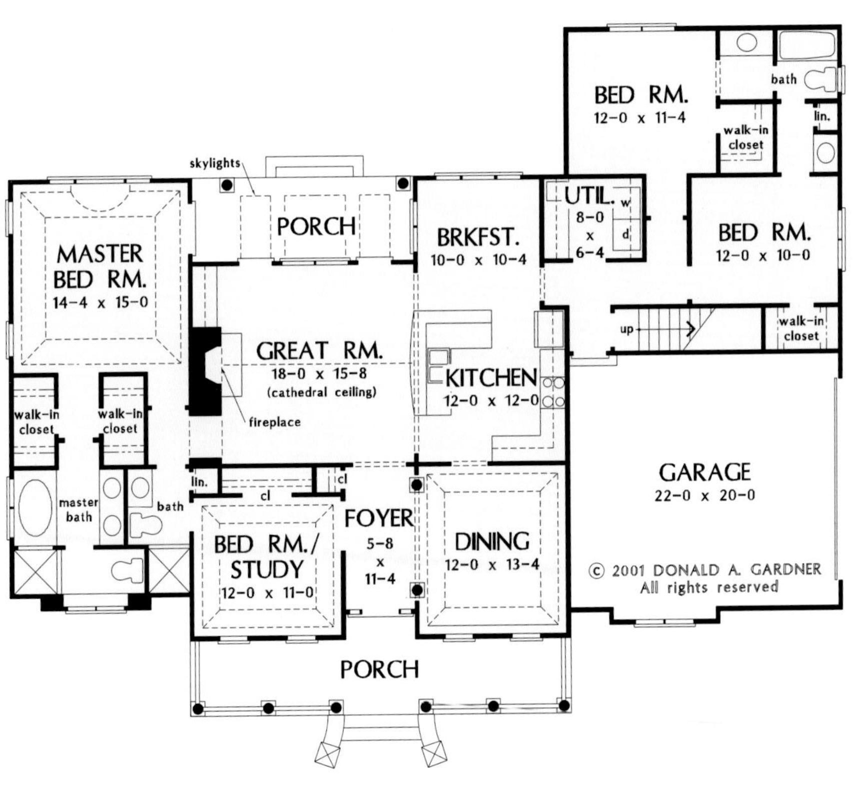

skylights
PORCH
MASTER BED RM.
14-4 x 15-0
BRKFST.
10-0 x 10-4
UTIL.
8-0 x 6-4
BED RM.
12-0 x 11-4
bath
walk-in closet
lin.
BED RM.
12-0 x 10-0
GREAT RM.
18-0 x 15-8
(cathedral ceiling)
fireplace
KITCHEN
12-0 x 12-0
up
walk-in closet
walk-in closet
walk-in closet
master bath
bath
lin.
cl
cl
FOYER
5-8 x 11-4
BED RM./ STUDY
12-0 x 11-0
DINING
12-0 x 13-4
GARAGE
22-0 x 20-0
© 2001 DONALD A. GARDNER All rights reserved
PORCH

FIRST FLOOR

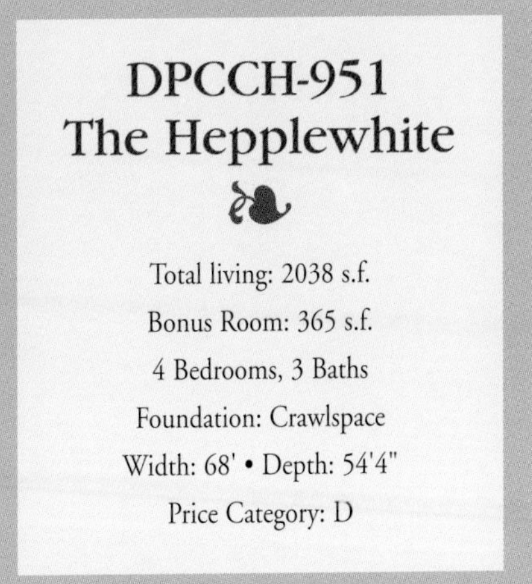

DPCCH-951
The Hepplewhite

Total living: 2038 s.f.
Bonus Room: 365 s.f.
4 Bedrooms, 3 Baths
Foundation: Crawlspace
Width: 68' • Depth: 54'4"
Price Category: D

ROOM TO ROAM

I love the fact that you can stand or sit in the front of the house and see all the way to the back. It helps bring the natural surroundings inside.

DPCCH-918
The Meadowsweet

Total living: 2211 s.f.

First Floor: 1476 s.f. • Second Floor: 735 s.f.

Bonus Room: 374 s.f.

4 Bedrooms, 2-1/2 Baths

Foundation: Crawlspace

Width: 48'4" • Depth: 51'4"

Price Category: D

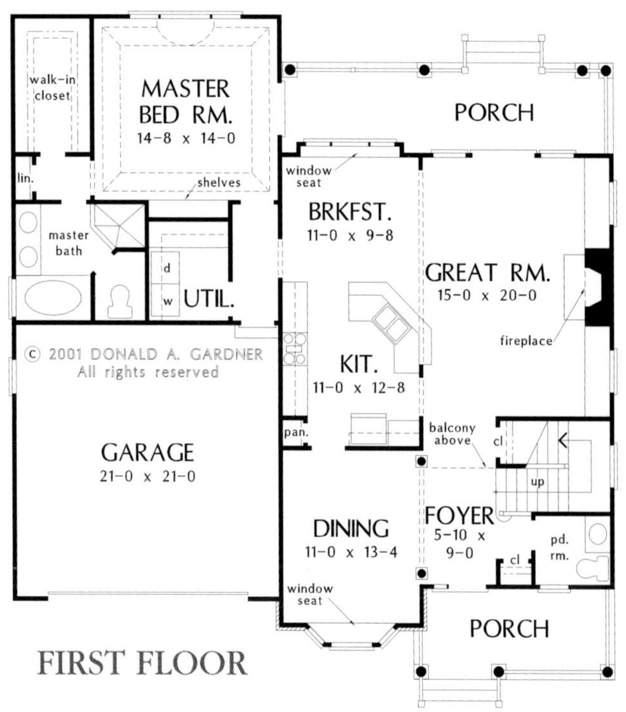

walk-in closet
MASTER BED RM.
14-8 x 14-0
PORCH
lin.
shelves
window seat
BRKFST.
11-0 x 9-8
master bath
GREAT RM.
15-0 x 20-0
d
w
UTIL.
© 2001 DONALD A. GARDNER
All rights reserved
fireplace
KIT.
11-0 x 12-8
GARAGE
21-0 x 21-0
pan.
balcony above
cl
up
DINING
11-0 x 13-4
FOYER
5-10 x 9-0
pd. rm.
cl
window seat
PORCH

FIRST FLOOR

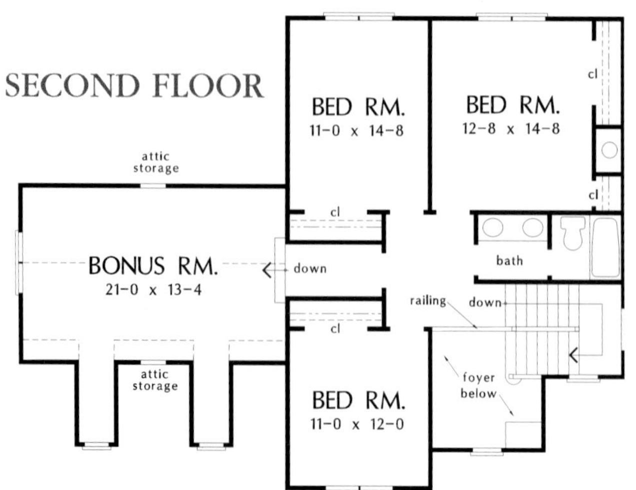

SECOND FLOOR
BED RM.
11-0 x 14-8
BED RM.
12-8 x 14-8
cl
attic storage
cl
cl
BONUS RM.
21-0 x 13-4
down
bath
railing
down
cl
attic storage
foyer below
BED RM.
11-0 x 12-0

ROOM TO ROAM

Long gone are the days of grandmother's small summer kitchen. In this home we're able to spread out and utilize the central island.

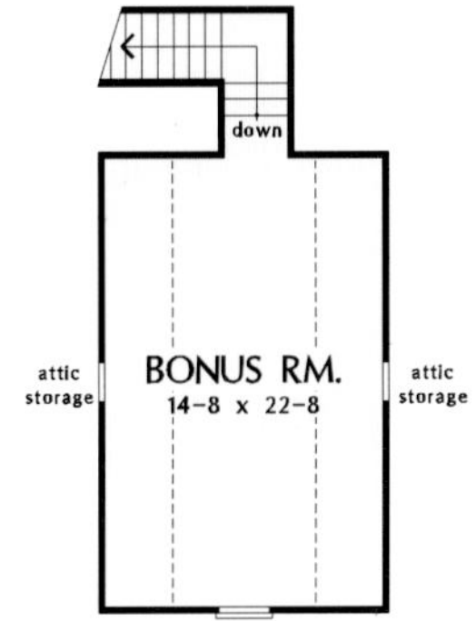
down
attic storage
BONUS RM.
14-8 x 22-8
attic storage

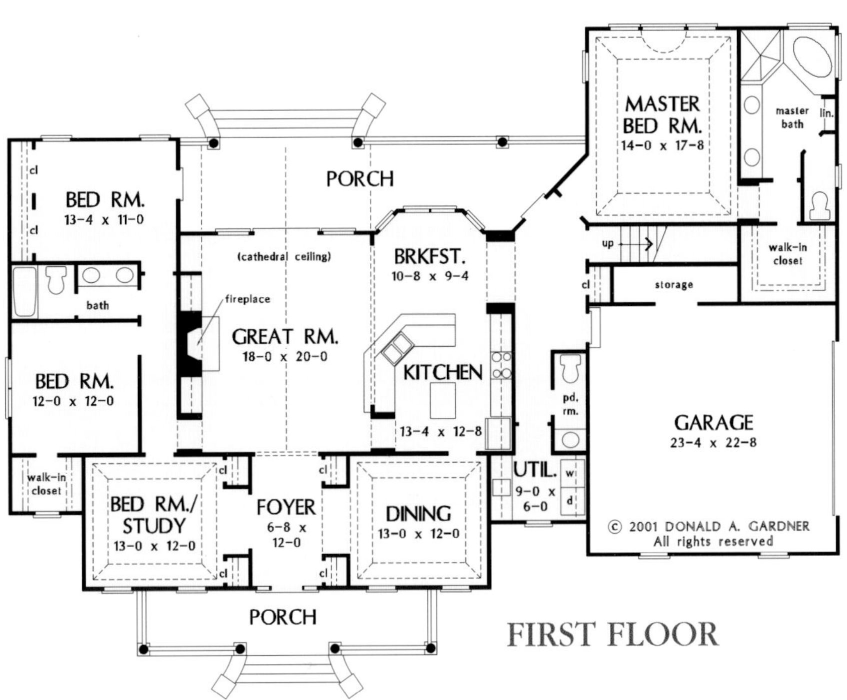
BED RM.
13-4 x 11-0
cl
bath
BED RM.
12-0 x 12-0
walk-in closet
PORCH
(cathedral ceiling)
fireplace
GREAT RM.
18-0 x 20-0
BRKFST.
10-8 x 9-4
KITCHEN
13-4 x 12-8
MASTER BED RM.
14-0 x 17-8
master bath
lin.
walk-in closet
up
storage
pd. rm.
GARAGE
23-4 x 22-8
UTIL.
9-0 x 6-0
w
d
BED RM./ STUDY
13-0 x 12-0
FOYER
6-8 x 12-0
DINING
13-0 x 12-0
PORCH
© 2001 DONALD A. GARDNER
All rights reserved

FIRST FLOOR

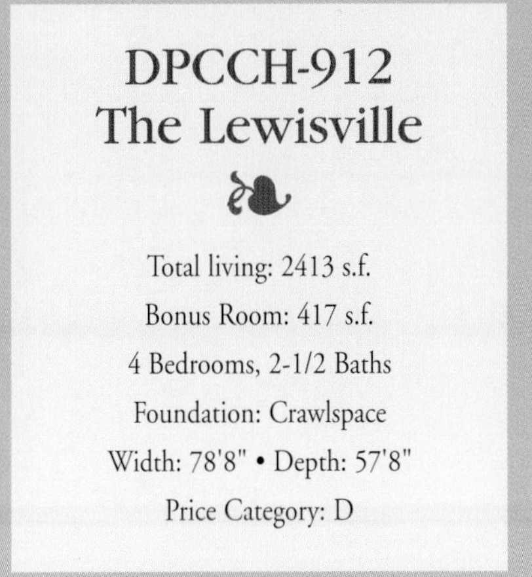

DPCCH-912
The Lewisville

Total living: 2413 s.f.

Bonus Room: 417 s.f.

4 Bedrooms, 2-1/2 Baths

Foundation: Crawlspace

Width: 78'8" • Depth: 57'8"

Price Category: D

ROOM TO ROAM

© 1997 Donald A. Gardner Architects, Inc.

Tonight's supper club theme is "family recipes." We'll set up buffet-style in the dining room and enjoy our casual meal in the great room like a large family gathering.

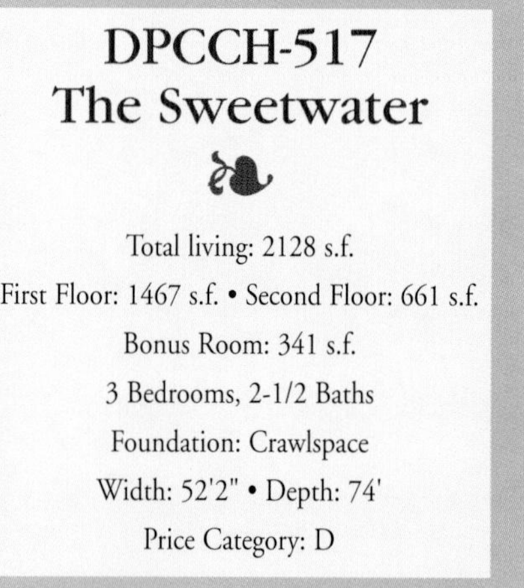

DPCCH-517
The Sweetwater

Total living: 2128 s.f.

First Floor: 1467 s.f. • Second Floor: 661 s.f.

Bonus Room: 341 s.f.

3 Bedrooms, 2-1/2 Baths

Foundation: Crawlspace

Width: 52'2" • Depth: 74'

Price Category: D

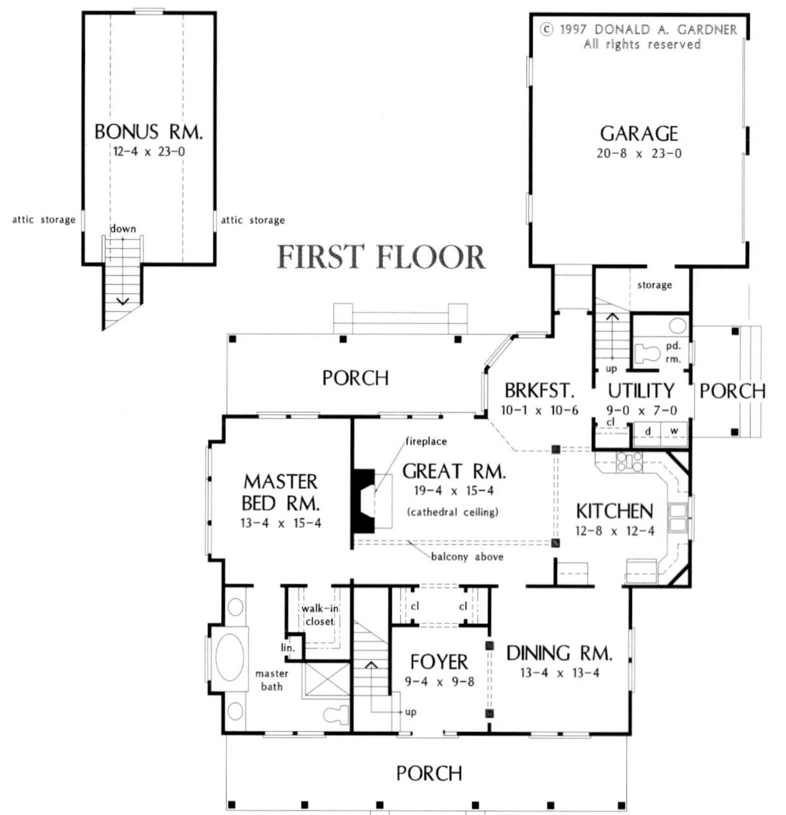

BONUS RM.
12-4 x 23-0
attic storage
down
attic storage
FIRST FLOOR
© 1997 DONALD A. GARDNER
All rights reserved
GARAGE
20-8 x 23-0
storage
pd. rm.
PORCH
BRKFST.
10-1 x 10-6
UTILITY
9-0 x 7-0
up
cl
d
w
PORCH
fireplace
MASTER BED RM.
13-4 x 15-4
GREAT RM.
19-4 x 15-4
(cathedral ceiling)
KITCHEN
12-8 x 12-4
balcony above
walk-in closet
cl
cl
lin.
master bath
FOYER
9-4 x 9-8
up
DINING RM.
13-4 x 13-4
PORCH

SECOND FLOOR

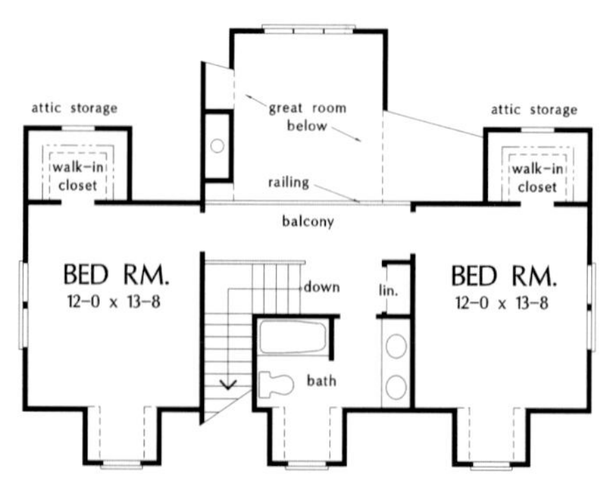

attic storage
great room below
attic storage
walk-in closet
railing
walk-in closet
balcony
BED RM.
12-0 x 13-8
down
lin.
BED RM.
12-0 x 13-8
bath

ROOM TO ROAM

I'll never forget the time the twins tried to fly the kite in the great room. One had the hair dryer; the other, a table fan.

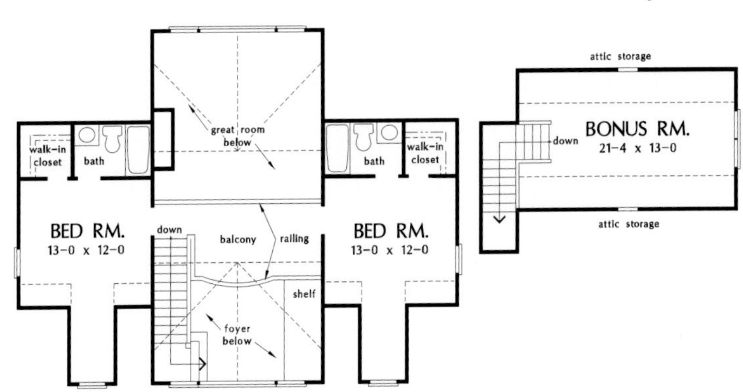
attic storage
BONUS RM.
21-4 x 13-0
down
attic storage
great room below
walk-in closet
bath
walk-in closet
bath
BED RM.
13-0 x 12-0
down
balcony
railing
BED RM.
13-0 x 12-0
shelf
foyer below

SECOND FLOOR

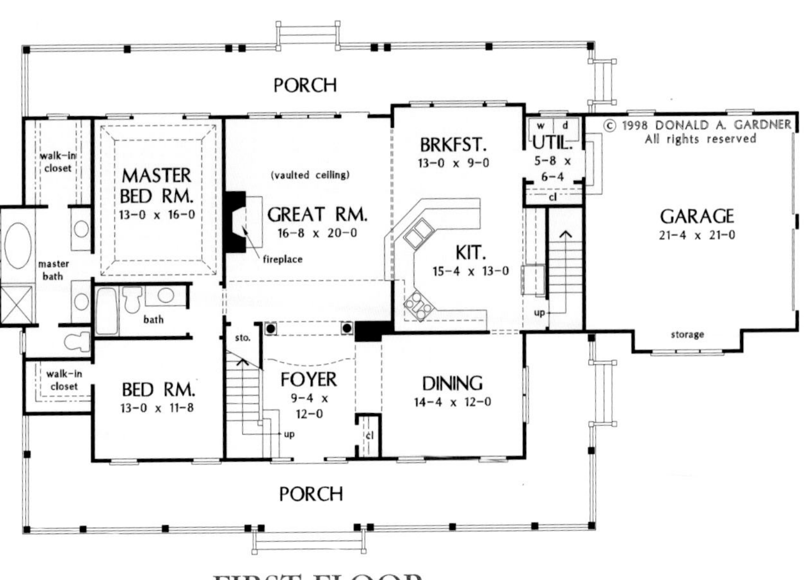
PORCH
walk-in closet
MASTER BED RM.
13-0 x 16-0
(vaulted ceiling)
GREAT RM.
16-8 x 20-0
fireplace
BRKFST.
13-0 x 9-0
w d
UTIL.
5-8 x 6-4
cl
© 1998 DONALD A. GARDNER
All rights reserved
GARAGE
21-4 x 21-0
KIT.
15-4 x 13-0
master bath
bath
up
storage
sto.
walk-in closet
BED RM.
13-0 x 11-8
FOYER
9-4 x 12-0
up
cl
DINING
14-4 x 12-0
PORCH

FIRST FLOOR

DPCCH-764
The Edisto

Total living: 2509 s.f.

First Floor: 1830 s.f. • Second Floor: 679 s.f.

Bonus Room: 346 s.f.

4 Bedrooms, 4 Baths

Foundation: Crawlspace

Width: 81'2" • Depth: 48'

Price Category: E

ROOM TO ROAM

© 1998 Donald A. Gardner, Inc.

Our built-in cabinetry displays all of our milkware and antique decoys. Since we didn't have to use furniture to house our collectibles, we had extra floor space for our trunks.

DPCCH-704
The Juniper

Total living: 2363 s.f.

First Floor: 1575 s.f. • Second Floor: 788 s.f.

Bonus Room: 251 s.f.

4 Bedrooms, 3-1/2 Baths

Foundation: Crawlspace

Width: 65' • Depth: 49'

Price Category: D

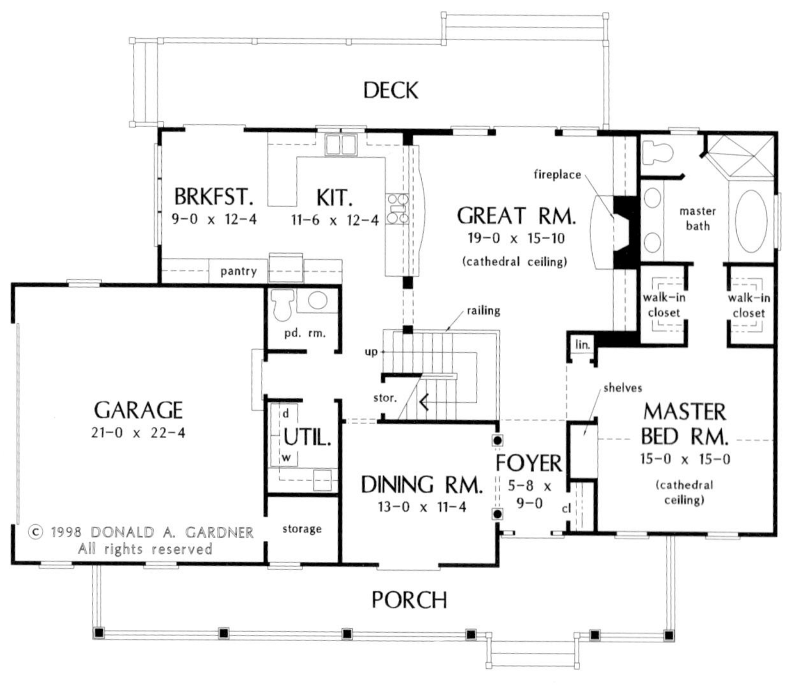
DECK
BRKFST.
9-0 x 12-4
KIT.
11-6 x 12-4
GREAT RM.
19-0 x 15-10
(cathedral ceiling)
fireplace
master bath
walk-in closet
walk-in closet
pantry
railing
pd. rm.
up
lin.
stor.
shelves
GARAGE
21-0 x 22-4
UTIL.
MASTER BED RM.
15-0 x 15-0
(cathedral ceiling)
DINING RM.
13-0 x 11-4
FOYER
5-8 x 9-0
cl
storage
© 1998 DONALD A. GARDNER
All rights reserved
PORCH

FIRST FLOOR

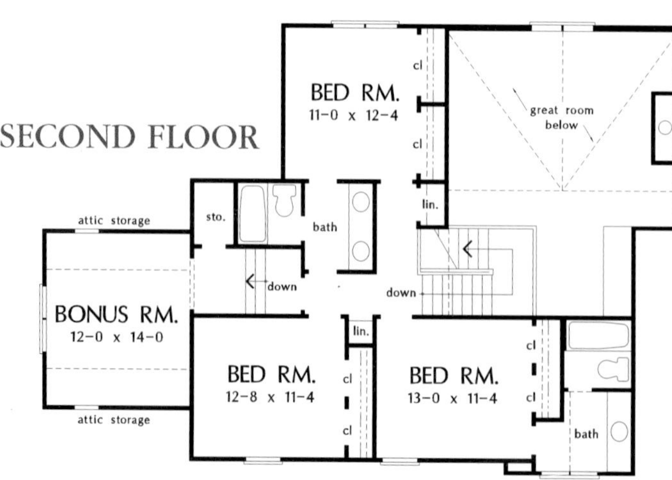
SECOND FLOOR
BED RM.
11-0 x 12-4
great room below
attic storage
sto.
bath
lin.
down
down
BONUS RM.
12-0 x 14-0
lin.
BED RM.
12-8 x 11-4
BED RM.
13-0 x 11-4
attic storage
bath

ROOM TO ROAM

Our dog and cat are like siblings. They take turns chasing each other all around the house, getting plenty of exercise.

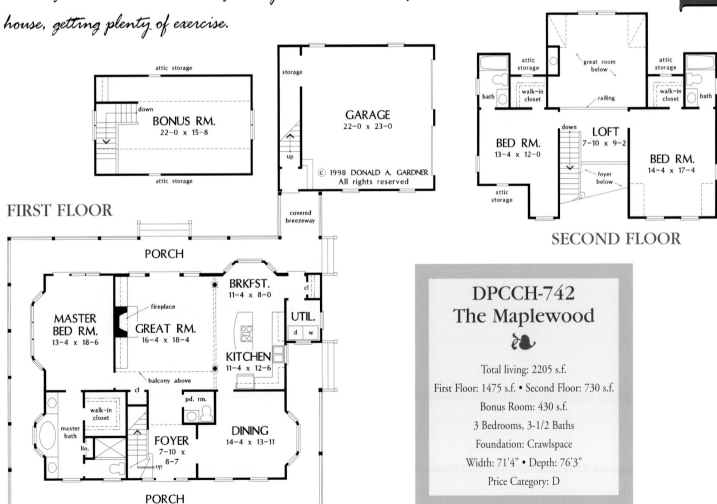

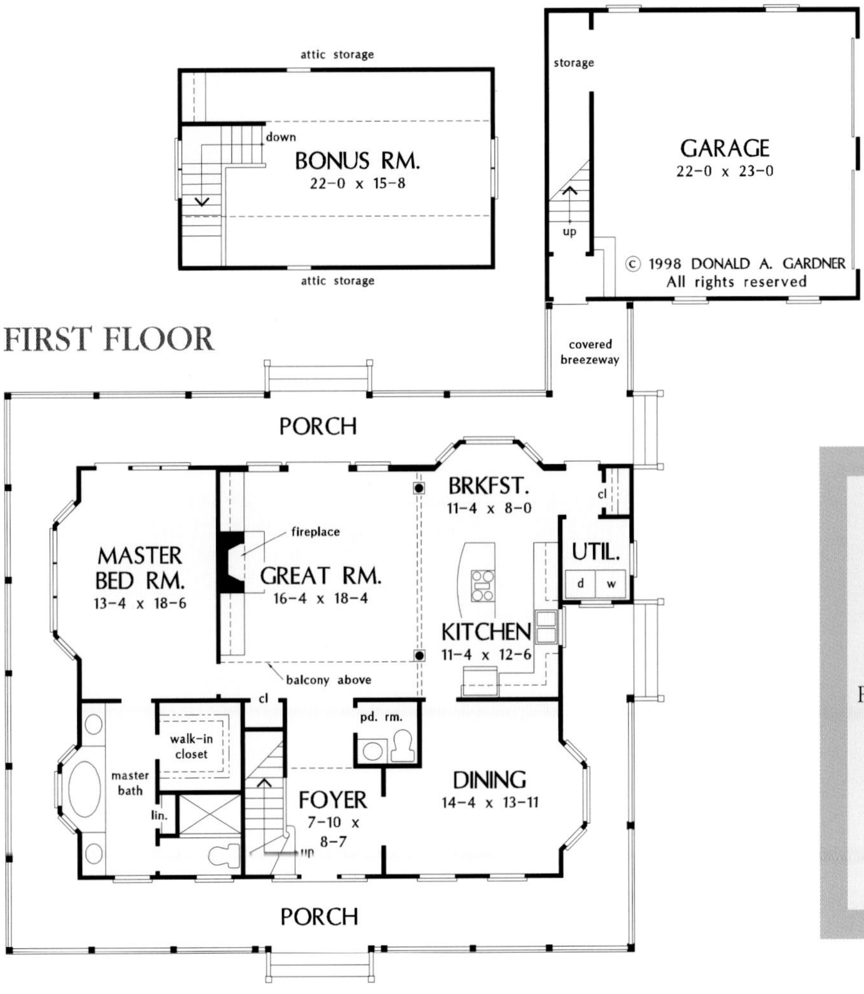

attic storage

BONUS RM.
22-0 x 15-8

down

attic storage

storage

GARAGE
22-0 x 23-0

up

FIRST FLOOR

covered breezeway

PORCH

BRKFST.
11-4 x 8-0

cl

UTIL.

d w

MASTER BED RM.
13-4 x 18-6

fireplace

GREAT RM.
16-4 x 18-4

KITCHEN
11-4 x 12-6

balcony above

cl

pd. rm.

walk-in closet

master bath

lin.

FOYER
7-10 x 8-7

up

DINING
14-4 x 13-11

PORCH

attic storage

great room below

attic storage

bath

walk-in closet

railing

walk-in closet

bath

down

LOFT
7-10 x 9-2

BED RM.
13-4 x 12-0

BED RM.
14-4 x 17-4

foyer below

attic storage

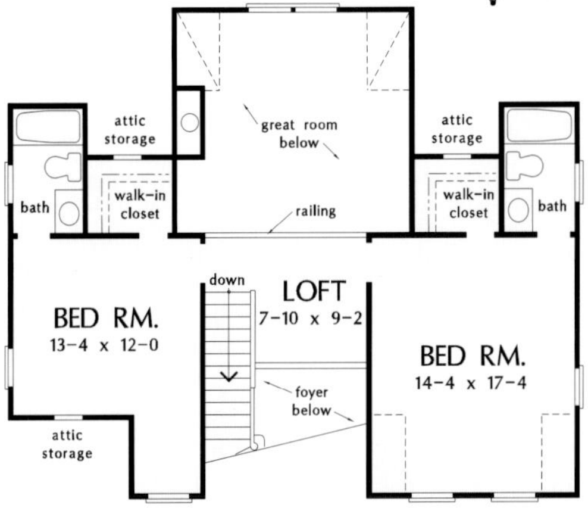

SECOND FLOOR

DPCCH-742
The Maplewood

Total living: 2205 s.f.

First Floor: 1475 s.f. • Second Floor: 730 s.f.

Bonus Room: 430 s.f.

3 Bedrooms, 3-1/2 Baths

Foundation: Crawlspace

Width: 71'4" • Depth: 76'3"

Price Category: D

ROOM TO ROAM

Call me old-fashioned, but I still beat and air my rugs. I take them to the rear porch, because it's so accessible.

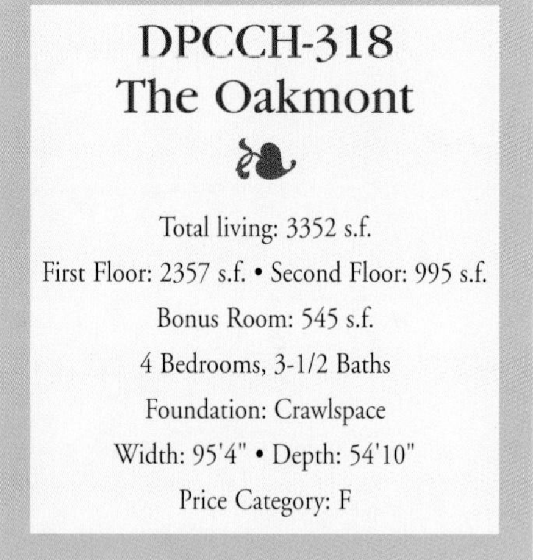

DPCCH-318
The Oakmont

Total living: 3352 s.f.

First Floor: 2357 s.f. • Second Floor: 995 s.f.

Bonus Room: 545 s.f.

4 Bedrooms, 3-1/2 Baths

Foundation: Crawlspace

Width: 95'4" • Depth: 54'10"

Price Category: F

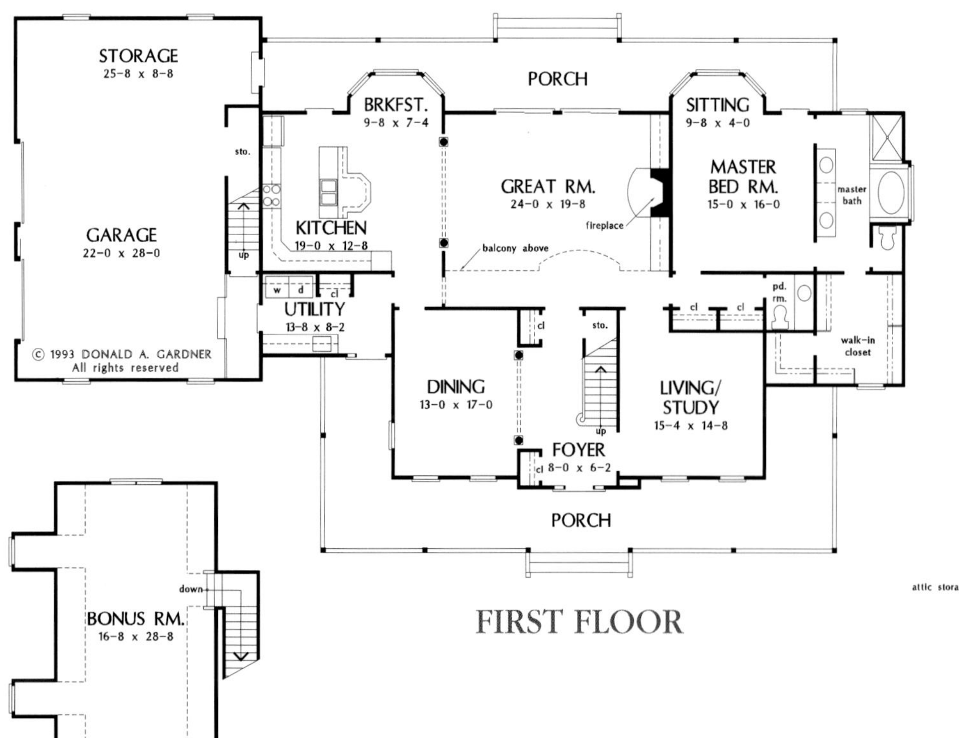
STORAGE
25-8 x 8-8
GARAGE
22-0 x 28-0
© 1993 DONALD A. GARDNER
All rights reserved
sto.
up
KITCHEN
19-0 x 12-8
w
d
UTILITY
13-8 x 8-2
BRKFST.
9-8 x 7-4
PORCH
GREAT RM.
24-0 x 19-8
fireplace
balcony above
SITTING
9-8 x 4-0
MASTER
BED RM.
15-0 x 16-0
master
bath
pd.
rm.
cl
cl
walk-in
closet
cl
sto.
DINING
13-0 x 17-0
up
FOYER
8-0 x 6-2
cl
LIVING/
STUDY
15-4 x 14-8
PORCH
down
BONUS RM.
16-8 x 28-8

FIRST FLOOR

SECOND FLOOR

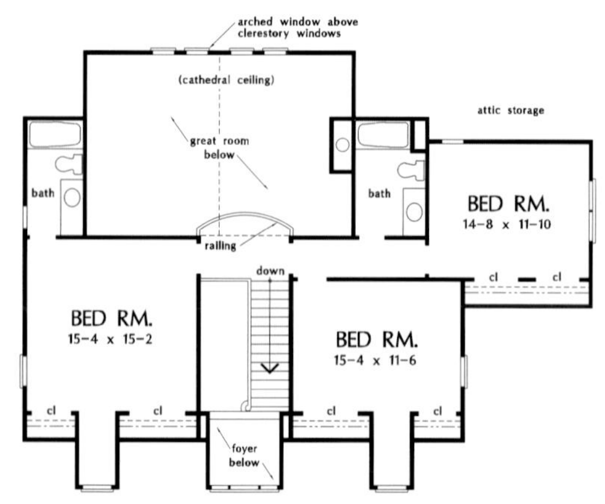
arched window above
clerestory windows
(cathedral ceiling)
great room
below
attic storage
attic storage
bath
bath
railing
BED RM.
14-8 x 11-10
down
cl
cl
BED RM.
15-4 x 15-2
BED RM.
15-4 x 11-6
cl
cl
cl
cl
foyer
below

ROOM TO ROAM

© 1989 Donald A. Gardner Architects, Inc.

When the floorplan's open, there's room for your favorite things. We have a salvaged pew that provides seating on one side of a long, pine table.

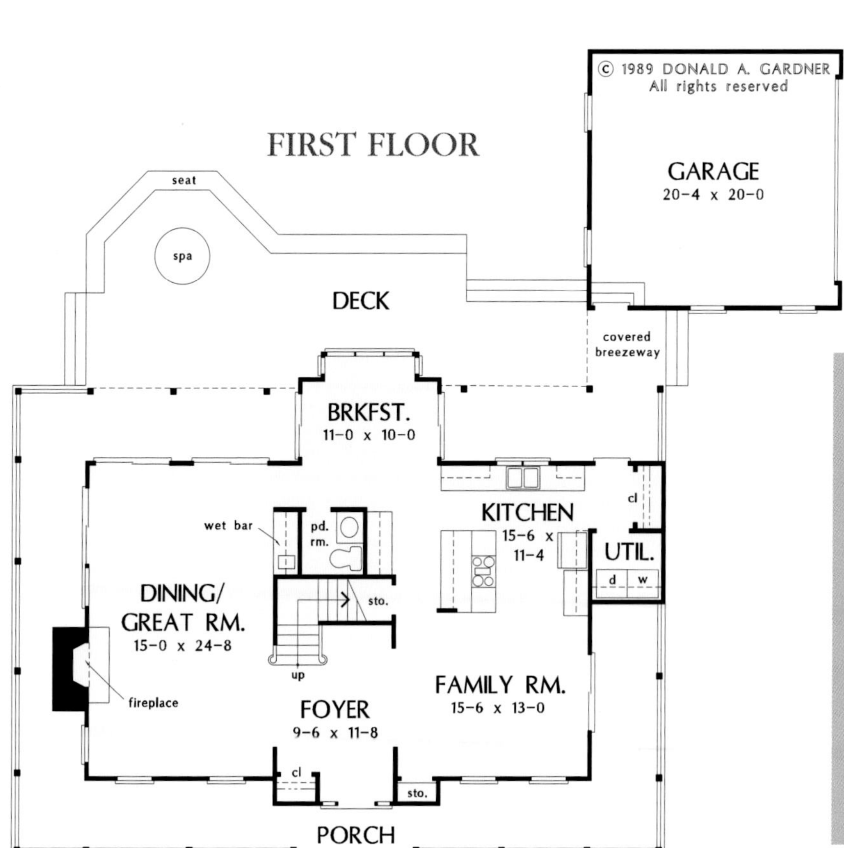
© 1989 DONALD A. GARDNER
All rights reserved
GARAGE
20-4 x 20-0
seat
spa
DECK
covered
breezeway
BRKFST.
11-0 x 10-0
KITCHEN
15-6 x
11-4
cl
UTIL.
d
w
wet bar
pd.
rm.
sto.
DINING/
GREAT RM.
15-0 x 24-8
up
fireplace
FOYER
9-6 x 11-8
FAMILY RM.
15-6 x 13-0
cl
sto.
PORCH

FIRST FLOOR

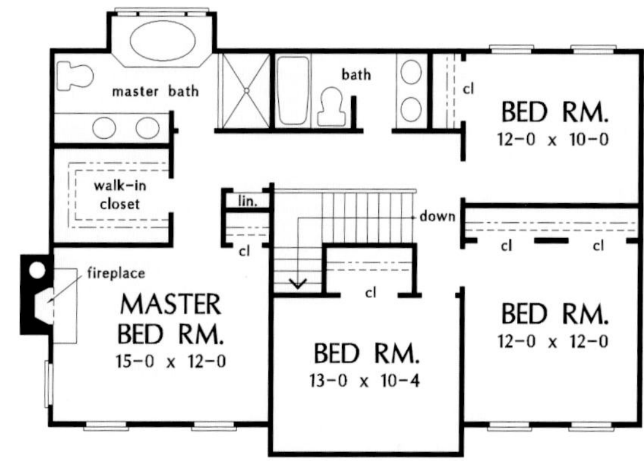
master bath
bath
cl
BED RM.
12-0 x 10-0
walk-in
closet
lin.
cl
down
cl
cl
fireplace
MASTER
BED RM.
15-0 x 12-0
cl
BED RM.
13-0 x 10-4
BED RM.
12-0 x 12-0

SECOND FLOOR

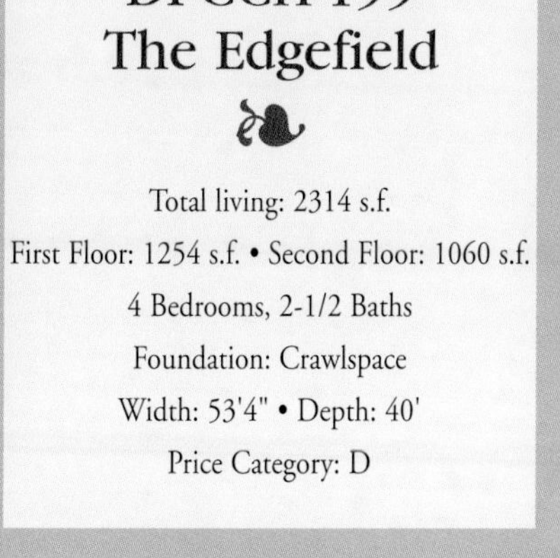

DPCCH-199
The Edgefield

Total living: 2314 s.f.

First Floor: 1254 s.f. • Second Floor: 1060 s.f.

4 Bedrooms, 2-1/2 Baths

Foundation: Crawlspace

Width: 53'4" • Depth: 40'

Price Category: D

ROOM TO ROAM

© 1995 Donald A. Gardner Architects, Inc.

My husband's just finished transforming the extra garage space into a woodworking shop, and he's had to show me every little thing — twice.

DPCCH-388
The Williston

Total living: 2370 s.f.

First Floor: 1778 s.f. • Second Floor: 592 s.f.

Bonus Room: 404 s.f.

3 Bedrooms, 2-1/2 Baths

Foundation: Crawlspace

Width: 81' • Depth: 44'2"

Price Category: D

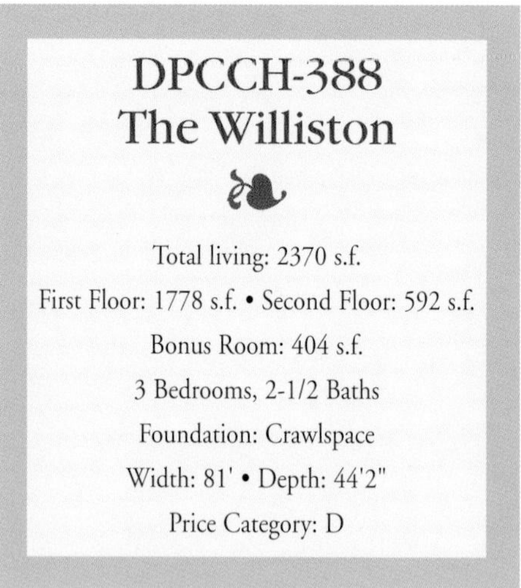
skylights
BONUS RM.
22-0 x 13-0
down

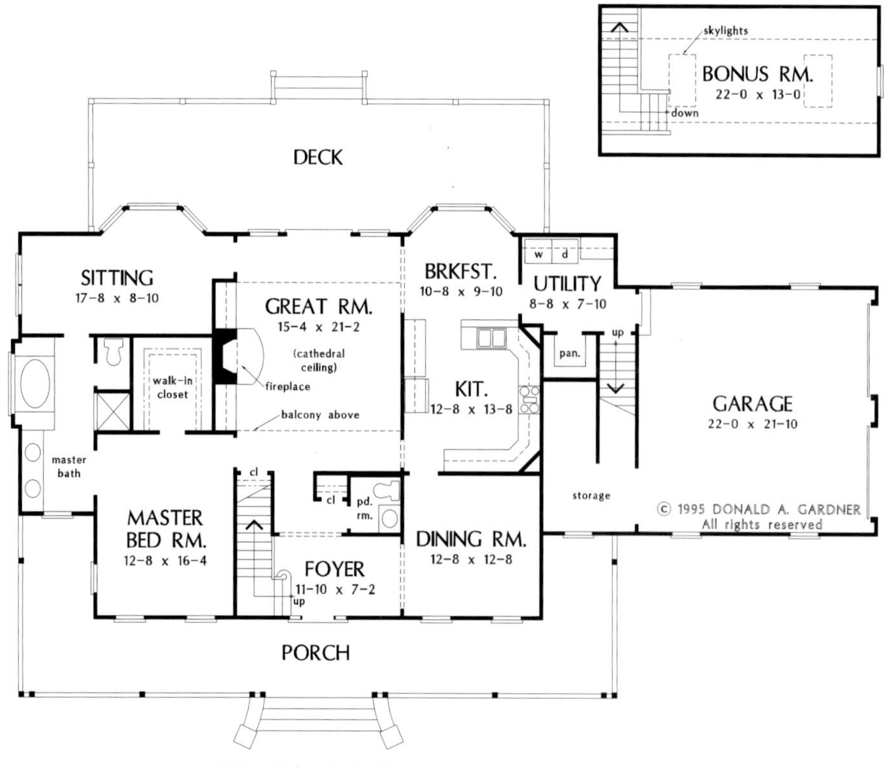
DECK
SITTING
17-8 x 8-10
GREAT RM.
15-4 x 21-2
(cathedral ceiling)
fireplace
balcony above
walk-in closet
master bath
BRKFST.
10-8 x 9-10
UTILITY
8-8 x 7-10
w d
pan.
up
KIT.
12-8 x 13-8
GARAGE
22-0 x 21-10
storage
cl
pd. rm.
MASTER BED RM.
12-8 x 16-4
FOYER
11-10 x 7-2
up
DINING RM.
12-8 x 12-8
© 1995 DONALD A. GARDNER
All rights reserved
PORCH

FIRST FLOOR

SECOND FLOOR

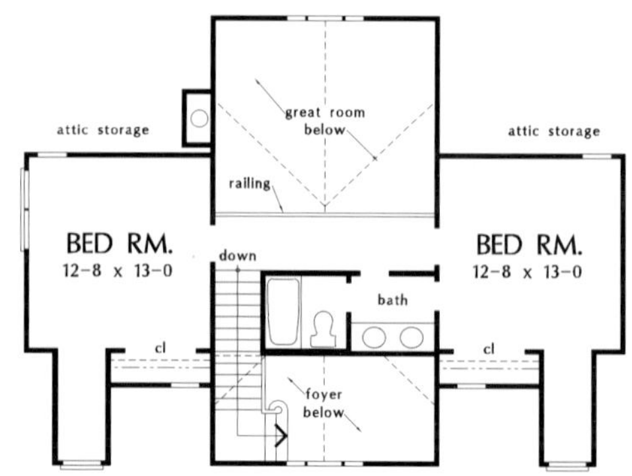
attic storage
great room below
railing
attic storage
BED RM.
12-8 x 13-0
down
BED RM.
12-8 x 13-0
bath
cl
cl
foyer below

ROOM TO ROAM

We have a large family that loves to get together.
A house seems so much warmer when
it's full of family and friends.

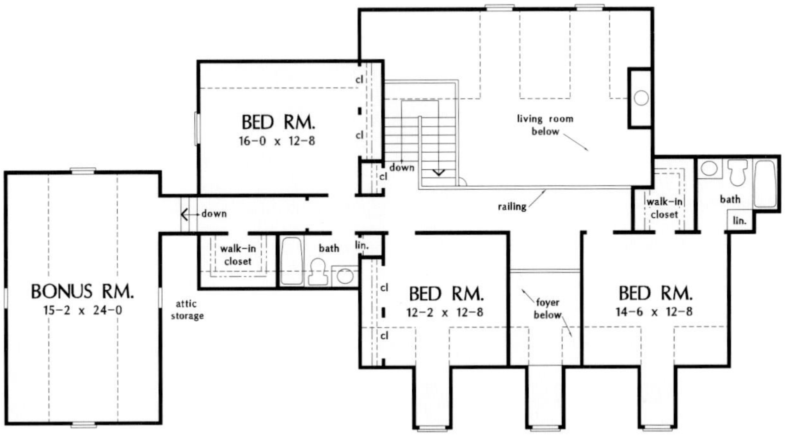

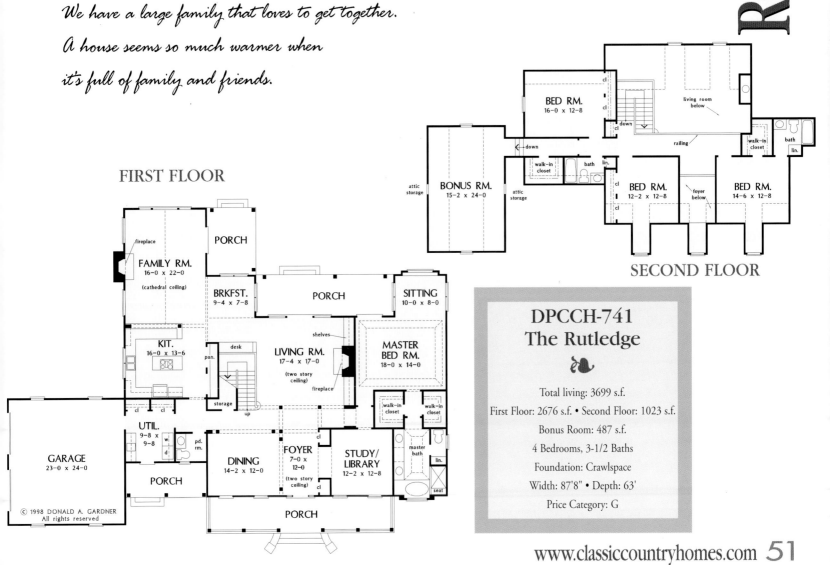

FIRST FLOOR

PORCH
fireplace
FAMILY RM.
16-0 x 22-0
(cathedral ceiling)
BRKFST.
9-4 x 7-8
PORCH
SITTING
10-0 x 8-0
KIT.
16-0 x 13-6
pan.
desk
shelves
LIVING RM.
17-4 x 17-0
(two story ceiling)
fireplace
MASTER BED RM.
18-0 x 14-0
storage
up
cl
cl
walk-in closet
walk-in closet
UTIL.
9-8 x 9-8
w
d
pd. rm.
DINING
14-2 x 12-0
FOYER
7-0 x 12-0
(two story ceiling)
cl
cl
STUDY/ LIBRARY
12-2 x 12-8
master bath
lin.
seat
GARAGE
23-0 x 24-0
PORCH
PORCH

SECOND FLOOR

BED RM.
16-0 x 12-8
cl
cl
cl
down
living room below
railing
walk-in closet
bath
lin.
down
walk-in closet
bath
lin.
attic storage
BONUS RM.
15-2 x 24-0
attic storage
cl
cl
BED RM.
12-2 x 12-8
foyer below
BED RM.
14-6 x 12-8

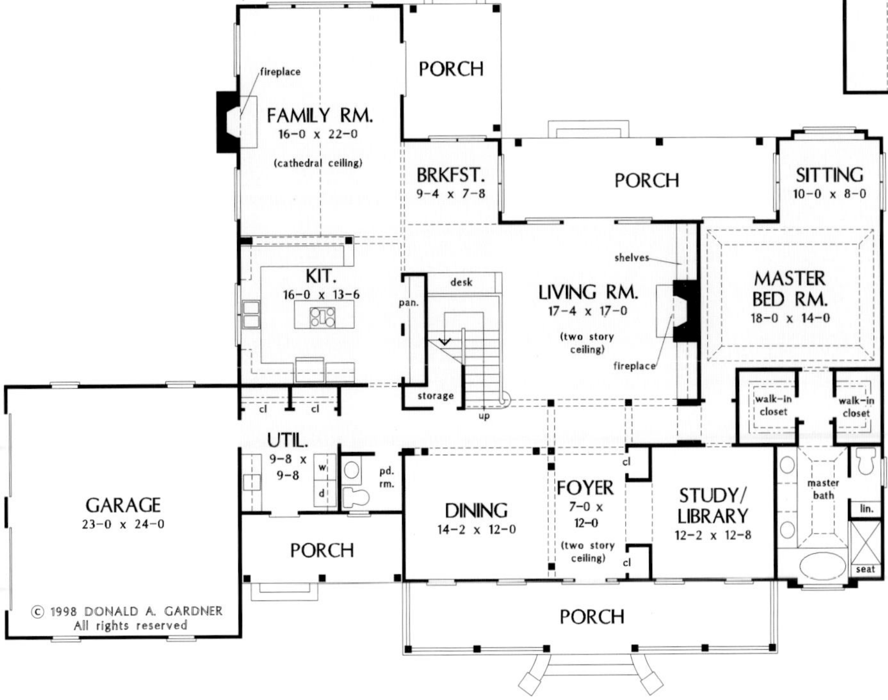

DPCCH-741
The Rutledge

Total living: 3699 s.f.
First Floor: 2676 s.f. • Second Floor: 1023 s.f.
Bonus Room: 487 s.f.
4 Bedrooms, 3-1/2 Baths
Foundation: Crawlspace
Width: 87'8" • Depth: 63'
Price Category: G

Neighborly Advice

Bonus rooms provide flexibility, and this section contains plans with bonus spaces ranging from one room to an entire floor. Depending on your needs, wants and budget, your bonus room can be finished during the house construction or at a later date. Use these points to help you decide:

How do you want to use it? How might your needs change? Ask yourself questions; then question your builder. Ask the price difference between finishing the bonus room during construction verses waiting. Ask what the cost would be if you just had the floor system installed. Ask what the cost would be to have the flooring, wiring/plumbing and drywall installed now with the fixtures and amenities added later. Ask what costs might go into demolition or retrofitting if you decided to wait completely. Come up with different scenarios. Once you have a number of options, decide which one best meets your agenda.

HIDDEN SPACES

HIDDEN SPACES

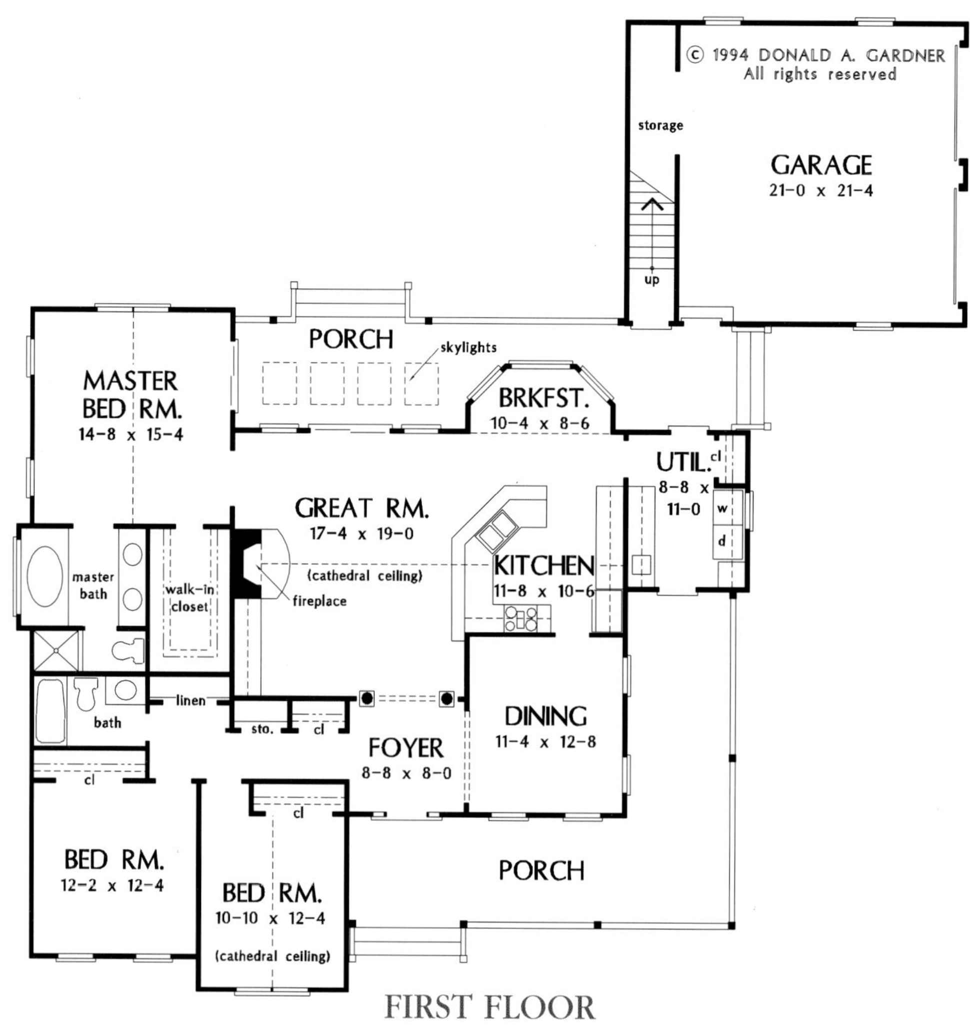

© 1994 DONALD A. GARDNER
All rights reserved
storage
GARAGE
21-0 x 21-4
up
PORCH
skylights
MASTER BED RM.
14-8 x 15-4
BRKFST.
10-4 x 8-6
UTIL.
8-8 x 11-0
cl
w
d
GREAT RM.
17-4 x 19-0
(cathedral ceiling)
fireplace
KITCHEN
11-8 x 10-6
master bath
walk-in closet
linen
bath
sto.
cl
DINING
11-4 x 12-8
FOYER
8-8 x 8-0
cl
cl
BED RM.
12-2 x 12-4
BED RM.
10-10 x 12-4
(cathedral ceiling)
PORCH

FIRST FLOOR

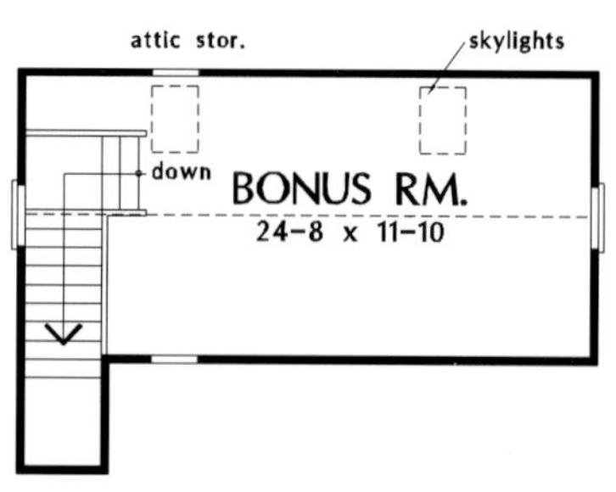

attic stor.
skylights
down
BONUS RM.
24-8 x 11-10

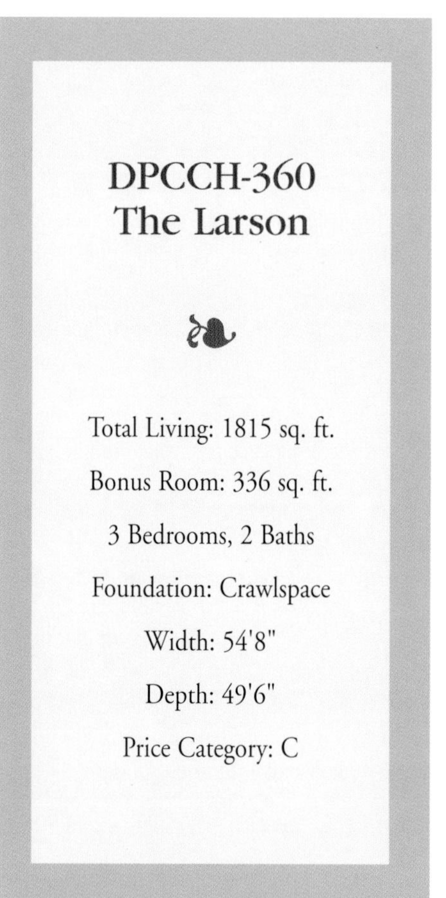

DPCCH-360
The Larson

Total Living: 1815 sq. ft.

Bonus Room: 336 sq. ft.

3 Bedrooms, 2 Baths

Foundation: Crawlspace

Width: 54'8"

Depth: 49'6"

Price Category: C

DESIGNER NOTE: *"Porches expand the living space and create wonderful 'rooms.' We wrapped this home's porch around the dining room and moved the garage to the back of the house."*

When you're working out of the house where clients often visit, it's important to have a dedicated office space, but more important, clients should feel at home. Using colors found at harvest time — earthy browns, ripe reds and deep greens — this room combines country style with a professional attitude.

The Larson

REAR

Photographed home may have been modified from the original construction documents.

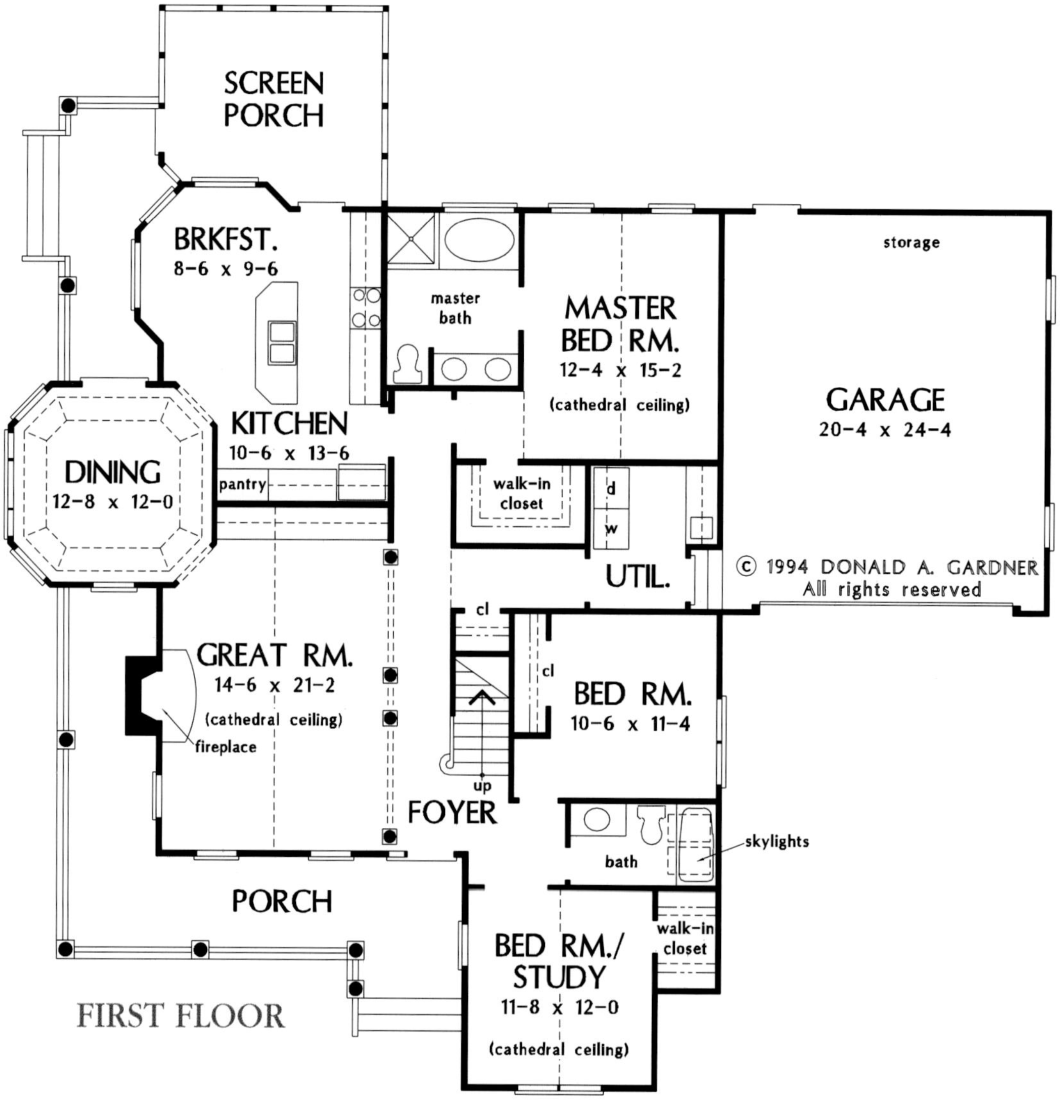

SCREEN PORCH

BRKFST.
8-6 x 9-6

KITCHEN
10-6 x 13-6

pantry

DINING
12-8 x 12-0

master bath

MASTER BED RM.
12-4 x 15-2
(cathedral ceiling)

storage

GARAGE
20-4 x 24-4

walk-in closet

d
w

UTIL.

cl

GREAT RM.
14-6 x 21-2
(cathedral ceiling)

fireplace

cl

BED RM.
10-6 x 11-4

up

FOYER

bath

skylights

PORCH

walk-in closet

BED RM./
STUDY
11-8 x 12-0
(cathedral ceiling)

FIRST FLOOR

BONUS RM.
14-2 x 17-10

down

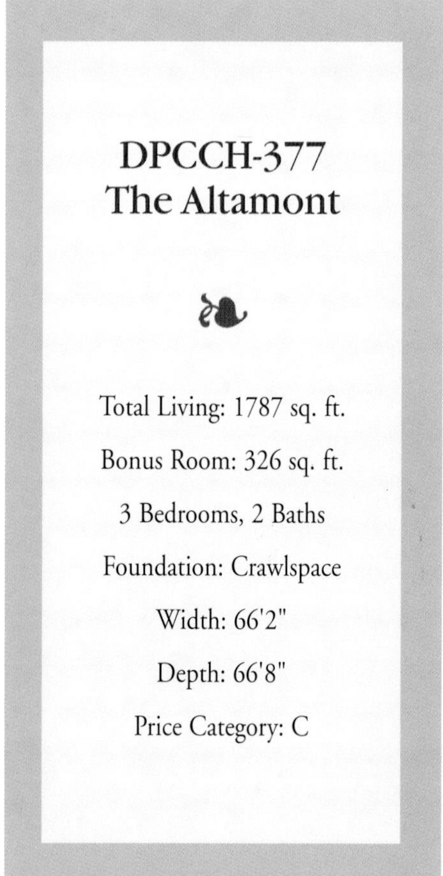

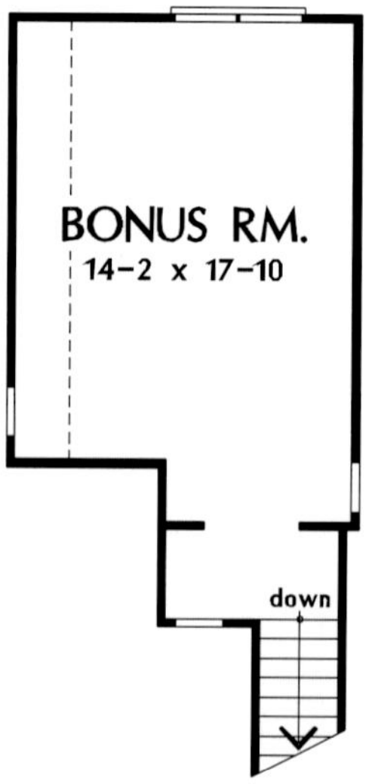

DPCCH-377
The Altamont

Total Living: 1787 sq. ft.

Bonus Room: 326 sq. ft.

3 Bedrooms, 2 Baths

Foundation: Crawlspace

Width: 66'2"

Depth: 66'8"

Price Category: C

DESIGNER NOTE: *"We thought that most homeowners would love to step outside, under a roof, from all the living spaces: great room, dining room, kitchen and breakfast room."*

There is a way to keep from tripping over toys — create a dedicated playroom in the bonus room. Games and toys may be scattered over the floor, but at least they are out of the way. Checkers are a favorite around here, along with coloring and video games. The kids share the playroom, and it helps keep their rooms a little more neat.

The Altamont

REAR

Photographed home may have been modified from the original construction documents.

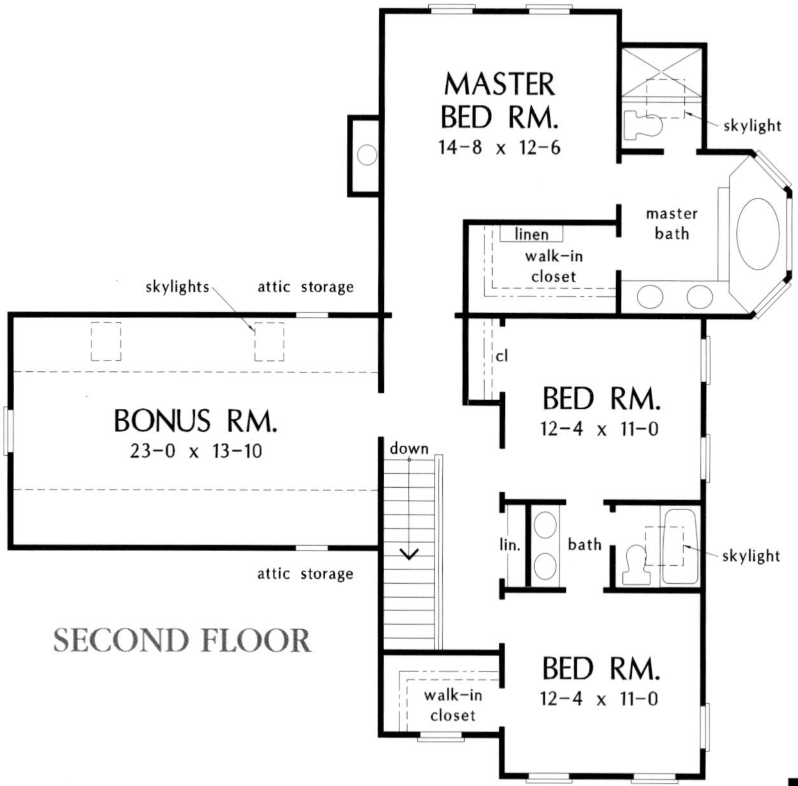

HIDDEN SPACES

MASTER BED RM. 14-8 x 12-6
skylight
master bath
linen
walk-in closet
skylights
attic storage
BONUS RM. 23-0 x 13-10
down
cl
BED RM. 12-4 x 11-0
lin.
bath
skylight
attic storage
BED RM. 12-4 x 11-0
walk-in closet

SECOND FLOOR

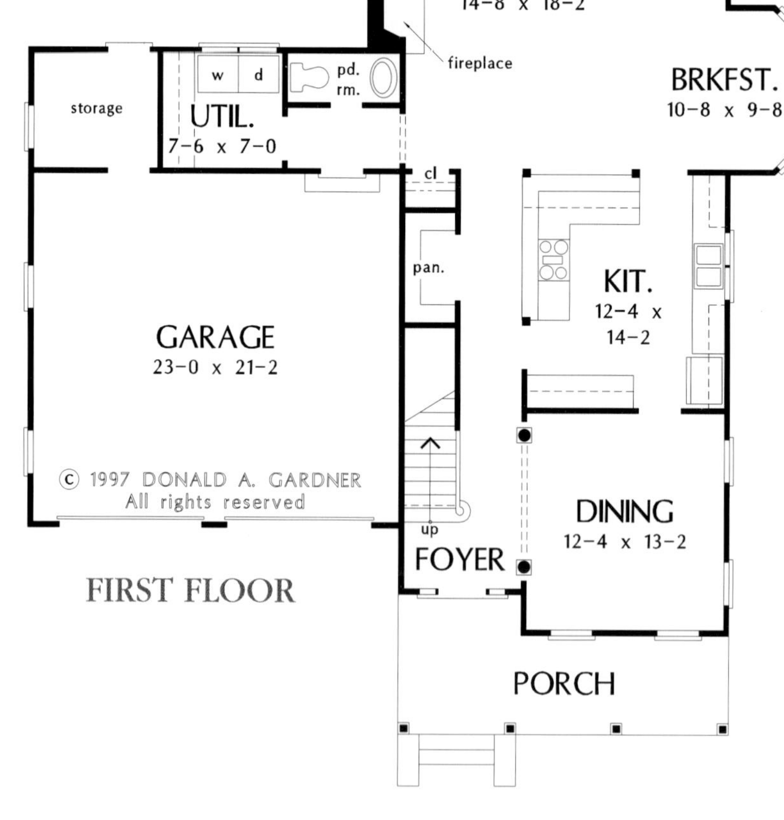

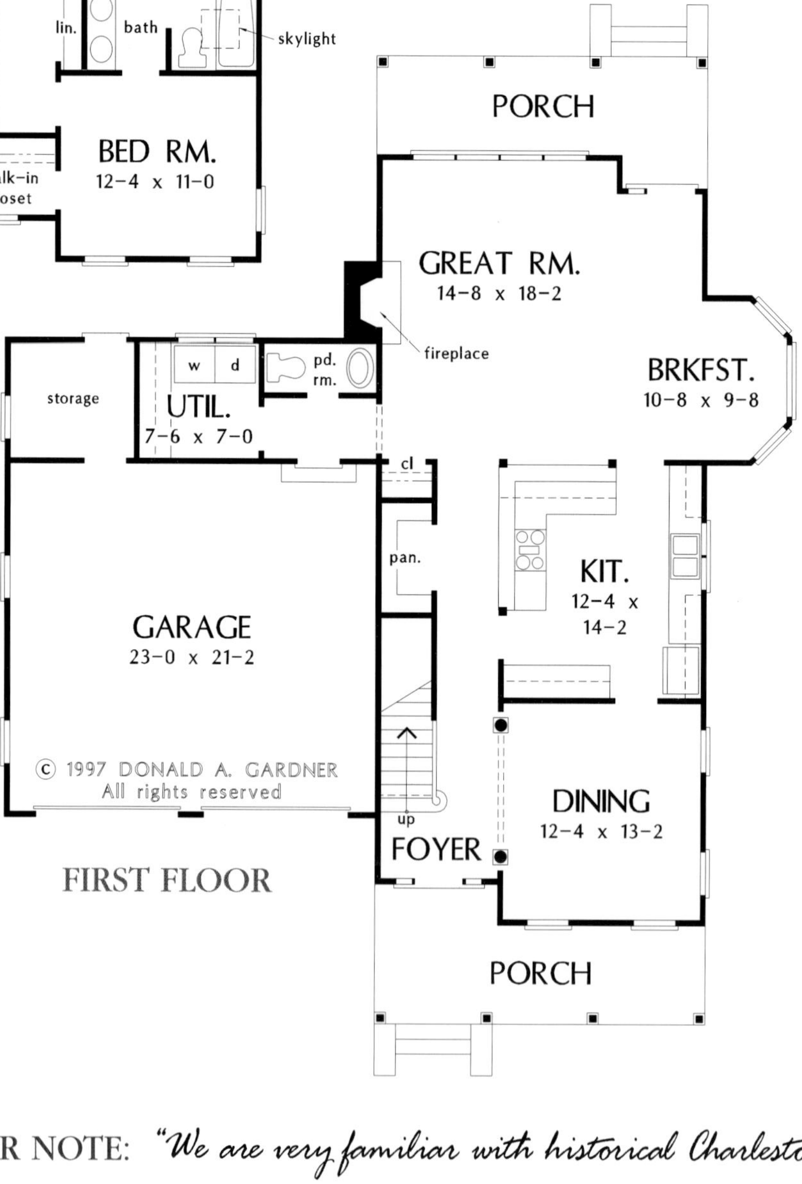

PORCH
GREAT RM. 14-8 x 18-2
fireplace
BRKFST. 10-8 x 9-8
storage
w
d
pd. rm.
UTIL. 7-6 x 7-0
cl
pan.
KIT. 12-4 x 14-2
GARAGE 23-0 x 21-2
© 1997 DONALD A. GARDNER
All rights reserved
up
FOYER
DINING 12-4 x 13-2
PORCH

FIRST FLOOR

DPCCH-486
The Waverly

Total Living: 2073 sq. ft.

First Floor: 1113 sq. ft.

Second Floor: 960 sq. ft.

Bonus Room: 338 sq. ft.

3 Bedrooms, 2-1/2 Baths

Foundation: Crawlspace

Width: 49'4"

Depth: 58'10"

Price Category: D

DESIGNER NOTE: *"We are very familiar with historical Charleston in our home state of South Carolina, and in this design we tried to achieve that same sense of charm and scale in a narrow footprint."*

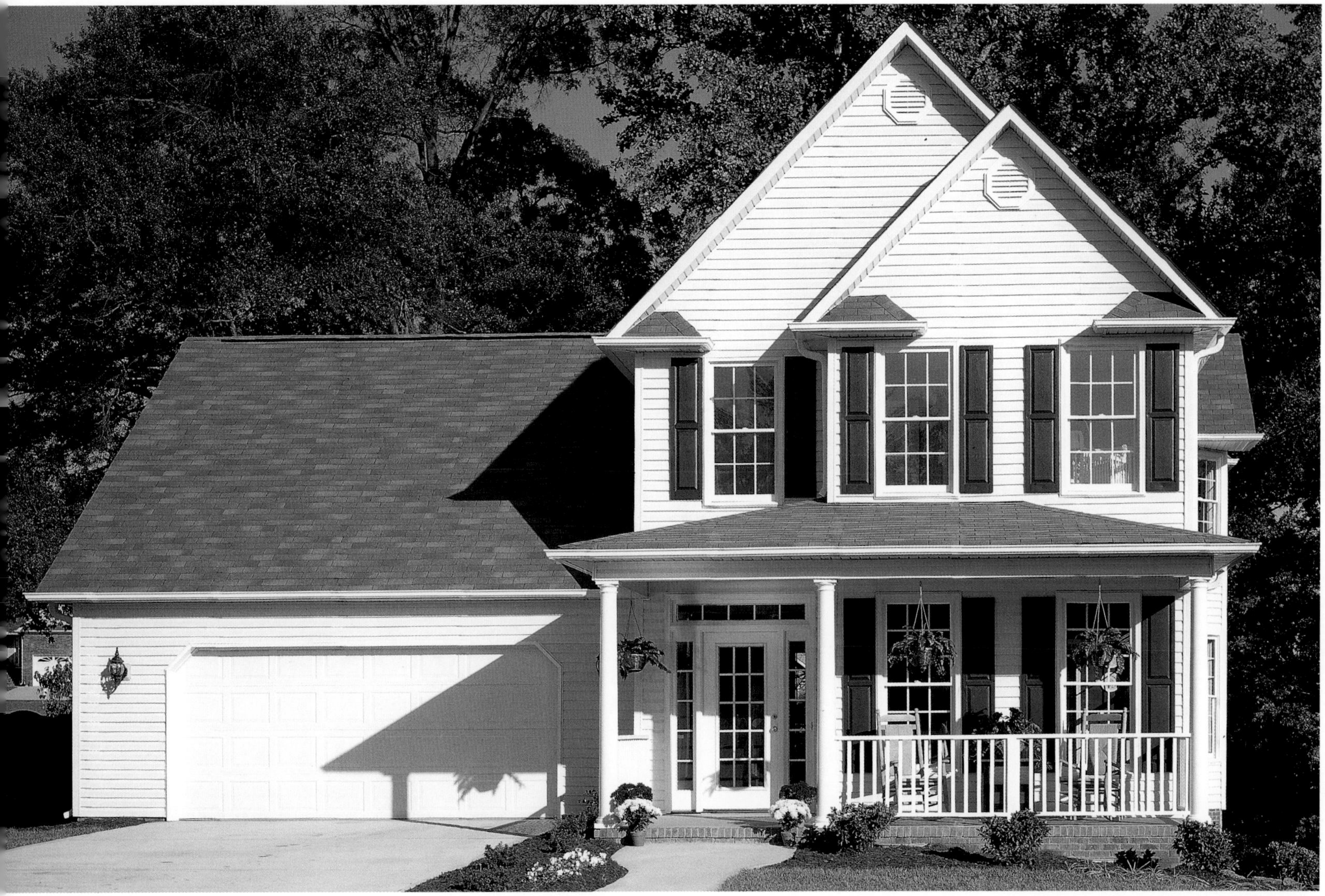

Our bonus room is a large nursery decorated with antique teddy bears. The sitting area has two large rocking chairs with an antique quilt rack. Mother's beautifully refurbished crib, alongside my aunt's wardrobe and washing stand, stands against the wall. It's funny how one person's hand-me-down is another person's heirloom.

REAR

Photographed home may have been modified from the original construction documents.

The Waverly

HIDDEN SPACES

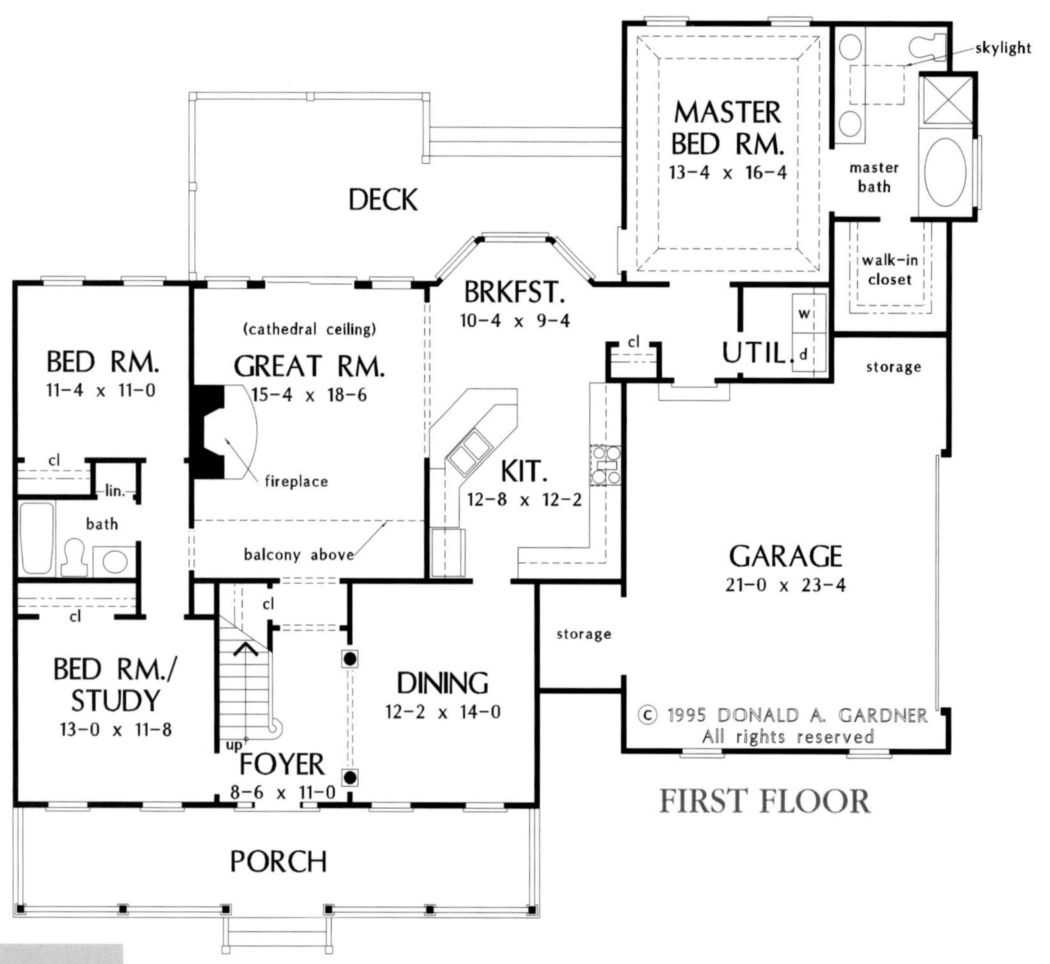

MASTER BED RM.
13-4 x 16-4
skylight
master bath
walk-in closet
DECK
BRKFST.
10-4 x 9-4
cl
UTIL.
w
d
storage
BED RM.
11-4 x 11-0
(cathedral ceiling)
GREAT RM.
15-4 x 18-6
fireplace
cl
lin.
bath
balcony above
KIT.
12-8 x 12-2
GARAGE
21-0 x 23-4
storage
cl
cl
BED RM./
STUDY
13-0 x 11-8
up
FOYER
8-6 x 11-0
DINING
12-2 x 14-0
© 1995 DONALD A. GARDNER
All rights reserved
FIRST FLOOR
PORCH

DPCCH-414
The Liberty Hill

Total Living: 1883 sq. ft.

First Floor: 1803 sq. ft.

Second Floor: 80 sq. ft.

Bonus Room: 918 sq. ft.

3 Bedrooms, 2 Baths

Foundation: Crawlspace

Width: 63'8"

Depth: 57'4"

Price Category: C

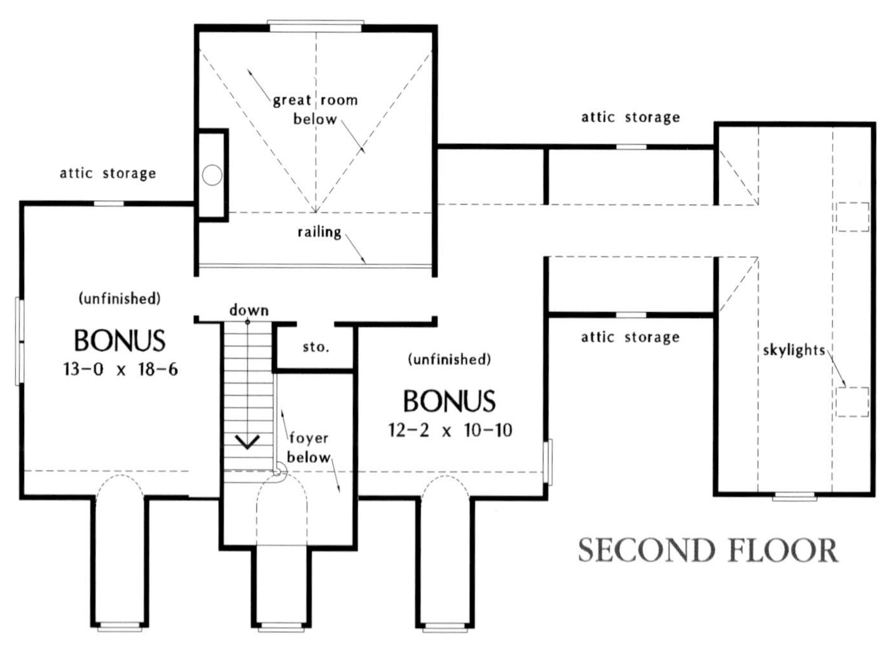

great room below
attic storage
attic storage
railing
(unfinished)
BONUS
13-0 x 18-6
down
sto.
(unfinished)
BONUS
12-2 x 10-10
attic storage
skylights
foyer below
SECOND FLOOR

DESIGNER NOTE: *"Did you ever wish you had another room? That's what we thought when we designed this home with bonus space that utilizes the entire attic."*

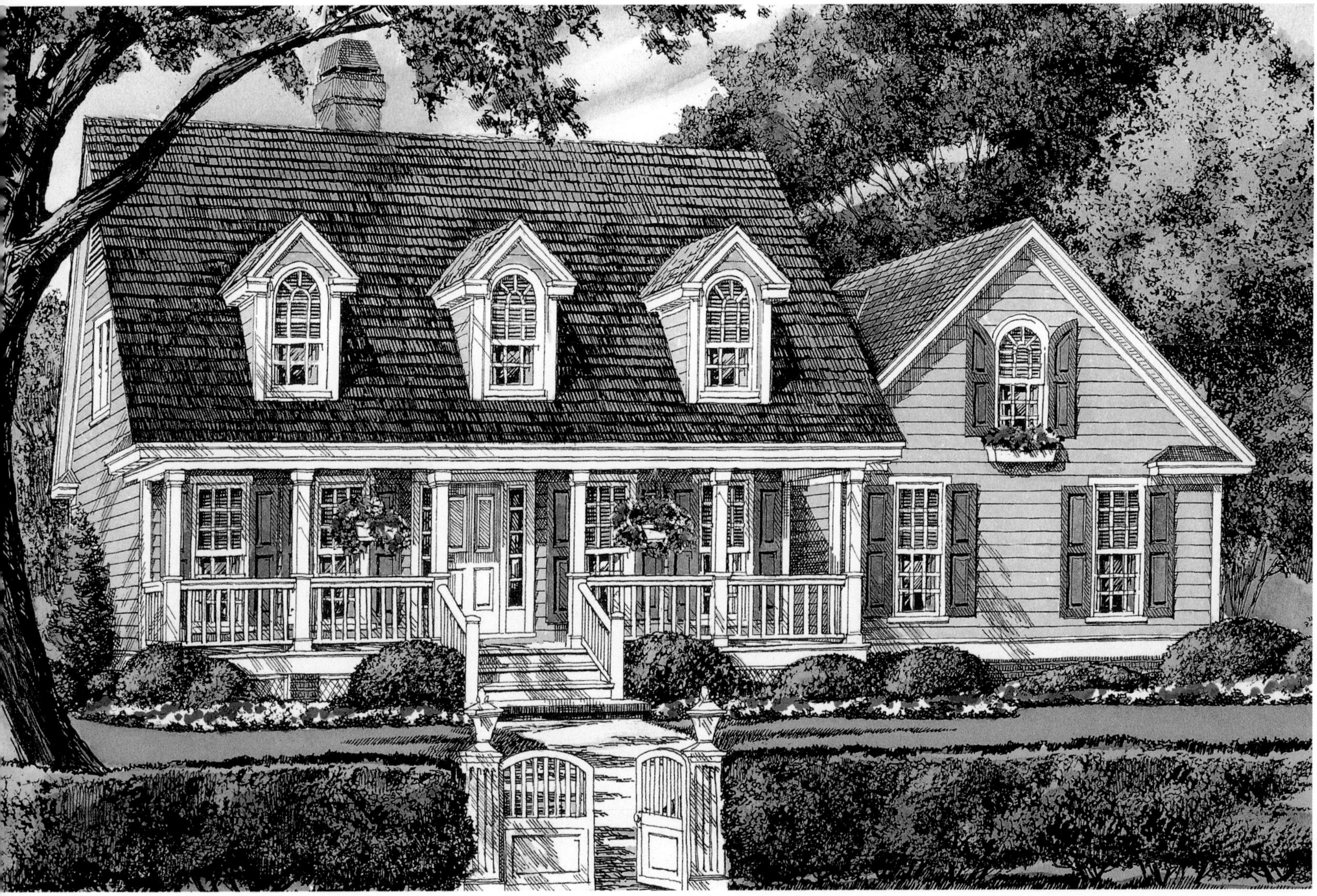

The entire upstairs was transformed for the kids: two bedrooms, two baths and plenty of game storage. Our son's room features a lodge theme with a matching private bath in hunter green and deep red. Our daughter chose a pale yellow and sage décor. Her bath is across from her room and is decorated with flowers and dragonflies.

The Liberty Hill

REAR

HIDDEN SPACES

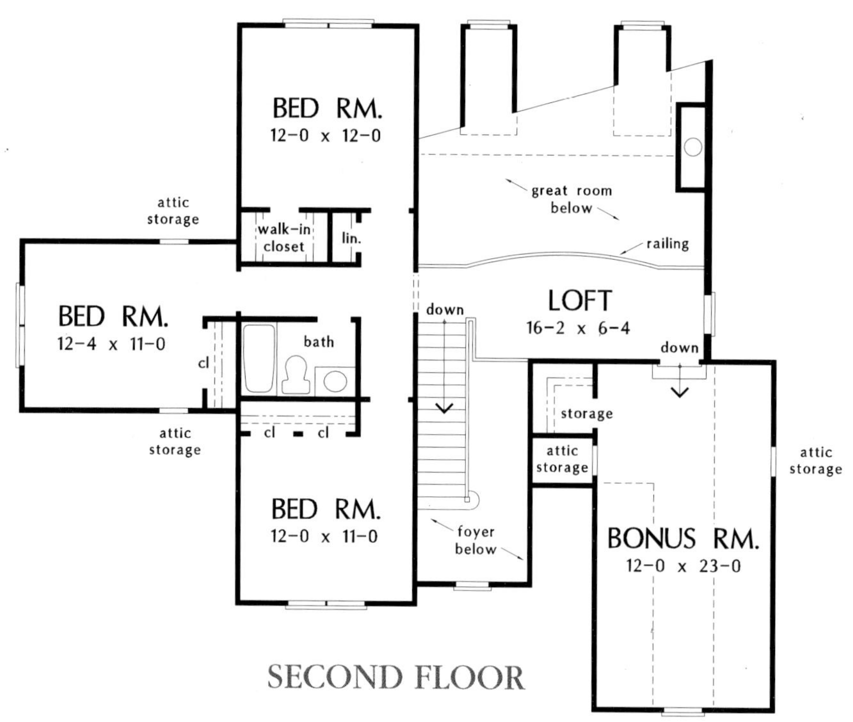

BED RM.
12-0 x 12-0
attic storage
walk-in closet
lin.
great room below
railing
BED RM.
12-4 x 11-0
bath
cl
LOFT
16-2 x 6-4
down
down
storage
attic storage
cl
cl
attic storage
attic storage
BED RM.
12-0 x 11-0
foyer below
BONUS RM.
12-0 x 23-0

SECOND FLOOR

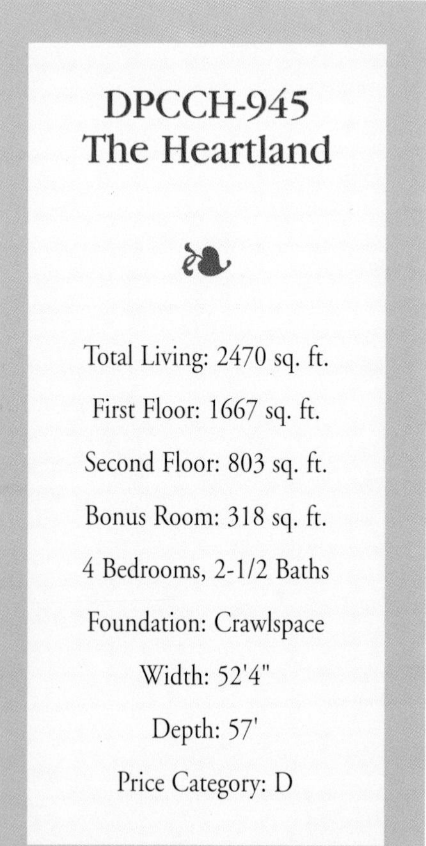

DPCCH-945
The Heartland

Total Living: 2470 sq. ft.

First Floor: 1667 sq. ft.

Second Floor: 803 sq. ft.

Bonus Room: 318 sq. ft.

4 Bedrooms, 2-1/2 Baths

Foundation: Crawlspace

Width: 52'4"

Depth: 57'

Price Category: D

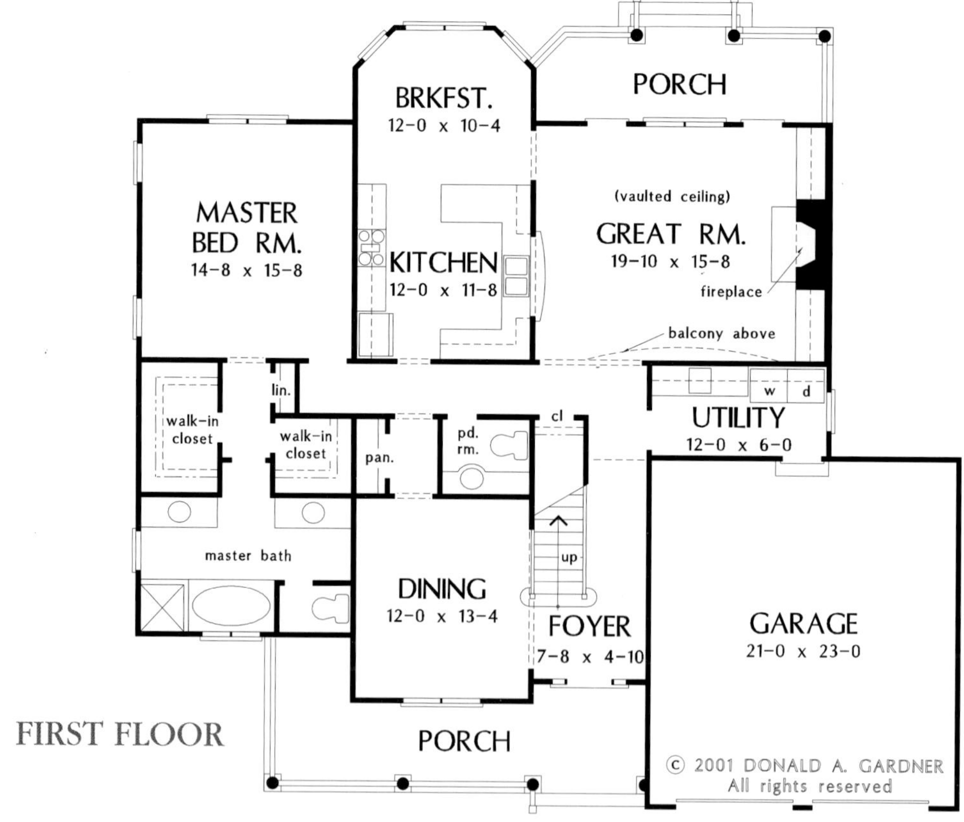

BRKFST.
12-0 x 10-4
PORCH
MASTER BED RM.
14-8 x 15-8
KITCHEN
12-0 x 11-8
(vaulted ceiling)
GREAT RM.
19-10 x 15-8
fireplace
balcony above
lin.
walk-in closet
walk-in closet
pan.
pd. rm.
cl
w d
UTILITY
12-0 x 6-0
master bath
up
DINING
12-0 x 13-4
FOYER
7-8 x 4-10
GARAGE
21-0 x 23-0
PORCH
© 2001 DONALD A. GARDNER
All rights reserved

FIRST FLOOR

DESIGNER NOTE: *"In designing this home, we had in mind the ideal family home: two dining spaces, a generous great room with overlooking loft, four bedrooms, a wrapping porch and a bonus space for the office, media or rec room."*

My wife and I like to watch old black and white movies, especially westerns. Although the kids watch them with us occasionally, they like teenage movies my wife and I don't always enjoy. Now the kids have a dedicated media room in the bonus room. They watch their movies and listen to their music up there, and we enjoy ours down here.

The Heartland

REAR

PORCH
BRKFST. 10-0 x 9-4
MASTER BED RM. 13-0 x 16-0
BED RM. 11-0 x 12-0
GREAT RM. 15-8 x 19-0
KIT. 10-0 x 12-0
BED RM. 11-0 x 12-0
FOYER 6-0 x 13-0
DINING 12-0 x 13-0
UTIL. 6-0 x 10-0
PORCH
BED RM./ STUDY 11-0 x 12-0
GARAGE 21-0 x 21-0

FIRST FLOOR

BONUS RM. 14-0 x 21-0

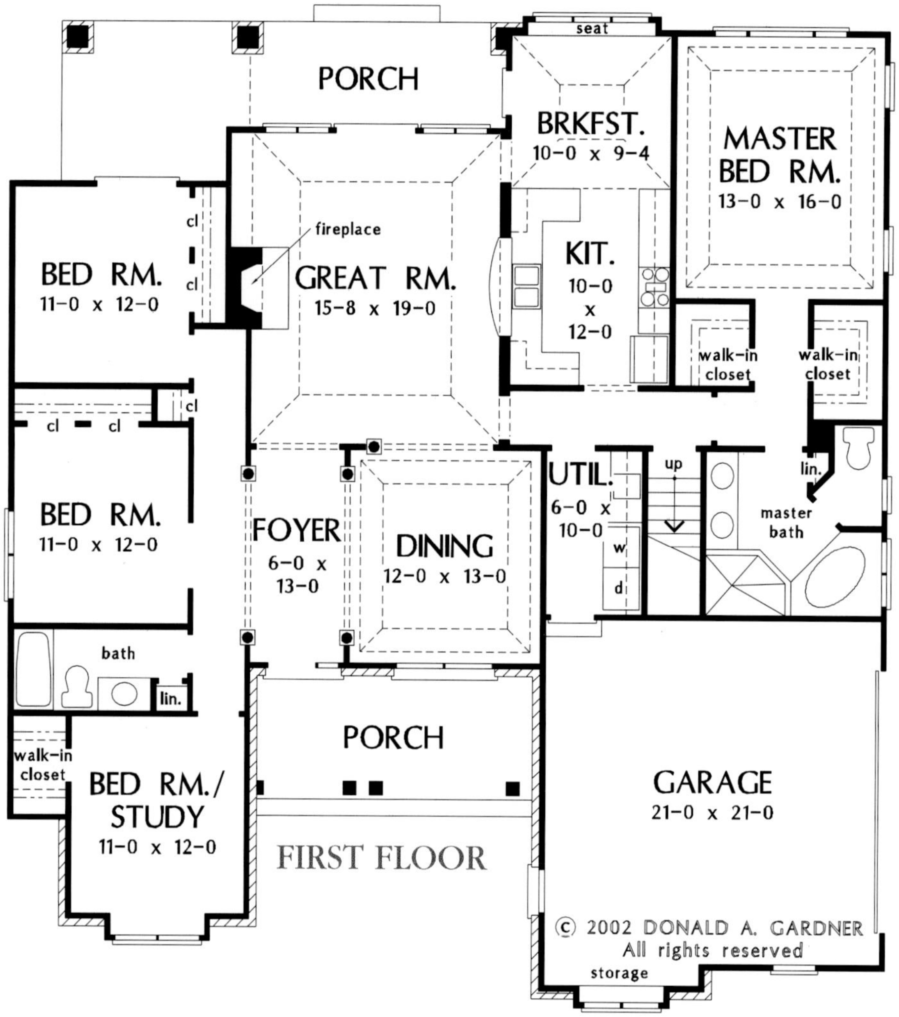

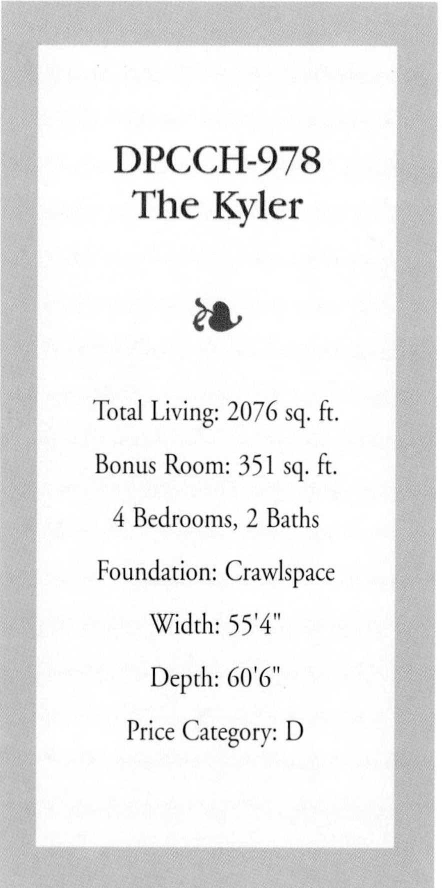

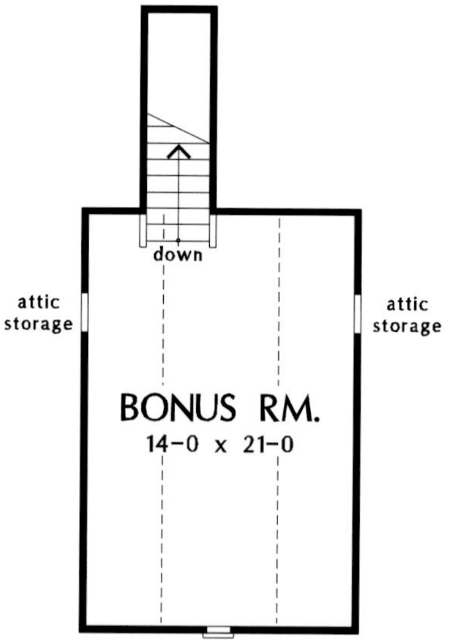

DPCCH-978
The Kyler

Total Living: 2076 sq. ft.

Bonus Room: 351 sq. ft.

4 Bedrooms, 2 Baths

Foundation: Crawlspace

Width: 55'4"

Depth: 60'6"

Price Category: D

DESIGNER NOTE: *"Traditional exteriors just say 'home.' This house features traditional elements such as gable brackets, shutters, brick and siding, arched porch beams, trimmed columns and a widow bay topped with a metal roof."*

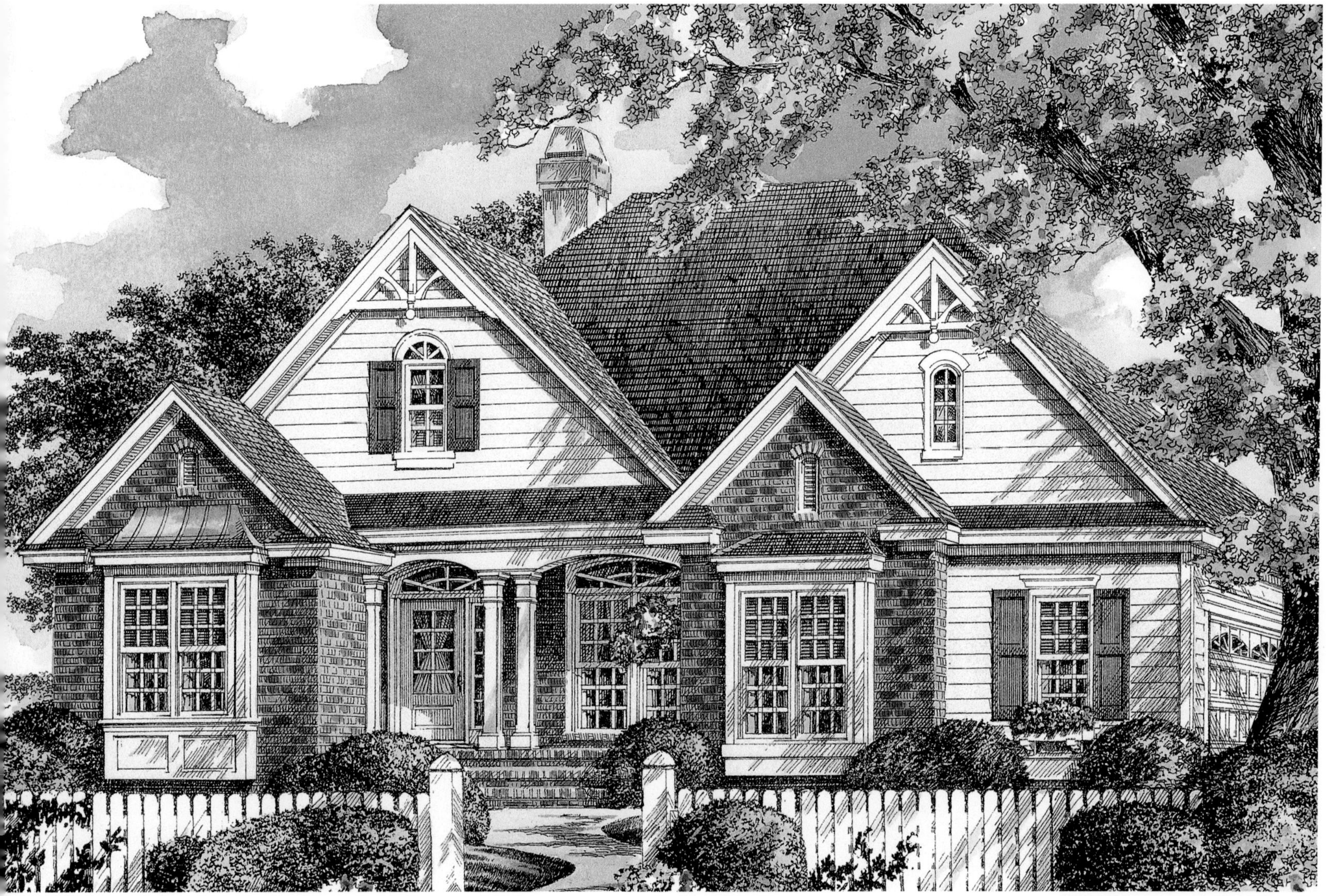

My husband played football for a small, rural high school team. They were state champions his senior year. When we decided to turn the bonus room into a home gym, I pulled out his old photos, trophies and jersey, using them to create a special area he would enjoy. He thinks it's great, saying he's inspired to be in that shape again.

The Kyler

REAR

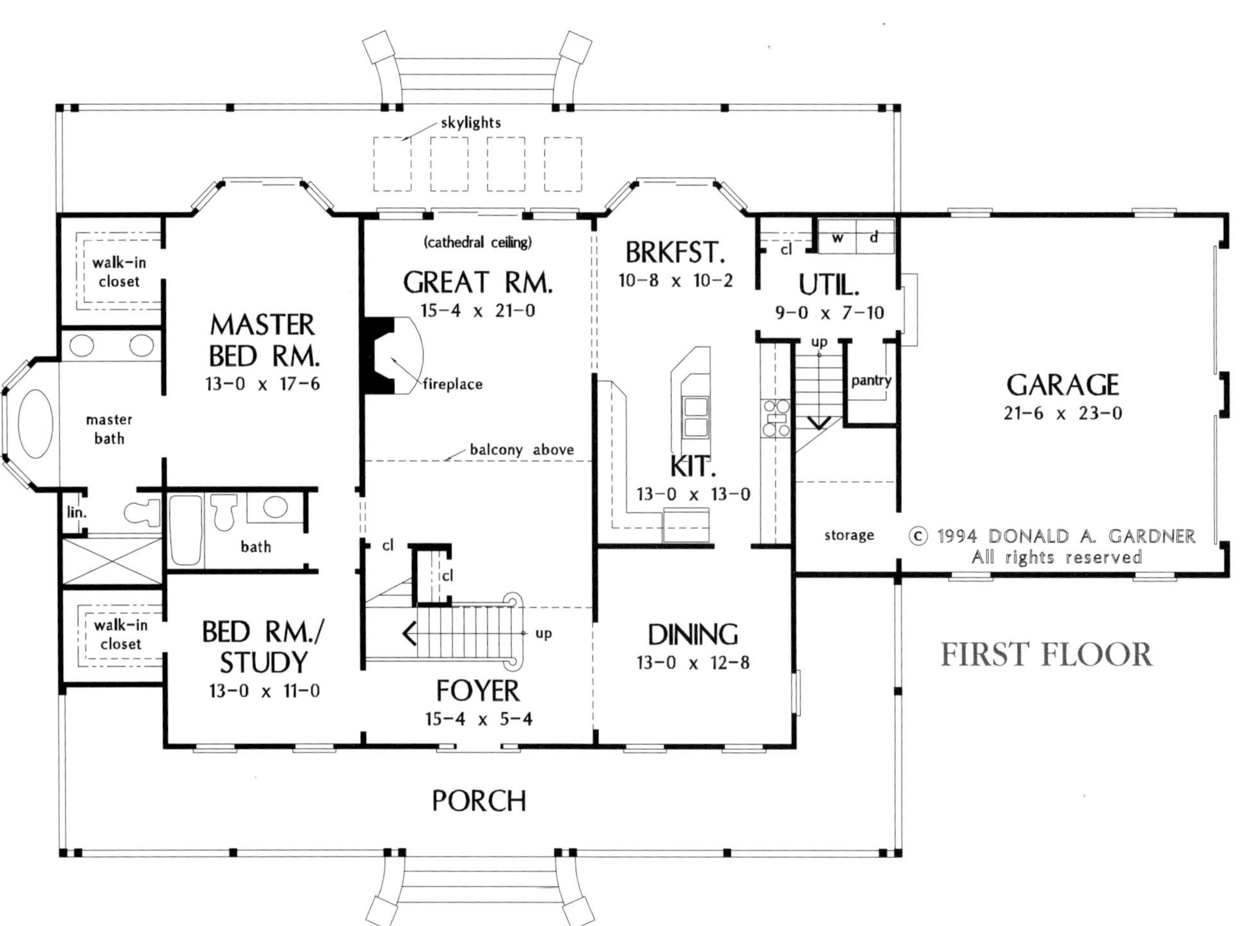
skylights
(cathedral ceiling)
GREAT RM.
15-4 x 21-0
fireplace
balcony above
walk-in closet
MASTER BED RM.
13-0 x 17-6
master bath
lin.
bath
walk-in closet
BED RM./ STUDY
13-0 x 11-0
cl
cl
up
FOYER
15-4 x 5-4
BRKFST.
10-8 x 10-2
KIT.
13-0 x 13-0
DINING
13-0 x 12-8
cl
w
d
UTIL.
9-0 x 7-10
up
pantry
storage
GARAGE
21-6 x 23-0
© 1994 DONALD A. GARDNER
All rights reserved
PORCH
FIRST FLOOR

DPCCH-370
The Dobbins

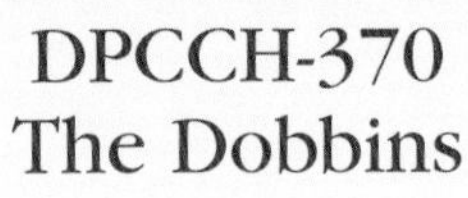

Total Living: 2435 sq. ft.

First Floor: 1841 sq. ft.

Second Floor: 594 sq. ft.

Bonus Room: 391 sq. ft.

4 Bedrooms, 3 Baths

Foundation: Crawlspace

Width: 82'2"

Depth: 48'10"

Price Category: D

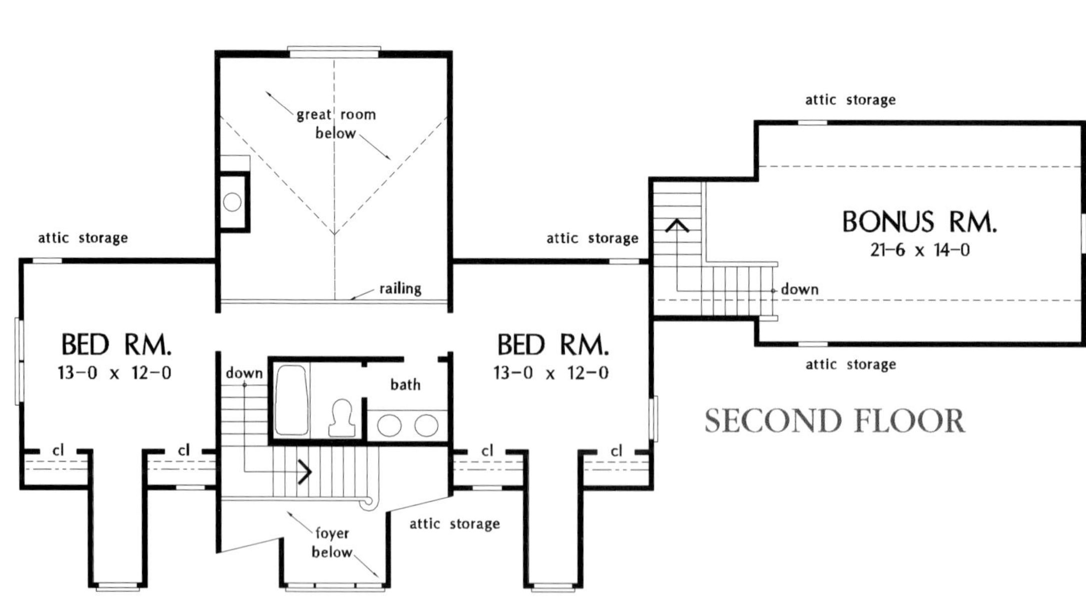
great room below
railing
attic storage
attic storage
attic storage
attic storage
attic storage
BED RM.
13-0 x 12-0
down
bath
BED RM.
13-0 x 12-0
cl
cl
cl
cl
foyer below
BONUS RM.
21-6 x 14-0
down
SECOND FLOOR

DESIGNER NOTE: *"Our customers love porches, so we nearly wrapped this entire house with one. We think it's just great."*

We have decided to hold the quilting bee in the bonus room from now on. As part of the new quilting room décor, we're going to hang three generations of quilts along the walls. A large center table will be perfect for quilting and conversation, and since the bonus room is near the kitchen, it will be easy to arrange refreshments.

The Dobbins

REAR

HIDDEN SPACES

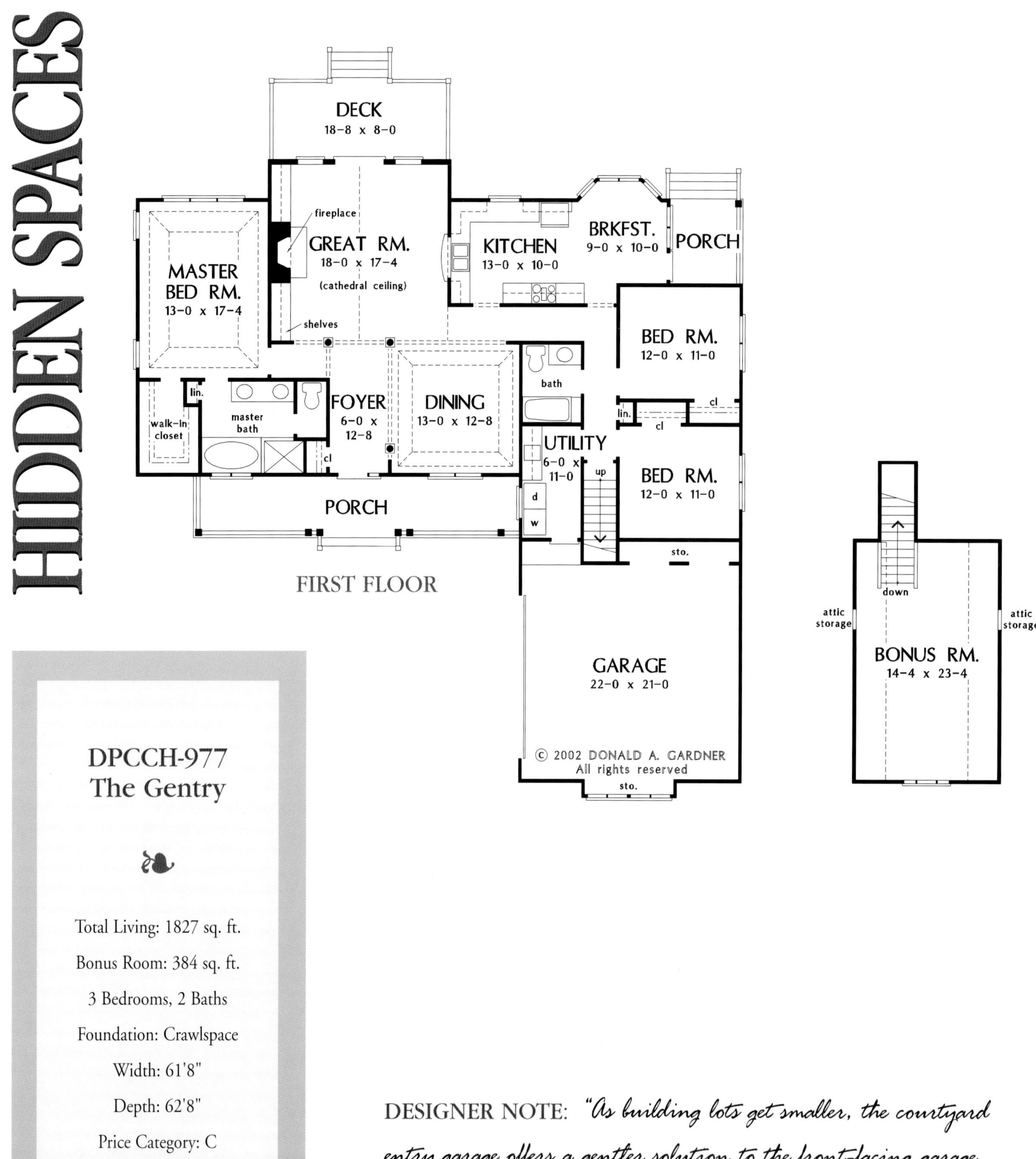
DECK
18-8 x 8-0
fireplace
GREAT RM.
18-0 x 17-4
(cathedral ceiling)
shelves
MASTER
BED RM.
13-0 x 17-4
KITCHEN
13-0 x 10-0
BRKFST.
9-0 x 10-0
PORCH
BED RM.
12-0 x 11-0
lin.
walk-in
closet
master
bath
cl
FOYER
6-0 x
12-8
DINING
13-0 x 12-8
bath
lin.
cl
cl
UTILITY
6-0 x
11-0
up
BED RM.
12-0 x 11-0
d
w
PORCH
sto.
FIRST FLOOR
GARAGE
22-0 x 21-0
© 2002 DONALD A. GARDNER
All rights reserved
sto.
down
attic
storage
attic
storage
BONUS RM.
14-4 x 23-4

DPCCH-977
The Gentry

Total Living: 1827 sq. ft.

Bonus Room: 384 sq. ft.

3 Bedrooms, 2 Baths

Foundation: Crawlspace

Width: 61'8"

Depth: 62'8"

Price Category: C

DESIGNER NOTE: *"As building lots get smaller, the courtyard entry garage offers a gentler solution to the front-facing garage. We added one to this design and kept the house as the focal point by incorporating a front porch and intersecting gable over the entry."*

The bonus room is an office with an antique desk, file cabinet and collection of old fans. Old typewriters and cabinetry help soften the modern look of the computer, while an old mail sack covers a trash can. Framed postcards from the late 1800s and early 1900s fill the walls, and reproduction lamps add plenty of light.

The Gentry

REAR

HIDDEN SPACES

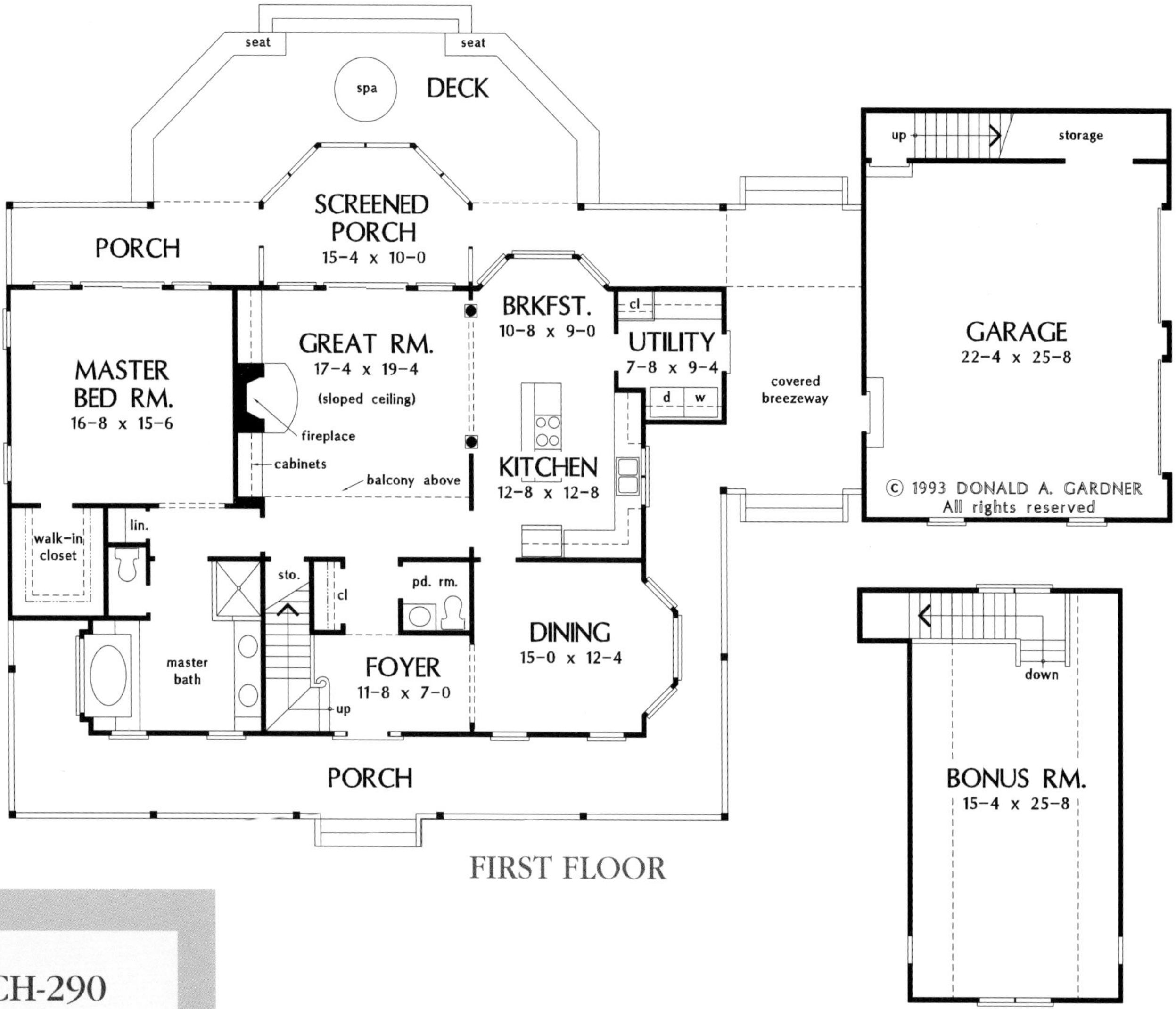

seat
seat
spa
DECK
PORCH
SCREENED PORCH 15-4 x 10-0
BRKFST. 10-8 x 9-0
cl
UTILITY 7-8 x 9-4
d
w
MASTER BED RM. 16-8 x 15-6
GREAT RM. 17-4 x 19-4 (sloped ceiling)
fireplace
cabinets
balcony above
KITCHEN 12-8 x 12-8
covered breezeway
walk-in closet
lin.
sto.
cl
pd. rm.
master bath
FOYER 11-8 x 7-0
up
DINING 15-0 x 12-4
PORCH
up
storage
GARAGE 22-4 x 25-8
© 1993 DONALD A. GARDNER
All rights reserved
down
BONUS RM. 15-4 x 25-8

FIRST FLOOR

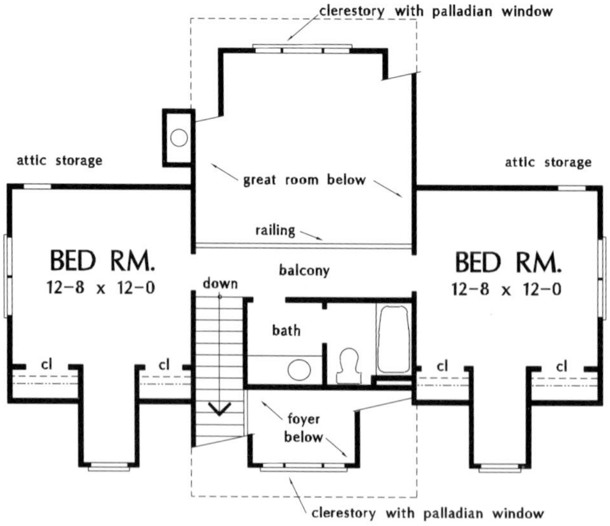

clerestory with palladian window
attic storage
great room below
attic storage
railing
BED RM. 12-8 x 12-0
balcony
down
BED RM. 12-8 x 12-0
bath
cl
cl
cl
cl
foyer below
clerestory with palladian window

SECOND FLOOR

DPCCH-290
The Burgess

Total Living: 2188 sq. ft.

First Floor: 1618 sq. ft.

Second Floor: 570 sq. ft.

Bonus Room: 495 sq. ft.

3 Bedrooms, 2-1/2 Baths

Foundation: Crawlspace

Width: 54'

Depth: 57'

Price Category: D

DESIGNER NOTE: *"When we designed this home we thought of the delightful farm houses from days gone by with their detached garages and wrapping porches."*

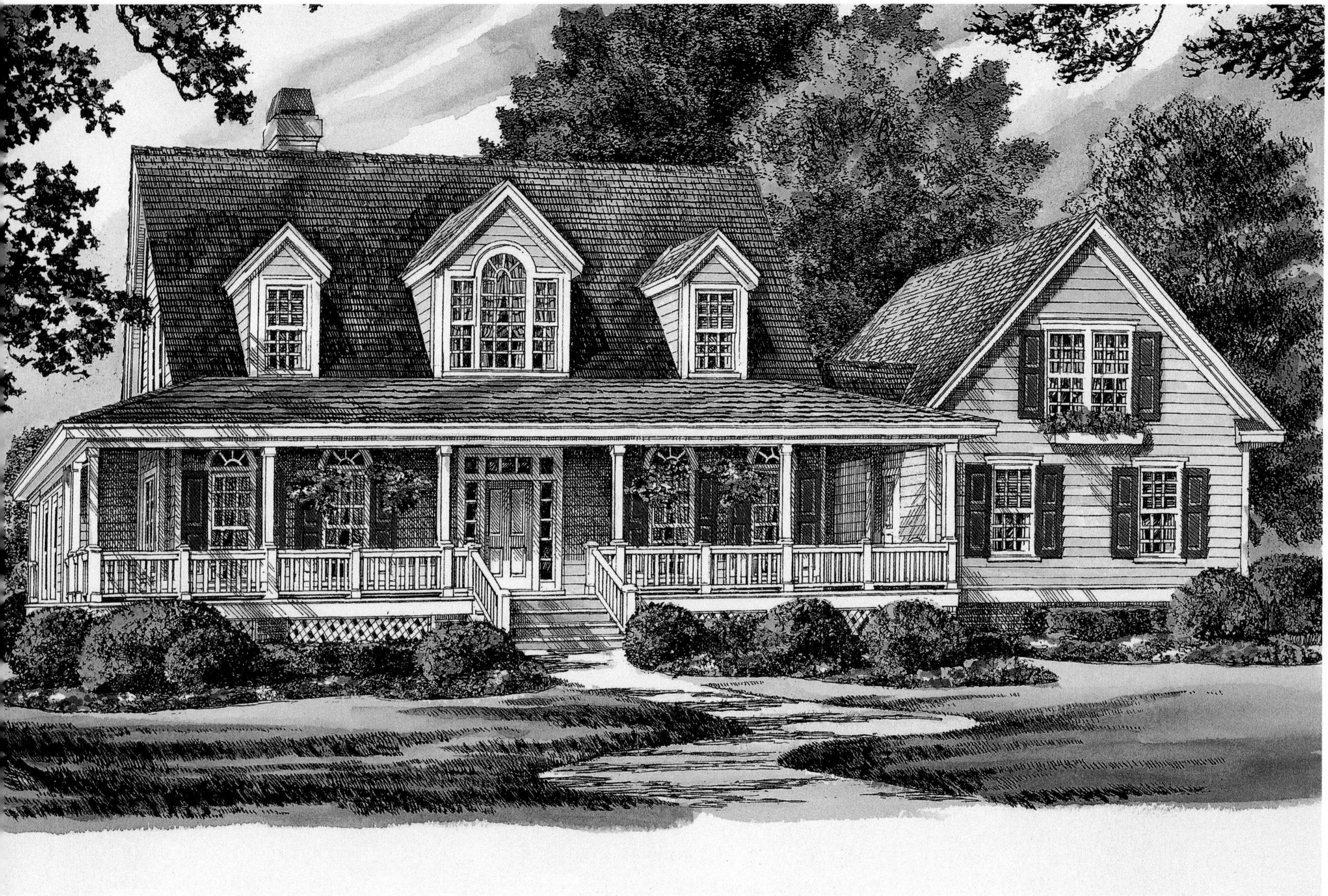

We put shelves along our bonus room walls and turned it into a massive storage area. It's very organized, and it's easy to find things. Seasonal decorations are in one area, and our tents, innertubes and fishing poles are in another. It makes packing for camping trips convenient, and the horseshoes and badminton set are there too.

The Burgess

REAR

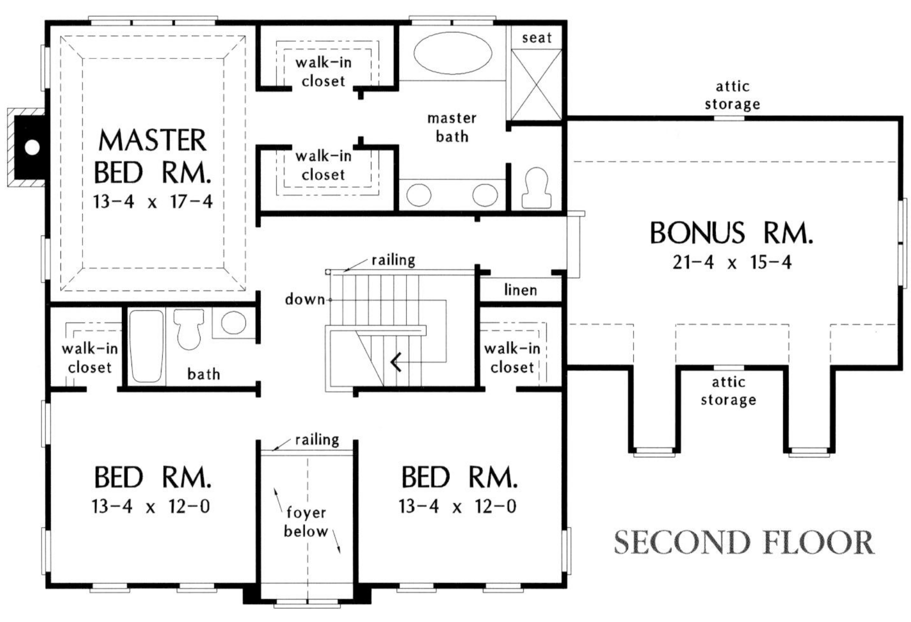

seat
walk-in closet
master bath
attic storage
MASTER BED RM. 13-4 x 17-4
walk-in closet
BONUS RM. 21-4 x 15-4
railing
linen
down
walk-in closet
bath
walk-in closet
attic storage
railing
BED RM. 13-4 x 12-0
foyer below
BED RM. 13-4 x 12-0
SECOND FLOOR

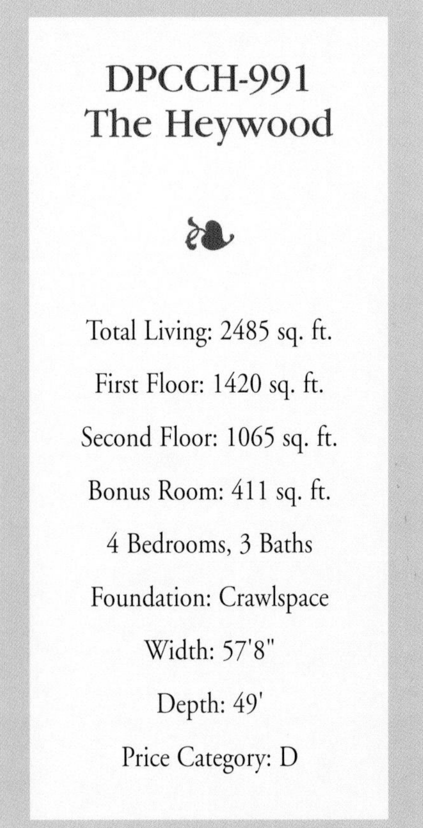

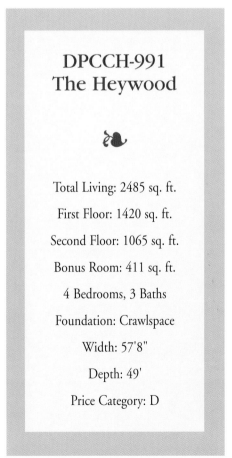

DPCCH-991
The Heywood

Total Living: 2485 sq. ft.

First Floor: 1420 sq. ft.

Second Floor: 1065 sq. ft.

Bonus Room: 411 sq. ft.

4 Bedrooms, 3 Baths

Foundation: Crawlspace

Width: 57'8"

Depth: 49'

Price Category: D

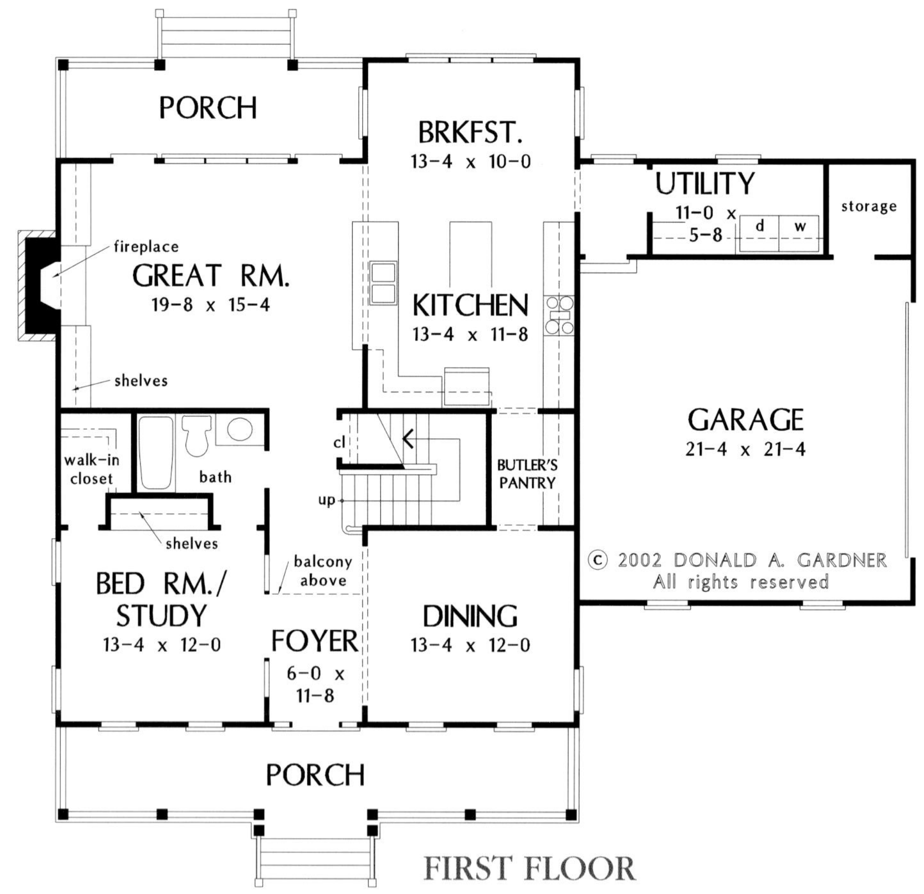

PORCH
BRKFST. 13-4 x 10-0
UTILITY 11-0 x 5-8
d
w
storage
fireplace
GREAT RM. 19-8 x 15-4
KITCHEN 13-4 x 11-8
shelves
GARAGE 21-4 x 21-4
walk-in closet
bath
cl
BUTLER'S PANTRY
up
shelves
balcony above
© 2002 DONALD A. GARDNER All rights reserved
BED RM./ STUDY 13-4 x 12-0
FOYER 6-0 x 11-8
DINING 13-4 x 12-0
PORCH
FIRST FLOOR

DESIGNER NOTE: *"We are consistently trying to combine uniqueness and efficiency into our homes. This design does both with style and grace."*

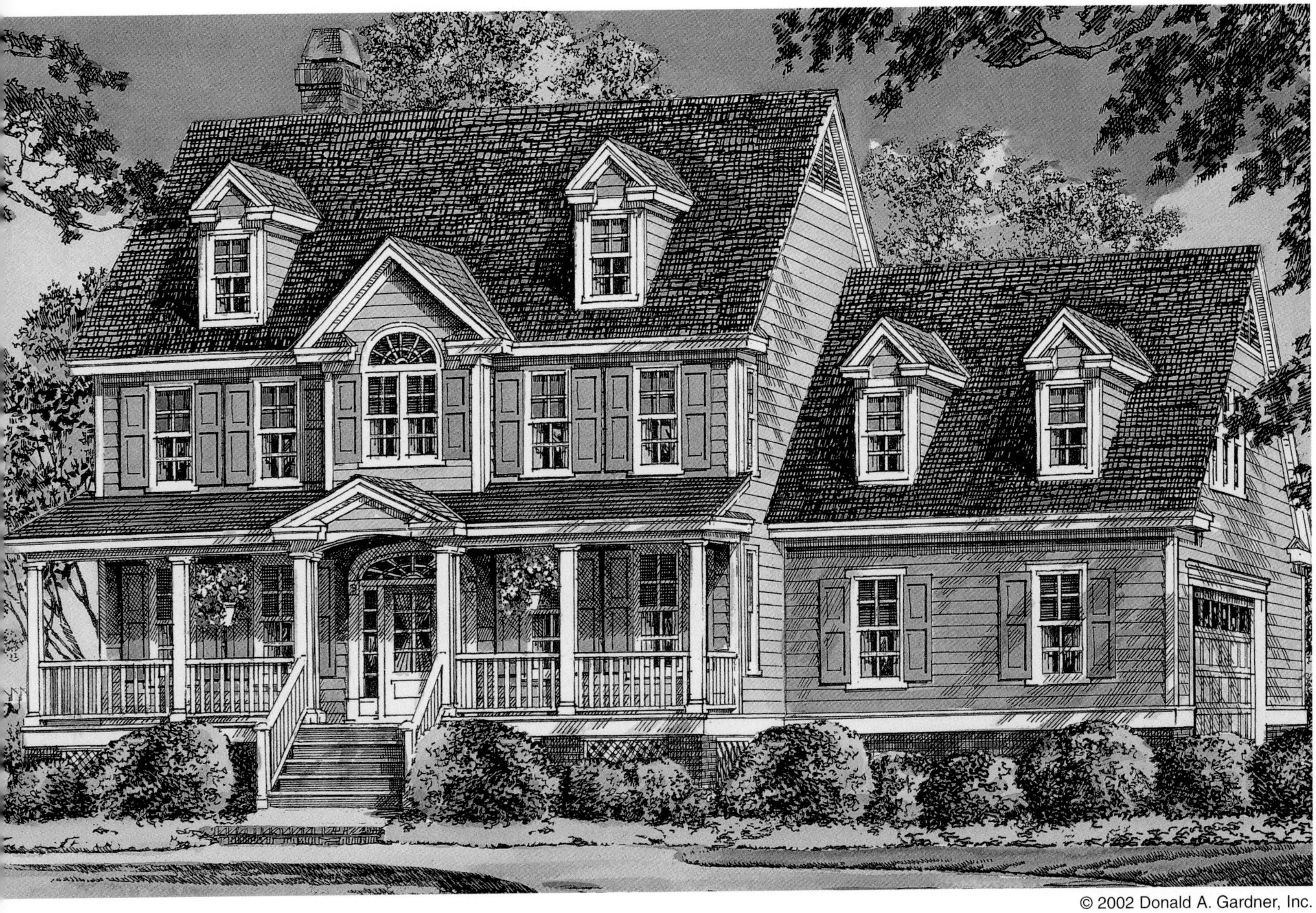

Today when I came home there was yarn all over the house. The kids had been playing in the backyard, and when I asked them how it happened, they didn't have any idea. After much research, we discovered the kitten had found my yarn in the bonus room. She must have played hard, because she was asleep next to my yarn basket.

The Heywood

REAR

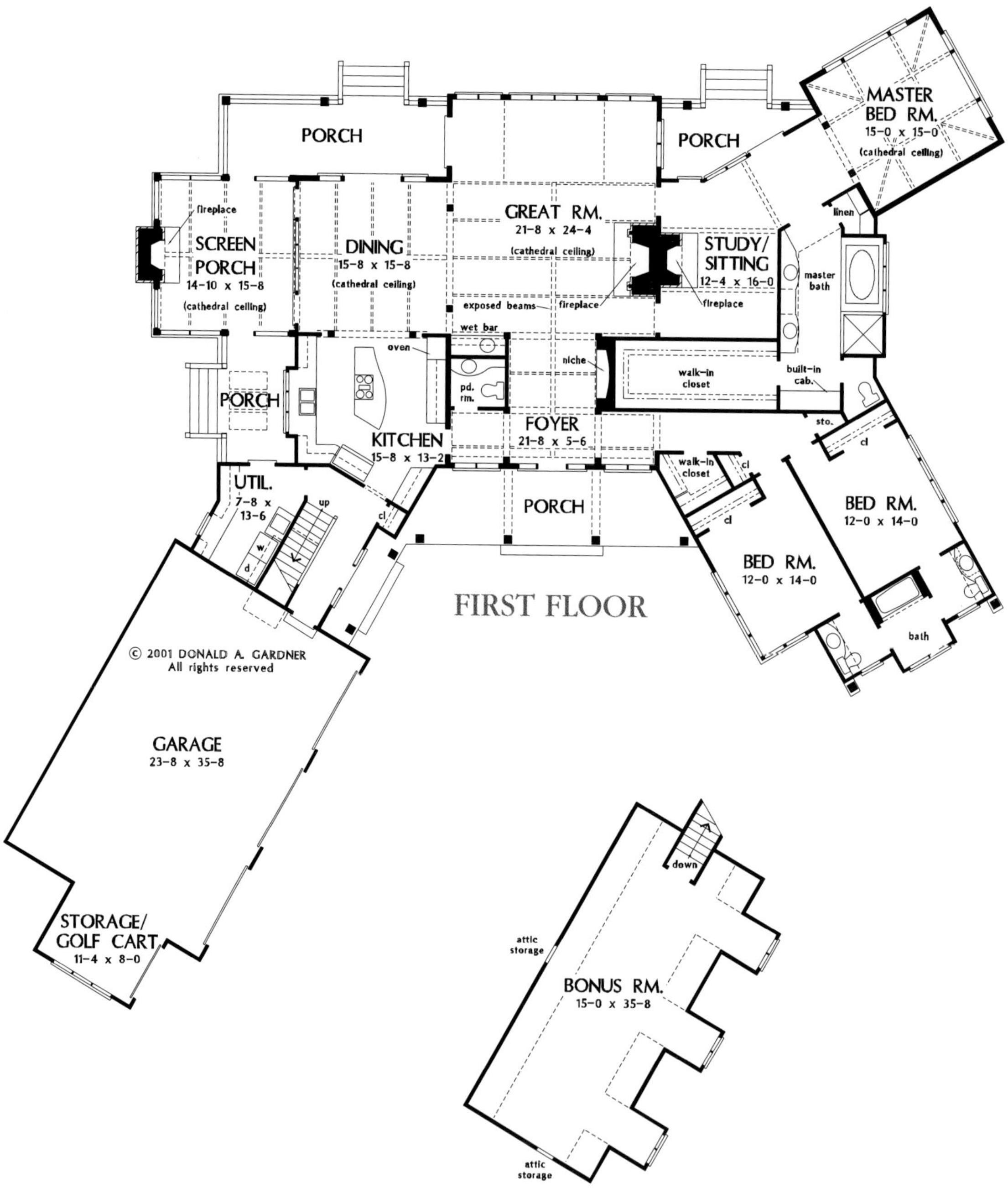

PORCH
PORCH
MASTER BED RM. 15-0 x 15-0 (cathedral ceiling)
fireplace
SCREEN PORCH 14-10 x 15-8 (cathedral ceiling)
DINING 15-8 x 15-8 (cathedral ceiling)
GREAT RM. 21-8 x 24-4 (cathedral ceiling)
STUDY/ SITTING 12-4 x 16-0
linen
master bath
exposed beams
fireplace
fireplace
wet bar
oven
pd. rm.
niche
walk-in closet
built-in cab.
PORCH
KITCHEN 15-8 x 13-2
FOYER 21-8 x 5-6
sto.
cl
UTIL. 7-8 x 13-6
up
cl
w
d
PORCH
walk-in closet
cl
cl
BED RM. 12-0 x 14-0
BED RM. 12-0 x 14-0
bath
FIRST FLOOR

GARAGE 23-8 x 35-8
STORAGE/ GOLF CART 11-4 x 8-0
down
attic storage
BONUS RM. 15-0 x 35-8
attic storage

DPCCH-959
The Cedar Creek

Total Living: 3188 sq. ft.

Bonus Room: 615 sq. ft.

3 Bedrooms, 2-1/2 Baths

Foundation: Crawlspace

Width: 106'4"

Depth: 104'1"

Price Category: F

DESIGNER NOTE: *"This home was designed for the lot that has an 180-degree view and for owners who enjoy an informal, yet sophisticated lifestyle."*

Our bonus room has been turned into a guest suite. With a morning kitchen and private bath, guests feel more comfortable and independent. They come and go as they please through the main house or service entrance, yet the suite is convenient to the gathering rooms. It's decorated with a lodge feel — complete with a feather bed.

The Cedar Creek

REAR

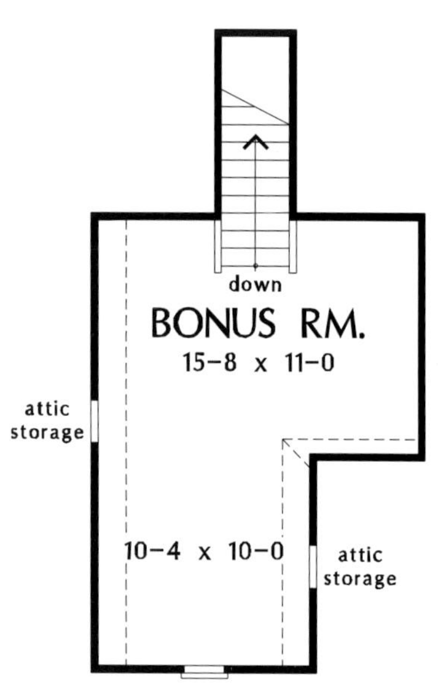
down
BONUS RM.
15–8 x 11–0
attic storage
10–4 x 10–0
attic storage

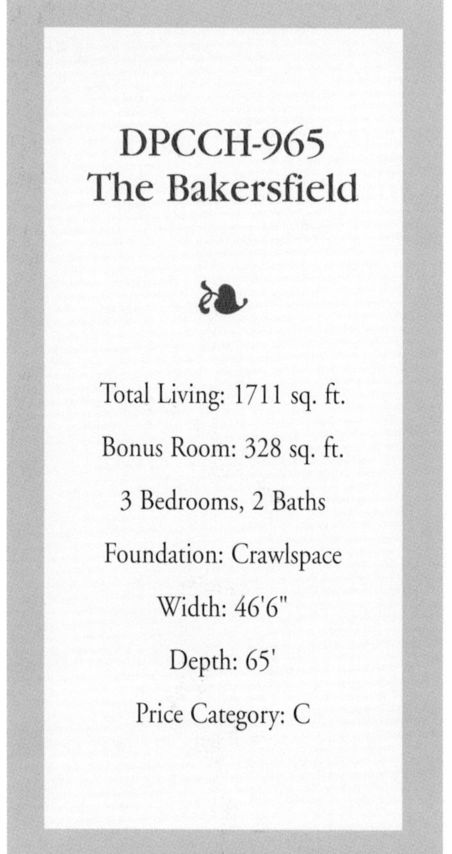

DPCCH-965
The Bakersfield

Total Living: 1711 sq. ft.

Bonus Room: 328 sq. ft.

3 Bedrooms, 2 Baths

Foundation: Crawlspace

Width: 46'6"

Depth: 65'

Price Category: C

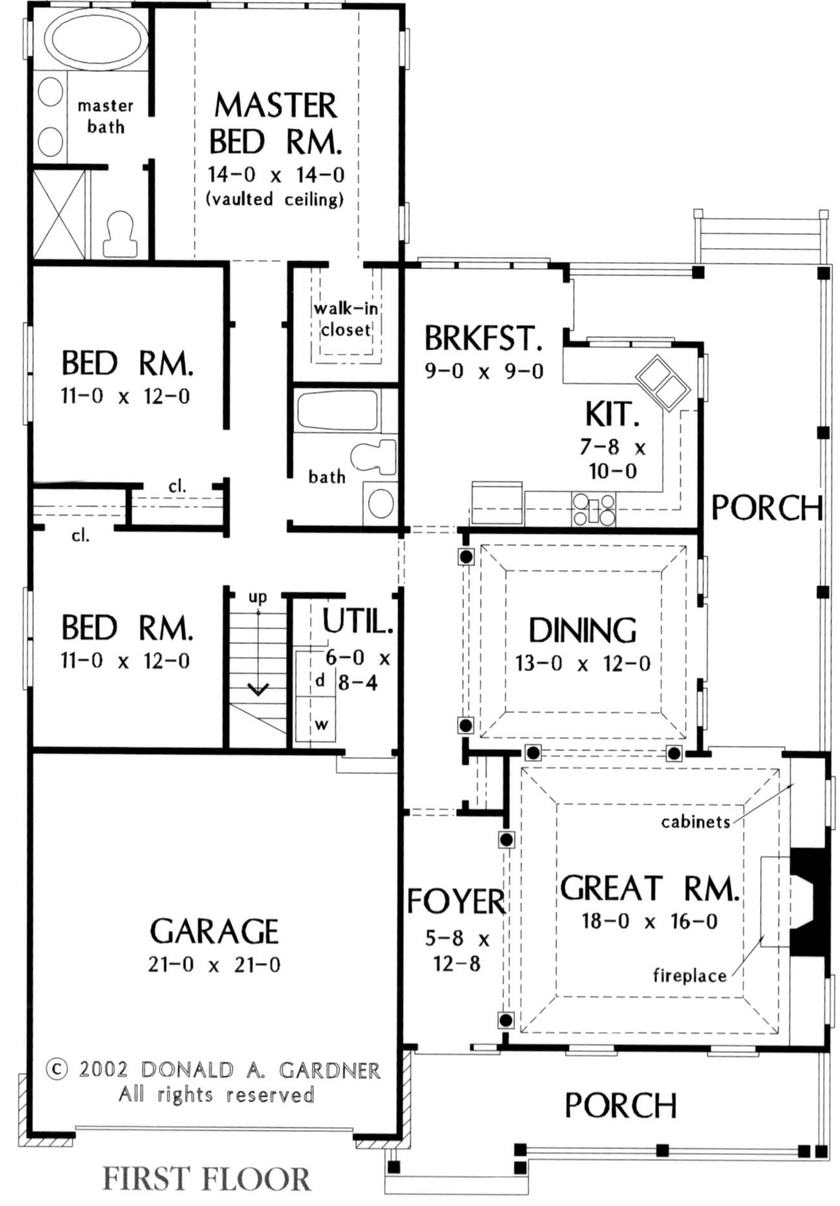
master bath
MASTER BED RM.
14–0 x 14–0
(vaulted ceiling)
walk–in closet
BRKFST.
9–0 x 9–0
KIT.
7–8 x 10–0
BED RM.
11–0 x 12–0
bath
cl.
cl.
PORCH
BED RM.
11–0 x 12–0
up
UTIL.
6–0 x 8–4
d
w
DINING
13–0 x 12–0
cabinets
GREAT RM.
18–0 x 16–0
fireplace
FOYER
5–8 x 12–8
GARAGE
21–0 x 21–0
© 2002 DONALD A. GARDNER
All rights reserved
PORCH

FIRST FLOOR

DESIGNER NOTE: *"The front of narrow homes are usually dominated by the garage. We designed a home where the garage is secondary and the impact comes from the living spaces."*

© 2002 Donald A. Gardner Inc.

The bonus room is an all-around craft room. We use it for scrapbooking, woodburning, basket weaving or whatever we might be into at the time. I recently took a stained glass class where we worked with lead; my husband just finished a woodcarving class. I think we're going to be adding a few more shelves for our supplies.

The Bakersfield

REAR

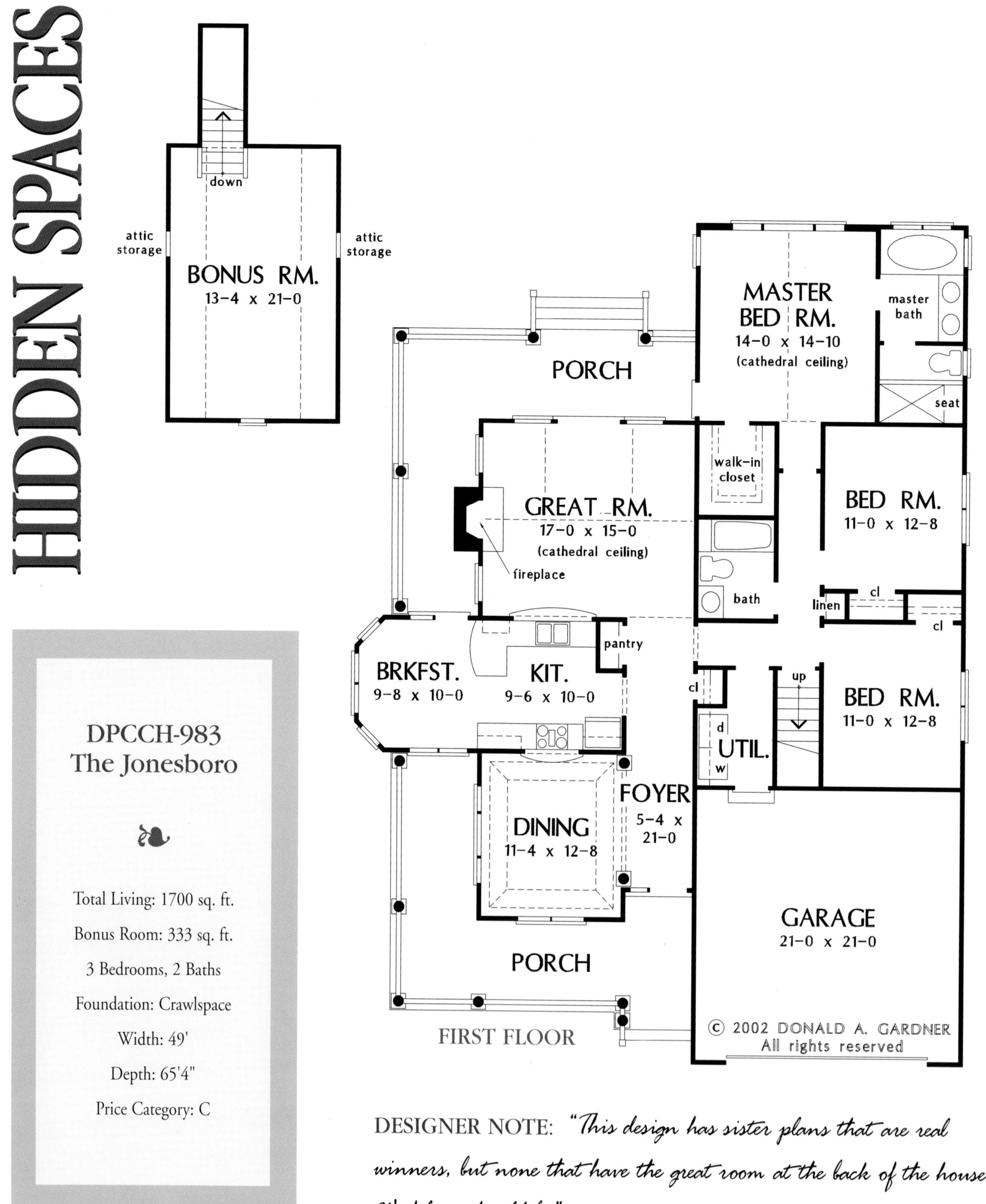

attic storage
attic storage
down
BONUS RM.
13-4 x 21-0
MASTER BED RM.
14-0 x 14-10
(cathedral ceiling)
master bath
seat
PORCH
walk-in closet
GREAT RM.
17-0 x 15-0
(cathedral ceiling)
fireplace
BED RM.
11-0 x 12-8
bath
linen
cl
cl
pantry
BRKFST.
9-8 x 10-0
KIT.
9-6 x 10-0
cl
up
BED RM.
11-0 x 12-8
d
w
UTIL.
FOYER
5-4 x 21-0
DINING
11-4 x 12-8
GARAGE
21-0 x 21-0
PORCH
FIRST FLOOR
© 2002 DONALD A. GARDNER
All rights reserved

DPCCH-983
The Jonesboro

Total Living: 1700 sq. ft.

Bonus Room: 333 sq. ft.

3 Bedrooms, 2 Baths

Foundation: Crawlspace

Width: 49'

Depth: 65'4"

Price Category: C

DESIGNER NOTE: *"This design has sister plans that are real winners, but none that have the great room at the back of the house. We felt it should be."*

It was a school play that transformed our bonus room. I volunteered to help turn two boys and one girl into George Washington, Abe Lincoln and the Statue of Liberty. I needed a lot of room to draw patterns, cut and sew. The bonus room gave me all the space I needed, and now it's my permanent sewing room.

REAR

The Jonesboro

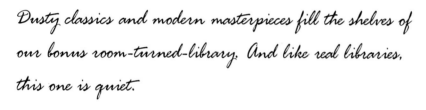

Dusty classics and modern masterpieces fill the shelves of our bonus room-turned-library. And like real libraries, this one is quiet.

DPCCH-927
The Pritchard

Total living: 2406 s.f.

First Floor: 1653 s.f. • Second Floor: 753 s.f.

Bonus Room: 349 s.f.

4 Bedrooms, 2-1/2 Baths

Foundation: Crawlspace

Width: 78' • Depth: 44'

Price Category: D

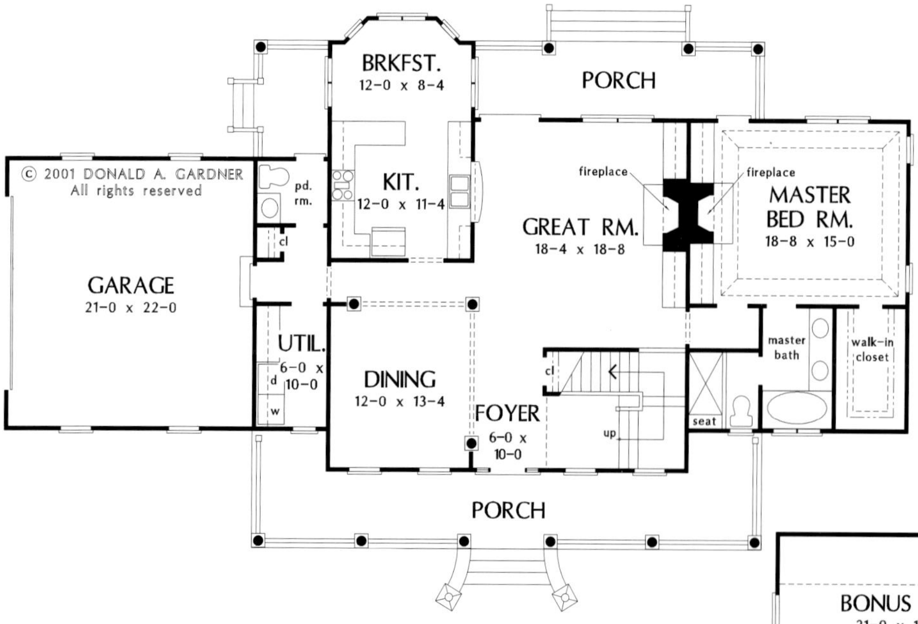

BRKFST. 12-0 x 8-4
PORCH
KIT. 12-0 x 11-4
pd. rm.
cl
fireplace
fireplace
GREAT RM. 18-4 x 18-8
MASTER BED RM. 18-8 x 15-0
GARAGE 21-0 x 22-0
UTIL. 6-0 x 10-0
d
w
DINING 12-0 x 13-4
cl
FOYER 6-0 x 10-0
up
seat
master bath
walk-in closet
PORCH

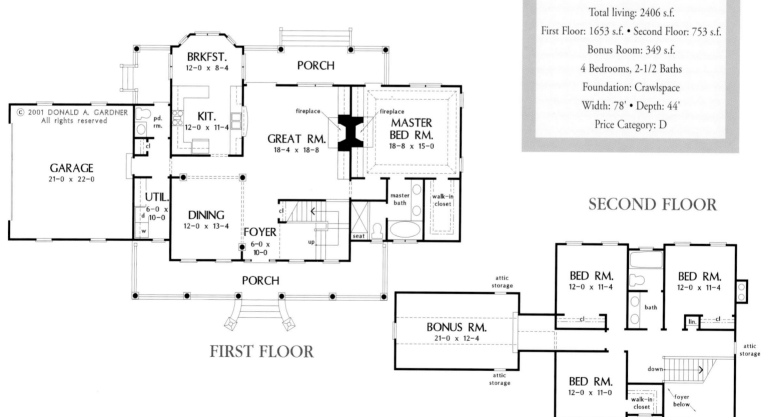

FIRST FLOOR

SECOND FLOOR

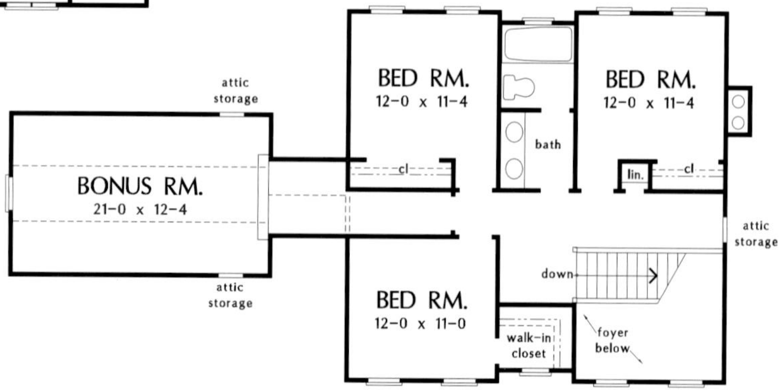

attic storage
BONUS RM. 21-0 x 12-4
attic storage
BED RM. 12-0 x 11-4
cl
bath
BED RM. 12-0 x 11-4
lin.
cl
attic storage
down
BED RM. 12-0 x 11-0
walk-in closet
foyer below

HIDDEN SPACES

An old-fashioned popcorn machine, a couple of rows of theatre seats and some old movie posters helped turn our bonus room into a 1940s movie theatre.

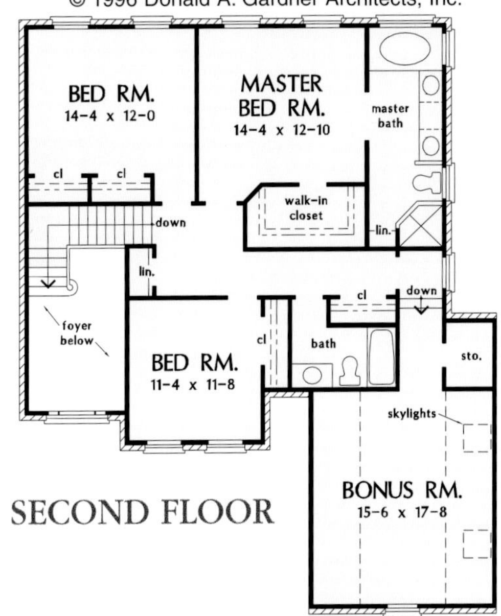

BED RM.
14-4 x 12-0
MASTER
BED RM.
14-4 x 12-10
master
bath
cl
cl
walk-in
closet
down
lin.
lin.
foyer
below
BED RM.
11-4 x 11-8
cl
cl
bath
down
sto.
skylights
BONUS RM.
15-6 x 17-8

SECOND FLOOR

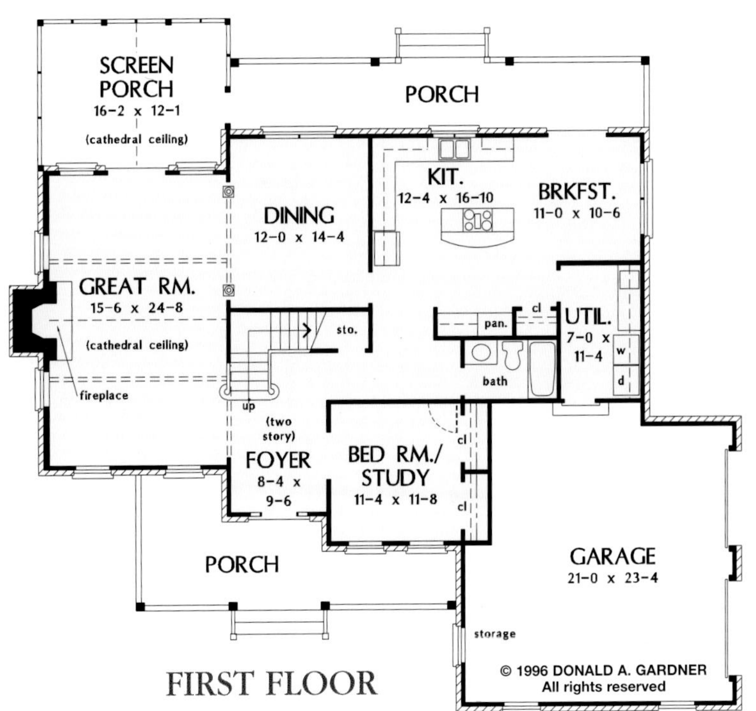

SCREEN
PORCH
16-2 x 12-1
(cathedral ceiling)
PORCH
DINING
12-0 x 14-4
KIT.
12-4 x 16-10
BRKFST.
11-0 x 10-6
GREAT RM.
15-6 x 24-8
(cathedral ceiling)
fireplace
sto.
pan.
cl
UTIL.
7-0 x
11-4
w
d
bath
up
(two
story)
FOYER
8-4 x
9-6
BED RM./
STUDY
11-4 x 11-8
cl
cl
PORCH
GARAGE
21-0 x 23-4
storage
© 1996 DONALD A. GARDNER
All rights reserved

FIRST FLOOR

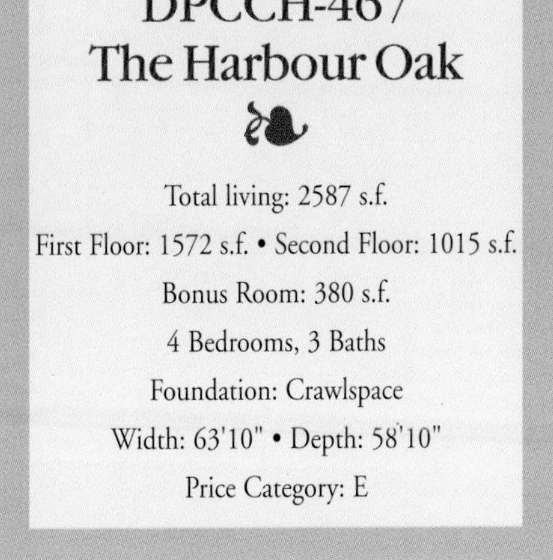

DPCCH-467
The Harbour Oak

Total living: 2587 s.f.

First Floor: 1572 s.f. • Second Floor: 1015 s.f.

Bonus Room: 380 s.f.

4 Bedrooms, 3 Baths

Foundation: Crawlspace

Width: 63'10" • Depth: 58'10"

Price Category: E

HIDDEN SPACES

We were afraid the kids heard the noise coming from the bonus room. We wanted to surprise them with the puppy this morning.

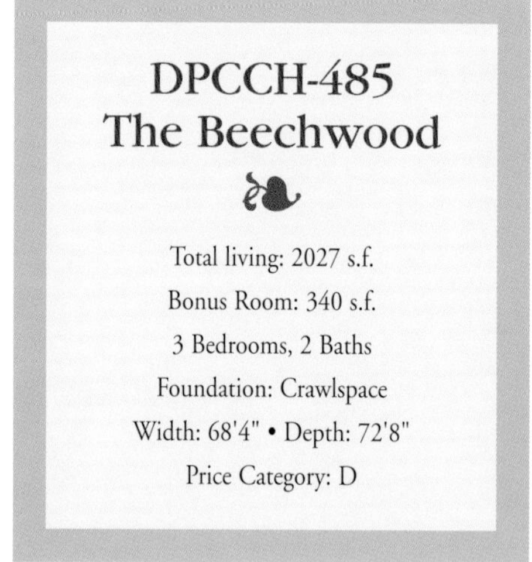

DPCCH-485
The Beechwood

Total living: 2027 s.f.

Bonus Room: 340 s.f.

3 Bedrooms, 2 Baths

Foundation: Crawlspace

Width: 68'4" • Depth: 72'8"

Price Category: D

FIRST FLOOR

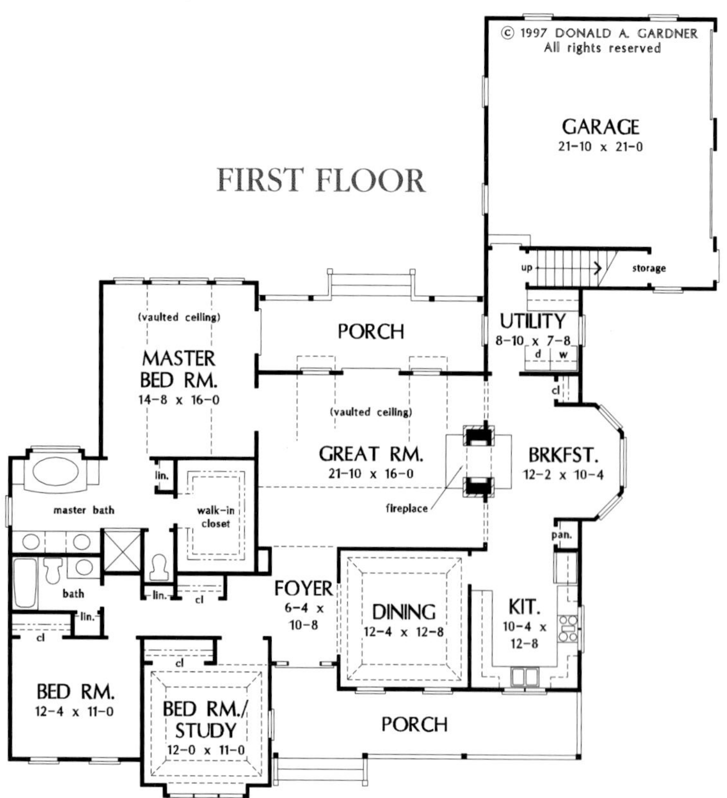
© 1997 DONALD A. GARDNER
All rights reserved
GARAGE
21-10 x 21-0
up
storage
UTILITY
8-10 x 7-8
d
w
cl
PORCH
(vaulted ceiling)
MASTER
BED RM.
14-8 x 16-0
(vaulted ceiling)
GREAT RM.
21-10 x 16-0
fireplace
BRKFST.
12-2 x 10-4
lin.
master bath
walk-in
closet
pan.
bath
lin.
cl
FOYER
6-4 x
10-8
DINING
12-4 x 12-8
KIT.
10-4 x
12-8
cl
BED RM.
12-4 x 11-0
BED RM./
STUDY
12-0 x 11-0
PORCH

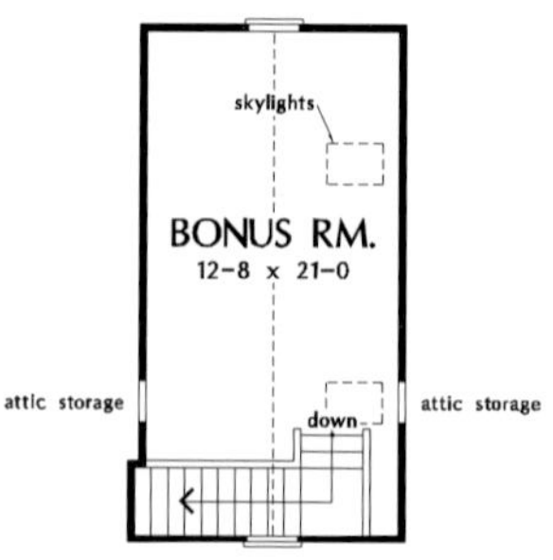
skylights
BONUS RM.
12-8 x 21-0
attic storage
down
attic storage

Our bonus room has a pool table, jukebox and wet bar. The bar seats are covered in old blue jeans, and we have framed posters all around.

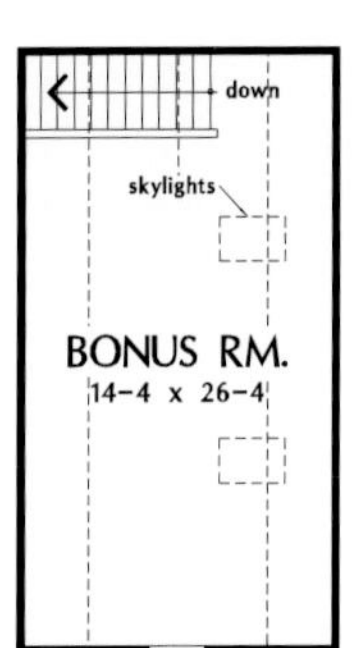
down
skylights
BONUS RM.
14-4 x 26-4

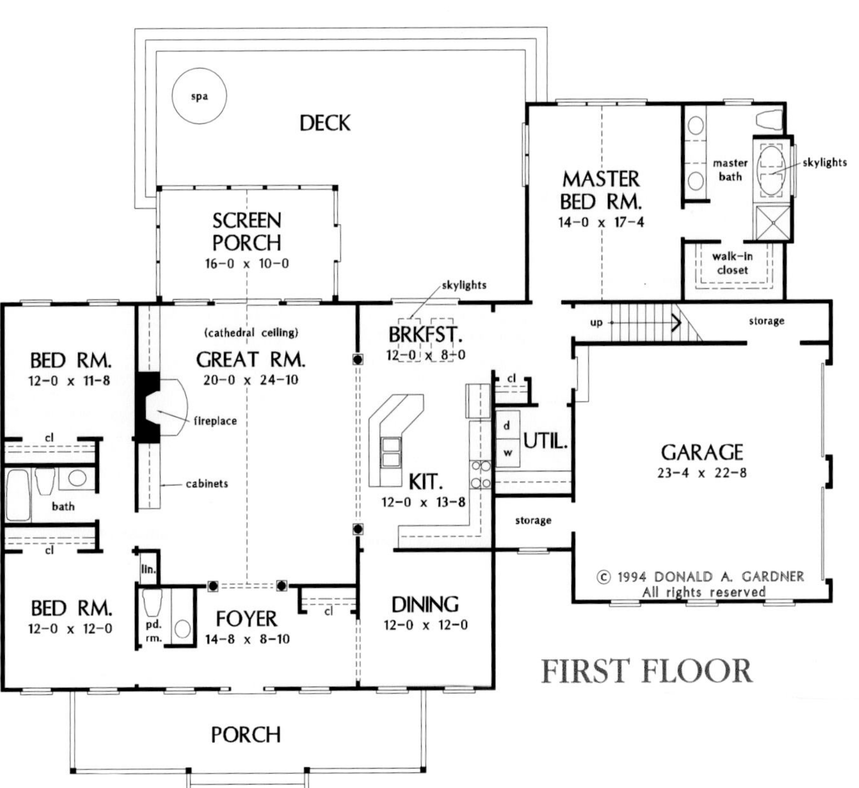
spa
DECK
SCREEN PORCH
16-0 x 10-0
MASTER BED RM.
14-0 x 17-4
master bath
skylights
walk-in closet
skylights
BED RM.
12-0 x 11-8
(cathedral ceiling)
GREAT RM.
20-0 x 24-10
BRKFST.
12-0 x 8-0
up
storage
fireplace
cl
d
w
UTIL.
GARAGE
23-4 x 22-8
bath
cabinets
KIT.
12-0 x 13-8
storage
cl
lin.
BED RM.
12-0 x 12-0
pd. rm.
FOYER
14-8 x 8-10
cl
DINING
12-0 x 12-0
© 1994 DONALD A. GARDNER
All rights reserved
PORCH

FIRST FLOOR

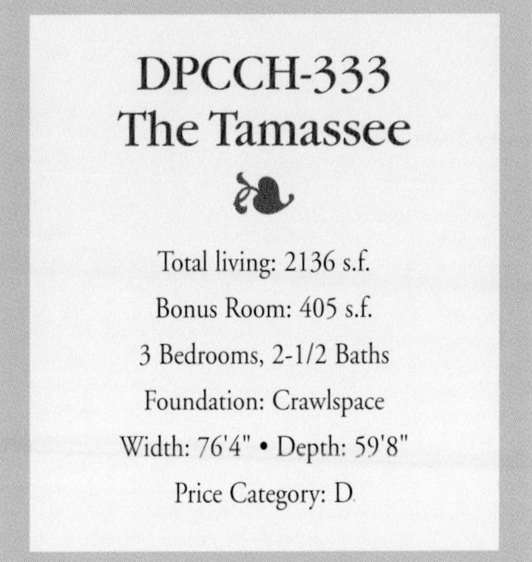

DPCCH-333
The Tamassee

Total living: 2136 s.f.

Bonus Room: 405 s.f.

3 Bedrooms, 2-1/2 Baths

Foundation: Crawlspace

Width: 76'4" • Depth: 59'8"

Price Category: D

HIDDEN SPACES

© 2001 Donald A. Gardner, Inc.

Today's rain canceled our backyard picnic, but didn't dampen our spirits. We placed gingham next to the kid's tent in the playroom and had a picnic without the ants.

DPCCH-915
The Remington

Total living: 1915 s.f.

Bonus Room: 364 s.f.

3 Bedrooms, 2 Baths

Foundation: Crawlspace

Width: 64'4" • Depth: 50'2"

Price Category: C

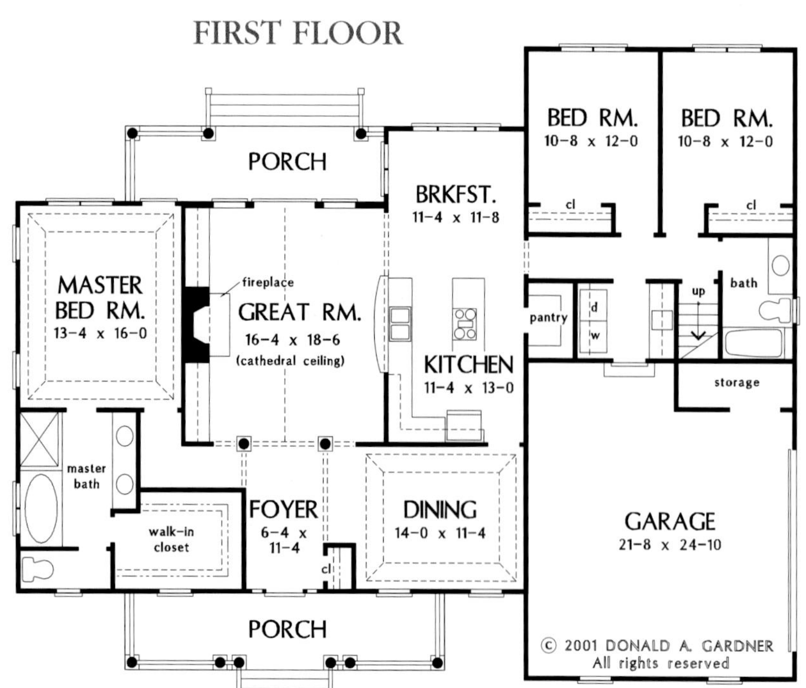
FIRST FLOOR
PORCH
BRKFST.
11-4 x 11-8
BED RM.
10-8 x 12-0
BED RM.
10-8 x 12-0
cl
cl
MASTER
BED RM.
13-4 x 16-0
fireplace
GREAT RM.
16-4 x 18-6
(cathedral ceiling)
pantry
d
w
up
bath
KITCHEN
11-4 x 13-0
storage
master
bath
walk-in
closet
FOYER
6-4 x
11-4
cl
DINING
14-0 x 11-4
GARAGE
21-8 x 24-10
PORCH
© 2001 DONALD A. GARDNER
All rights reserved

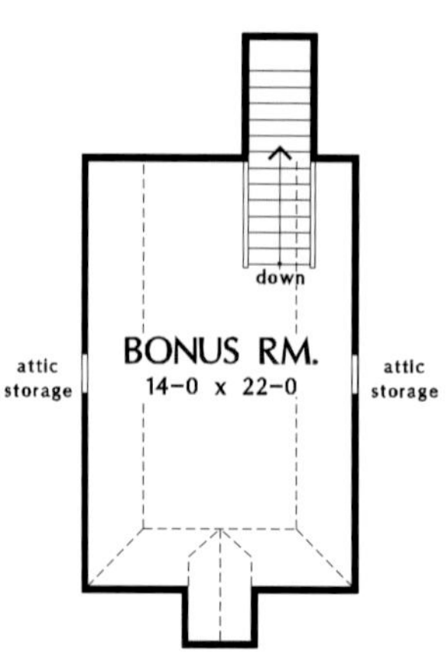
down
attic
storage
BONUS RM.
14-0 x 22-0
attic
storage

© 1996 Donald A. Gardner Architects, Inc.

HIDDEN SPACES

After attending a craft fair, we decided to try our hand at pottery. We purchased a small kiln and turned the bonus room into a pottery studio.

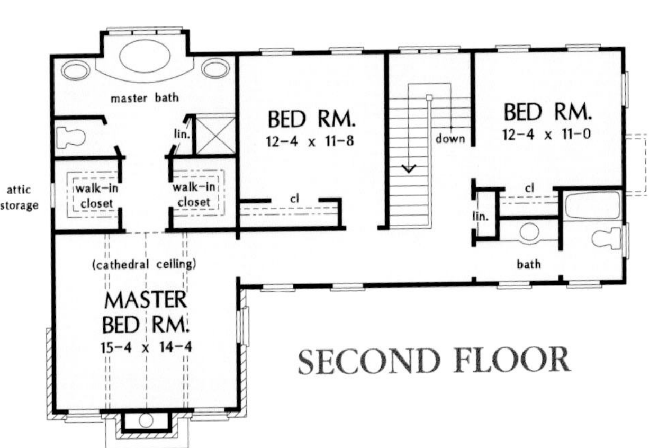

master bath
lin.
BED RM.
12-4 x 11-8
down
BED RM.
12-4 x 11-0
attic storage
walk-in closet
walk-in closet
cl
cl
lin.
bath
(cathedral ceiling)
MASTER BED RM.
15-4 x 14-4

SECOND FLOOR

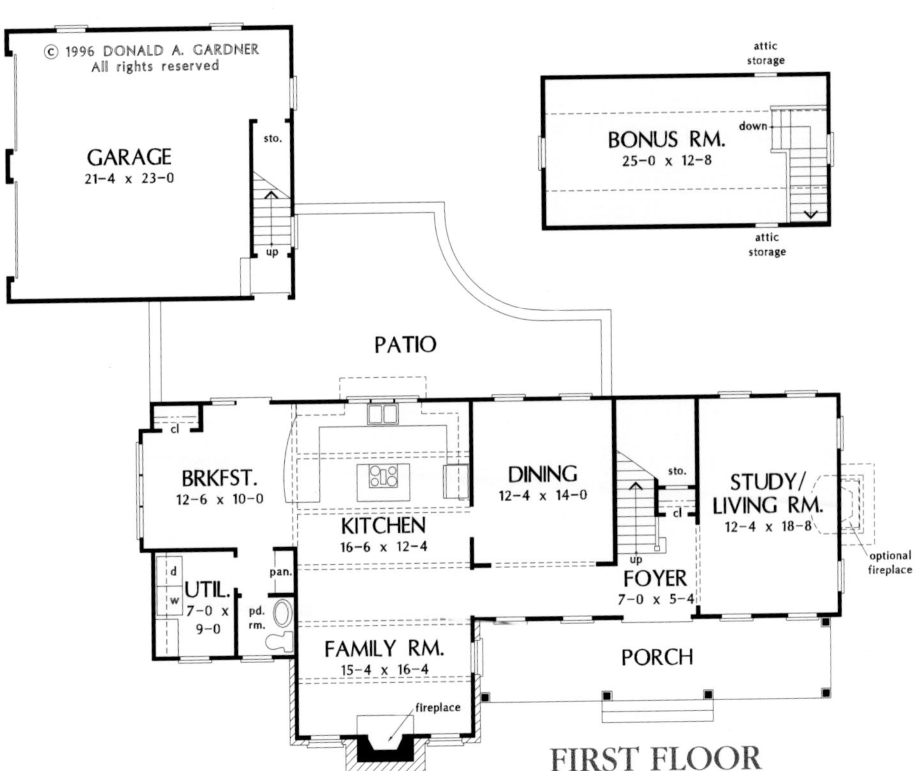

© 1996 DONALD A. GARDNER
All rights reserved
GARAGE
21-4 x 23-0
sto.
up
attic storage
BONUS RM.
25-0 x 12-8
down
attic storage
PATIO
cl
BRKFST.
12-6 x 10-0
DINING
12-4 x 14-0
sto.
STUDY/ LIVING RM.
12-4 x 18-8
KITCHEN
16-6 x 12-4
cl
up
optional fireplace
pan.
UTIL.
7-0 x 9-0
pd. rm.
FOYER
7-0 x 5-4
FAMILY RM.
15-4 x 16-4
PORCH
fireplace

FIRST FLOOR

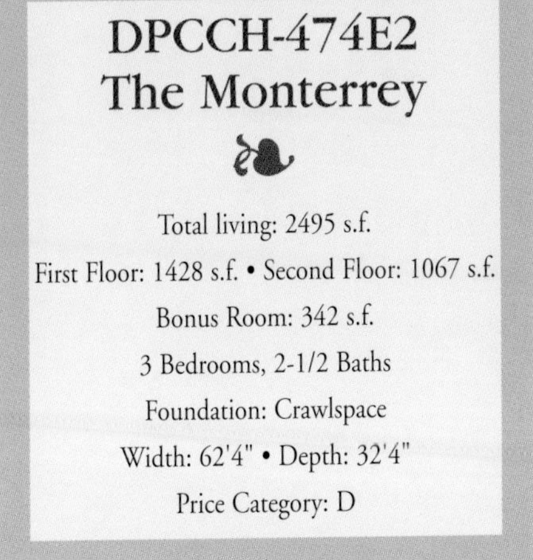

DPCCH-474E2
The Monterrey

Total living: 2495 s.f.

First Floor: 1428 s.f. • Second Floor: 1067 s.f.

Bonus Room: 342 s.f.

3 Bedrooms, 2-1/2 Baths

Foundation: Crawlspace

Width: 62'4" • Depth: 32'4"

Price Category: D

HIDDEN SPACES

© 1998 Donald A. Gardner, Inc.

When my mother-in-law came to live with us, we turned the bonus room into our teenager's suite and moved mom into the other first-floor suite.

DPCCH-736
The Silverleaf

Total living: 3371 s.f.

First Floor: 2623 s.f. • Second Floor: 748 s.f.

Bonus Room: 738 s.f.

4 Bedrooms, 4-1/2 Baths

Foundation: Crawlspace

Width: 85'8" • Depth: 51'4"

Price Category: F

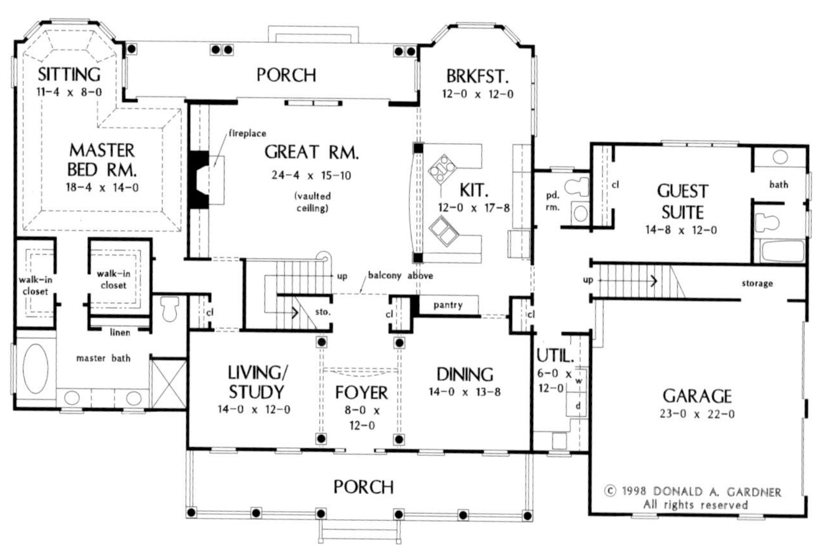
SITTING
11-4 x 8-0
PORCH
BRKFST.
12-0 x 12-0
MASTER
BED RM.
18-4 x 14-0
fireplace
GREAT RM.
24-4 x 15-10
(vaulted ceiling)
KIT.
12-0 x 17-8
pd. rm.
cl
GUEST
SUITE
14-8 x 12-0
bath
walk-in closet
walk-in closet
up
balcony above
pantry
storage
sto.
cl
linen
master bath
LIVING/
STUDY
14-0 x 12-0
FOYER
8-0 x 12-0
DINING
14-0 x 13-8
UTIL.
6-0 x 12-0
GARAGE
23-0 x 22-0
PORCH
© 1998 DONALD A. GARDNER
All rights reserved

FIRST FLOOR

SECOND FLOOR

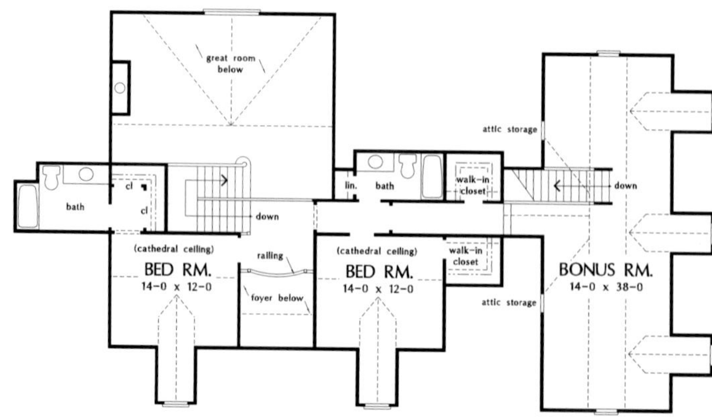
great room below
attic storage
bath
cl
down
lin.
bath
walk-in closet
down
(cathedral ceiling)
BED RM.
14-0 x 12-0
railing
foyer below
(cathedral ceiling)
BED RM.
14-0 x 12-0
walk-in closet
BONUS RM.
14-0 x 38-0
attic storage

HIDDEN SPACES

Whether you call it a fiddle or violin, it can be hard on your ears while they're learning to play, so we transformed the bonus room into a soundproof practice room for the kids.

attic storage
MASTER BED RM.
16-2 x 14-0
skylight
master bath
lin.
BED RM.
11-10 x 11-0
cl
down
skylights
BONUS RM.
21-4 x 15-8
walk-in closets
bath
attic storage
cl
down
lin.
cl
BED RM.
11-10 x 11-2
railing
BED RM.
11-10 x 11-2

SECOND FLOOR

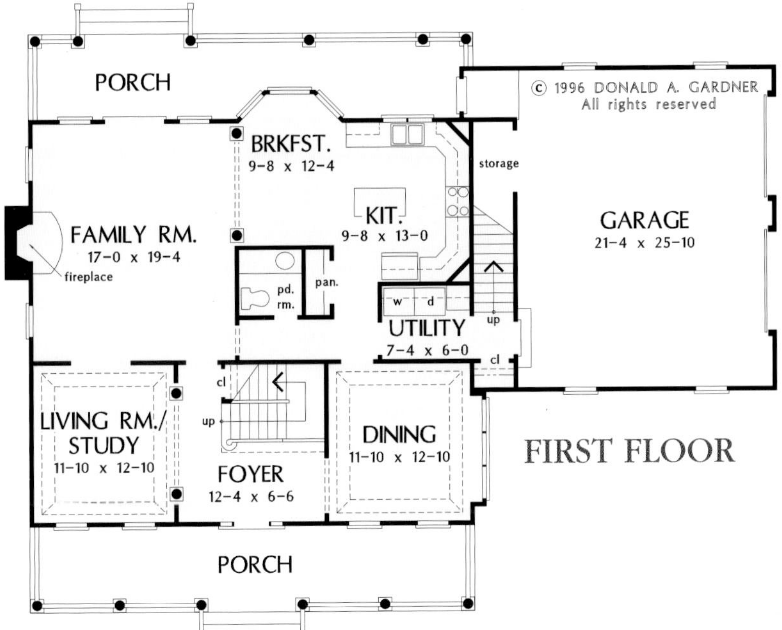
PORCH
© 1996 DONALD A. GARDNER
All rights reserved
BRKFST.
9-8 x 12-4
storage
KIT.
9-8 x 13-0
GARAGE
21-4 x 25-10
FAMILY RM.
17-0 x 19-4
fireplace
pd. rm.
pan.
w
d
UTILITY
7-4 x 6-0
up
cl
cl
up
LIVING RM./ STUDY
11-10 x 12-10
FOYER
12-4 x 6-6
DINING
11-10 x 12-10
PORCH

FIRST FLOOR

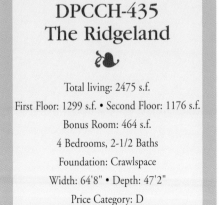

DPCCH-435
The Ridgeland

Total living: 2475 s.f.

First Floor: 1299 s.f. • Second Floor: 1176 s.f.

Bonus Room: 464 s.f.

4 Bedrooms, 2-1/2 Baths

Foundation: Crawlspace

Width: 64'8" • Depth: 47'2"

Price Category: D

HIDDEN SPACES

We turned the bonus room into a music room. We encased a guitar, banjo and fiddle in a massive shadow box. It sets a mood.

DPCCH-354
The Ammons

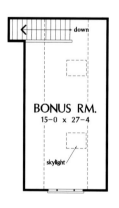

Total living: 2123 s.f.

Bonus Room: 439 s.f.

3 Bedrooms, 2-1/2 Baths

Foundation: Crawlspace

Width: 77' • Depth: 53'8"

Price Category: D

FIRST FLOOR

PORCH

(cathedral ceiling)
MASTER BED RM.
15–4 x 20–0

master bath

skylights

fireplace

walk-in closet

BED RM.
14–0 x 11–8

(cathedral ceiling)
GREAT RM.
17–4 x 19–2

fireplace

BRKFST.
11–4 x 9–2

cl

up

storage

cl

lin.

bath

KIT.
11–4 x 12–8

pantry

d w

UTIL.

GARAGE
24–8 x 23–8

cl

BED RM./ STUDY
13–8 x 12–4

FOYER
6–4 x 12–4

cl

DINING
15–8 x 12–4

pd. rm.

© 1994 DONALD A. GARDNER
All rights reserved

PORCH

down

BONUS RM.
15–0 x 27–4

skylight

HIDDEN SPACES

© 1999 Donald A. Gardner, Inc.

We had a lot of collectibles and no place to put them. Our bonus room became a family room as well as a place to display our collections.

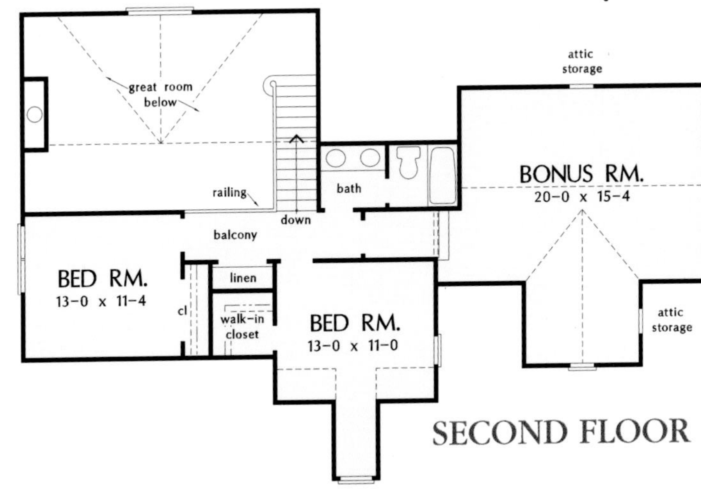

great room below
railing
down
balcony
bath
attic storage
BONUS RM.
20-0 x 15-4
BED RM.
13-0 x 11-4
linen
cl
walk-in closet
BED RM.
13-0 x 11-0
attic storage

SECOND FLOOR

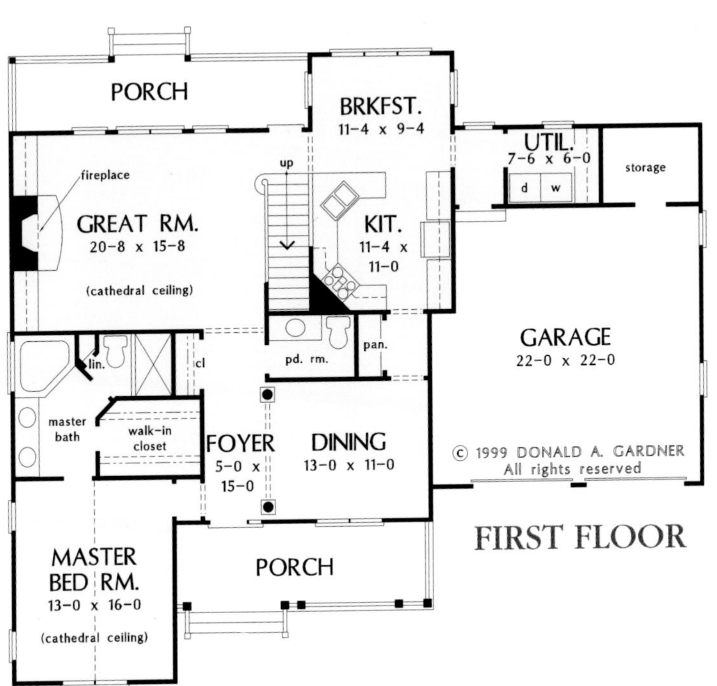

PORCH
BRKFST.
11-4 x 9-4
UTIL.
7-6 x 6-0
d
w
storage
up
fireplace
GREAT RM.
20-8 x 15-8
(cathedral ceiling)
KIT.
11-4 x 11-0
GARAGE
22-0 x 22-0
lin.
cl
pd. rm.
pan.
master bath
walk-in closet
FOYER
5-0 x 15-0
DINING
13-0 x 11-0
© 1999 DONALD A. GARDNER All rights reserved
MASTER BED RM.
13-0 x 16-0
(cathedral ceiling)
PORCH

FIRST FLOOR

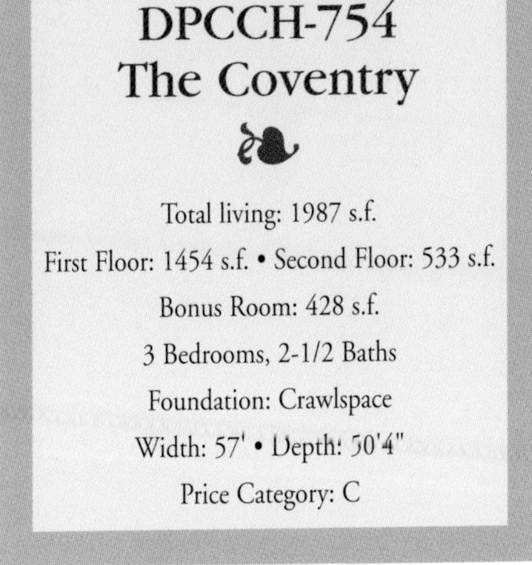

DPCCH-754
The Coventry

Total living: 1987 s.f.

First Floor: 1454 s.f. • Second Floor: 533 s.f.

Bonus Room: 428 s.f.

3 Bedrooms, 2-1/2 Baths

Foundation: Crawlspace

Width: 57' • Depth: 50'4"

Price Category: C

HIDDEN SPACES

We were upstairs in the bonus room when the mail arrived. His letter came. He would be coming home soon, and we were so excited.

DPCCH-955
The Lochaven

Total living: 2080 s.f.

Bonus Room: 348 s.f.

4 Bedrooms, 2 Baths

Foundation: Crawlspace

Width: 63'8" • Depth: 54'4"

Price Category: D

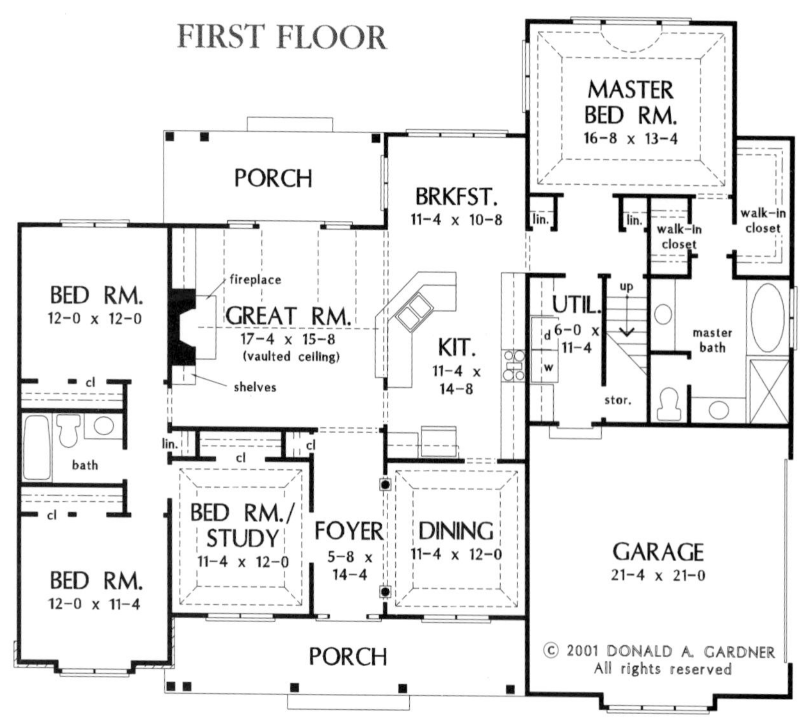
FIRST FLOOR
MASTER BED RM.
16-8 x 13-4
PORCH
BRKFST.
11-4 x 10-8
lin.
lin.
walk-in closet
walk-in closet
BED RM.
12-0 x 12-0
fireplace
GREAT RM.
17-4 x 15-8
(vaulted ceiling)
shelves
KIT.
11-4 x 14-8
UTIL.
6-0 x 11-4
up
d
w
master bath
stor.
cl
bath
cl
lin.
cl
cl
BED RM./ STUDY
11-4 x 12-0
FOYER
5-8 x 14-4
DINING
11-4 x 12-0
GARAGE
21-4 x 21-0
BED RM.
12-0 x 11-4
PORCH
© 2001 DONALD A. GARDNER
All rights reserved

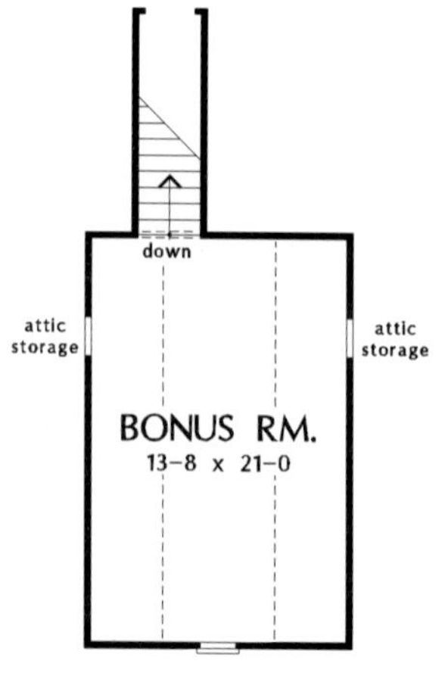
down
attic storage
attic storage
BONUS RM.
13-8 x 21-0

We built the garage first, transforming the bonus room into a studio apartment, and lived there while our house was being built.

PORCH
BRKFST.
9-4 x 9-4
up
GREAT RM.
22-0 x 19-10
(cathedral ceiling)
shelves
fireplace
balcony above
sto.
PORCH
MASTER
BED RM.
17-0 x 17-0
KITCHEN
18-4 x 14-8
pantry
pd. rm.
cl
walk-in closet
bath
lin.
master bath
UTIL.
9-10 x 12-0
w
d
DINING
13-2 x 14-0
FOYER
7-0 x 14-0
BED RM./
STUDY
13-6 x 14-0
walk-in closet
PORCH

FIRST FLOOR

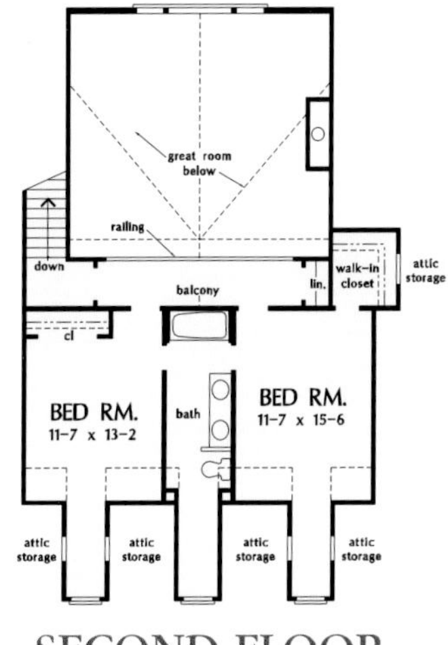
great room below
railing
down
balcony
lin.
walk-in closet
attic storage
cl
BED RM.
11-7 x 13-2
bath
BED RM.
11-7 x 15-6
attic storage
attic storage
attic storage
attic storage

SECOND FLOOR

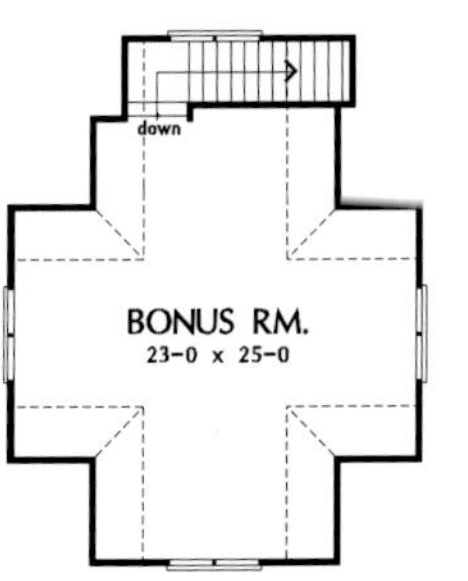
down
BONUS RM.
23-0 x 25-0

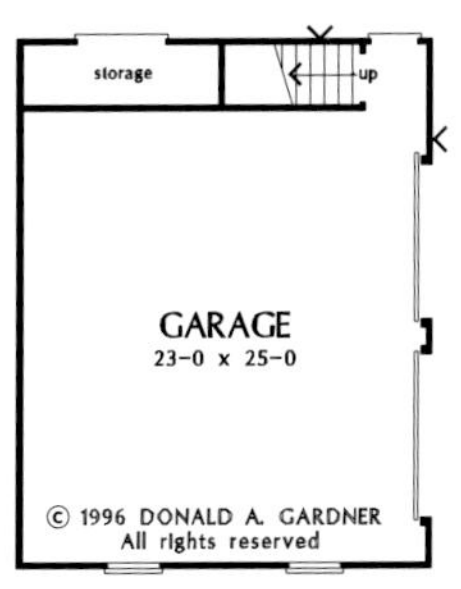
storage
up
GARAGE
23-0 x 25-0
© 1996 DONALD A. GARDNER
All rights reserved

DPCCH-461
The Marquette Manor

Total living: 3238 s.f.

First Floor: 2516 s.f. • Second Floor: 722 s.f.

Bonus Room: 513 s.f.

4 Bedrooms, 3-1/2 Baths

Foundation: Crawlspace

Width: 72' • Depth: 60'7"

Price Category: F

Neighborly Advice

Glasswork has done the same job for centuries: allow two-way viewing and permit natural light inside. But in the old days, having a lot of windows and glass doors meant higher power bills. That isn't true anymore, and this section presents plans that feature picturesque windows, French doors and the like. While looking at these plans, remember today's benefits of glasswork:

Energy-efficient windows, transoms and French doors help reduce electric bills by decreasing the amount of heating/cooling loss from a home, minimizing the affect of outside temperatures and keeping out harmful rays. With more natural light coming into the house, the lighting cost is decreased, because the need for artificial light is reduced. Glasswork also visually expands interior space without the density of walls, eliminating barriers between the home and its natural surroundings. And with the variety of window shapes, sizes and styles available, a brighter home is more affordable.

FRAMING VIEWS

FRAMING VIEWS

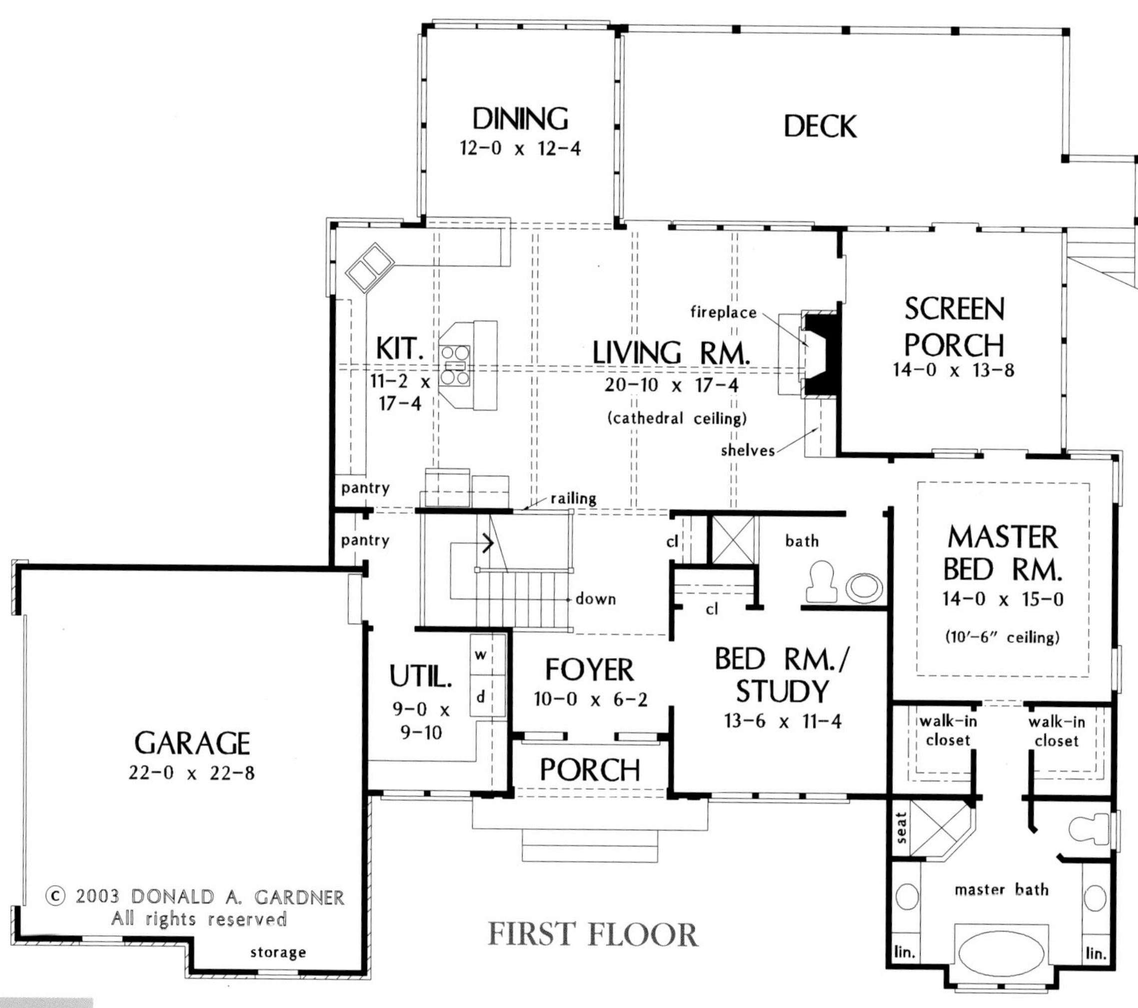
DINING
12-0 x 12-4
DECK
KIT.
11-2 x 17-4
fireplace
LIVING RM.
20-10 x 17-4
(cathedral ceiling)
shelves
SCREEN PORCH
14-0 x 13-8
pantry
railing
pantry
cl
bath
MASTER BED RM.
14-0 x 15-0
(10'-6" ceiling)
down
cl
UTIL.
9-0 x 9-10
w
d
FOYER
10-0 x 6-2
BED RM./ STUDY
13-6 x 11-4
walk-in closet
walk-in closet
GARAGE
22-0 x 22-8
PORCH
seat
master bath
© 2003 DONALD A. GARDNER
All rights reserved
storage
lin.
lin.

FIRST FLOOR

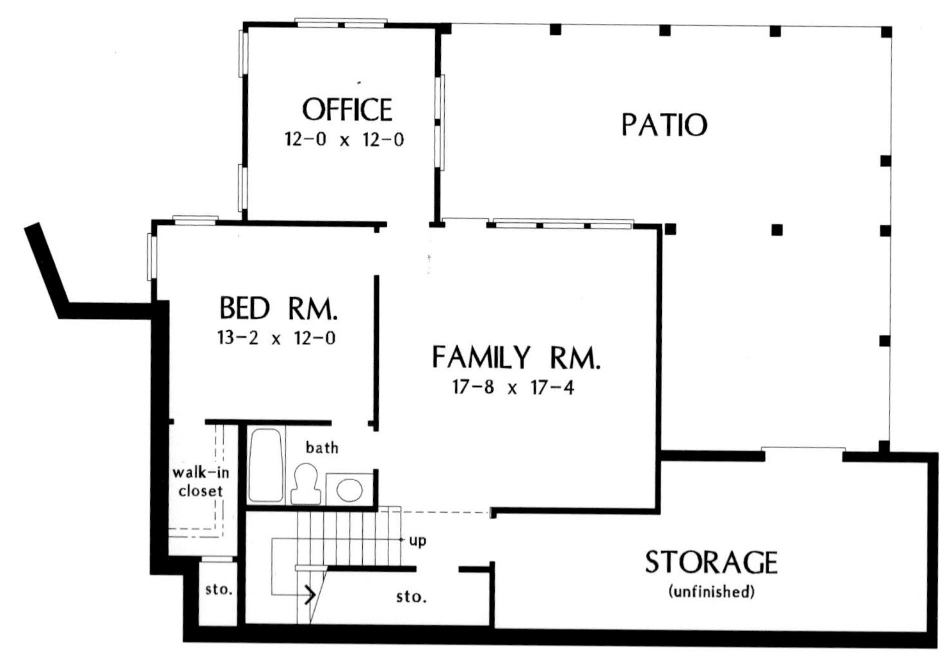
OFFICE
12-0 x 12-0
PATIO
BED RM.
13-2 x 12-0
FAMILY RM.
17-8 x 17-4
bath
walk-in closet
up
STORAGE
(unfinished)
sto.
sto.

BASEMENT FLOOR

DPCCH-1012
The Colridge

Total Living: 2652 sq. ft.

First Floor: 1732 sq. ft.

Basement Floor: 920 sq. ft.

3 Bedrooms, 3 Baths

Foundation: Hillside Walkout

Width: 70'6"

Depth: 59'6"

Price Category: E

DESIGNER NOTE: *"Here we pictured a hillside lot overlooking the lake or mountain views beyond. Such a house had to have a craftsman exterior."*

The rear wall of windows brings the outdoors inside. When I was young, I used to sit at a big picture window and watch my papa drive his tractor in the field. There was an apple tree at the back of the property, and at the end of the day, papa would always have an apple for me in the front pocket of his overalls.

The Colbridge

REAR

Photographed home may have been modified from the original construction documents.

FRAMING VIEWS

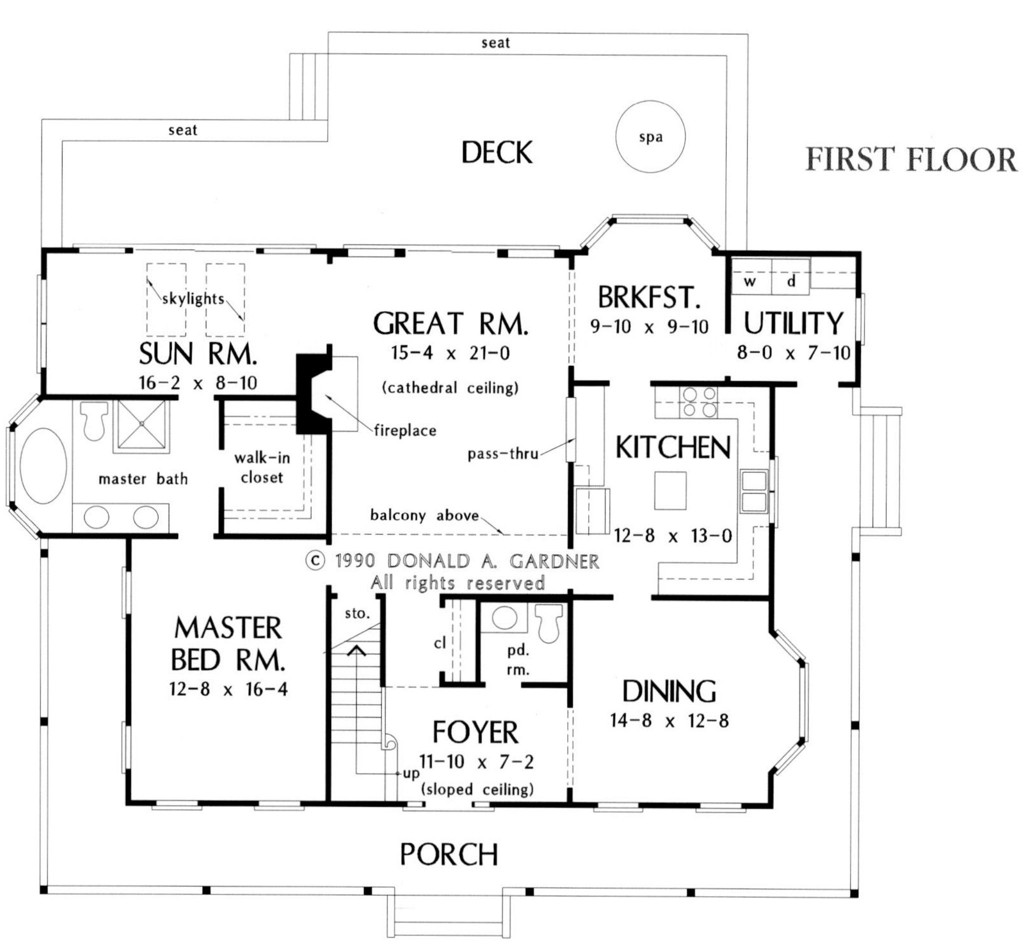
seat
seat
DECK
spa
FIRST FLOOR
skylights
SUN RM.
16-2 x 8-10
GREAT RM.
15-4 x 21-0
(cathedral ceiling)
BRKFST.
9-10 x 9-10
w d
UTILITY
8-0 x 7-10
fireplace
walk-in closet
master bath
pass-thru
KITCHEN
12-8 x 13-0
balcony above
© 1990 DONALD A. GARDNER
All rights reserved
sto.
cl
pd. rm.
MASTER BED RM.
12-8 x 16-4
DINING
14-8 x 12-8
FOYER
11-10 x 7-2
(sloped ceiling)
up
PORCH

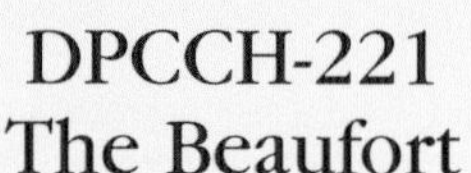

DPCCH-221
The Beaufort

Total Living: 2218 sq. ft.

First Floor: 1651 sq. ft.

Second Floor: 567 sq. ft.

3 Bedrooms, 2-1/2 Baths

Foundation: Crawlspace

Width: 55'

Depth: 42'4"

Price Category: D

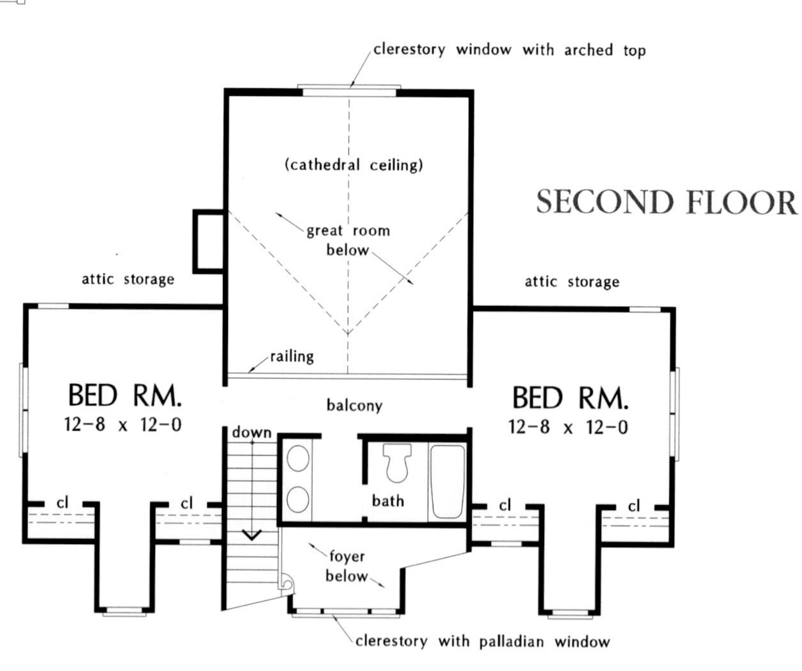
clerestory window with arched top
(cathedral ceiling)
SECOND FLOOR
great room below
attic storage
attic storage
railing
BED RM.
12-8 x 12-0
balcony
BED RM.
12-8 x 12-0
down
bath
cl
cl
cl
cl
foyer below
clerestory with palladian window

DESIGNER NOTE: *"We tried to imagine how many ways you could use a 'sunroom,' and with this design we'll let you decide."*

A comfortable chair, knitted throw and copy of the *Farmer's Almanac* are all it takes to make a dormer alcove into a quaint reading retreat for guests. My old hope chest doubles as an ottoman, so they can prop their feet up and really relax. For added ambiance, the window frames the trees by day and the stars by night.

The Beaufort

REAR

Photographed home may have been modified from the original construction documents.

FRAMING VIEWS

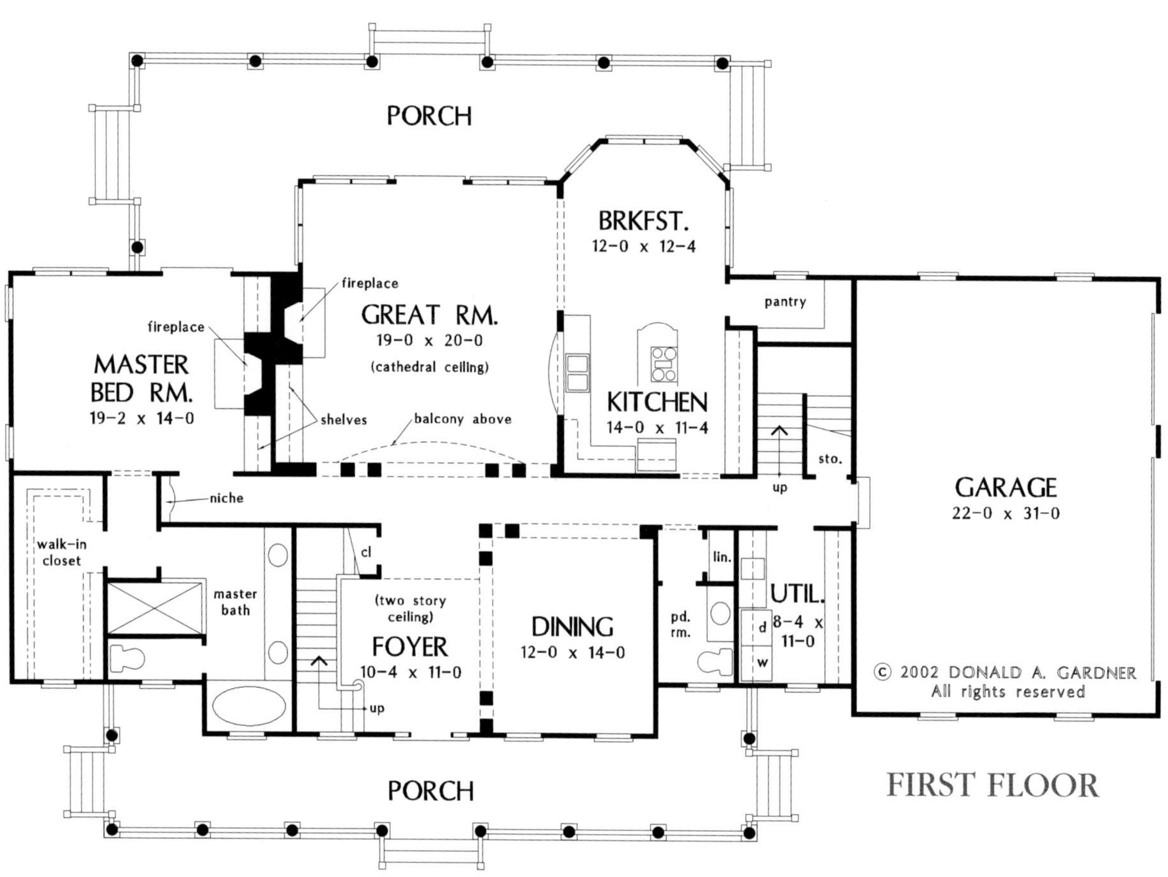

PORCH
BRKFST.
12-0 x 12-4
fireplace
GREAT RM.
19-0 x 20-0
(cathedral ceiling)
pantry
fireplace
MASTER
BED RM.
19-2 x 14-0
KITCHEN
14-0 x 11-4
shelves
balcony above
sto.
up
niche
GARAGE
22-0 x 31-0
walk-in
closet
cl
lin.
master
bath
(two story
ceiling)
FOYER
10-4 x 11-0
DINING
12-0 x 14-0
pd.
rm.
UTIL.
8-4 x
11-0
d
w
up
© 2002 DONALD A. GARDNER
All rights reserved
PORCH
FIRST FLOOR

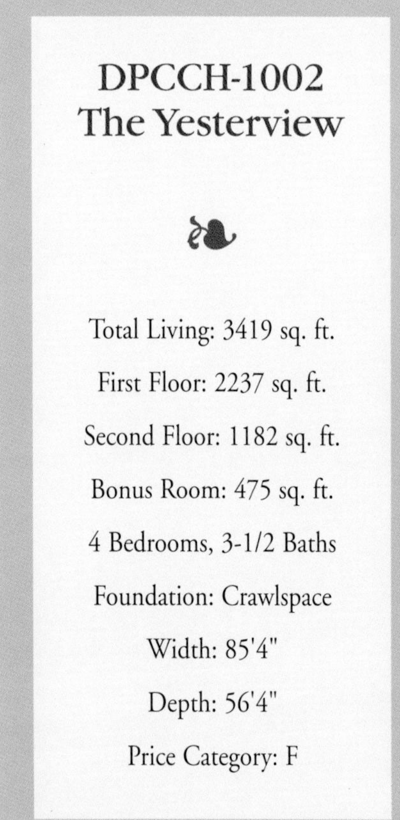

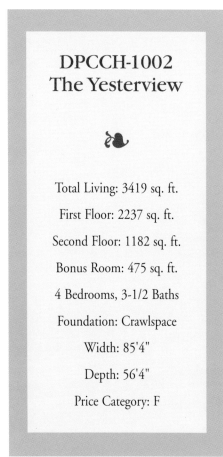

DPCCH-1002
The Yesterview

Total Living: 3419 sq. ft.

First Floor: 2237 sq. ft.

Second Floor: 1182 sq. ft.

Bonus Room: 475 sq. ft.

4 Bedrooms, 3-1/2 Baths

Foundation: Crawlspace

Width: 85'4"

Depth: 56'4"

Price Category: F

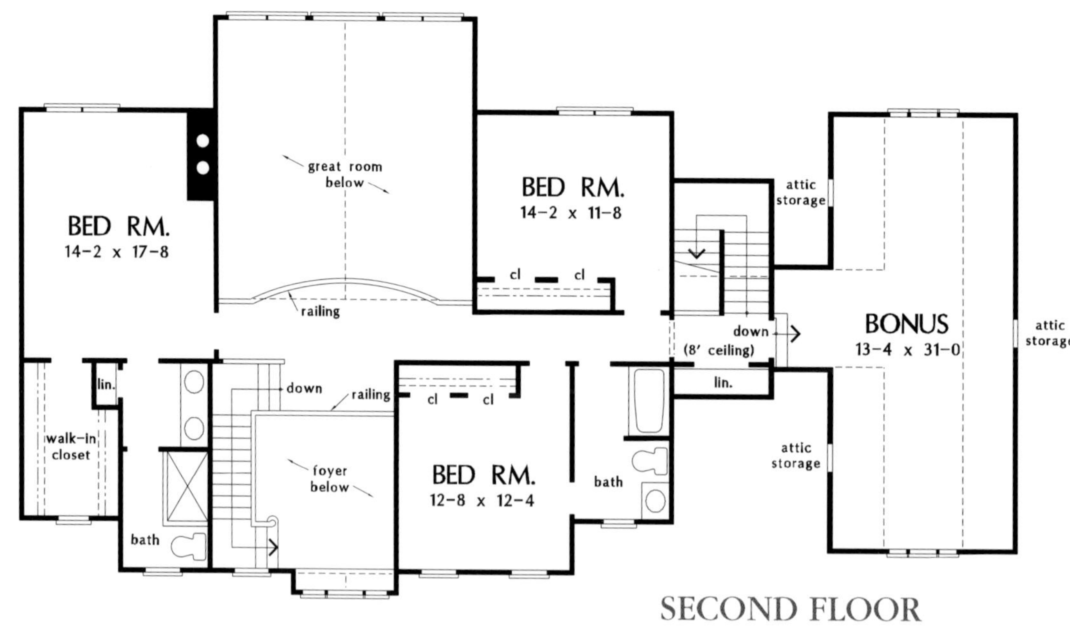

great room
below
BED RM.
14-2 x 11-8
attic
storage
BED RM.
14-2 x 17-8
cl
cl
railing
down
(8' ceiling)
BONUS
13-4 x 31-0
attic
storage
lin.
down
railing
lin.
walk-in
closet
cl
cl
attic
storage
foyer
below
BED RM.
12-8 x 12-4
bath
bath
SECOND FLOOR

DESIGNER NOTE: *"We thought of Texas-size rooms inside a strong, Southern style exterior when we designed this house."*

Standing on the second-floor balcony, looking through the front Palladian, you can see the long, tree-lined road to the house. When you turn around, looking out the rear transom and adjacent windows, you see what looks like an endless field of corn. Row after row — as far as the eye can see — seem to join heaven and earth.

The Yesterview

REAR

FRAMING VIEWS

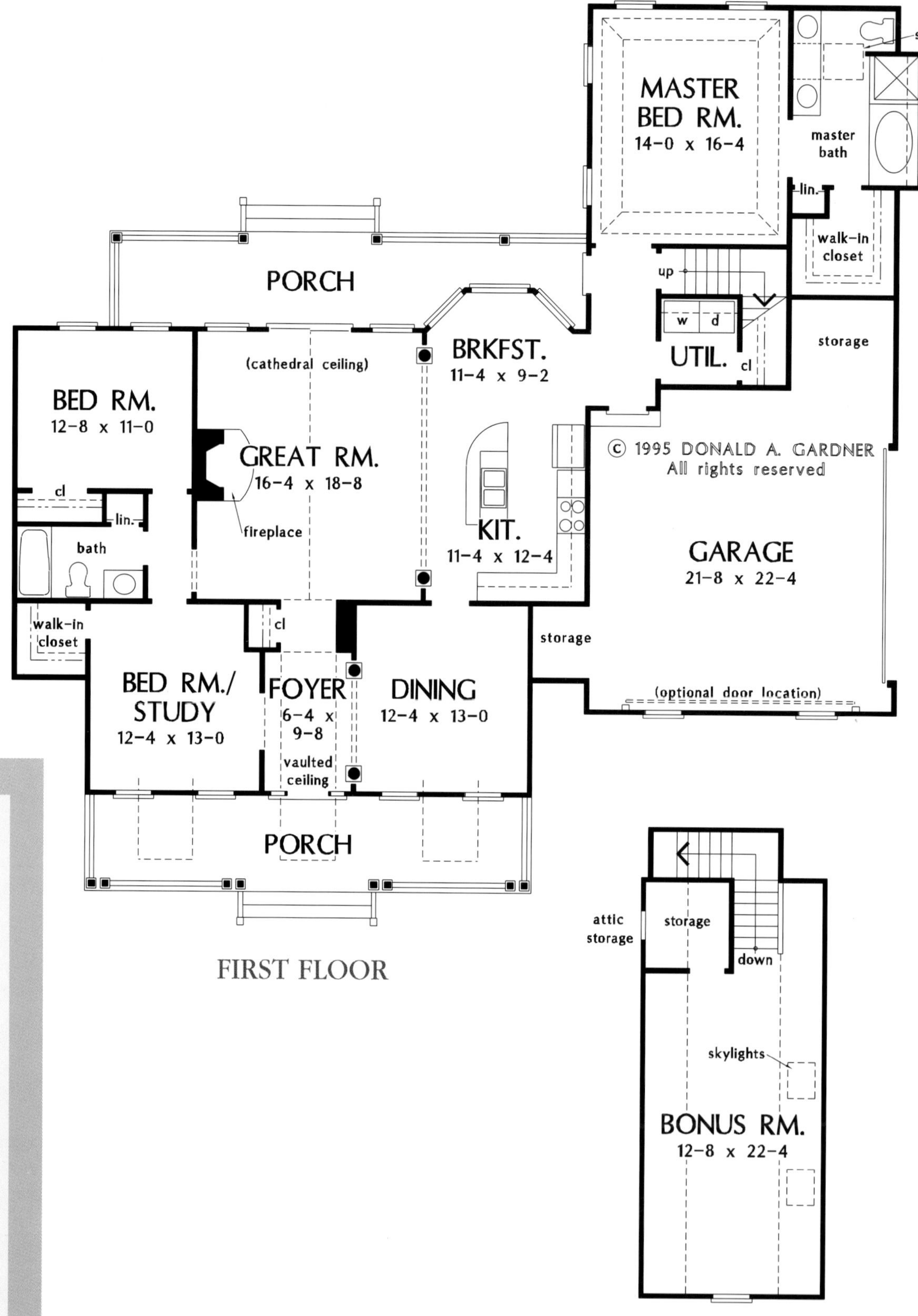
skylight
MASTER BED RM.
14-0 x 16-4
master bath
lin.
walk-in closet
PORCH
up
w d
UTIL.
cl
storage
BRKFST.
11-4 x 9-2
(cathedral ceiling)
BED RM.
12-8 x 11-0
GREAT RM.
16-4 x 18-8
fireplace
cl
lin.
bath
© 1995 DONALD A. GARDNER
All rights reserved
KIT.
11-4 x 12-4
GARAGE
21-8 x 22-4
walk-in closet
cl
storage
BED RM./ STUDY
12-4 x 13-0
FOYER
6-4 x 9-8
vaulted ceiling
DINING
12-4 x 13-0
(optional door location)
PORCH
attic storage
storage
down
skylights
BONUS RM.
12-8 x 22-4

FIRST FLOOR

DPCCH-393
The Georgetown

Total Living: 1832 sq. ft.

Bonus Room: 425 sq. ft.

3 Bedrooms, 2 Baths

Foundation: Crawlspace

Width: 65'4"

Depth: 62'

Price Category: C

DESIGNER NOTE: *"As seen in this design, we've learned the importance of an inviting front porch and the value of repeating a familiar detail such as a dormer."*

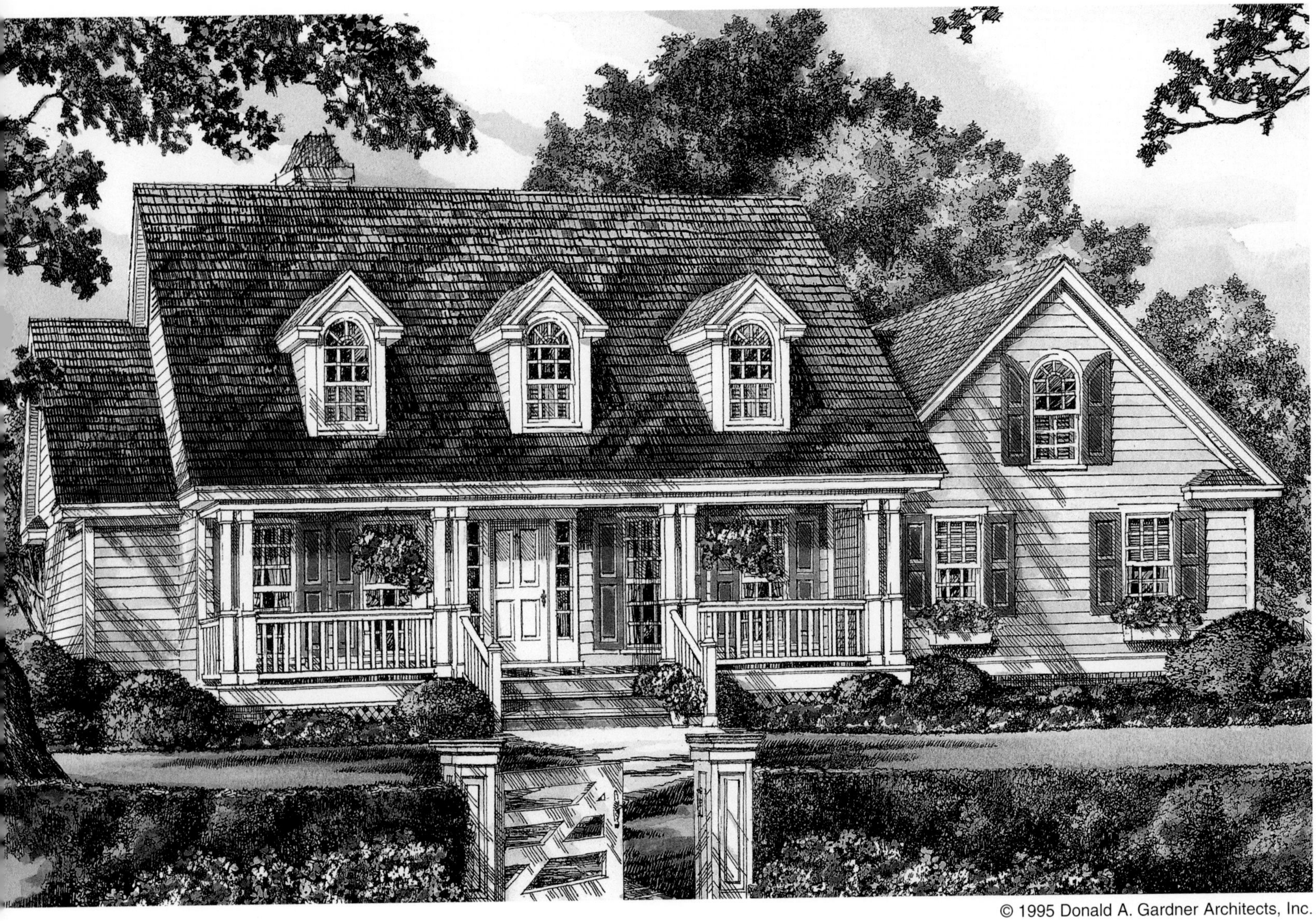

In a way, the dormers mimic our mountainous surroundings. From the bottom of the driveway, they look like tiny houses on a far-away mountainside. But I love the dormers most in winter when it snows. Each is capped with a blanket of white, and the house almost looks like a gingerbread house with icing.

The Georgetown

REAR

FRAMING VIEWS

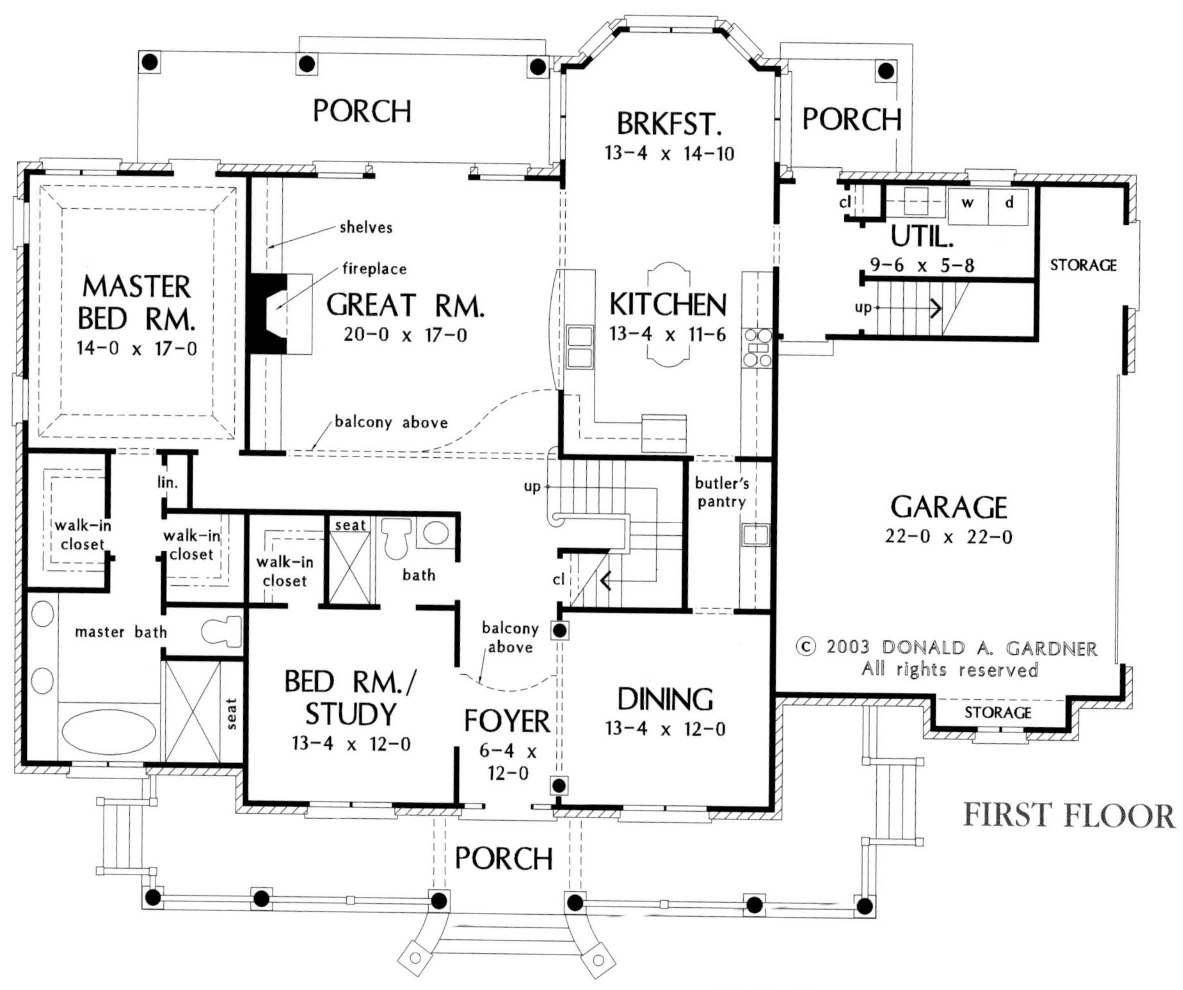
PORCH
BRKFST.
13-4 x 14-10
PORCH
cl
w
d
UTIL.
9-6 x 5-8
STORAGE
up
shelves
fireplace
MASTER
BED RM.
14-0 x 17-0
GREAT RM.
20-0 x 17-0
KITCHEN
13-4 x 11-6
balcony above
up
butler's
pantry
lin.
walk-in
closet
walk-in
closet
walk-in
closet
seat
bath
cl
GARAGE
22-0 x 22-0
master bath
balcony
above
© 2003 DONALD A. GARDNER
All rights reserved
BED RM./
STUDY
13-4 x 12-0
FOYER
6-4 x
12-0
DINING
13-4 x 12-0
STORAGE
seat
FIRST FLOOR
PORCH

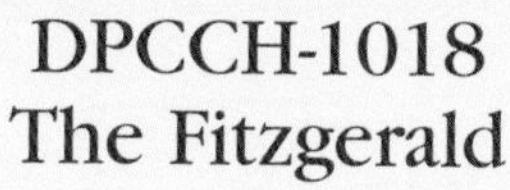

DPCCH-1018
The Fitzgerald

Total Living: 3196 sq. ft.

First Floor: 2215 sq. ft.

Second Floor: 981 sq. ft.

Bonus Room: 402 sq. ft.

5 Bedrooms, 4 Baths

Foundation: Crawlspace

Width: 71'11"

Depth: 55'10"

Price Category: F

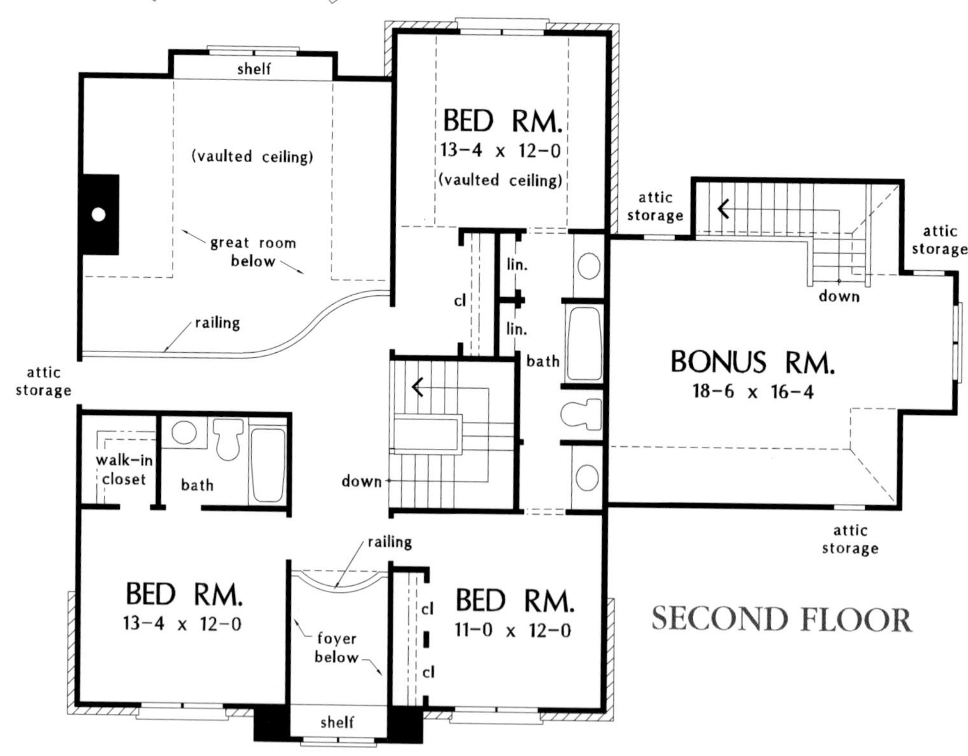
shelf
(vaulted ceiling)
great room
below
railing
BED RM.
13-4 x 12-0
(vaulted ceiling)
attic
storage
attic
storage
lin.
cl
lin.
bath
down
BONUS RM.
18-6 x 16-4
attic
storage
walk-in
closet
bath
down
attic
storage
railing
BED RM.
13-4 x 12-0
foyer
below
cl
BED RM.
11-0 x 12-0
cl
shelf
SECOND FLOOR

DESIGNER NOTE: *"For this design, we thought of the estate homeowner sitting on the front porch and greeting neighbors or viewing the golf course from the breakfast room."*

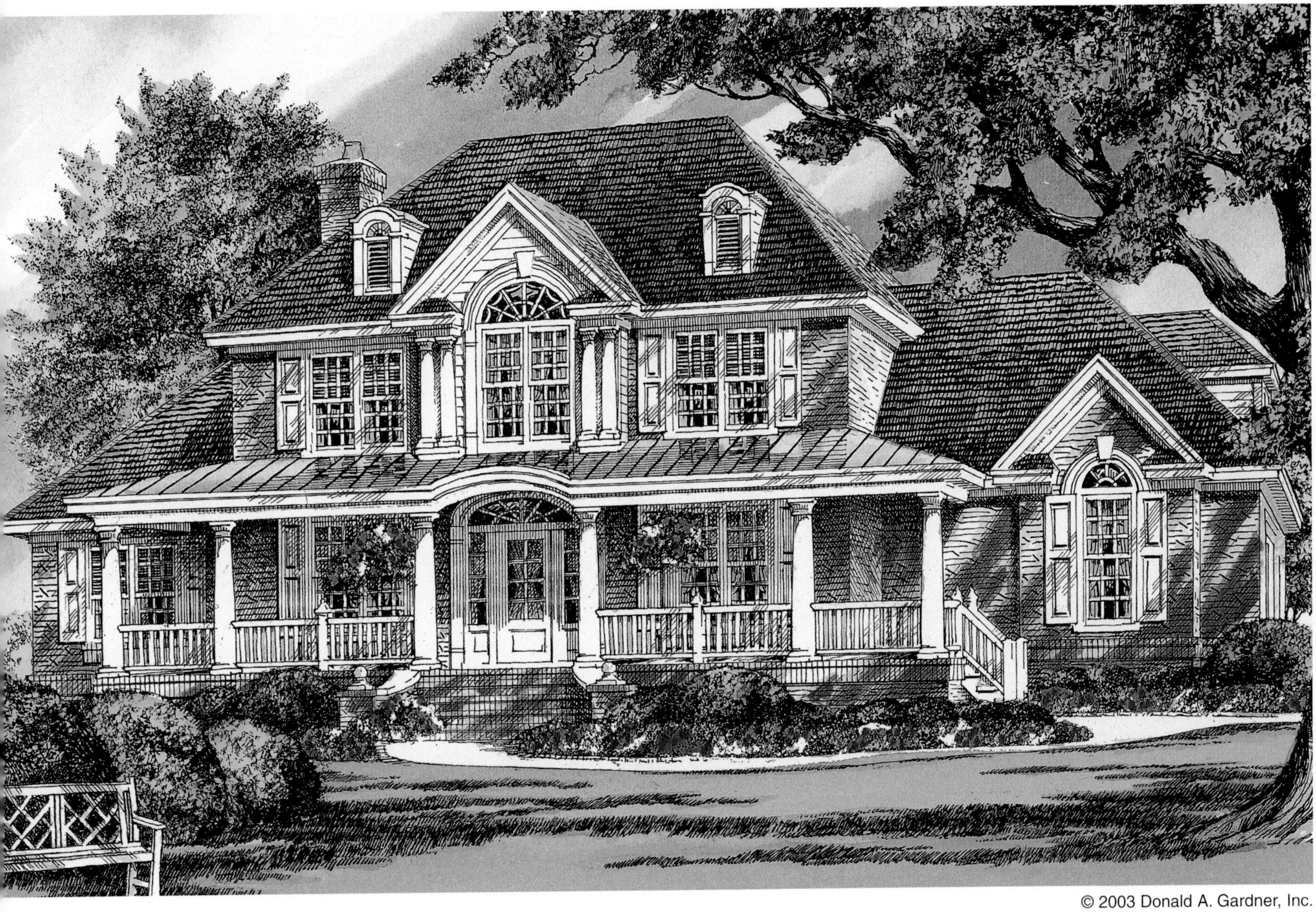

We're avid bird watchers, and we were straightening up the garage when we heard them. We looked up through the transom, and there they were — Canadian Geese in migration. We walked outside and watched them continue their journey. This is the first time we've seen them since we moved here. We had no idea we were in their path.

The Fitzgerald

REAR

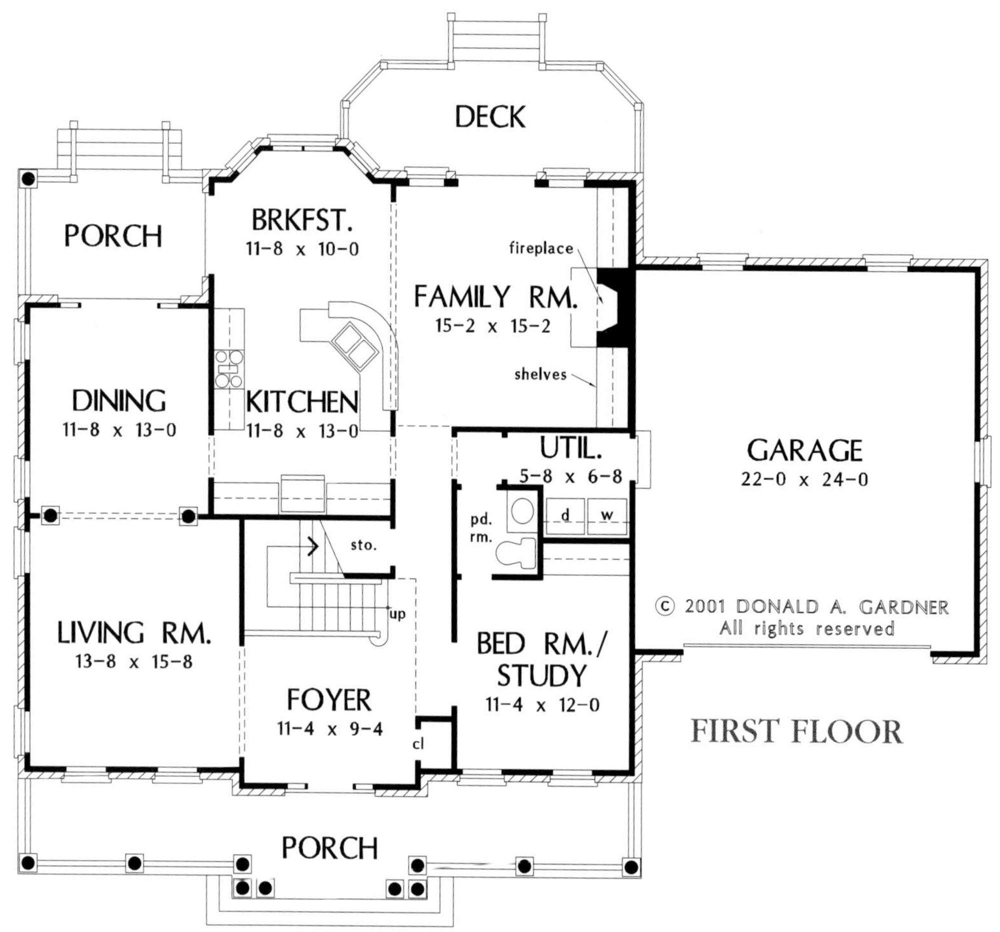
DECK
PORCH
BRKFST.
11-8 x 10-0
fireplace
FAMILY RM.
15-2 x 15-2
shelves
DINING
11-8 x 13-0
KITCHEN
11-8 x 13-0
UTIL.
5-8 x 6-8
d
w
pd. rm.
GARAGE
22-0 x 24-0
sto.
up
LIVING RM.
13-8 x 15-8
© 2001 DONALD A. GARDNER
All rights reserved
BED RM./ STUDY
11-4 x 12-0
FOYER
11-4 x 9-4
cl
PORCH

FIRST FLOOR

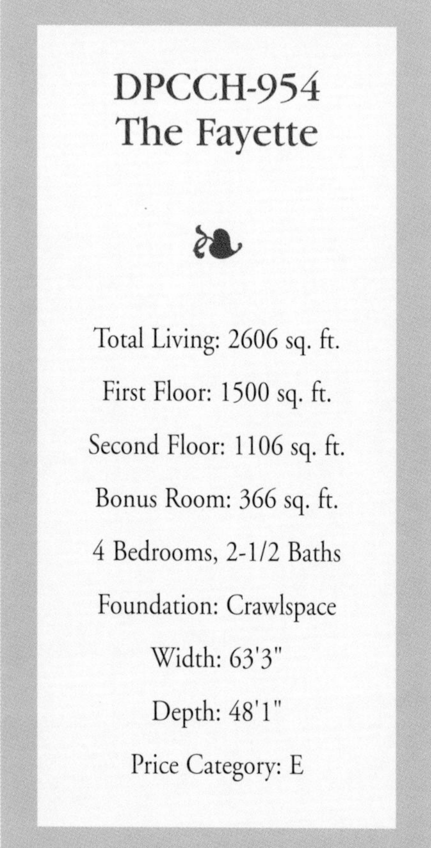

DPCCH-954
The Fayette

Total Living: 2606 sq. ft.

First Floor: 1500 sq. ft.

Second Floor: 1106 sq. ft.

Bonus Room: 366 sq. ft.

4 Bedrooms, 2-1/2 Baths

Foundation: Crawlspace

Width: 63'3"

Depth: 48'1"

Price Category: E

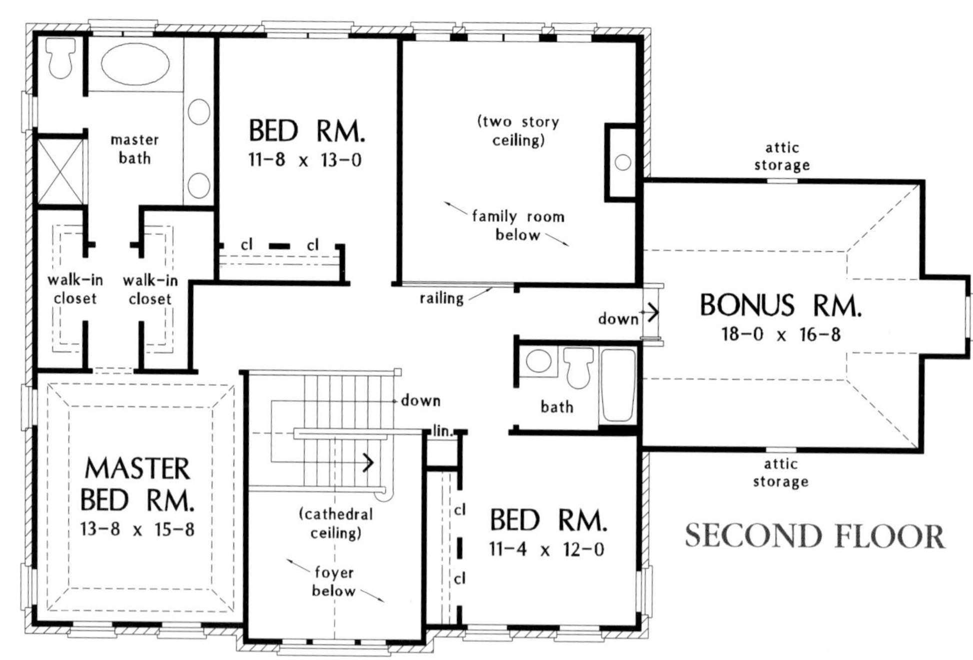
master bath
BED RM.
11-8 x 13-0
(two story ceiling)
family room below
attic storage
cl
cl
walk-in closet
walk-in closet
railing
down
BONUS RM.
18-0 x 16-8
bath
down
lin.
attic storage
MASTER BED RM.
13-8 x 15-8
(cathedral ceiling)
foyer below
cl
cl
BED RM.
11-4 x 12-0

SECOND FLOOR

DESIGNER NOTE: *"We had in mind regal, Georgian-style homes when we created this home. We added some special emphasis to the entry in order to say 'welcome.'"*

This house was built on an old cotton field. Although the cotton's gone, on bright, sunny days, you can look through the transoms and see white cottony, clouds against a vibrant blue sky. To me, it's almost as if the clouds are a reminder of what was once here.

The Fayette

REAR

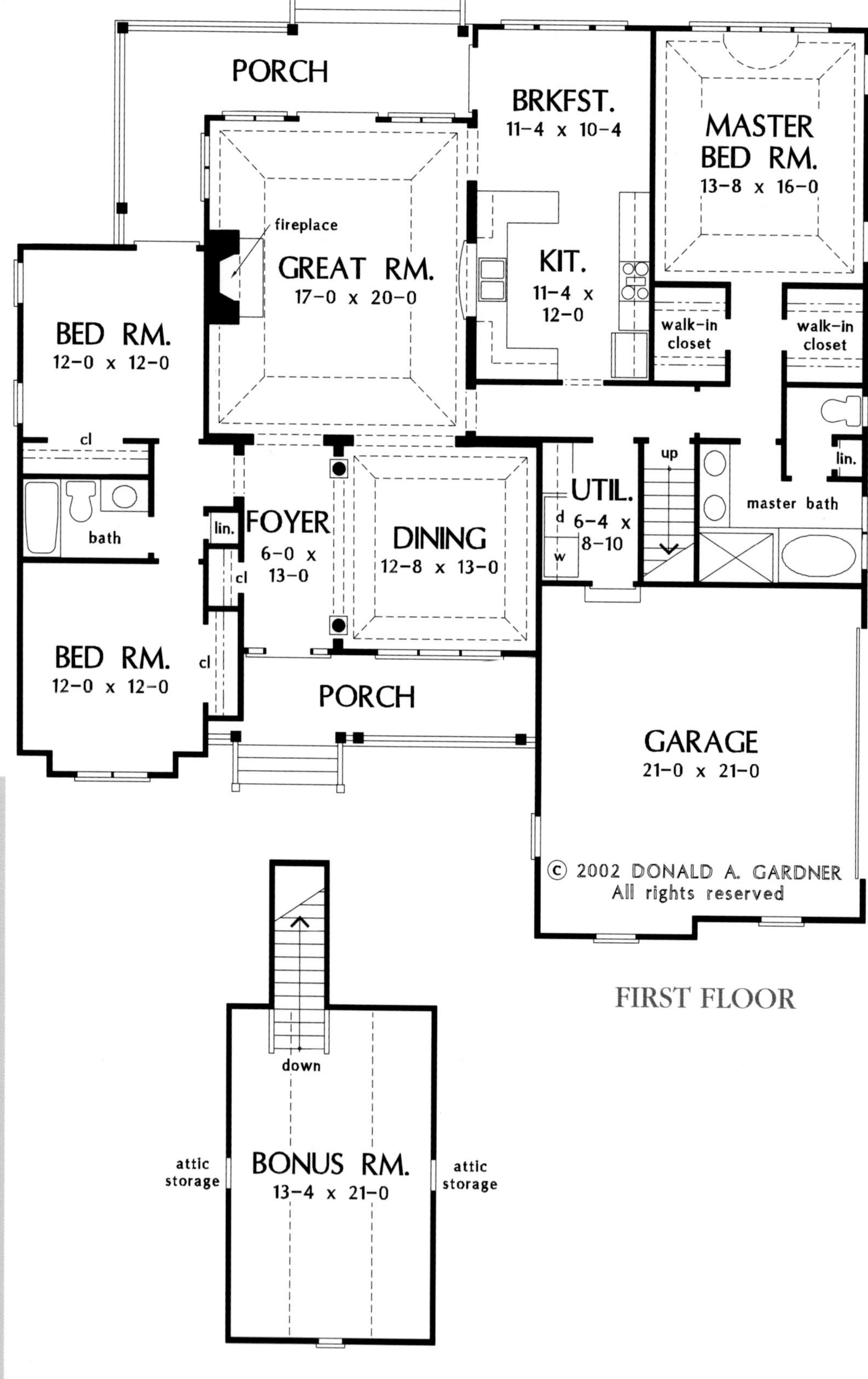
PORCH
BRKFST.
11-4 x 10-4
MASTER
BED RM.
13-8 x 16-0
fireplace
GREAT RM.
17-0 x 20-0
KIT.
11-4 x
12-0
BED RM.
12-0 x 12-0
walk-in
closet
walk-in
closet
cl
up
lin.
bath
UTIL.
6-4 x
8-10
d
w
master bath
lin.
FOYER
6-0 x
13-0
cl
DINING
12-8 x 13-0
BED RM.
12-0 x 12-0
cl
PORCH
GARAGE
21-0 x 21-0
© 2002 DONALD A. GARDNER
All rights reserved
FIRST FLOOR
down
attic
storage
BONUS RM.
13-4 x 21-0
attic
storage

DPCCH-992
The Gillespie

Total Living: 1955 sq. ft.

Bonus Room: 329 sq. ft.

3 Bedrooms, 2 Baths

Foundation: Crawlspace

Width: 56'

Depth: 58'4"

Price Category: C

DESIGNER NOTE: *"More light and more view make for a truly 'great' room. So, in this design, we tried to open up two walls of the room to the outdoors."*

I had a summer cold last July fourth, so instead of having a hamburger from the grill, I had traditional chicken soup in bed. But the kids did the sweetest thing. They went out into the field with their dad and lit fireworks, so I could see them through the transom and windows. It was such a special gesture that I didn't mind being sick.

The Gillespie

REAR

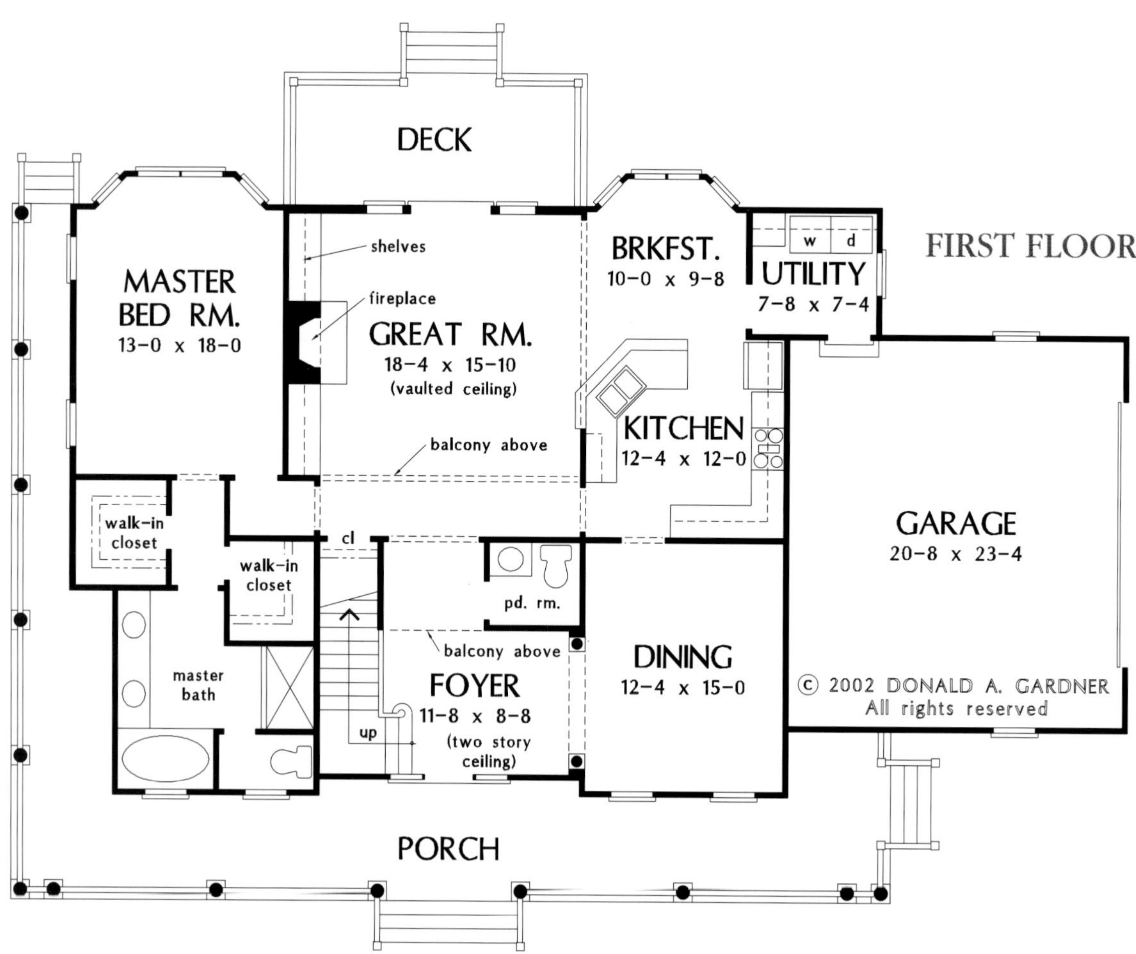
DECK
FIRST FLOOR
MASTER BED RM. 13-0 x 18-0
shelves
fireplace
GREAT RM. 18-4 x 15-10 (vaulted ceiling)
balcony above
BRKFST. 10-0 x 9-8
w d
UTILITY 7-8 x 7-4
KITCHEN 12-4 x 12-0
GARAGE 20-8 x 23-4
walk-in closet
walk-in closet
cl
pd. rm.
master bath
balcony above
FOYER 11-8 x 8-8 (two story ceiling)
up
DINING 12-4 x 15-0
© 2002 DONALD A. GARDNER All rights reserved
PORCH

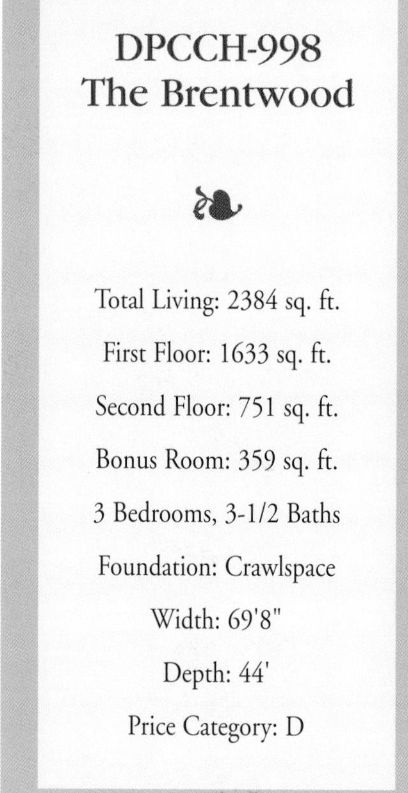

DPCCH-998
The Brentwood

Total Living: 2384 sq. ft.

First Floor: 1633 sq. ft.

Second Floor: 751 sq. ft.

Bonus Room: 359 sq. ft.

3 Bedrooms, 3-1/2 Baths

Foundation: Crawlspace

Width: 69'8"

Depth: 44'

Price Category: D

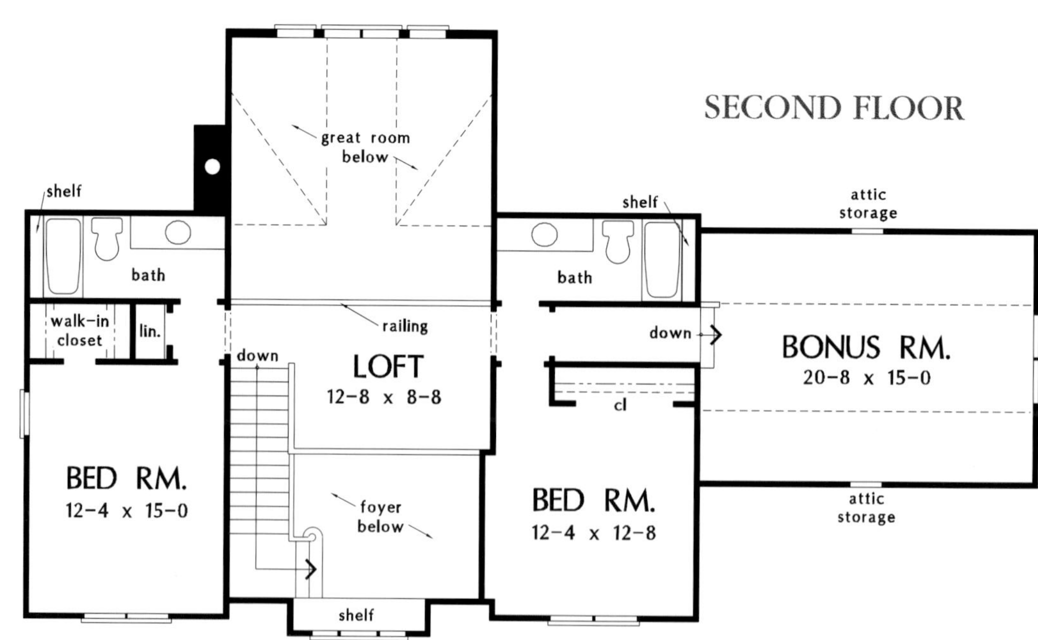
SECOND FLOOR
great room below
shelf
bath
shelf
bath
attic storage
walk-in closet
lin.
railing
down
LOFT 12-8 x 8-8
down
BONUS RM. 20-8 x 15-0
cl
BED RM. 12-4 x 15-0
foyer below
BED RM. 12-4 x 12-8
attic storage
shelf

DESIGNER NOTE: *"Most of our wraparound-porch plans are one-and-a-half stories, but with this home we wanted a true two-story look."*

It finished storming a few minutes ago, and now there's a huge rainbow that's visible through the rear transom. I don't think I've seen one that big since I was a child. It stretches beyond the split-rail fence and looks like it ends somewhere in the middle of the pasture. I know the science, but there's still something magical about a rainbow.

The Brentwood

REAR

FRAMING VIEWS

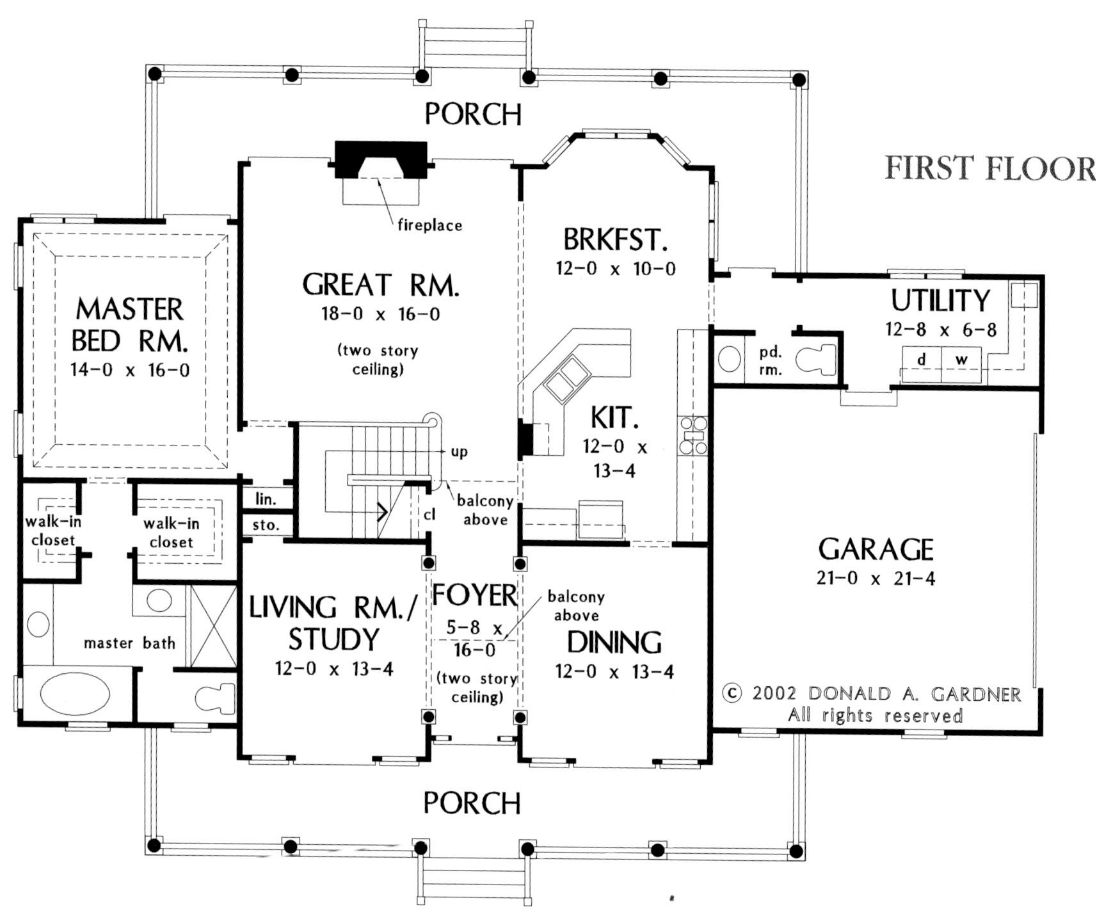
PORCH
FIRST FLOOR
fireplace
BRKFST.
12-0 x 10-0
MASTER
BED RM.
14-0 x 16-0
GREAT RM.
18-0 x 16-0
(two story
ceiling)
UTILITY
12-8 x 6-8
pd.
rm.
d
w
KIT.
12-0 x
13-4
up
balcony
above
lin.
sto.
cl
walk-in
closet
walk-in
closet
GARAGE
21-0 x 21-4
master bath
LIVING RM./
STUDY
12-0 x 13-4
FOYER
5-8 x
16-0
(two story
ceiling)
balcony
above
DINING
12-0 x 13-4
© 2002 DONALD A. GARDNER
All rights reserved
PORCH

DPCCH-971
The Southerland

Total Living: 2521 sq. ft.

First Floor: 1798 sq. ft.

Second Floor: 723 sq. ft.

Bonus Room: 349 sq. ft.

4 Bedrooms, 3-1/2 Baths

Foundation: Crawlspace

Width: 66'8"

Depth: 49'8"

Price Category: E

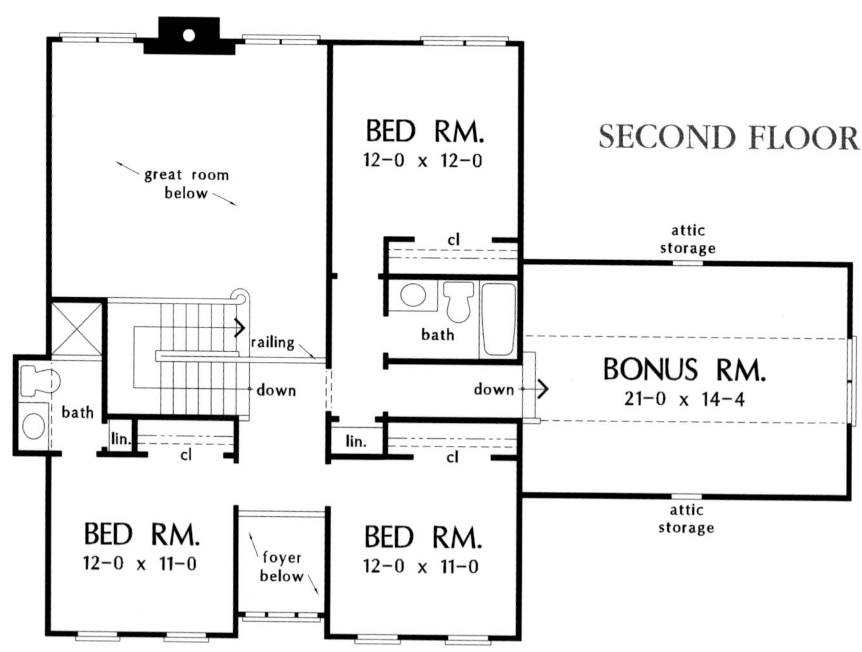
BED RM.
12-0 x 12-0
SECOND FLOOR
great room
below
cl
attic
storage
bath
railing
down
BONUS RM.
21-0 x 14-4
down
bath
lin.
cl
lin.
cl
attic
storage
BED RM.
12-0 x 11-0
foyer
below
BED RM.
12-0 x 11-0

DESIGNER NOTE: *"We wanted to create a smaller version of a popular design but keep all of the components that made it so strong in the first place."*

Our old hound dog always knows when we're eating. He'll make his rounds to all the French doors until he finds a spot where he can see us. Waiting patiently until we're finished, he'll bark once or twice to remind us to give him some of our table scraps. He always gets a little. His face and demeanor are just so hard to resist.

The Southerland

REAR

FRAMING VIEWS

FIRST FLOOR

SCREEN PORCH 15-4 x 13-6
PORCH
BRKFST. 9-8 x 10-4
KIT. 9-8 x 11-0
BED RM. 12-8 x 11-0
MASTER BED RM. 13-0 x 16-0
master bath
walk-in closet
UTIL. 9-0 x 6-0
DINING 13-8 x 12-0
GREAT RM. 15-0 x 20-8 (cathedral ceiling)
fireplace
FOYER
GARAGE 22-8 x 22-0
PORCH
railing
BED RM./ STUDY 12-8 x 12-0 (cathedral ceiling)

SECOND FLOOR

BONUS RM. 16-8 x 17-4
BONUS RM. 26-4 x 14-0
attic storage
down

DPCCH-1014
The Zeller

Total Living: 2005 sq. ft.

Bonus Room: 827 sq. ft.

3 Bedrooms, 2 Baths

Foundation: Crawlspace

Width: 66'4"

Depth: 64'10"

Price Category: D

DESIGNER NOTE: *"Every home should have a sense of uniqueness, and here we emphasized the dining room and wrapped it with two porches."*

I sat in the glassed breakfast area watching my grandbaby outside playing hopscotch. No matter how the world changes, some things are still fun to a child: climbing trees, skipping stones and playing marbles. I won't be climbing any trees today, but I might go out there and try a little hopscotch. I used to be pretty good.

The Zeller

REAR

FRAMING VIEWS

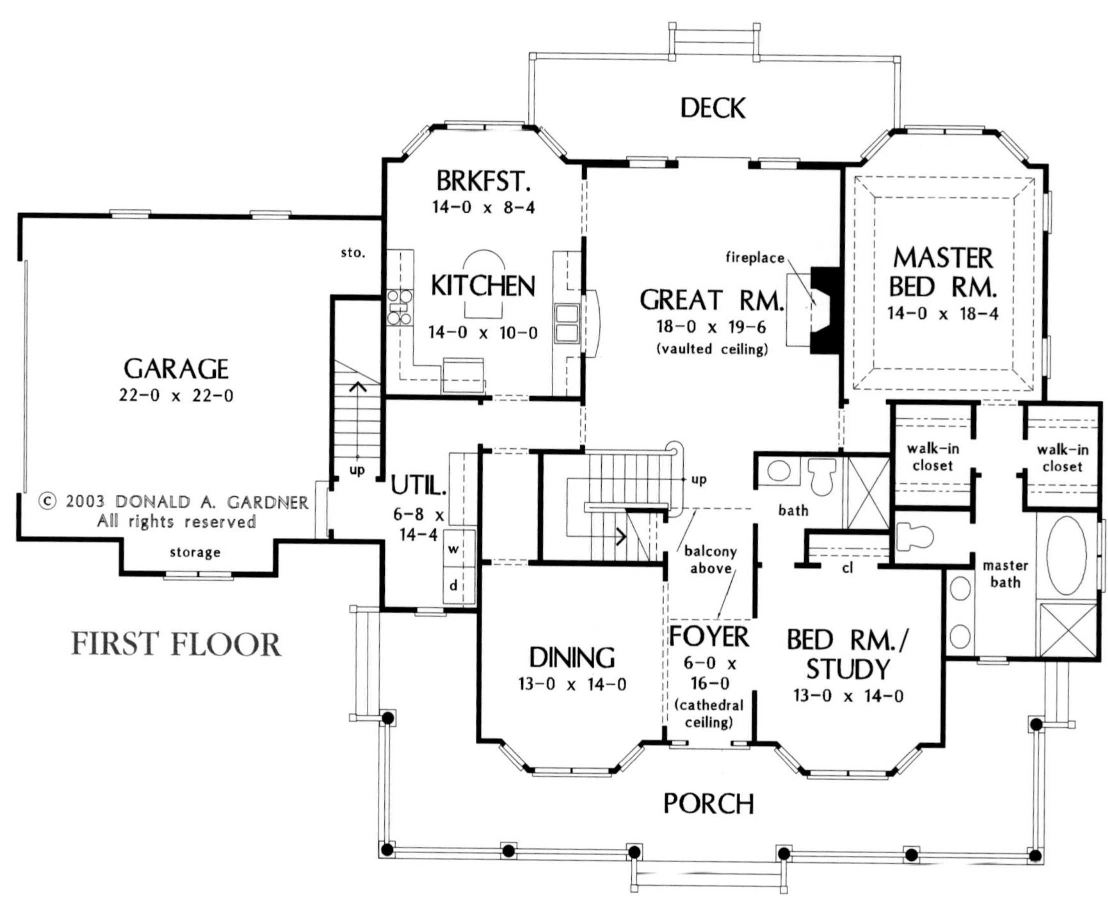
DECK
BRKFST.
14-0 x 8-4
KITCHEN
14-0 x 10-0
sto.
GARAGE
22-0 x 22-0
© 2003 DONALD A. GARDNER
All rights reserved
storage
up
UTIL.
6-8 x
14-4
w
d
fireplace
GREAT RM.
18-0 x 19-6
(vaulted ceiling)
MASTER
BED RM.
14-0 x 18-4
walk-in
closet
walk-in
closet
up
bath
balcony
above
cl
master
bath
DINING
13-0 x 14-0
FOYER
6-0 x
16-0
(cathedral
ceiling)
BED RM./
STUDY
13-0 x 14-0
PORCH

FIRST FLOOR

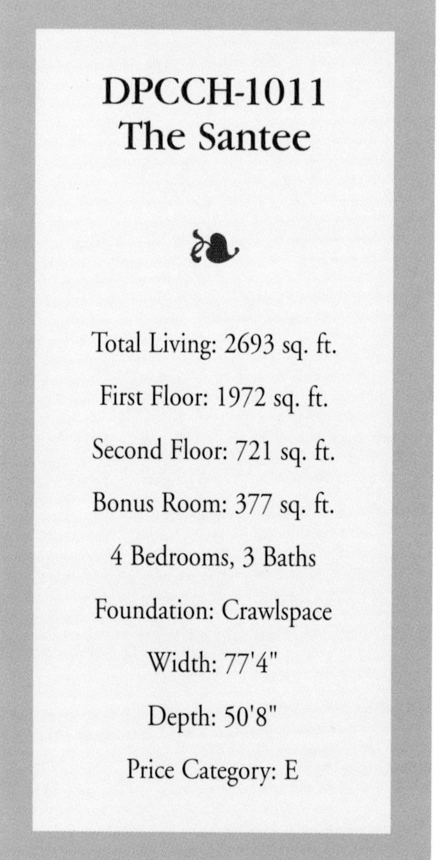

DPCCH-1011
The Santee

Total Living: 2693 sq. ft.

First Floor: 1972 sq. ft.

Second Floor: 721 sq. ft.

Bonus Room: 377 sq. ft.

4 Bedrooms, 3 Baths

Foundation: Crawlspace

Width: 77'4"

Depth: 50'8"

Price Category: E

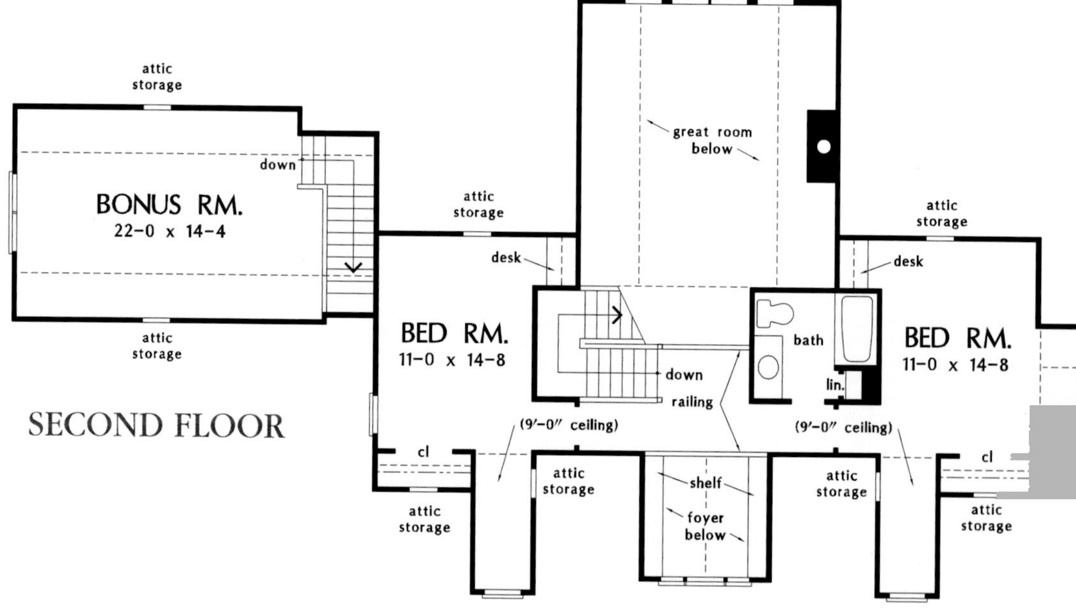
attic
storage
down
BONUS RM.
22-0 x 14-4
attic
storage
great room
below
attic
storage
attic
storage
desk
desk
BED RM.
11-0 x 14-8
bath
BED RM.
11-0 x 14-8
down
railing
lin.
(9'-0" ceiling)
(9'-0" ceiling)
cl
cl
attic
storage
shelf
attic
storage
foyer
below
attic
storage
attic
storage

SECOND FLOOR

DESIGNER NOTE: *"When designing this home we wanted to give special emphasis to the entry and expanded the center dormer to include a Palladian window."*

Although they tried not to make a sound, they couldn't help but wake me. I got up when they came in to kiss me goodbye. As I walked them to the door, I could see how excited they were. I sat at the bay window and watched them drive down the dirt road early this morning. The first fishing trip is almost like a rite of passage.

The Santee

REAR

We hung the tire swing from a limb on the big oak in the backyard, so we can see it through the French doors.

DPCCH-762
The Saddlebrook

Total living: 2356 s.f.

First Floor: 1718 s.f. • Second Floor: 638 s.f.

Bonus Room: 341 s.f.

4 Bedrooms, 3 Baths

Foundation: Crawlspace

Width: 71' • Depth: 42'8"

Price Category: D

DECK
MASTER BED RM. 16-0 x 13-0
(cathedral ceiling)
fireplace
GREAT RM. 17-0 x 16-4
up
BRKFST. 11-8 x 10-4
cl
w d
UTIL.
storage
KIT. 11-8 x 12-0
pan.
GARAGE 21-0 x 23-4
walk-in closet
walk-in closet
master bath
bath
lin.
cl
sto.
cl
BED RM./ STUDY 11-8 x 11-0
FOYER 8-8 x 11-4
DINING 11-8 x 13-4
© 1998 DONALD A. GARDNER All rights reserved
PORCH

FIRST FLOOR

SECOND FLOOR

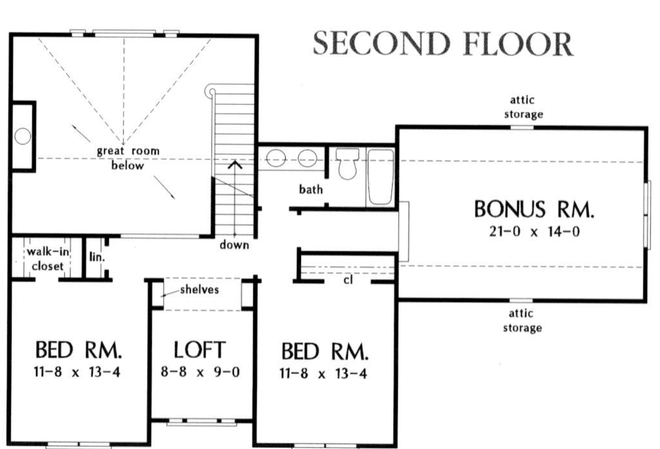
great room below
down
bath
attic storage
BONUS RM. 21-0 x 14-0
attic storage
walk-in closet
lin.
shelves
cl
BED RM. 11-8 x 13-4
LOFT 8-8 x 9-0
BED RM. 11-8 x 13-4

This morning a crop duster flew by several times with a banner that read "Will you marry me M.K.?" I went to the balcony and looked out the Palladian to read it.

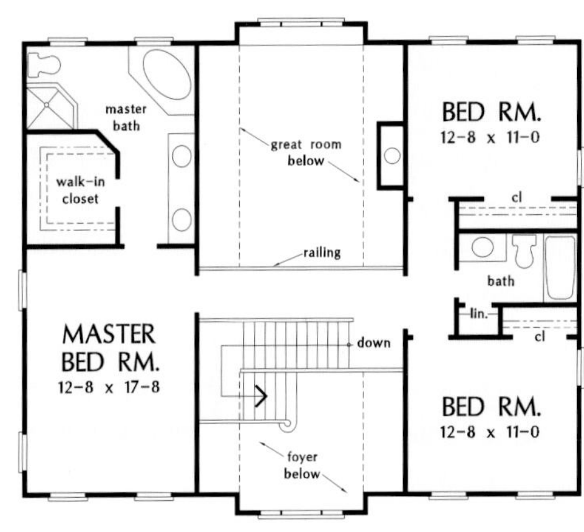
master bath
walk-in closet
great room below
railing
BED RM.
12-8 x 11-0
cl
bath
lin.
cl
MASTER BED RM.
12-8 x 17-8
down
BED RM.
12-8 x 11-0
foyer below

SECOND FLOOR

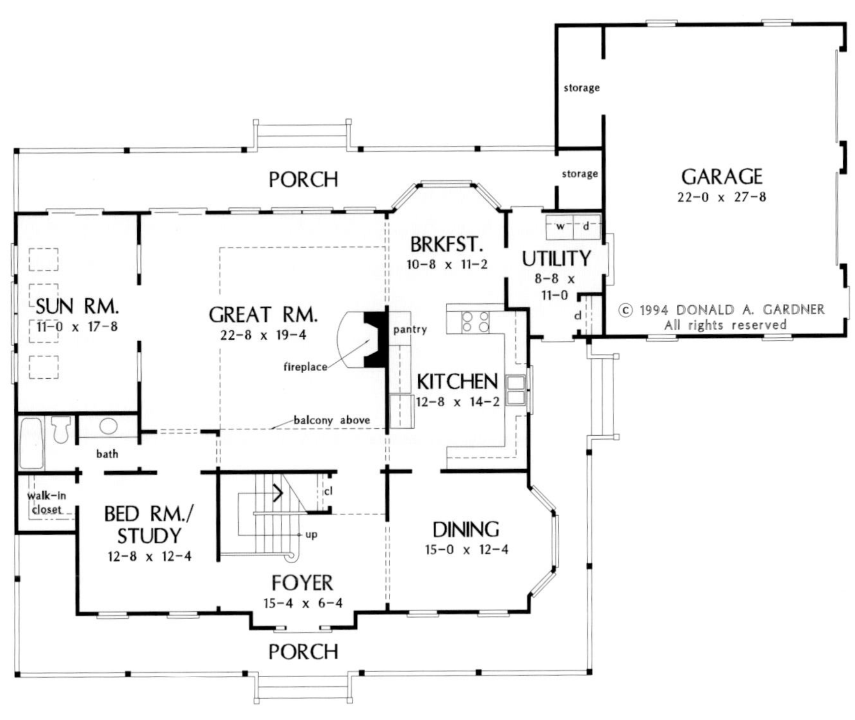
storage
storage
GARAGE
22-0 x 27-8
PORCH
BRKFST.
10-8 x 11-2
UTILITY
8-8 x 11-0
w
d
SUN RM.
11-0 x 17-8
GREAT RM.
22-8 x 19-4
fireplace
pantry
KITCHEN
12-8 x 14-2
© 1994 DONALD A. GARDNER
All rights reserved
balcony above
bath
walk-in closet
cl
BED RM./ STUDY
12-8 x 12-4
up
DINING
15-0 x 12-4
FOYER
15-4 x 6-4
PORCH

FIRST FLOOR

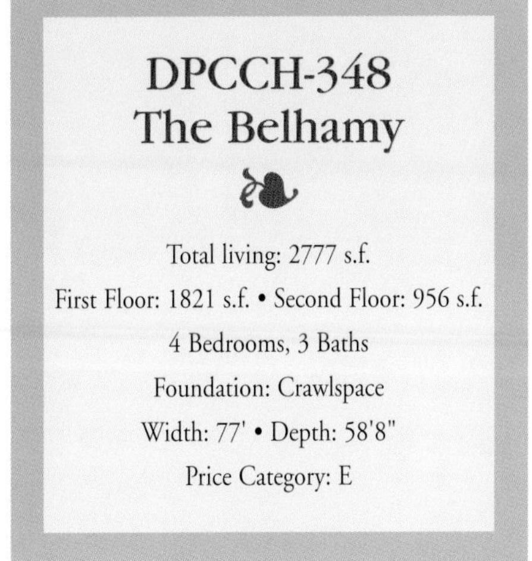

DPCCH-348
The Belhamy

Total living: 2777 s.f.

First Floor: 1821 s.f. • Second Floor: 956 s.f.

4 Bedrooms, 3 Baths

Foundation: Crawlspace

Width: 77' • Depth: 58'8"

Price Category: E

It isn't strange to look out a back window or French door and see a cow in the backyard. Our fence doesn't always keep them out.

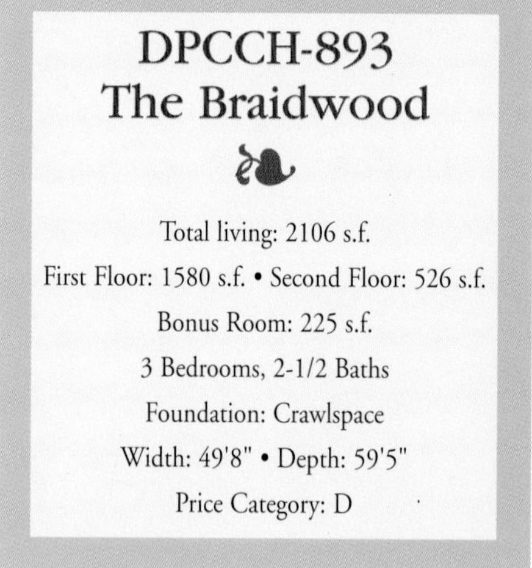

DPCCH-893
The Braidwood

Total living: 2106 s.f.

First Floor: 1580 s.f. • Second Floor: 526 s.f.

Bonus Room: 225 s.f.

3 Bedrooms, 2-1/2 Baths

Foundation: Crawlspace

Width: 49'8" • Depth: 59'5"

Price Category: D

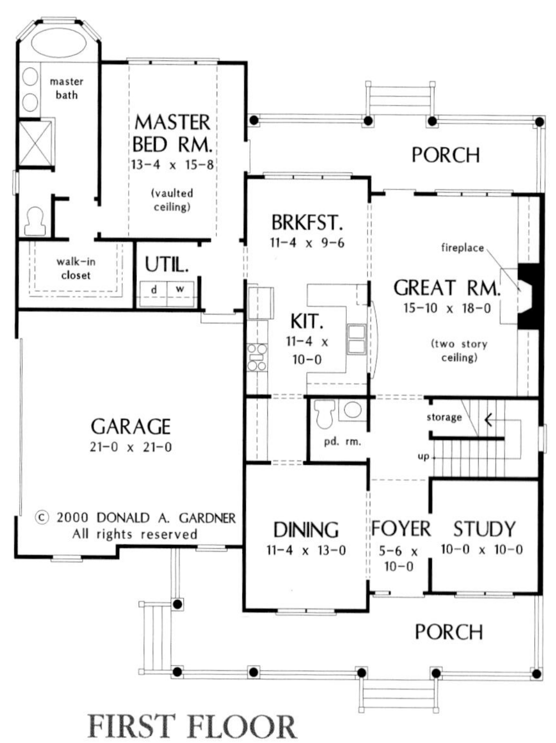
master bath
MASTER BED RM. 13-4 x 15-8 (vaulted ceiling)
PORCH
walk-in closet
UTIL.
d w
BRKFST. 11-4 x 9-6
fireplace
GREAT RM. 15-10 x 18-0 (two story ceiling)
KIT. 11-4 x 10-0
GARAGE 21-0 x 21-0
pd. rm.
storage
up
© 2000 DONALD A. GARDNER All rights reserved
DINING 11-4 x 13-0
FOYER 5-6 x 10-0
STUDY 10-0 x 10-0
PORCH

FIRST FLOOR

SECOND FLOOR

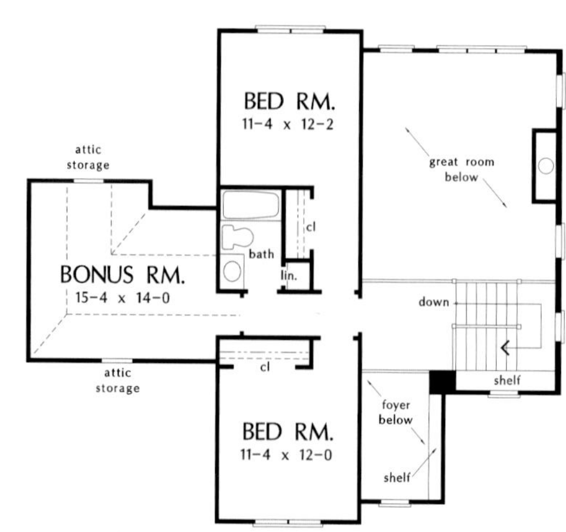
BED RM. 11-4 x 12-2
attic storage
great room below
cl
bath
lin.
BONUS RM. 15-4 x 14-0
down
cl
attic storage
shelf
foyer below
BED RM. 11-4 x 12-0
shelf

The clerestory in the great room reminds me of sunsets over the ocean. It seems that the sun lingers for a brief time before disappearing for the evening.

BED RM.
12-4 x 11-8
walk-in closet
bath
BED RM.
12-4 x 12-0
lin.
sto.
walk-in closet
down
great room below

SECOND FLOOR

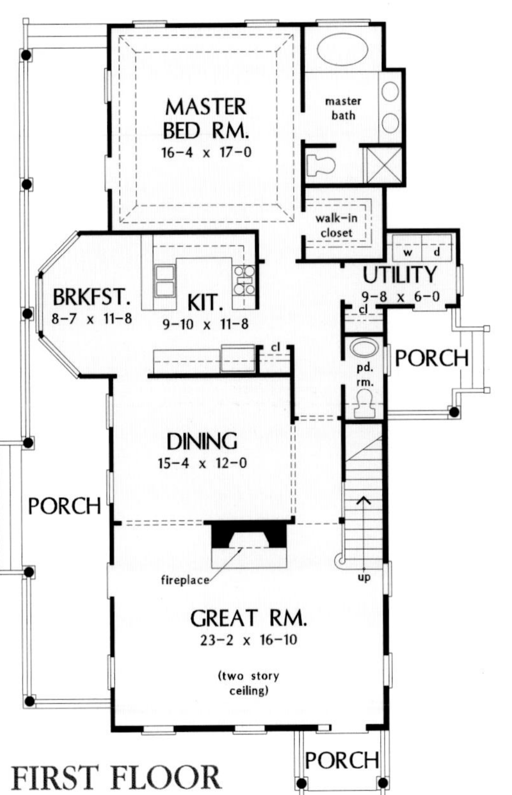
MASTER BED RM.
16-4 x 17-0
master bath
walk-in closet
UTILITY
9-8 x 6-0
w
d
cl
BRKFST.
8-7 x 11-8
KIT.
9-10 x 11-8
cl
pd. rm.
PORCH
DINING
15-4 x 12-0
PORCH
fireplace
up
GREAT RM.
23-2 x 16-10
(two story ceiling)
PORCH

FIRST FLOOR

GARAGE
22-4 x 25-4

DPCCH-492
The Savannah

Total living: 2105 s.f.

First Floor: 1545 s.f. • Second Floor: 560 s.f.

3 Bedrooms, 2-1/2 Baths

Foundation: Crawlspace

Width: 38' • Depth: 64'4"

Price Category: D

We put a large American flag on the front of our house. You can see it from the dining room's curved window and the upstairs Palladian.

DPCCH-964
The Yarborough

Total living: 2222 s.f.

First Floor: 1684 s.f. • Second Floor: 538 s.f.

Bonus Room: 415 s.f.

3 Bedrooms, 2-1/2 Baths

Foundation: Crawlspace

Width: 46'3" • Depth: 64'7"

Price Category: D

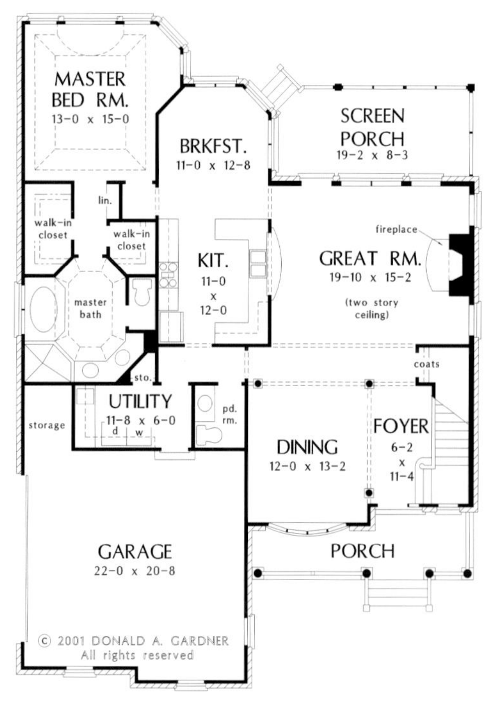

MASTER BED RM.
13-0 x 15-0
walk-in closet
lin.
walk-in closet
master bath
sto.
BRKFST.
11-0 x 12-8
SCREEN PORCH
19-2 x 8-3
KIT.
11-0 x 12-0
fireplace
GREAT RM.
19-10 x 15-2
(two story ceiling)
coats
storage
UTILITY
11-8 x 6-0
d w
pd. rm.
DINING
12-0 x 13-2
FOYER
6-2 x 11-4
GARAGE
22-0 x 20-8
PORCH
© 2001 DONALD A. GARDNER
All rights reserved

FIRST FLOOR

BED RM.
11-0 x 13-0
great room below
cl
attic storage
railing
down
bath
cl
foyer below
BED RM.
12-0 x 12-0
(vaulted ceiling)
BONUS RM.
12-0 x 27-0
attic storage
attic storage

SECOND FLOOR

You can lie on your back and look up at the stars without going outside. The rear clerestory captures them and displays them under the cathedral ceiling.

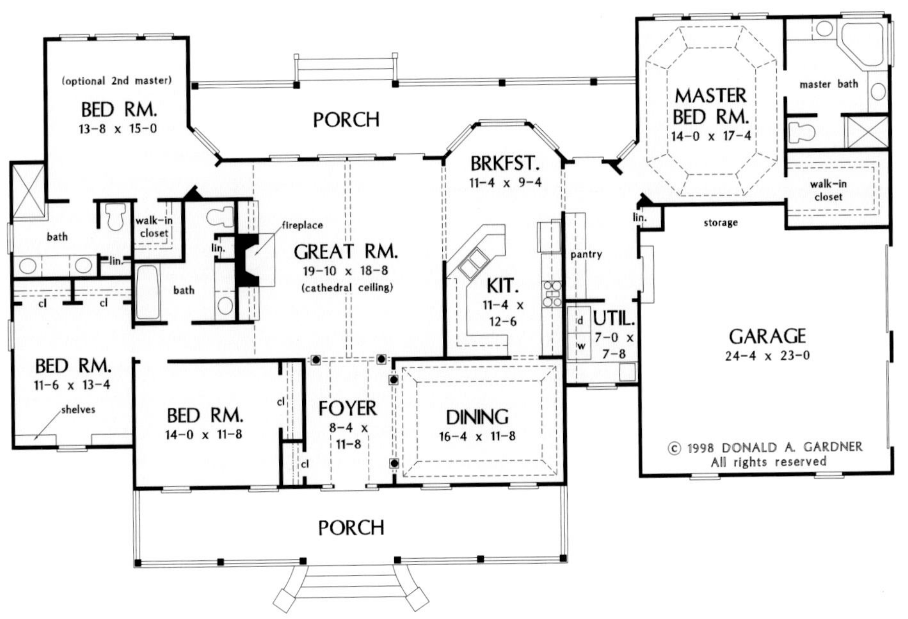

(optional 2nd master)
BED RM.
13-8 x 15-0
PORCH
BRKFST.
11-4 x 9-4
MASTER
BED RM.
14-0 x 17-4
master bath
walk-in
closet
bath
walk-in
closet
lin.
fireplace
GREAT RM.
19-10 x 18-8
(cathedral ceiling)
lin.
bath
KIT.
11-4 x
12-6
pantry
lin.
storage
UTIL.
7-0 x
7-8
d
w
GARAGE
24-4 x 23-0
cl
cl
BED RM.
11-6 x 13-4
shelves
BED RM.
14-0 x 11-8
cl
FOYER
8-4 x
11-8
cl
DINING
16-4 x 11-8
© 1998 DONALD A. GARDNER
All rights reserved
PORCH

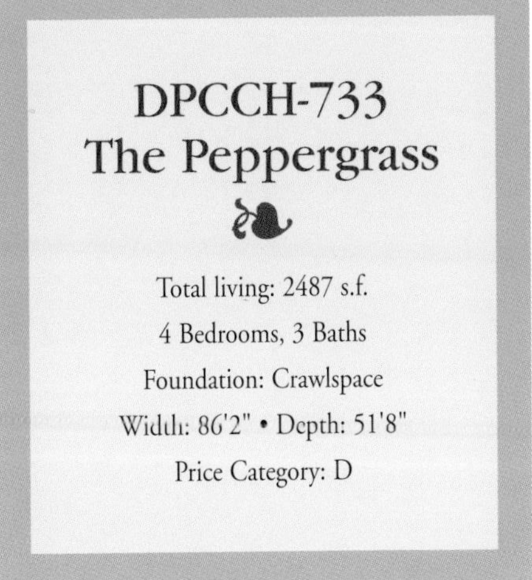

DPCCH-733
The Peppergrass

Total living: 2487 s.f.

4 Bedrooms, 3 Baths

Foundation: Crawlspace

Width: 86'2" • Depth: 51'8"

Price Category: D

We put an antique school desk in the dormer alcove. It's our granddaughter's favorite place to play school with her dolls.

DPCCH-849
The Azalea Crossing

Total living: 2482 s.f.

First Floor: 1706 s.f. • Second Floor: 776 s.f.

Bonus Room: 414 s.f.

4 Bedrooms, 2-1/2 Baths

Foundation: Crawlspace

Width: 54'8"• Depth: 43'

Price Category: D

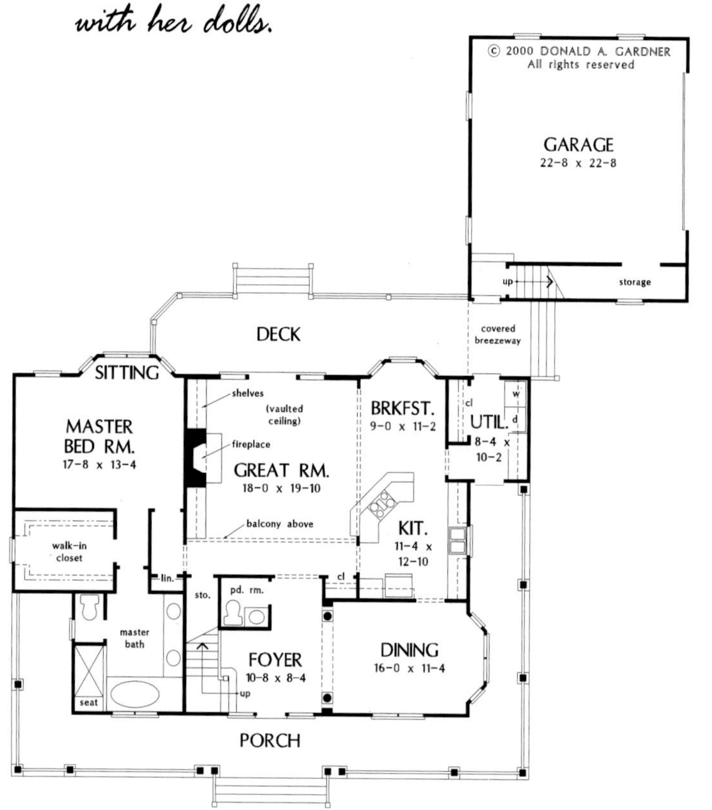
© 2000 DONALD A. GARDNER
All rights reserved
GARAGE
22-8 x 22-8
up
storage
DECK
covered breezeway
SITTING
MASTER BED RM.
17-8 x 13-4
shelves
(vaulted ceiling)
fireplace
GREAT RM.
18-0 x 19-10
balcony above
BRKFST.
9-0 x 11-2
UTIL.
8-4 x 10-2
KIT.
11-4 x 12-10
walk-in closet
lin.
sto.
pd. rm.
cl
master bath
seat
FOYER
10-8 x 8-4
up
DINING
16-0 x 11-4
PORCH

FIRST FLOOR

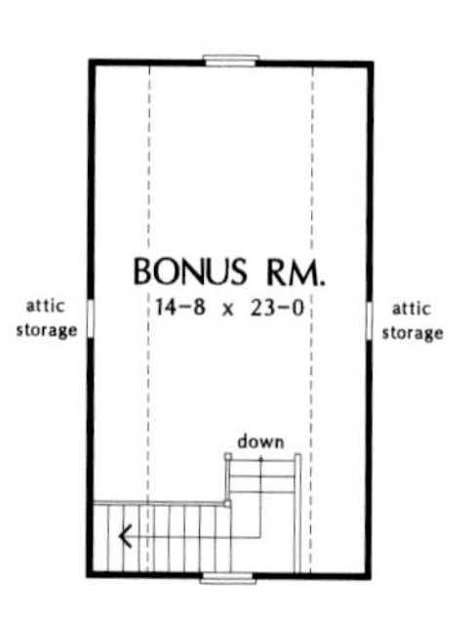
attic storage
BONUS RM.
14-8 x 23-0
attic storage
down

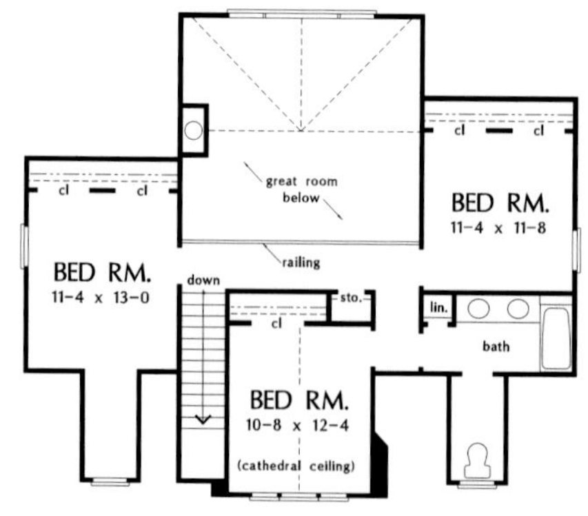
great room below
railing
cl
BED RM.
11-4 x 11-8
BED RM.
11-4 x 13-0
down
sto.
lin.
bath
BED RM.
10-8 x 12-4
(cathedral ceiling)

SECOND FLOOR

I don't know if they saw it through the French doors or if the aroma drifted outside, but five minutes later, half the apple pie was gone.

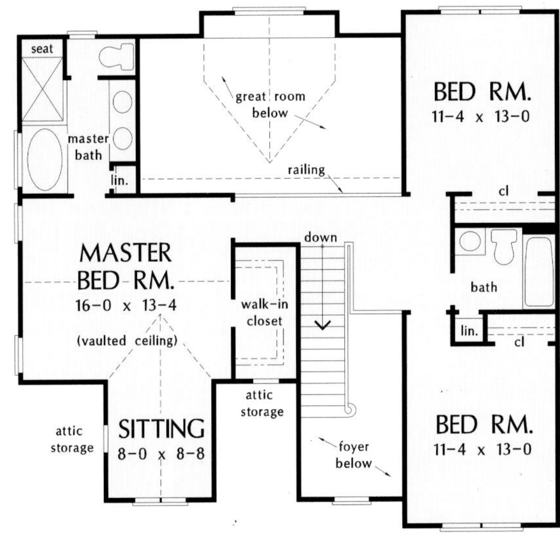
seat
master bath
lin.
great room below
railing
BED RM.
11-4 x 13-0
cl
MASTER BED RM.
16-0 x 13-4
(vaulted ceiling)
walk-in closet
down
bath
lin.
cl
attic storage
SITTING
8-0 x 8-8
attic storage
foyer below
BED RM.
11-4 x 13-0

SECOND FLOOR

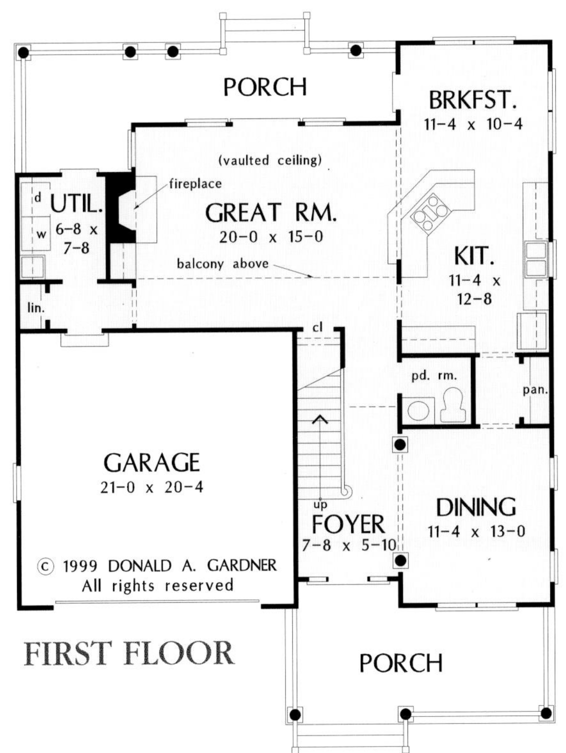
PORCH
BRKFST.
11-4 x 10-4
(vaulted ceiling)
fireplace
UTIL.
6-8 x 7-8
d
w
GREAT RM.
20-0 x 15-0
balcony above
KIT.
11-4 x 12-8
lin.
cl
pd. rm.
pan.
GARAGE
21-0 x 20-4
up
FOYER
7-8 x 5-10
DINING
11-4 x 13-0
© 1999 DONALD A. GARDNER
All rights reserved
PORCH

FIRST FLOOR

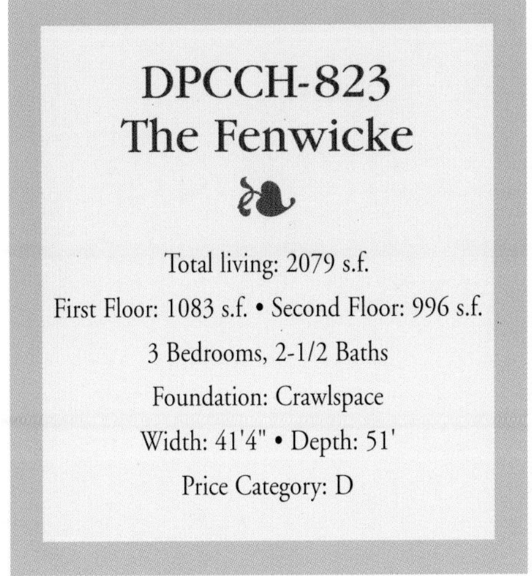

DPCCH-823
The Fenwicke

Total living: 2079 s.f.

First Floor: 1083 s.f. • Second Floor: 996 s.f.

3 Bedrooms, 2-1/2 Baths

Foundation: Crawlspace

Width: 41'4" • Depth: 51'

Price Category: D

We have a wren nest in our hanging basket off the upstairs porch. Looking through the French doors, you can watch the mother feed her babies.

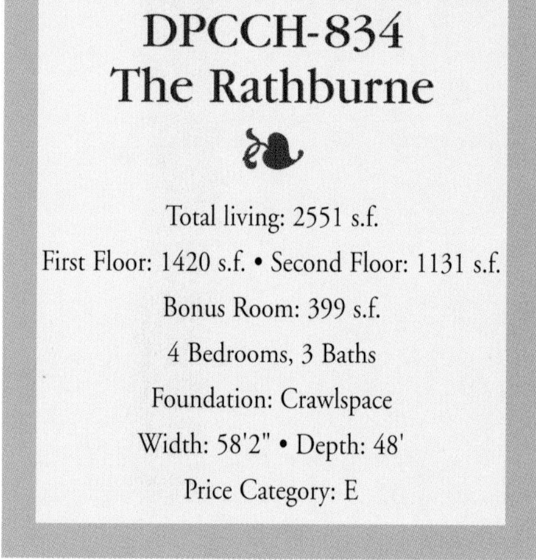

DPCCH-834
The Rathburne

Total living: 2551 s.f.

First Floor: 1420 s.f. • Second Floor: 1131 s.f.

Bonus Room: 399 s.f.

4 Bedrooms, 3 Baths

Foundation: Crawlspace

Width: 58'2" • Depth: 48'

Price Category: E

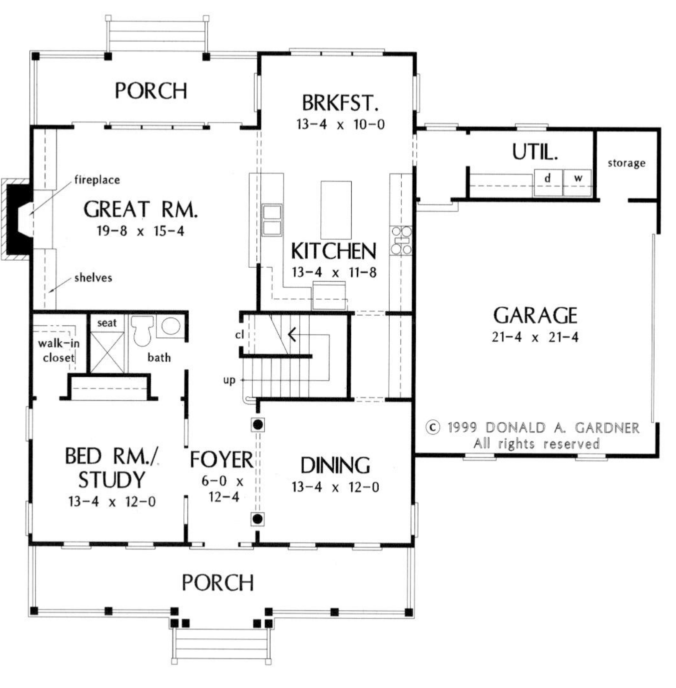
PORCH
BRKFST.
13-4 x 10-0
UTIL.
d
w
storage
fireplace
GREAT RM.
19-8 x 15-4
KITCHEN
13-4 x 11-8
shelves
GARAGE
21-4 x 21-4
seat
walk-in
closet
bath
cl
up
© 1999 DONALD A. GARDNER
All rights reserved
BED RM./
STUDY
13-4 x 12-0
FOYER
6-0 x
12-4
DINING
13-4 x 12-0
PORCH

FIRST FLOOR

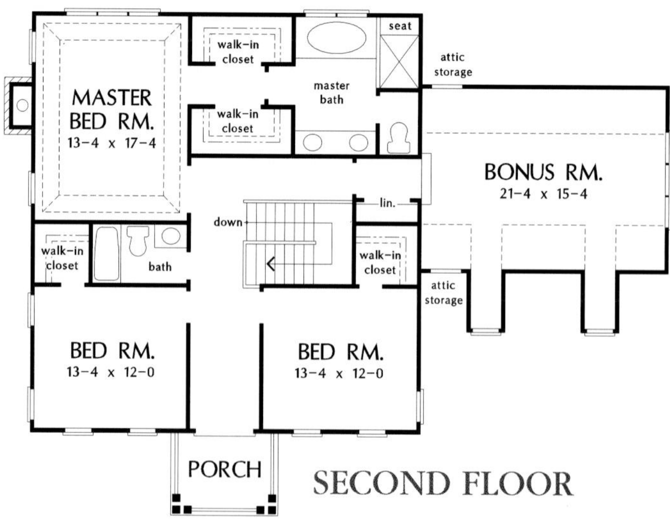
walk-in
closet
seat
attic
storage
master
bath
MASTER
BED RM.
13-4 x 17-4
walk-in
closet
BONUS RM.
21-4 x 15-4
lin.
down
walk-in
closet
bath
walk-in
closet
attic
storage
BED RM.
13-4 x 12-0
BED RM.
13-4 x 12-0
PORCH

SECOND FLOOR

He threw pebbles at my daughter's bay window, but it was my son that opened her window and told him to come back the next day without his guitar.

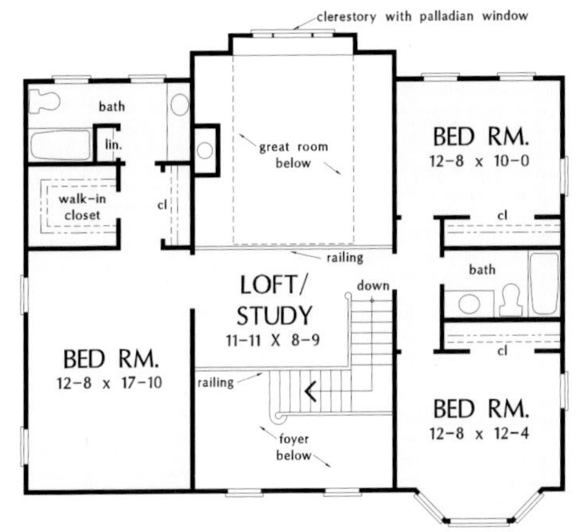
clerestory with palladian window
bath
lin.
walk-in closet
cl
great room below
BED RM.
12-8 x 10-0
cl
bath
railing
down
LOFT/ STUDY
11-11 X 8-9
BED RM.
12-8 x 17-10
railing
cl
BED RM.
12-8 x 12-4
foyer below

SECOND FLOOR

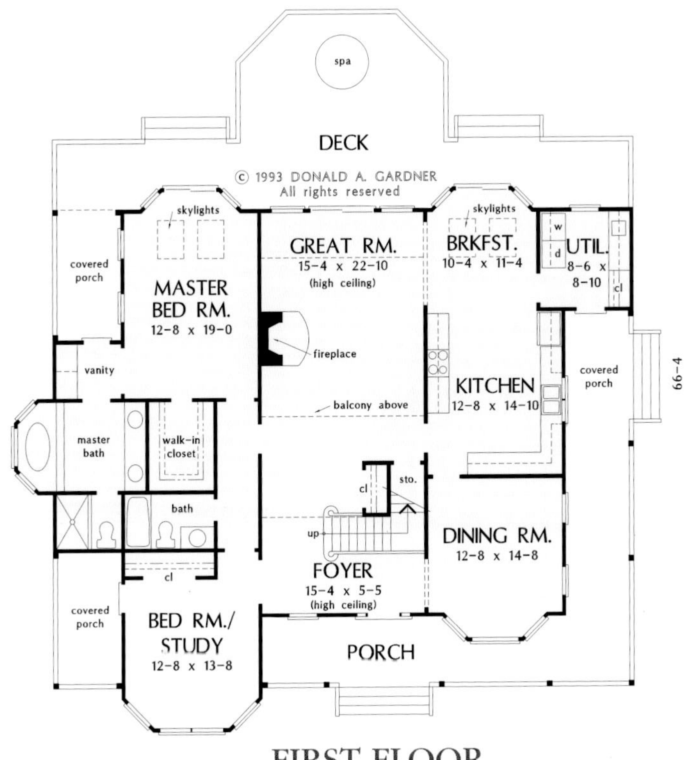
spa
DECK
© 1993 DONALD A. GARDNER
All rights reserved
skylights
skylights
covered porch
MASTER BED RM.
12-8 x 19-0
GREAT RM.
15-4 x 22-10
(high ceiling)
BRKFST.
10-4 x 11-4
w
d
UTIL.
8-6 x 8-10
cl
fireplace
vanity
KITCHEN
12-8 x 14-10
covered porch
66-4
balcony above
master bath
walk-in closet
cl
sto.
bath
up
DINING RM.
12-8 x 14-8
cl
FOYER
15-4 x 5-5
(high ceiling)
covered porch
BED RM./ STUDY
12-8 x 13-8
PORCH

FIRST FLOOR

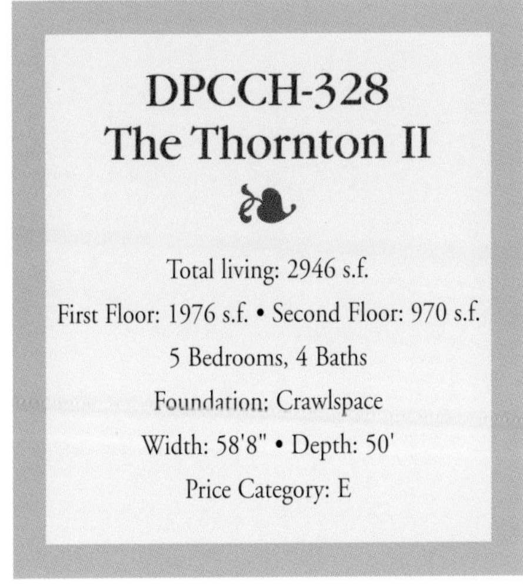

DPCCH-328
The Thornton II

Total living: 2946 s.f.

First Floor: 1976 s.f. • Second Floor: 970 s.f.

5 Bedrooms, 4 Baths

Foundation: Crawlspace

Width: 58'8" • Depth: 50'

Price Category: E

This morning the sun came streaming through the Palladian window over the foyer. It signaled the perfect day to pick berries.

DPCCH-405
The Pineville

Total living: 2203 s.f.

First Floor: 1561 s.f. • Second Floor: 642 s.f.

Bonus Room: 324 s.f.

3 Bedrooms, 2-1/2 Baths

Foundation: Crawlspace

Width: 68' • Depth: 50'4"

Price Category: D

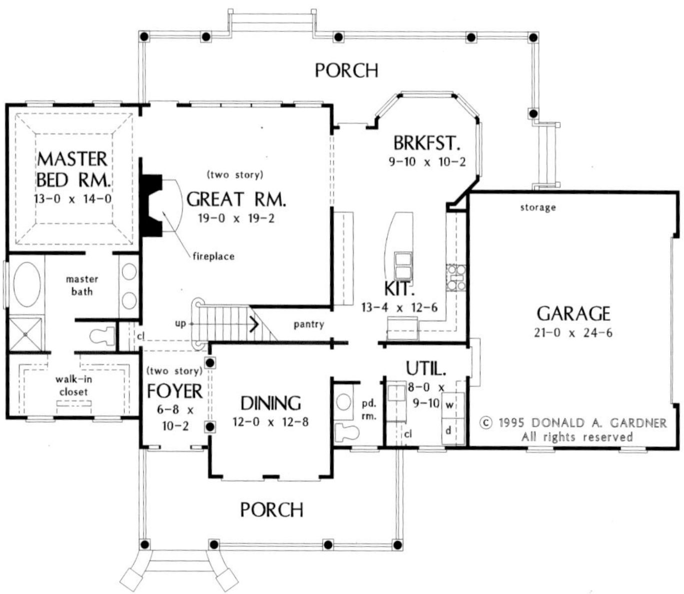
PORCH
MASTER BED RM. 13-0 x 14-0
(two story) GREAT RM. 19-0 x 19-2
fireplace
BRKFST. 9-10 x 10-2
storage
master bath
KIT. 13-4 x 12-6
GARAGE 21-0 x 24-6
up
pantry
cl
walk-in closet
(two story) FOYER 6-8 x 10-2
DINING 12-0 x 12-8
pd. rm.
UTIL. 8-0 x 9-10
w
d
cl
© 1995 DONALD A. GARDNER All rights reserved
PORCH

FIRST FLOOR

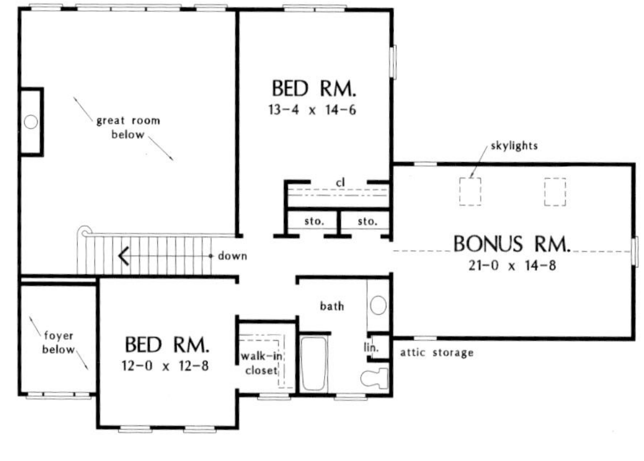
great room below
BED RM. 13-4 x 14-6
skylights
cl
sto.
sto.
down
BONUS RM. 21-0 x 14-8
bath
foyer below
BED RM. 12-0 x 12-8
walk-in closet
lin.
attic storage

SECOND FLOOR

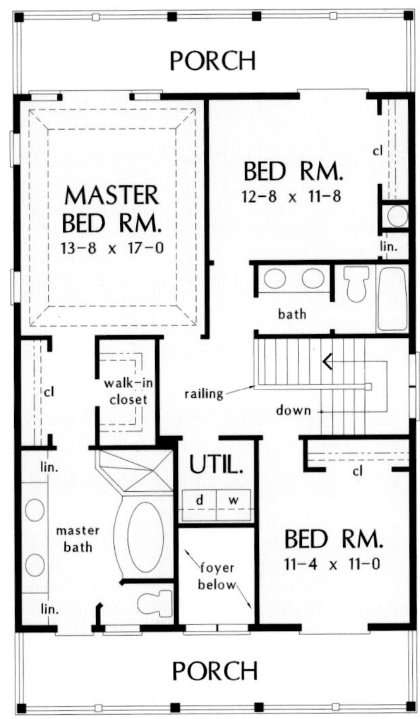
PORCH
MASTER
BED RM.
13-8 x 17-0
BED RM.
12-8 x 11-8
cl
lin.
bath
cl
walk-in
closet
railing
down
lin.
UTIL.
d w
cl
master
bath
BED RM.
11-4 x 11-0
foyer
below
lin.
PORCH

SECOND FLOOR

I grew up on a coastal farm. Our "bar-be-ques" were oyster roasts. When the sun lights the house, we rate our days by saying whether or not it's a good day for an oyster roast.

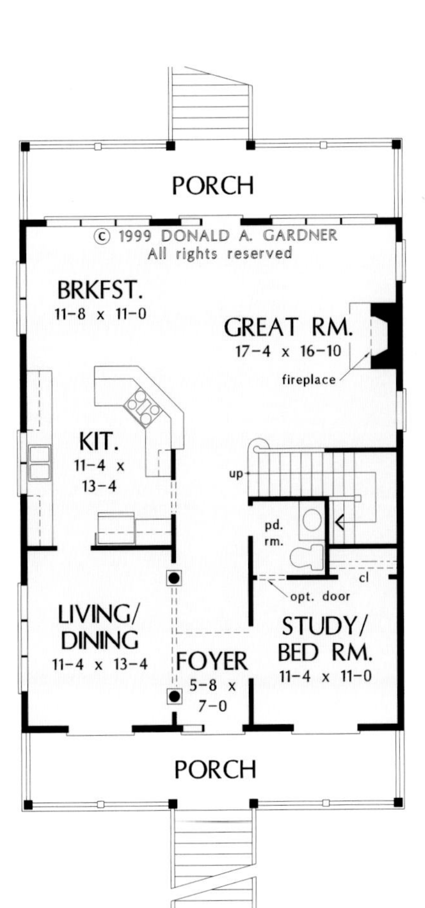
PORCH
© 1999 DONALD A. GARDNER
All rights reserved
BRKFST.
11-8 x 11-0
GREAT RM.
17-4 x 16-10
fireplace
KIT.
11-4 x
13-4
up
pd.
rm.
cl
opt. door
LIVING/
DINING
11-4 x 13-4
FOYER
5-8 x
7-0
STUDY/
BED RM.
11-4 x 11-0
PORCH

FIRST FLOOR

DPCCH-756
The Summercrest

Total living: 2228 s.f.

First Floor: 1170 s.f. • Second Floor: 1058 s.f.

4 Bedrooms, 2-1/2 Baths

Foundation: Post/Pier

Width: 30' • Depth: 51'

Price Category: D

Neighborly Advice

There's nothing quite like taking in a quiet afternoon on the porch or filling a deck with the laughter of friends. Outdoor living areas can turn a homestead into a fifty-two-week vacation spot every year. Spending at least a few minutes outside everyday helps invigorate the body, mind and spirit. But if you need more proof, read on:

The right amount of sun enables your body to make vitamin D, lowers your blood sugar and blood pressure, while increasing your energy and circulation. And don't forget fresh air. Fresh air helps circulation, improves the function of your skin, strengthens your immune system and helps fight diseases. So relaxing on a porch is never a waste of time. It's one of the best things you can do to maintain a healthy lifestyle.

SHADY SPOTS

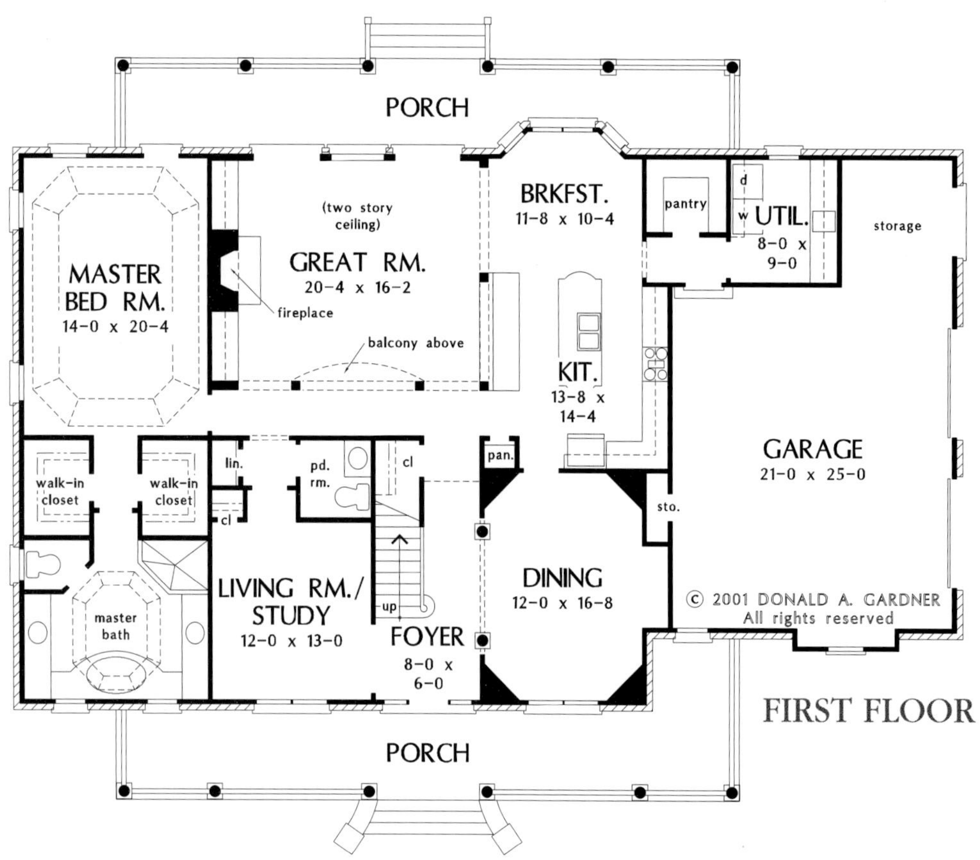
PORCH
BRKFST.
11-8 x 10-4
pantry
d
w
UTIL.
8-0 x 9-0
storage
(two story ceiling)
GREAT RM.
20-4 x 16-2
fireplace
balcony above
MASTER BED RM.
14-0 x 20-4
KIT.
13-8 x 14-4
GARAGE
21-0 x 25-0
walk-in closet
walk-in closet
lin.
cl
pd. rm.
cl
pan.
sto.
master bath
LIVING RM./ STUDY
12-0 x 13-0
up
FOYER
8-0 x 6-0
DINING
12-0 x 16-8
© 2001 DONALD A. GARDNER
All rights reserved
PORCH

FIRST FLOOR

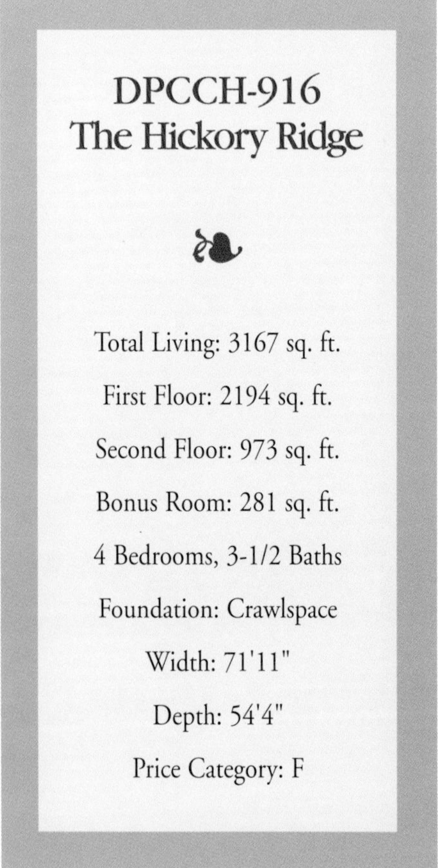

DPCCH-916
The Hickory Ridge

Total Living: 3167 sq. ft.

First Floor: 2194 sq. ft.

Second Floor: 973 sq. ft.

Bonus Room: 281 sq. ft.

4 Bedrooms, 3-1/2 Baths

Foundation: Crawlspace

Width: 71'11"

Depth: 54'4"

Price Category: F

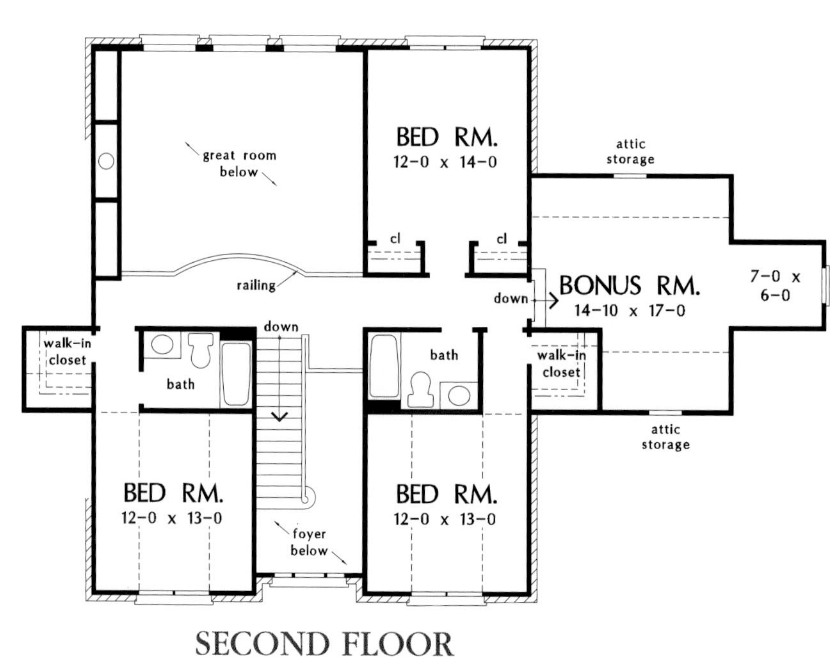
great room below
BED RM.
12-0 x 14-0
attic storage
cl
cl
railing
down
BONUS RM.
14-10 x 17-0
7-0 x 6-0
down
walk-in closet
bath
bath
walk-in closet
attic storage
BED RM.
12-0 x 13-0
foyer below
BED RM.
12-0 x 13-0

SECOND FLOOR

DESIGNER NOTE: *"You told us over and over again to do this concept in a brick version. We finally did it."*

There's nothing like a lazy day spent on the front porch swing, except sharing it with a loved one. Conversation is enhanced by sipping ice-cold glasses of tea topped with sprigs of freshly picked mint. It's the kind of day when talking stops to listen to the birds, and the sweet, subtle fragrance of gardenias and roses drift with the breeze.

The Hickory Ridge

REAR

Photographed home may have been modified from the original construction documents.

SHADY SPOTS

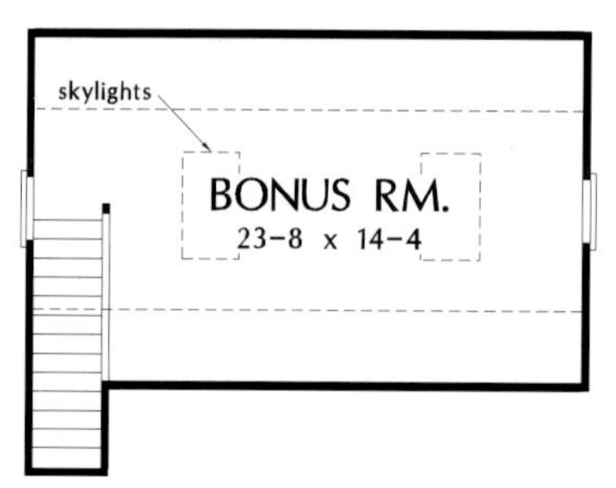
skylights
BONUS RM.
23–8 x 14–4

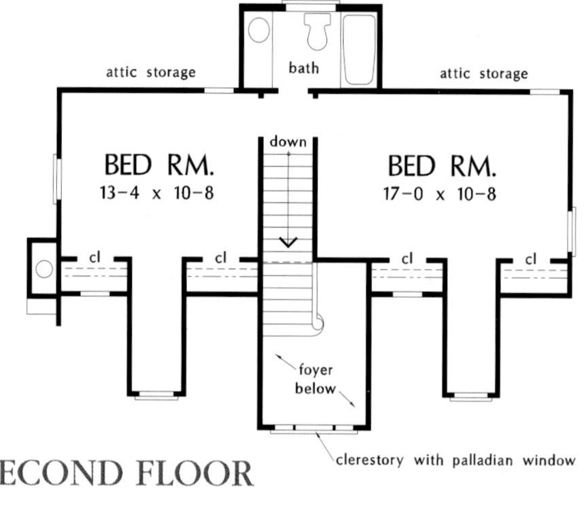
attic storage
bath
attic storage
down
BED RM.
13–4 x 10–8
BED RM.
17–0 x 10–8
cl
cl
cl
cl
foyer below
clerestory with palladian window
SECOND FLOOR

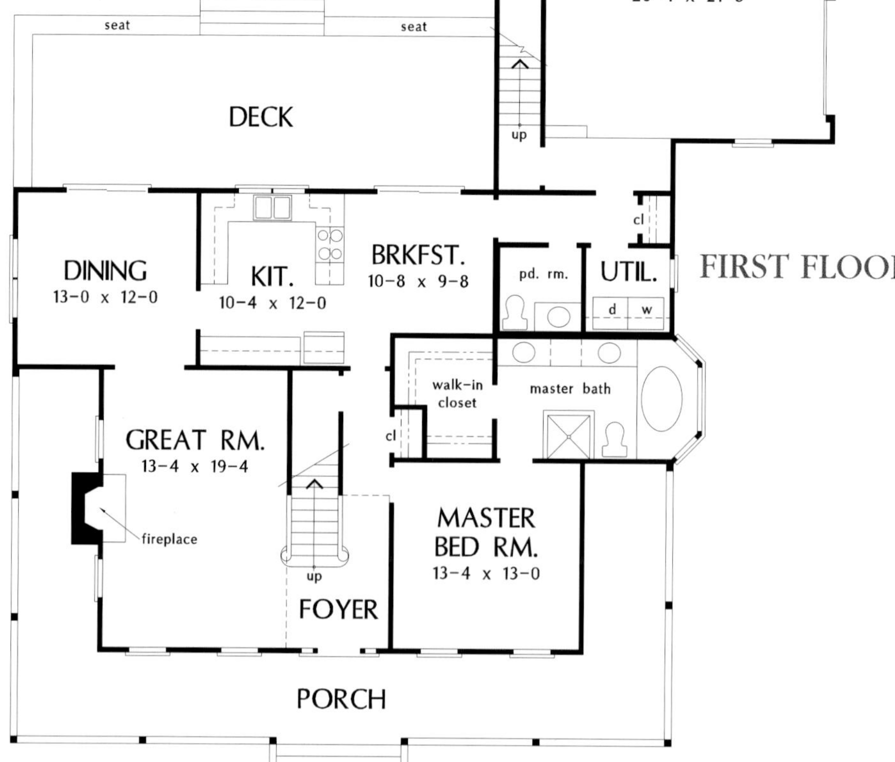
© 1991 DONALD A. GARDNER
All rights reserved
storage
GARAGE
20–4 x 21–8
seat
seat
DECK
up
cl
DINING
13–0 x 12–0
KIT.
10–4 x 12–0
BRKFST.
10–8 x 9–8
pd. rm.
UTIL.
d
w
walk-in closet
master bath
cl
GREAT RM.
13–4 x 19–4
fireplace
up
FOYER
MASTER BED RM.
13–4 x 13–0
PORCH
FIRST FLOOR

DPCCH-235
The Merrifield

Total Living: 1898 sq. ft.

First Floor: 1356 sq. ft.

Second Floor: 542 sq. ft.

Bonus Room: 393 sq. ft.

3 Bedrooms, 2-1/2 Baths

Foundation: Crawlspace

Width: 59'

Depth: 64'4"

Price Category: C

DESIGNER NOTE: *"We designed this home to incorporate the best features of a traditional farmhouse with wraparound porch."*

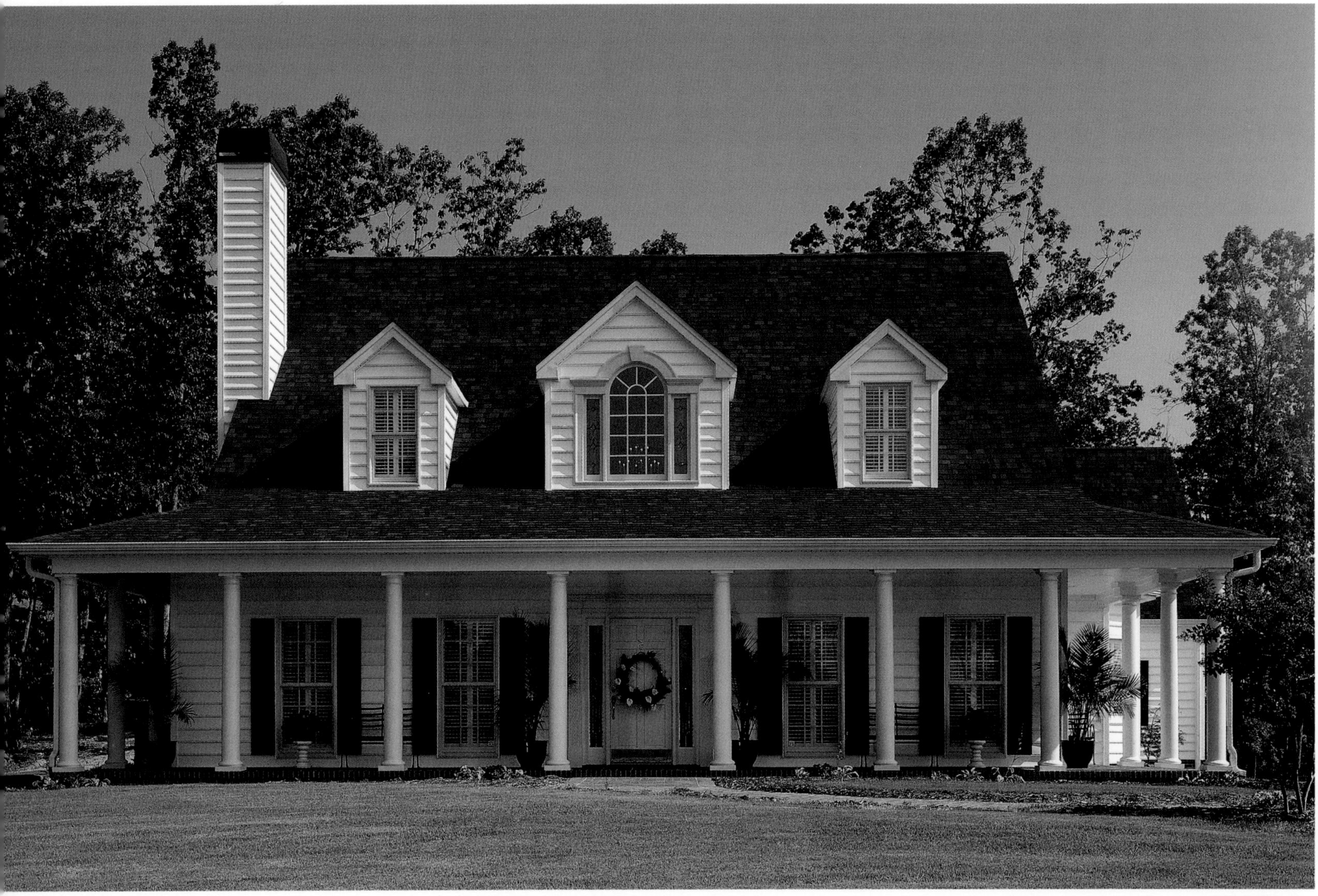

My grandpa used to sit on his front porch and whittle. He could make the most elaborate walking sticks. Thinking that whittling was a lot like work, I once asked him why he worked hard all day and came home to do more work on his sticks. He told me this was his way of relaxing. I didn't understand then, but I do now.

The Merrifield

REAR

Photographed home may have been modified from the original construction documents.

SHADY SPOTS

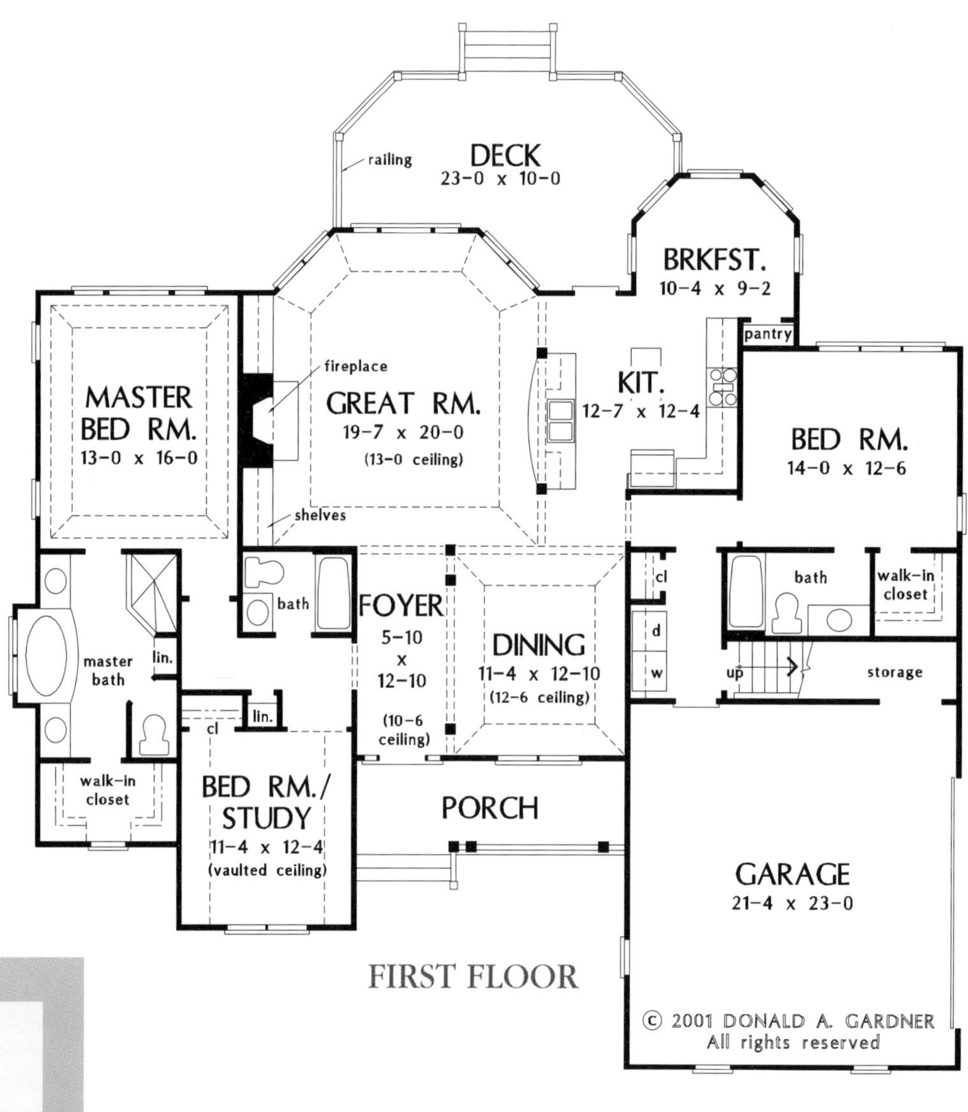

railing
DECK
23-0 x 10-0
BRKFST.
10-4 x 9-2
pantry
fireplace
MASTER BED RM.
13-0 x 16-0
GREAT RM.
19-7 x 20-0
(13-0 ceiling)
KIT.
12-7 x 12-4
BED RM.
14-0 x 12-6
shelves
bath
FOYER
5-10 x 12-10
(10-6 ceiling)
DINING
11-4 x 12-10
(12-6 ceiling)
cl
d
w
bath
walk-in closet
up
storage
master bath
lin.
lin.
cl
walk-in closet
BED RM./ STUDY
11-4 x 12-4
(vaulted ceiling)
PORCH
GARAGE
21-4 x 23-0
FIRST FLOOR
© 2001 DONALD A. GARDNER
All rights reserved

DPCCH-802
The Longleaf

Total Living: 1971 sq. ft.

Bonus Room: 358 sq. ft.

3 Bedrooms, 3 Baths

Foundation: Crawlspace

Width: 62'6"

Depth: 57'2"

Price Category: C

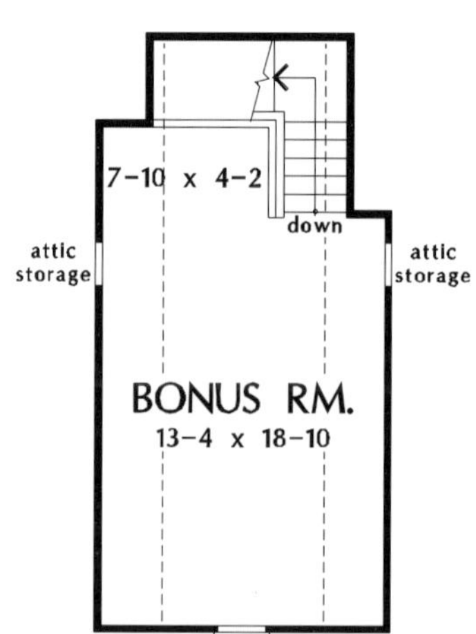

7-10 x 4-2
down
attic storage
attic storage
BONUS RM.
13-4 x 18-10

DESIGNER NOTE: *"This design is all about flow-through living spaces. From front porch to foyer to dining room to great room to kitchen to breakfast to rear deck, this is how most of us live."*

Weekends are made for family, friends and spicy, smoked bar-be-que. But we believe weekdays should be fun and festive too, so after work, we sometimes prepare a picnic and walk no further than the back porch. We stay outside until the sun goes down. It gives us the opportunity to spend quality time together and takes away work stress.

The Longleaf

REAR

Photographed home may have been modified from the original construction documents.

SHADY SPOTS

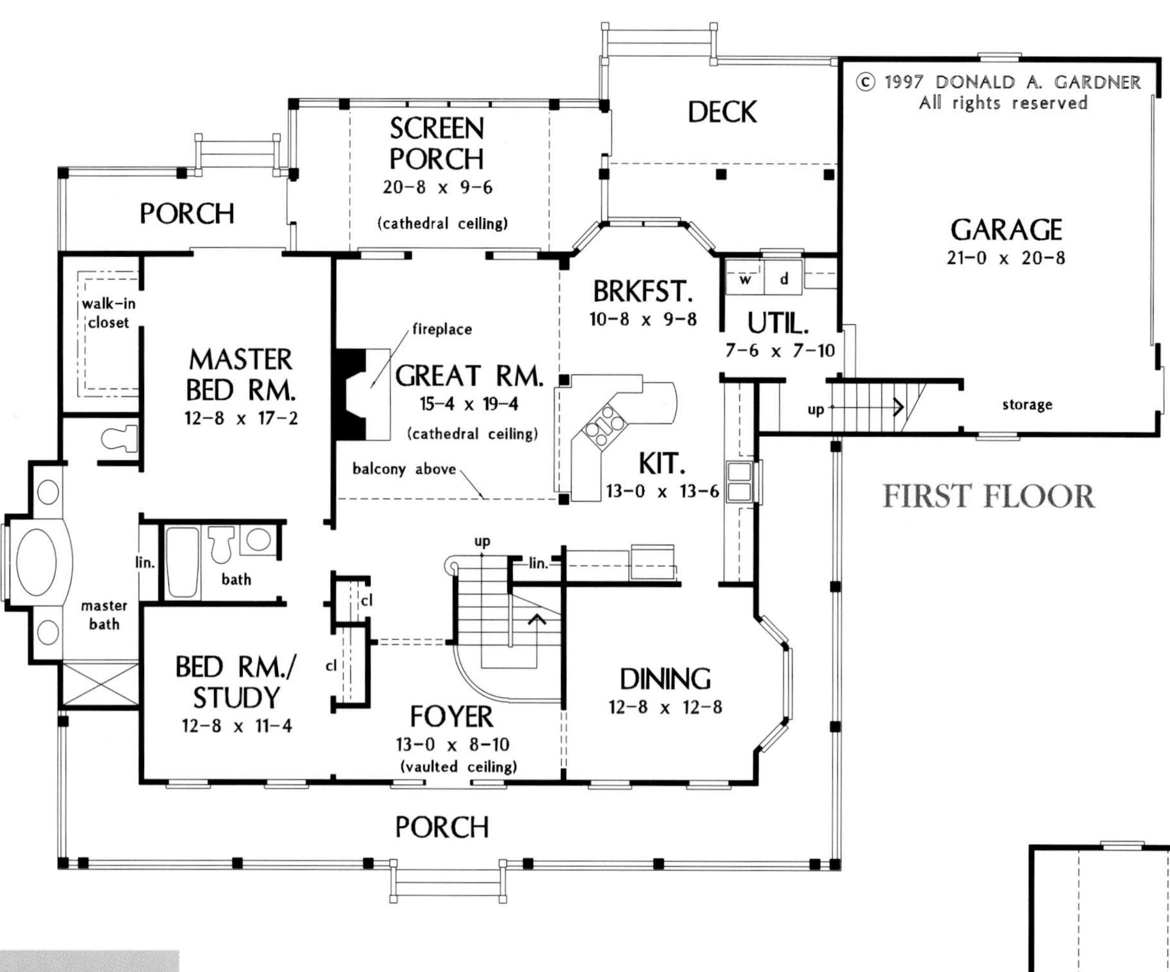

© 1997 DONALD A. GARDNER
All rights reserved
DECK
SCREEN PORCH
20-8 x 9-6
(cathedral ceiling)
PORCH
GARAGE
21-0 x 20-8
walk-in closet
MASTER BED RM.
12-8 x 17-2
fireplace
GREAT RM.
15-4 x 19-4
(cathedral ceiling)
balcony above
BRKFST.
10-8 x 9-8
UTIL.
7-6 x 7-10
w
d
up
storage
KIT.
13-0 x 13-6
FIRST FLOOR
lin.
bath
up
lin.
master bath
cl
cl
BED RM./ STUDY
12-8 x 11-4
FOYER
13-0 x 8-10
(vaulted ceiling)
DINING
12-8 x 12-8
PORCH

DPCCH-524
The Peachtree

Total Living: 2298 sq. ft.

First Floor: 1743 sq. ft.

Second Floor: 555 sq. ft.

Bonus Room: 350 sq. ft.

4 Bedrooms, 3 Baths

Foundation: Crawlspace

Width: 78'

Depth: 53'2"

Price Category: D

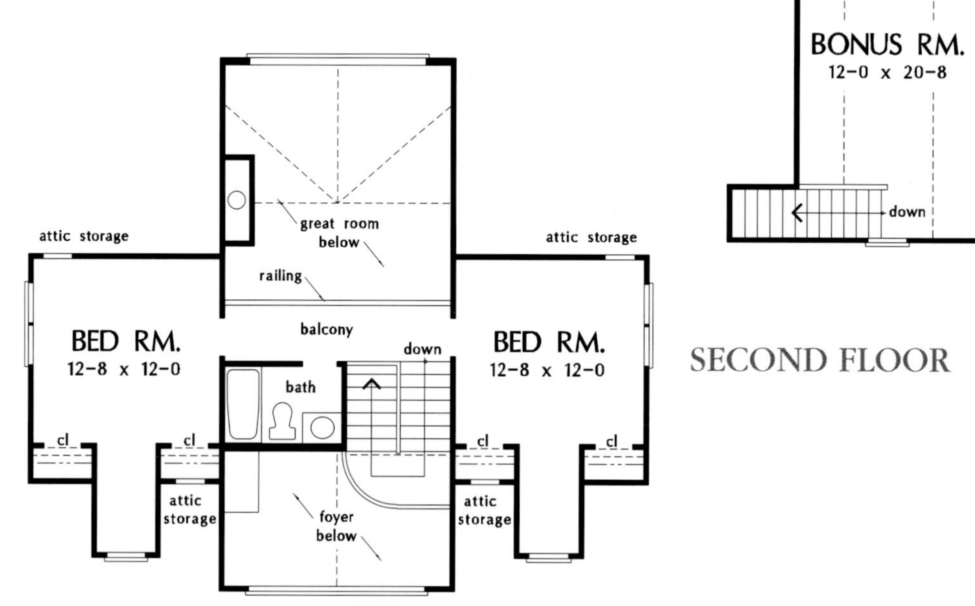

BONUS RM.
12-0 x 20-8
down
great room below
attic storage
attic storage
railing
balcony
BED RM.
12-8 x 12-0
down
BED RM.
12-8 x 12-0
SECOND FLOOR
bath
cl
cl
cl
cl
attic storage
foyer below
attic storage

DESIGNER NOTE: *"In this design, we wanted to show off the feature stair and allow the foyer and great room to blend together."*

The kids just couldn't understand why tadpoles aren't supposed to live in the house. First they wanted them in their rooms. Then they suggested the bonus room, and finally they offered to let them live in our master suite where they would visit. We ended up building a tadpole pond right off the deck. In just a few months, we had frogs.

The Peachtree

REAR

SHADY SPOTS

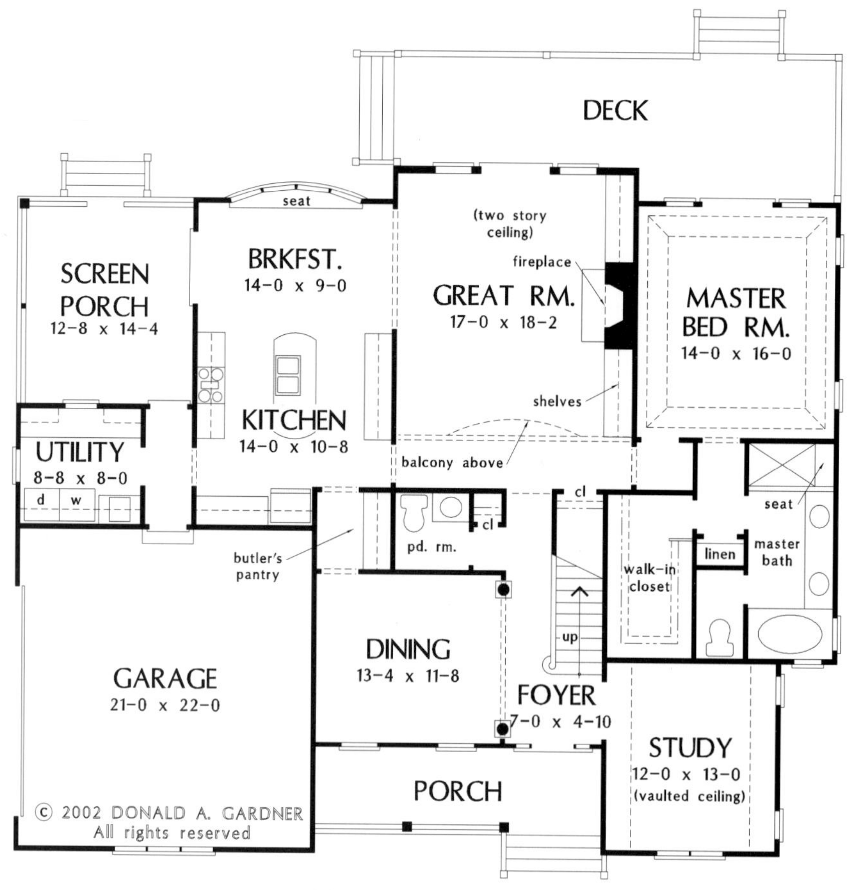
DECK
seat
SCREEN PORCH
12-8 x 14-4
BRKFST.
14-0 x 9-0
(two story ceiling)
fireplace
GREAT RM.
17-0 x 18-2
MASTER BED RM.
14-0 x 16-0
shelves
KITCHEN
14-0 x 10-8
UTILITY
8-8 x 8-0
d
w
balcony above
cl
seat
pd. rm.
linen
master bath
walk-in closet
butler's pantry
up
DINING
13-4 x 11-8
GARAGE
21-0 x 22-0
FOYER
7-0 x 4-10
STUDY
12-0 x 13-0
(vaulted ceiling)
PORCH
© 2002 DONALD A. GARDNER
All rights reserved

FIRST FLOOR

DPCCH-966
The Coltraine

Total Living: 2466 sq. ft.

First Floor: 1856 sq. ft.

Second Floor: 610 sq. ft.

Bonus Room: 322 sq. ft.

3 Bedrooms, 2-1/2 Baths

Foundation: Crawlspace

Width: 59'

Depth: 47'8"

Price Category: D

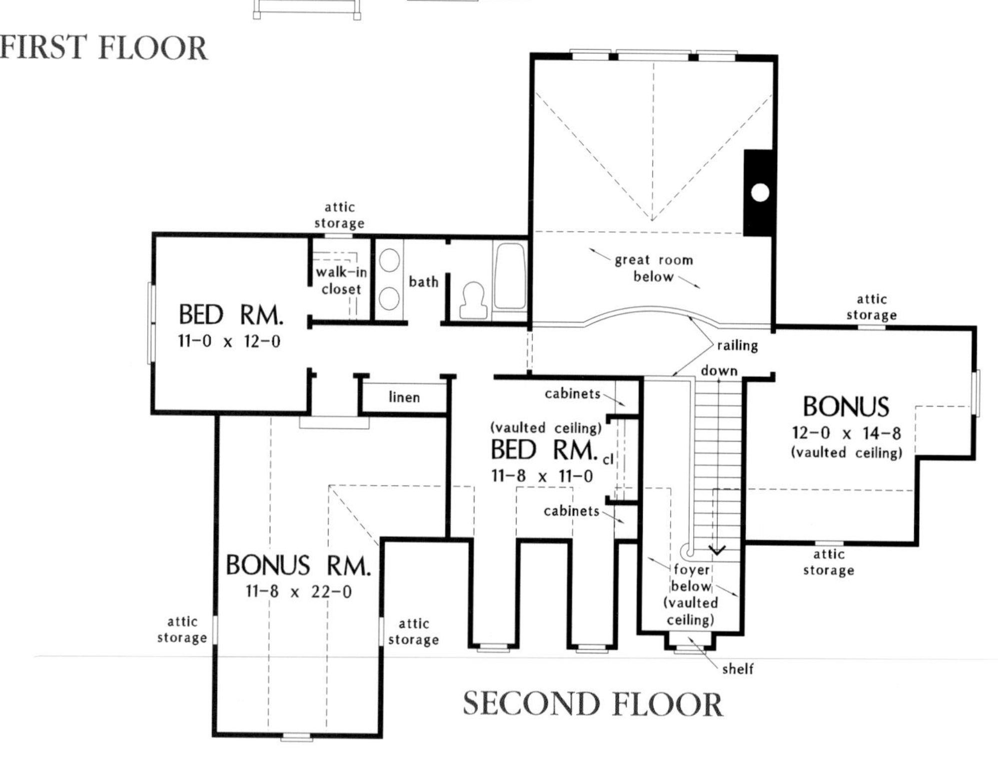
attic storage
walk-in closet
bath
great room below
BED RM.
11-0 x 12-0
attic storage
railing
down
linen
cabinets
(vaulted ceiling)
BED RM.
11-8 x 11-0
cl
cabinets
BONUS
12-0 x 14-8
(vaulted ceiling)
attic storage
BONUS RM.
11-8 x 22-0
attic storage
attic storage
foyer below (vaulted ceiling)
shelf

SECOND FLOOR

DESIGNER NOTE: *"Here we incorporated the screened porch into the main body of the house but in a location that didn't block views from inside. And, everyone knows, two bonus rooms are better than one."*

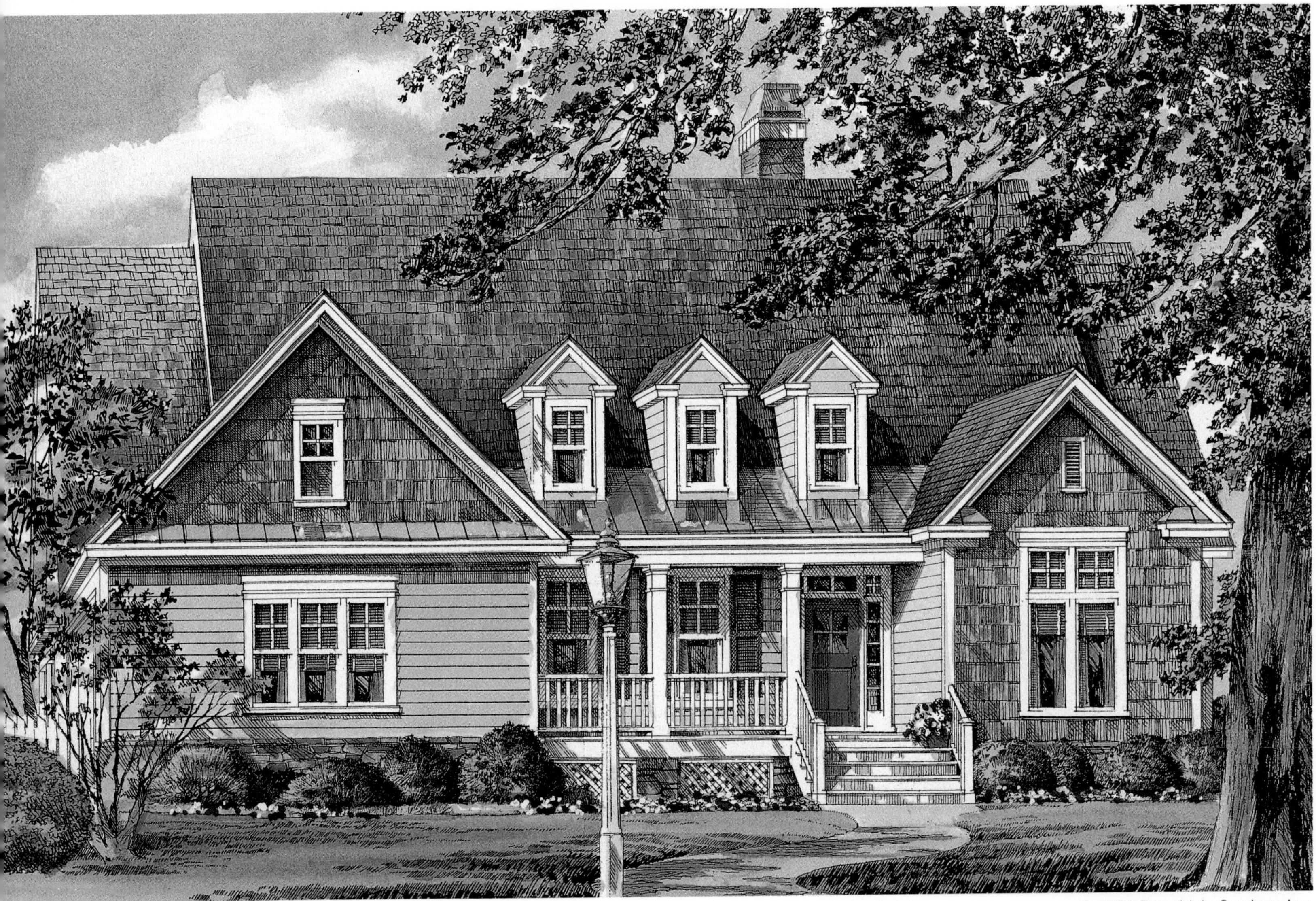

I love to sit in the screened porch and feel the breeze, look outside and hear the sounds while I'm cracking pecans, shelling peas or peeling apples. In the right setting, even work can be made into fun. Maybe it's just me, but I think the fresh air adds to the flavor. It certainly enhances my mood.

The Coltraine

REAR

SHADY SPOTS

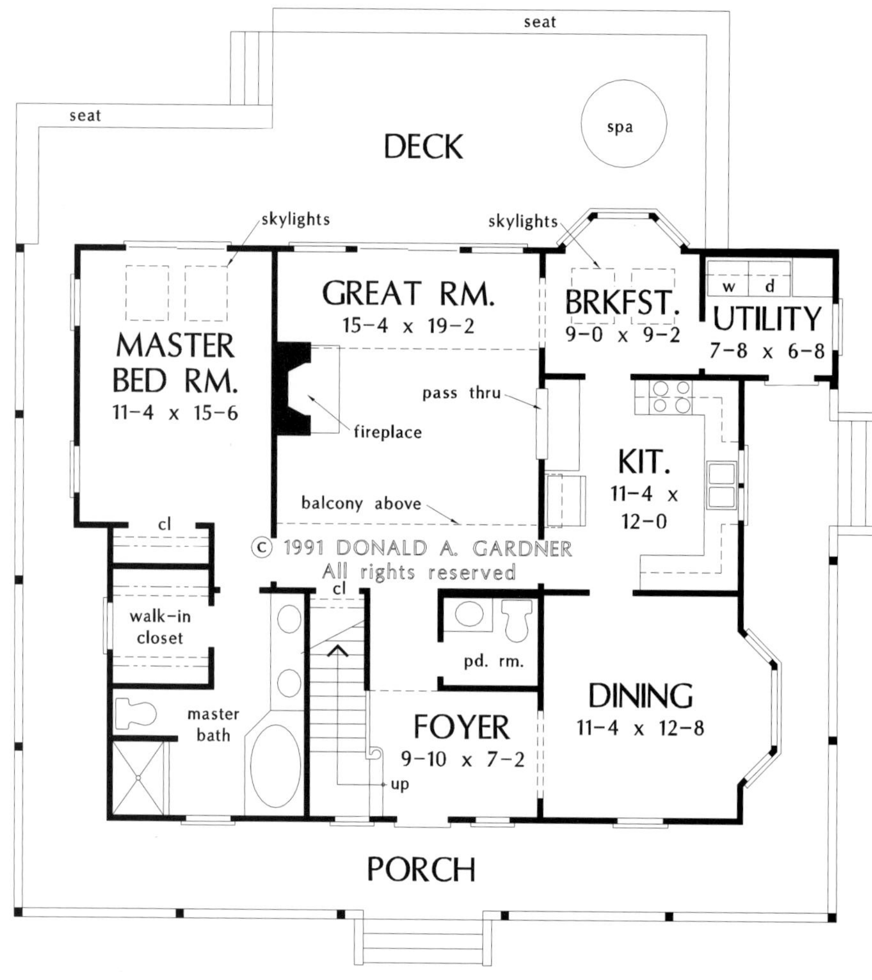

seat
seat
DECK
spa
skylights
skylights
GREAT RM.
15-4 x 19-2
BRKFST.
9-0 x 9-2
w d
UTILITY
7-8 x 6-8
MASTER
BED RM.
11-4 x 15-6
pass thru
fireplace
KIT.
11-4 x
12-0
balcony above
cl
© 1991 DONALD A. GARDNER
All rights reserved
cl
walk-in
closet
pd. rm.
DINING
11-4 x 12-8
master
bath
FOYER
9-10 x 7-2
up
PORCH

FIRST FLOOR

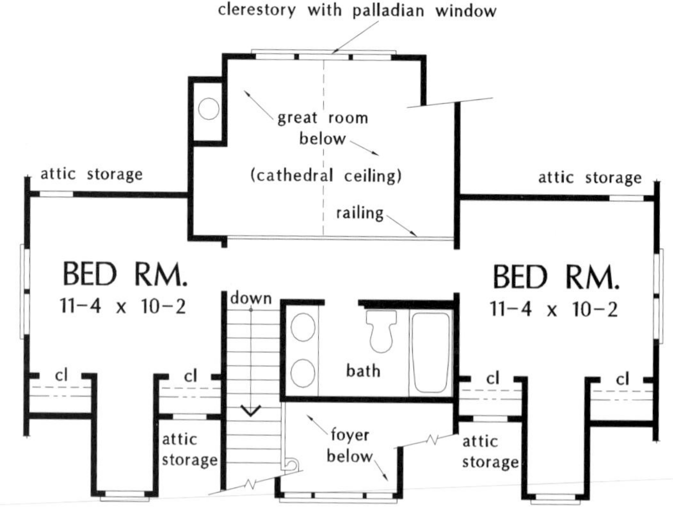

clerestory with palladian window
great room
below
(cathedral ceiling)
railing
attic storage
attic storage
BED RM.
11-4 x 10-2
down
bath
BED RM.
11-4 x 10-2
cl
cl
cl
cl
attic
storage
foyer
below
attic
storage

SECOND FLOOR

DPCCH-236
The Morninglory

Total Living: 1778 sq. ft.

First Floor: 1325 sq. ft.

Second Floor: 453 sq. ft.

3 Bedrooms, 2-1/2 Baths

Foundation: Crawlspace

Width: 48'4

Depth: 40'4"

Price Category: C

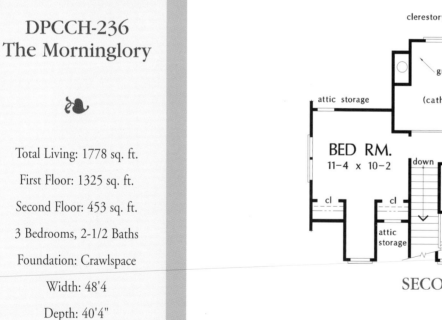

DESIGNER NOTE: *"We sought to create a comfortable, charming, country home that took full advantage of the attic space and presented a new twist on the triple-dormer theme."*

Last night we sat on the porch and watched a thunderstorm come our way. The thunder rumbled in the distance, gradually getting closer and closer. Flashes of lightening eventually joined the thunder. The temperature cooled, and the rain started to mist. We went inside about five minutes before the skies opened up.

The Morninglory

REAR

SHADY SPOTS

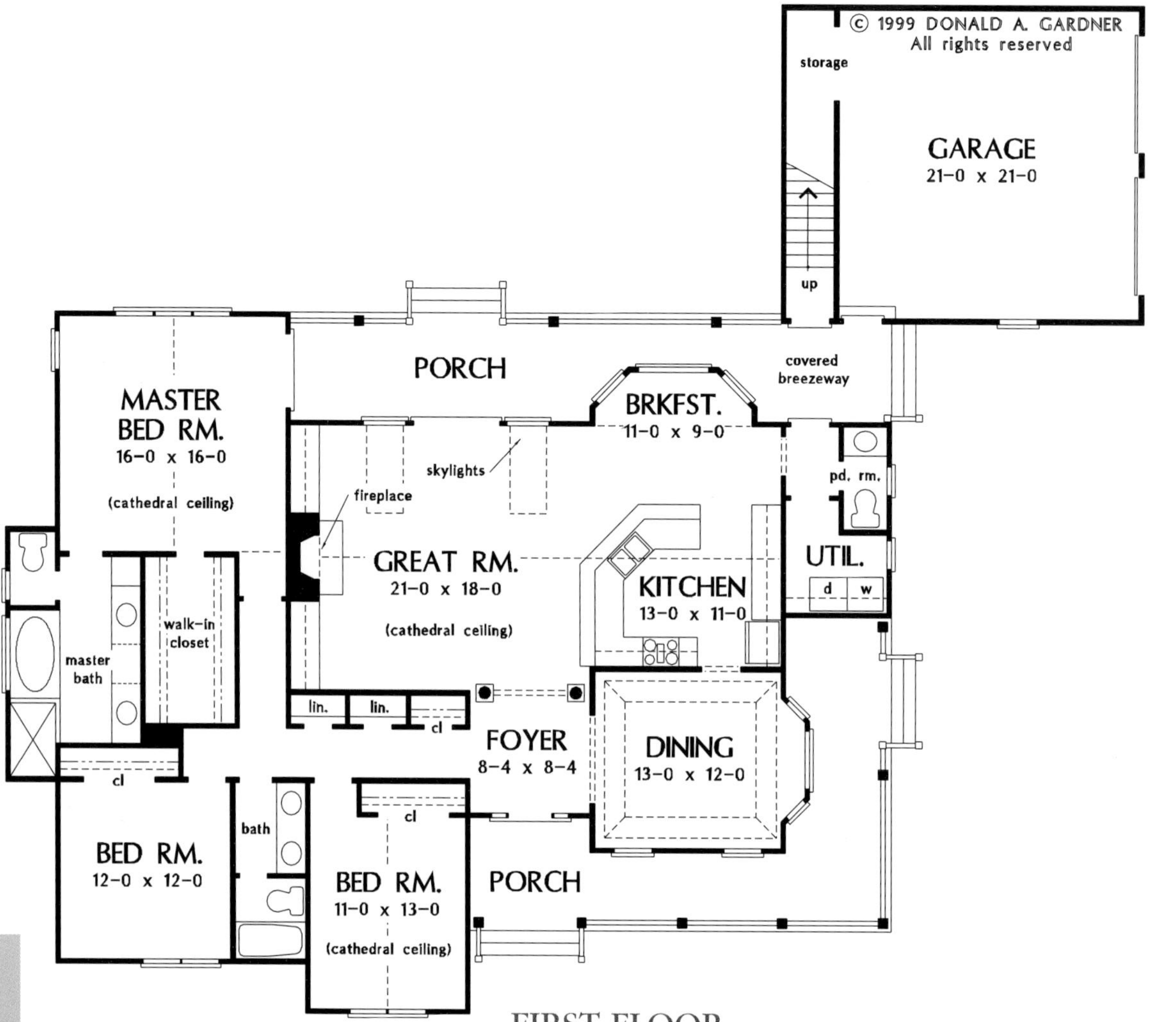

storage

GARAGE
21-0 x 21-0

up

PORCH

covered breezeway

MASTER BED RM.
16-0 x 16-0
(cathedral ceiling)

BRKFST.
11-0 x 9-0

skylights

fireplace

pd. rm.

GREAT RM.
21-0 x 18-0
(cathedral ceiling)

UTIL.

d w

KITCHEN
13-0 x 11-0

master bath

walk-in closet

lin. lin. cl

FOYER
8-4 x 8-4

DINING
13-0 x 12-0

cl

cl

bath

BED RM.
12-0 x 12-0

BED RM.
11-0 x 13-0
(cathedral ceiling)

PORCH

FIRST FLOOR

DPCCH-759
The Northwyke

Total Living: 2078 sq. ft.

Bonus Room: 339 sq. ft.

3 Bedrooms, 2-1/2 Baths

Foundation: Crawlspace

Width: 62'2"

Depth: 47'8"

Price Category: D

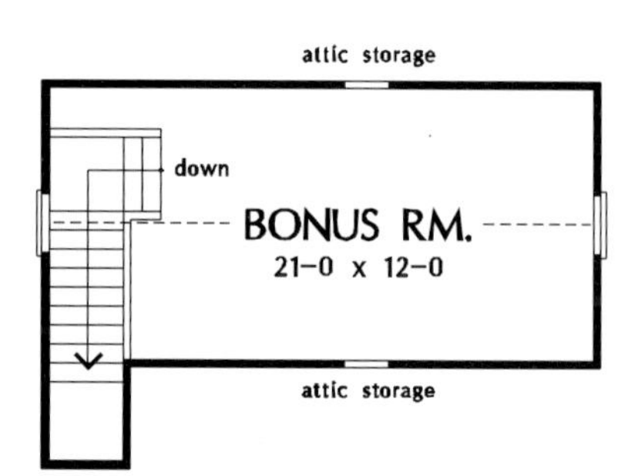
attic storage
down
BONUS RM.
21-0 x 12-0
attic storage

DESIGNER NOTE: *"For this design we wanted to gather the bedrooms to one side of the home for the young family but give the master suite just the right amount of privacy."*

The kids caught crawdads in the creek behind the house this morning. Later when I went to the back porch, I was surprised to find an empty bucket and four wet, muddy shoes full of crawdads. The kids spent the rest of the day running around the yard with bare feet. It reminded me of when I was young, except I never touched a crawdad.

The Northwyke

REAR

SHADY SPOTS

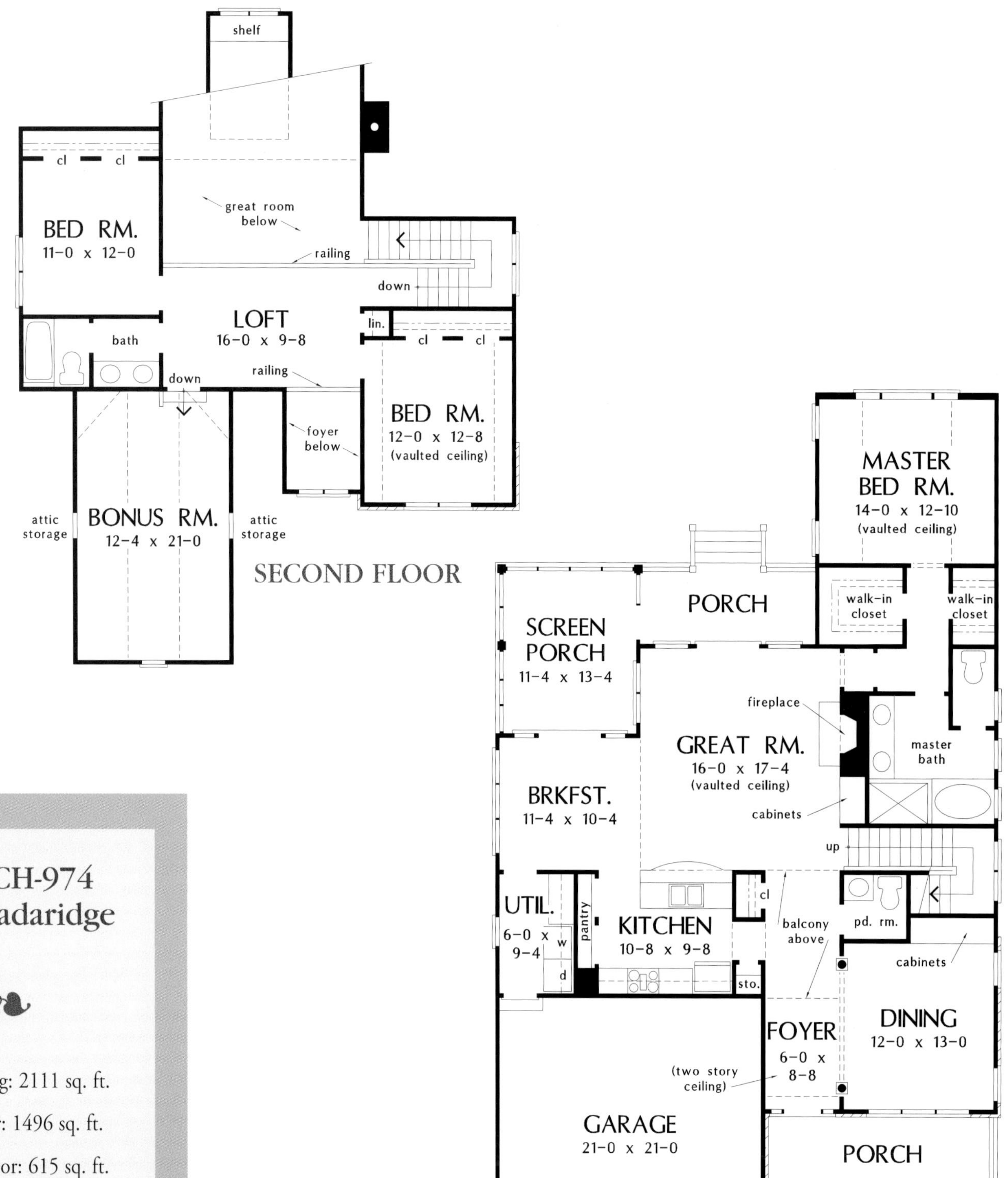

shelf
cl
cl
BED RM.
11-0 x 12-0
great room below
railing
down
LOFT
16-0 x 9-8
lin.
cl
cl
bath
down
railing
foyer below
BED RM.
12-0 x 12-8
(vaulted ceiling)
attic storage
BONUS RM.
12-4 x 21-0
attic storage
SECOND FLOOR
MASTER BED RM.
14-0 x 12-10
(vaulted ceiling)
walk-in closet
walk-in closet
PORCH
SCREEN PORCH
11-4 x 13-4
fireplace
GREAT RM.
16-0 x 17-4
(vaulted ceiling)
master bath
BRKFST.
11-4 x 10-4
cabinets
up
UTIL.
6-0 x 9-4
w
d
pantry
KITCHEN
10-8 x 9-8
cl
balcony above
pd. rm.
cabinets
sto.
FOYER
6-0 x 8-8
DINING
12-0 x 13-0
(two story ceiling)
GARAGE
21-0 x 21-0
PORCH
© 2002 DONALD A. GARDNER
All rights reserved
FIRST FLOOR

DPCCH-974
The Madaridge

Total Living: 2111 sq. ft.

First Floor: 1496 sq. ft.

Second Floor: 615 sq. ft.

Bonus Room: 277 sq. ft.

3 Bedrooms, 2-1/2 Baths

Foundation: Crawlspace

Width: 40'4"

Depth: 70'

Price Category: D

DESIGNER NOTE: *"We designed this home for those who have a tight lot but want a stately, two-story appearance enhanced with stone and multiple gables."*

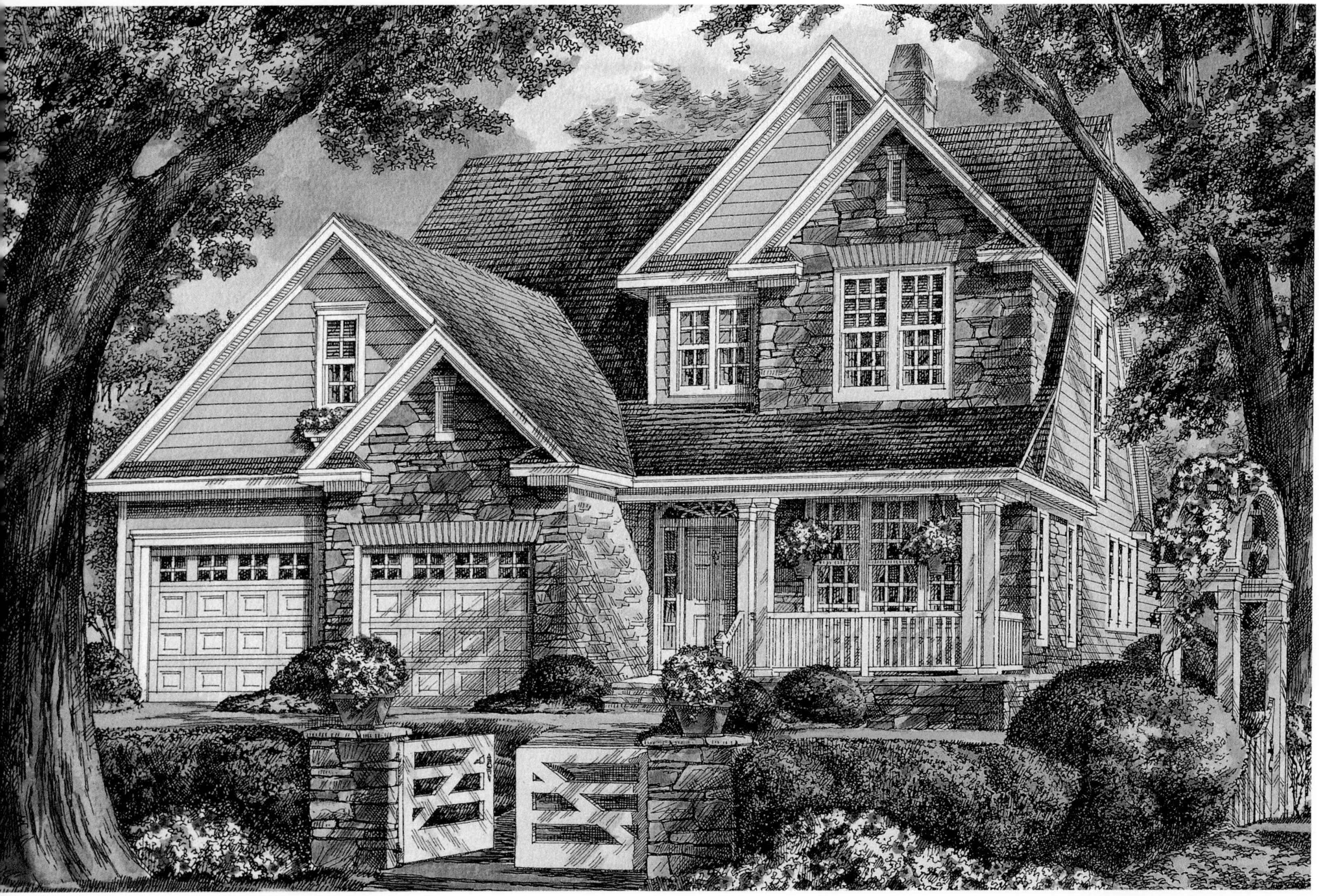

A restored or reproduction wood burning stove creates a charming outdoor kitchen in a screened porch. It didn't take me long to learn the cooking process, and you won't believe how incredible food tastes when it's slow-cooked over wood. I think it's easier to maintain than a grill, and it will certainly last longer.

The Madaridge

REAR

SHADY SPOTS

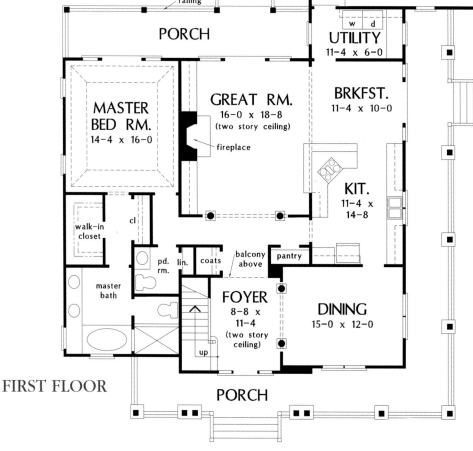

DPCCH-984
The Trotterville

BED RM.
11-4 x 12-8
great room below
attic storage
cl
railing
BED RM.
12-0 x 11-0
railing
dn
railing
cl
cl
bath
lin.
cl
attic storage
foyer below
cl
cl
BED RM.
12-8 x 11-0
SECOND FLOOR
GARAGE
21-0 x 22-0
© 2002 DONALD A. GARDNER
All rights reserved
railing
PORCH
w d
UTILITY
11-4 x 6-0
MASTER BED RM.
14-4 x 16-0
GREAT RM.
16-0 x 18-8
(two story ceiling)
fireplace
BRKFST.
11-4 x 10-0
KIT.
11-4 x 14-8
walk-in closet
cl
pd. rm.
lin.
coats
balcony above
pantry
master bath
FOYER
8-8 x 11-4
(two story ceiling)
up
DINING
15-0 x 12-0
FIRST FLOOR
PORCH

Total Living: 2490 sq. ft.

First Floor: 1687 sq. ft.

Second Floor: 803 sq. ft.

4 Bedrooms, 2-1/2 Baths

Foundation: Crawlspace

Width: 52'8"

Depth: 67'

Price Category: D

DESIGNER NOTE: *"Meshing old ideas, such as rear garage and craftsman detailing, with a contemporary lifestyle plan was our motivation when designing this home."*

When we first saw this house we thought about farm life and fresh laundry drying in the sun. Having modern conveniences, we really didn't need a clothesline, but for an old-time feel, we put two posts and a rope in the backyard to resemble a small, rustic clothesline. We use it to dry flowers from our cutting garden.

REAR

The Trotterville

SHADY SPOTS

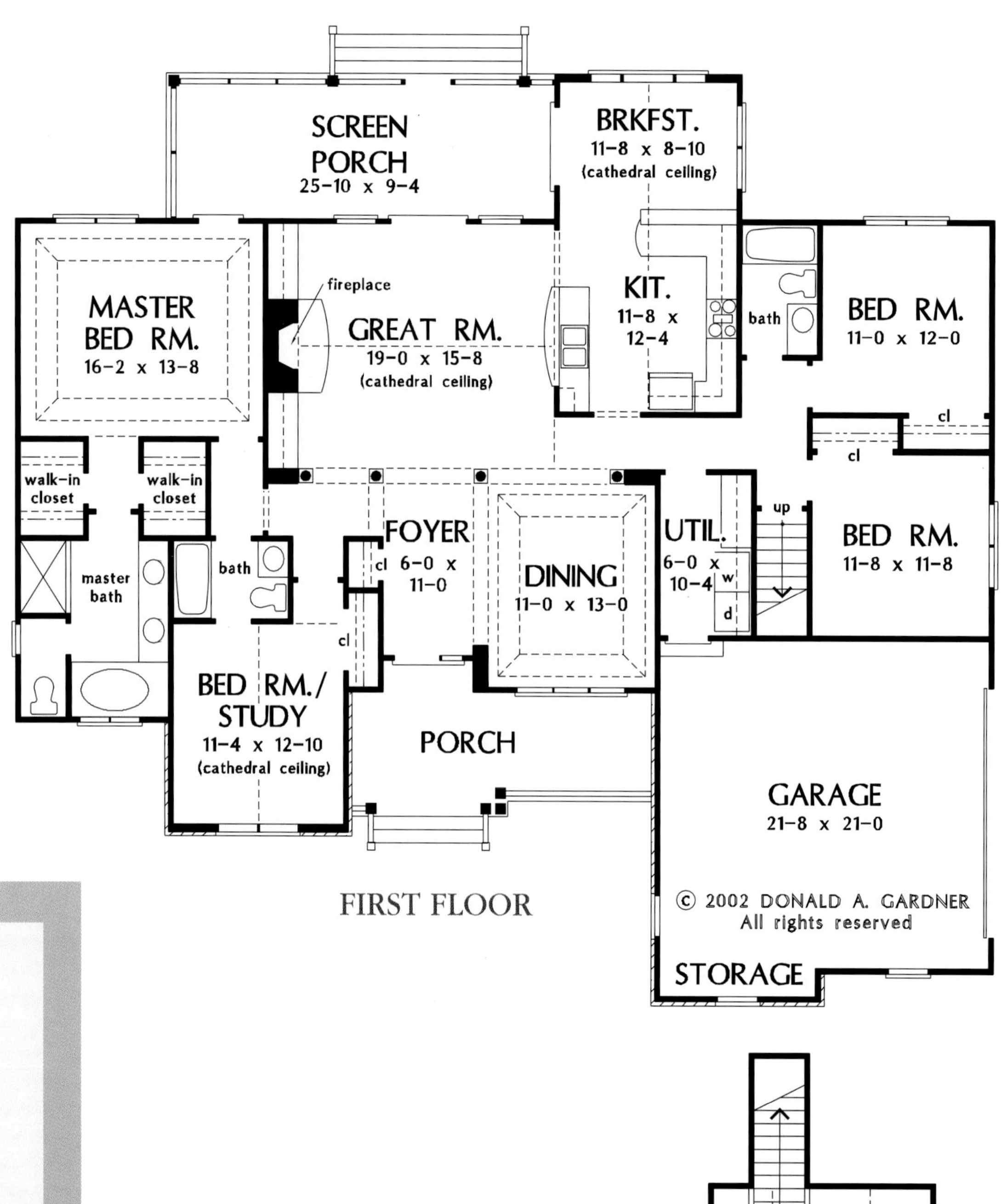
SCREEN PORCH
25-10 x 9-4
BRKFST.
11-8 x 8-10
(cathedral ceiling)
MASTER BED RM.
16-2 x 13-8
fireplace
GREAT RM.
19-0 x 15-8
(cathedral ceiling)
KIT.
11-8 x 12-4
bath
BED RM.
11-0 x 12-0
cl
cl
walk-in closet
walk-in closet
master bath
bath
FOYER
6-0 x 11-0
cl
DINING
11-0 x 13-0
UTIL.
6-0 x 10-4
w
d
up
BED RM.
11-8 x 11-8
cl
BED RM./ STUDY
11-4 x 12-10
(cathedral ceiling)
PORCH
GARAGE
21-8 x 21-0
© 2002 DONALD A. GARDNER
All rights reserved
STORAGE
FIRST FLOOR
down
attic storage
BONUS RM.
14-4 x 21-0
attic storage

DPCCH-967
The Satchwell

Total Living: 2097 sq. ft.

Bonus Room: 352 sq. ft.

4 Bedrooms, 3 Baths

Foundation: Crawlspace

Width: 64'10"

Depth: 59'6"

Price Category: D

DESIGNER NOTE: *"We thought of that homeowner who prefers single-level living and flexible spaces when we created this home design."*

We have a metal roof over our screened porch. I love to sit out there when it rains. It reminds me of my childhood. I spent many of my early days sitting in the barn listening to the rain hammer the old tin roof. The sound lulls me to sleep. Now everyone knows where to find me when it's raining, and they let me enjoy my nap.

The Satchwell

REAR

SHADY SPOTS

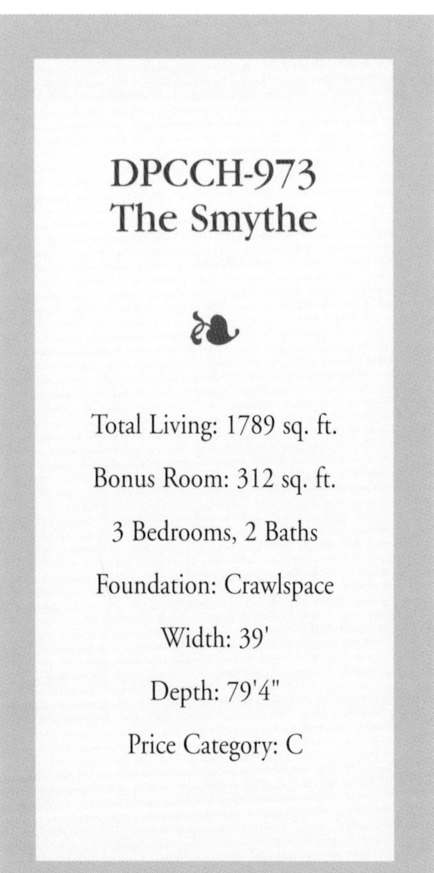

DPCCH-973
The Smythe

Total Living: 1789 sq. ft.

Bonus Room: 312 sq. ft.

3 Bedrooms, 2 Baths

Foundation: Crawlspace

Width: 39'

Depth: 79'4"

Price Category: C

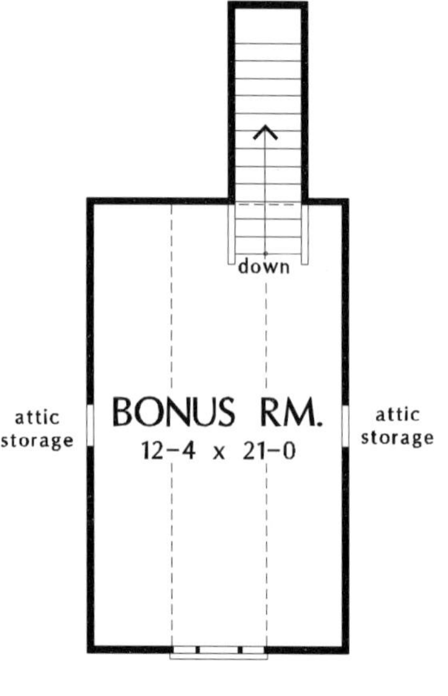

down
attic storage
BONUS RM.
12-4 x 21-0
attic storage

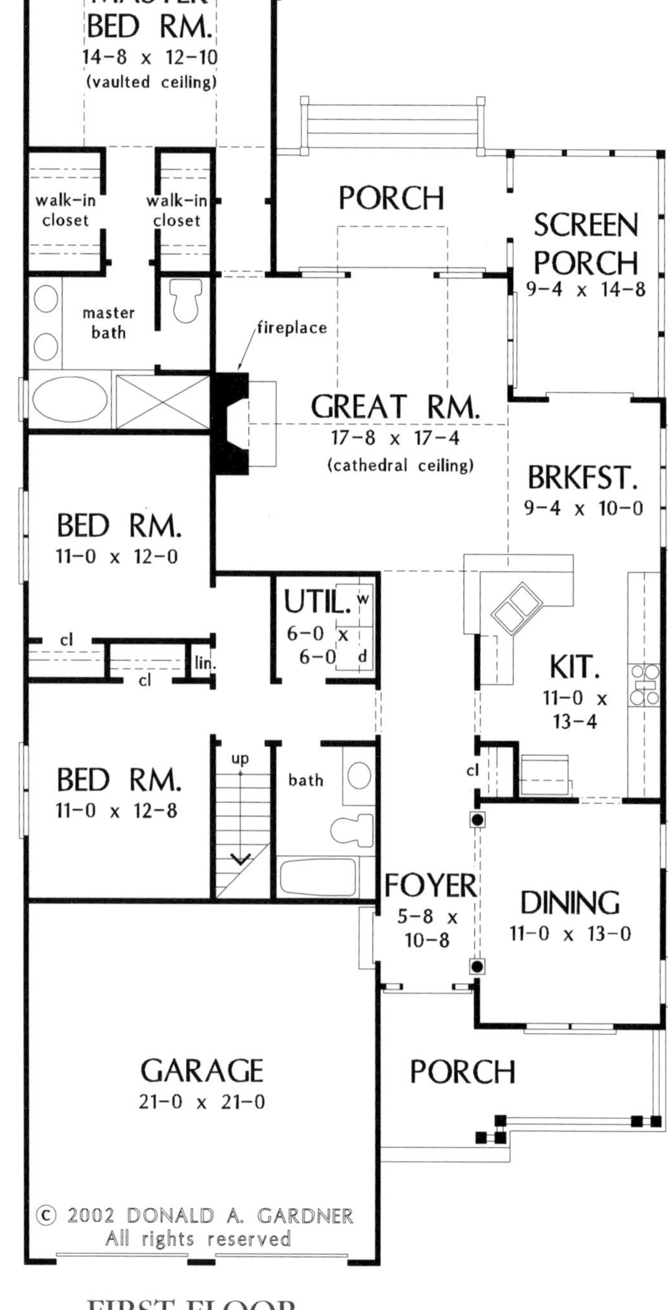

MASTER BED RM.
14-8 x 12-10
(vaulted ceiling)
walk-in closet
walk-in closet
master bath
PORCH
SCREEN PORCH
9-4 x 14-8
fireplace
GREAT RM.
17-8 x 17-4
(cathedral ceiling)
BRKFST.
9-4 x 10-0
BED RM.
11-0 x 12-0
UTIL.
6-0 x 6-0
w
d
cl
cl
lin.
KIT.
11-0 x 13-4
BED RM.
11-0 x 12-8
up
bath
cl
FOYER
5-8 x 10-8
DINING
11-0 x 13-0
GARAGE
21-0 x 21-0
PORCH
© 2002 DONALD A. GARDNER
All rights reserved

FIRST FLOOR

DESIGNER NOTE: *"We wanted to keep this design under 40-feet wide but give it all those special features: front porch, bonus room, screened porch, three bedrooms, open great room/kitchen/breakfast area."*

We take full advantage of the screened porch, enjoying it most of the year. For added comfort we drink ice-cold lemonade on hot days or steamy cocoa on the cool ones. We're planning to glass in the porch to make a four-season room. It will be a good investment, because we spend so much time here.

The Smythe

REAR

SHADY SPOTS

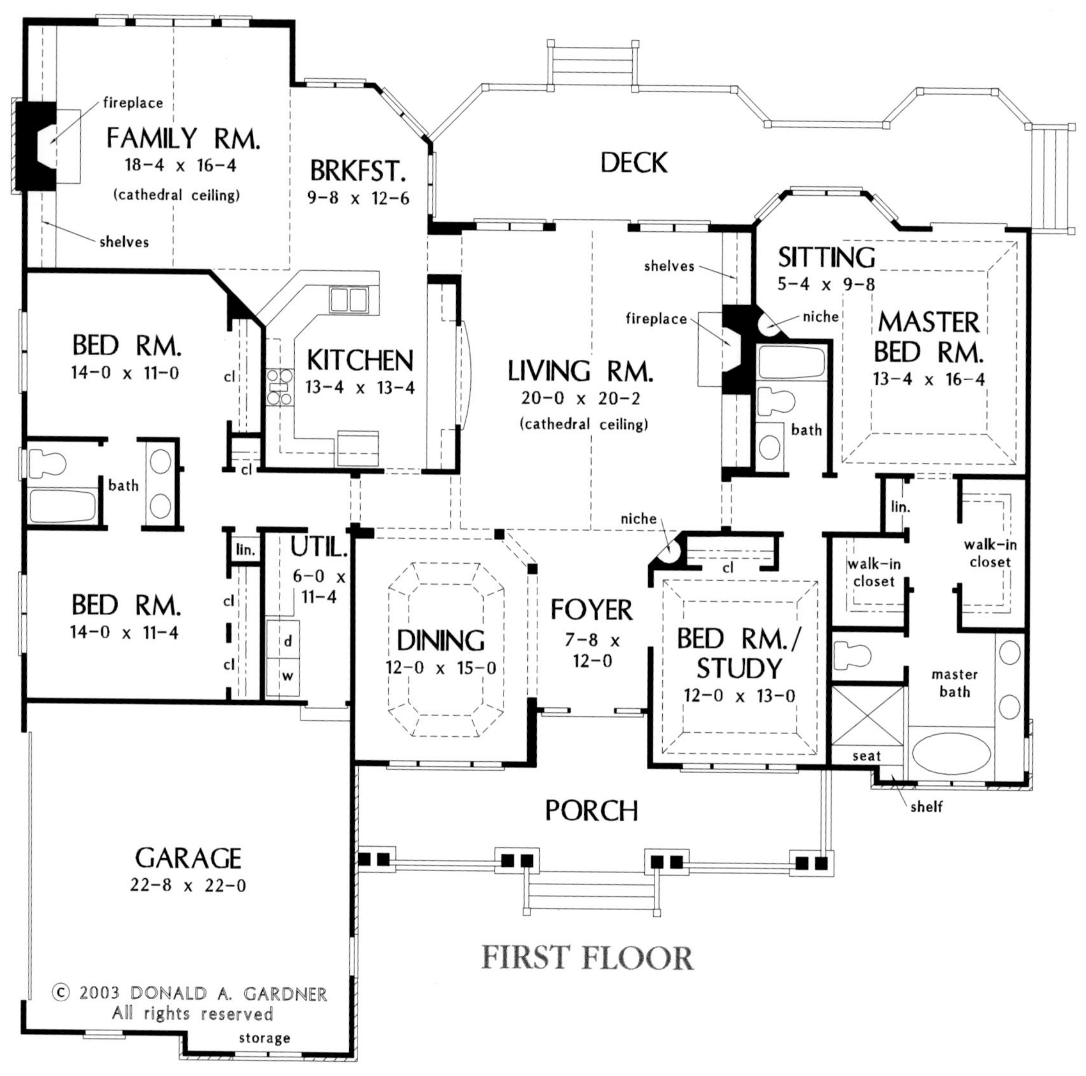

FAMILY RM.
18-4 x 16-4
(cathedral ceiling)
fireplace
shelves
BRKFST.
9-8 x 12-6
DECK
KITCHEN
13-4 x 13-4
LIVING RM.
20-0 x 20-2
(cathedral ceiling)
shelves
fireplace
SITTING
5-4 x 9-8
niche
MASTER BED RM.
13-4 x 16-4
bath
BED RM.
14-0 x 11-0
cl
bath
BED RM.
14-0 x 11-4
lin.
UTIL.
6-0 x 11-4
d
w
DINING
12-0 x 15-0
FOYER
7-8 x 12-0
niche
BED RM./ STUDY
12-0 x 13-0
lin.
walk-in closet
walk-in closet
master bath
seat
shelf
PORCH
GARAGE
22-8 x 22-0
storage
FIRST FLOOR

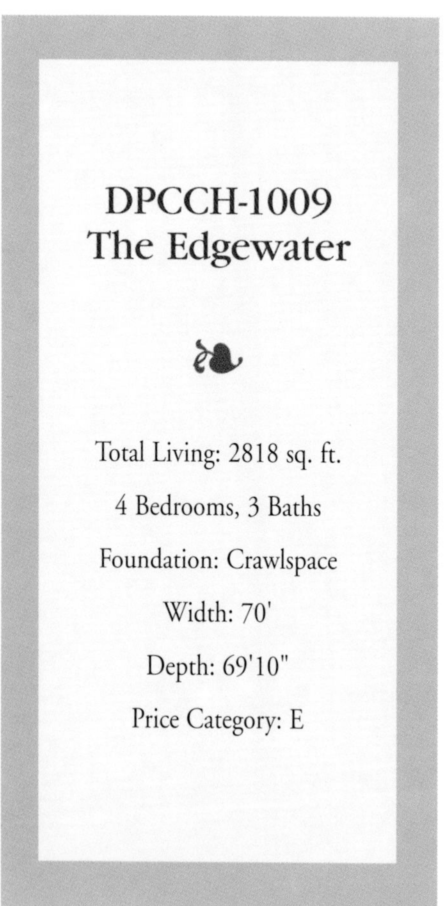

DPCCH-1009
The Edgewater

Total Living: 2818 sq. ft.

4 Bedrooms, 3 Baths

Foundation: Crawlspace

Width: 70'

Depth: 69'10"

Price Category: E

DESIGNER NOTE: *"We thought growing families would appreciate a home that had two entertaining spaces. So, we gave this plan separate living and family rooms and created a dramatic, well-appointed exterior."*

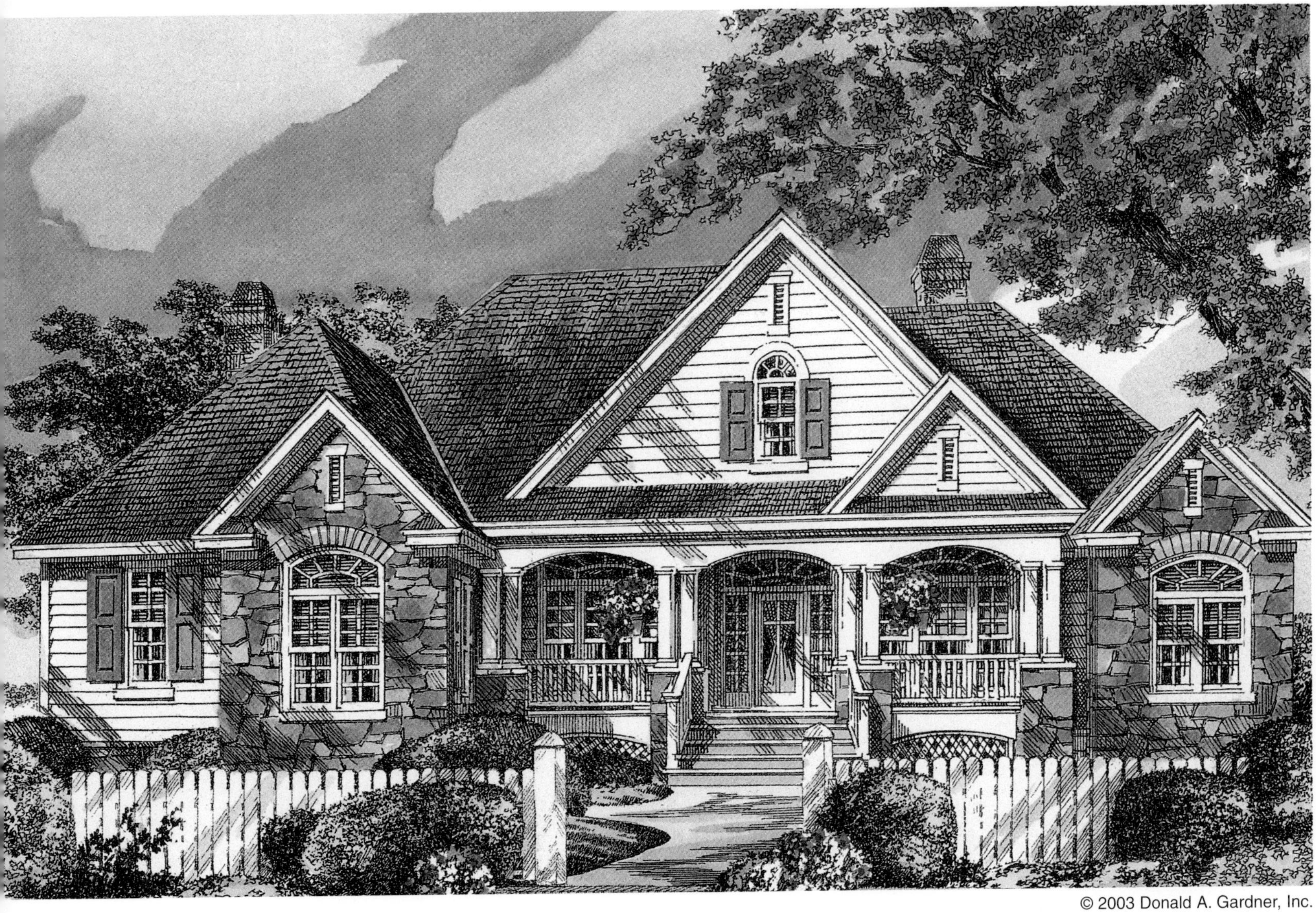

The sun went down as we finished planting our herb garden in the window box. Our hands smelled of rosemary and lemon thyme. We spent the rest of the evening outside, and every now and then the breeze would drift by with the scent of herbs. We often open the windows to let the wind bring the fragrances inside the house.

The Edgewater

REAR

We stopped by the farmer's market for a bushel of green beans. We snapped them on the porch while listening to a new bluegrass band.

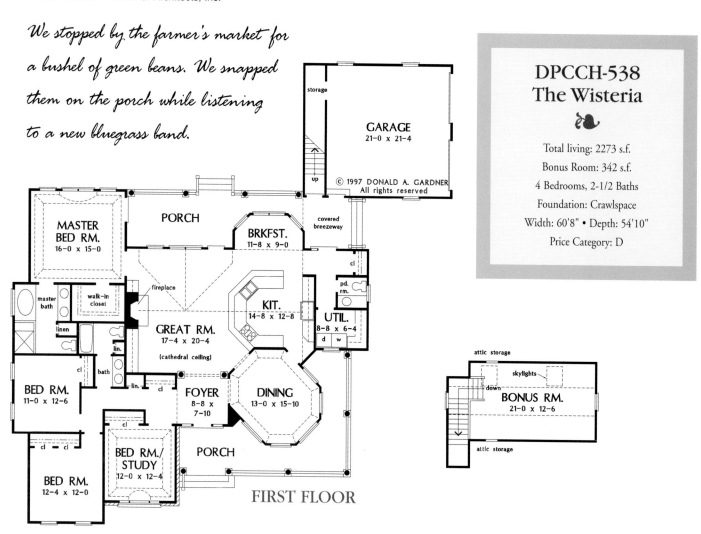

DPCCH-538
The Wisteria

Total living: 2273 s.f.

Bonus Room: 342 s.f.

4 Bedrooms, 2-1/2 Baths

Foundation: Crawlspace

Width: 60'8" • Depth: 54'10"

Price Category: D

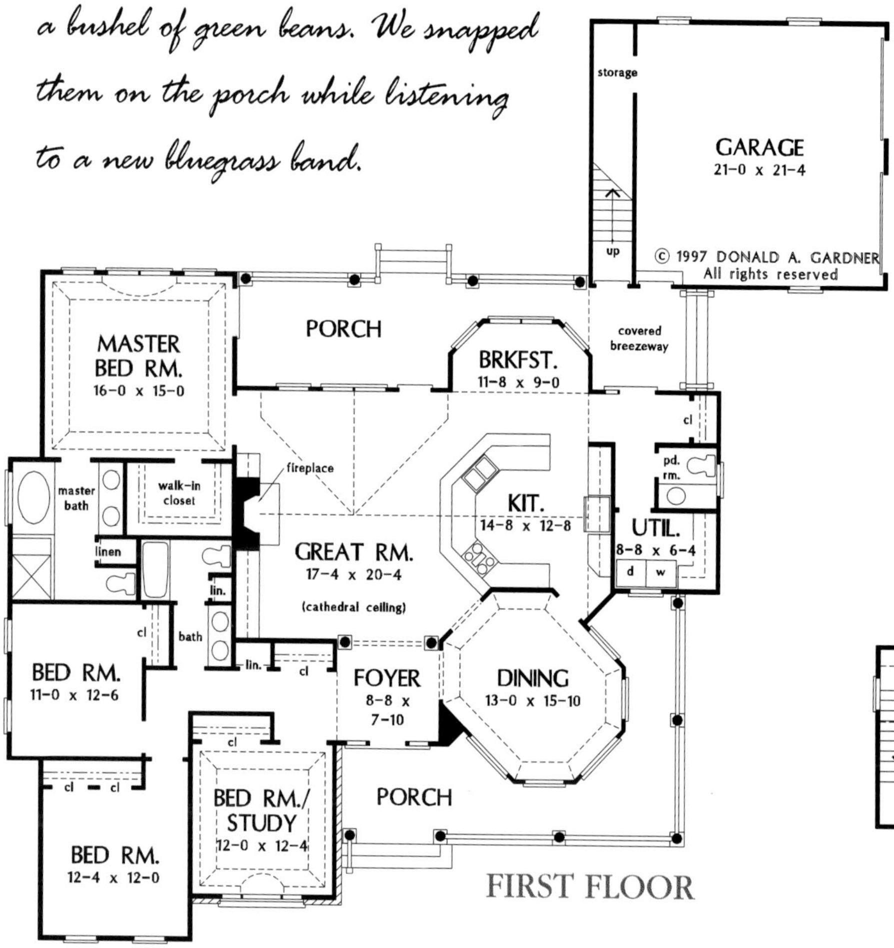

storage

GARAGE
21-0 x 21-4

up

PORCH

covered breezeway

MASTER BED RM.
16-0 x 15-0

BRKFST.
11-8 x 9-0

cl

fireplace

master bath

walk-in closet

KIT.
14-8 x 12-8

pd. rm.

UTIL.
8-8 x 6-4

d w

linen

GREAT RM.
17-4 x 20-4
(cathedral ceiling)

lin.

cl

bath

BED RM.
11-0 x 12-6

lin.

cl

FOYER
8-8 x 7-10

DINING
13-0 x 15-10

cl

cl cl

BED RM./ STUDY
12-0 x 12-4

PORCH

BED RM.
12-4 x 12-0

FIRST FLOOR

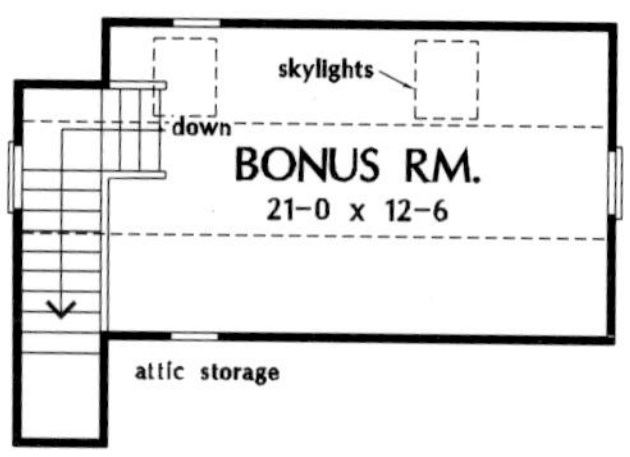

attic storage

skylights

down

BONUS RM.
21-0 x 12-6

attic storage

We moved an old baker's rack to our porch to use as a planting shelf. Annuals are planted in mason jars to provide color.

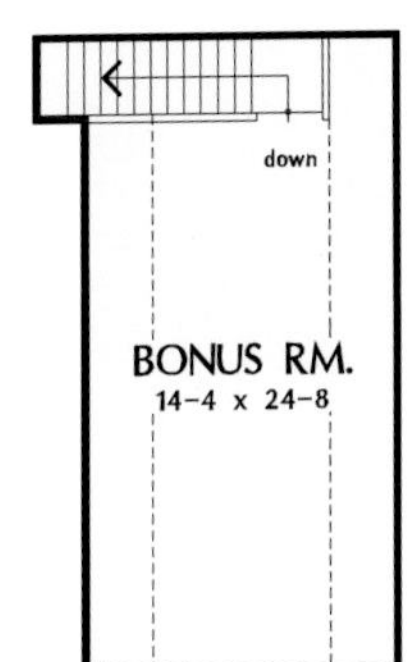
down
BONUS RM.
14-4 x 24-8

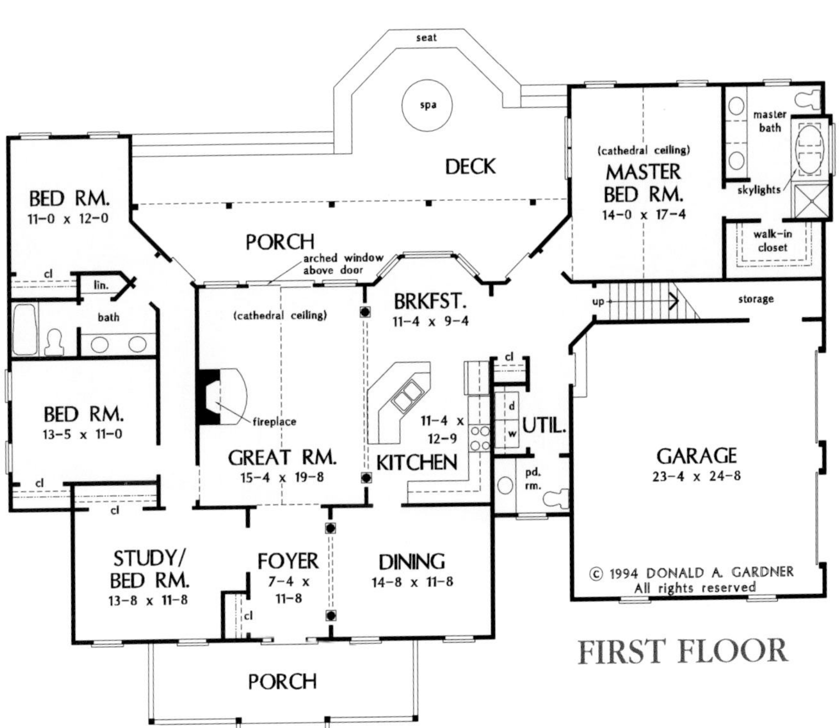
seat
spa
DECK
BED RM.
11-0 x 12-0
PORCH
arched window above door
BRKFST.
11-4 x 9-4
(cathedral ceiling)
MASTER BED RM.
14-0 x 17-4
master bath
skylights
walk-in closet
up
storage
cl
lin.
bath
(cathedral ceiling)
BED RM.
13-5 x 11-0
fireplace
GREAT RM.
15-4 x 19-8
11-4 x 12-9
KITCHEN
cl
d
w
UTIL.
pd. rm.
GARAGE
23-4 x 24-8
cl
cl
STUDY/ BED RM.
13-8 x 11-8
FOYER
7-4 x 11-8
cl
DINING
14-8 x 11-8
© 1994 DONALD A. GARDNER All rights reserved
PORCH

FIRST FLOOR

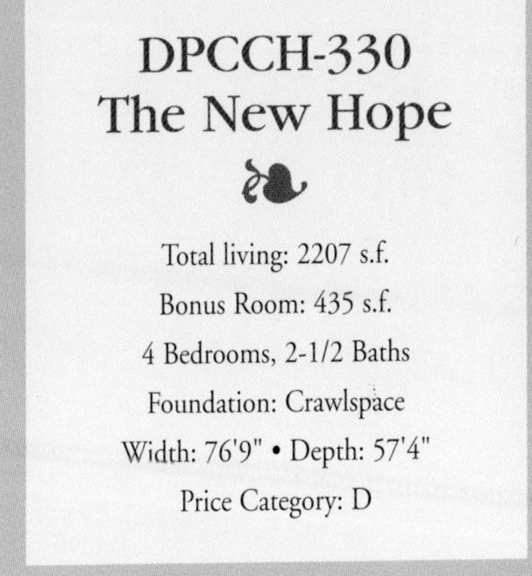

DPCCH-330
The New Hope

Total living: 2207 s.f.

Bonus Room: 435 s.f.

4 Bedrooms, 2-1/2 Baths

Foundation: Crawlspace

Width: 76'9" • Depth: 57'4"

Price Category: D

SHADY SPOTS

One of the nicest things about a cool Fall day is curling up with a quilt and taking an afternoon nap on the screened porch. You feel really refreshed when you awaken.

DPCCH-703
The Orchard Park

Total living: 2042 s.f.
Bonus Room: 475 s.f.
3 Bedrooms, 2-1/2 Baths
Foundation: Crawlspace
Width: 75'11" • Depth: 56'7"
Price Category: D

FIRST FLOOR

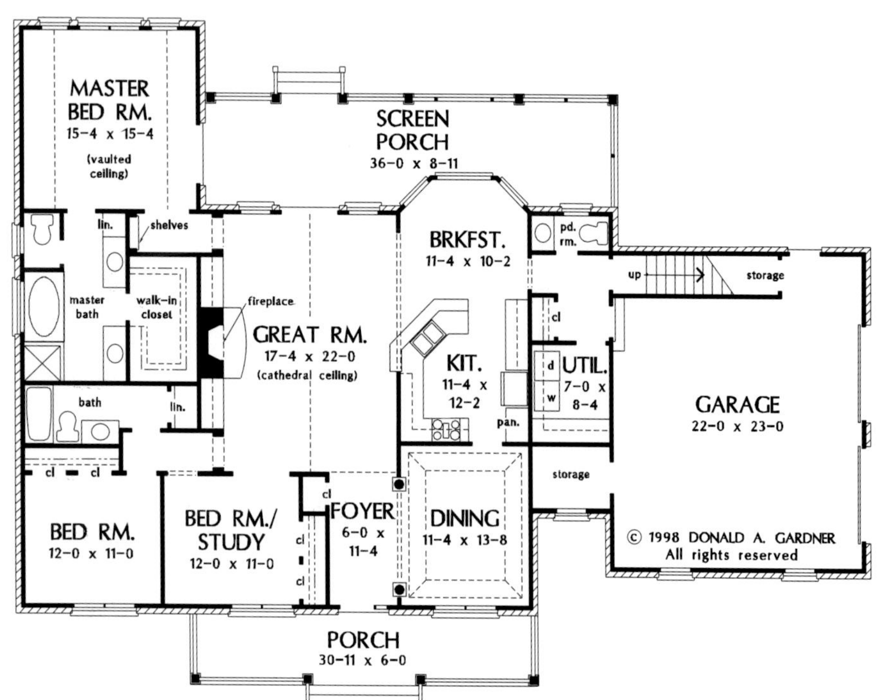
MASTER BED RM.
15-4 x 15-4
(vaulted ceiling)
SCREEN PORCH
36-0 x 8-11
lin.
shelves
BRKFST.
11-4 x 10-2
pd. rm.
up
storage
master bath
walk-in closet
fireplace
GREAT RM.
17-4 x 22-0
(cathedral ceiling)
KIT.
11-4 x 12-2
cl
d
w
UTIL.
7-0 x 8-4
GARAGE
22-0 x 23-0
bath
lin.
pan.
storage
cl
cl
BED RM.
12-0 x 11-0
BED RM./ STUDY
12-0 x 11-0
FOYER
6-0 x 11-4
DINING
11-4 x 13-8
© 1998 DONALD A. GARDNER
All rights reserved
PORCH
30-11 x 6-0

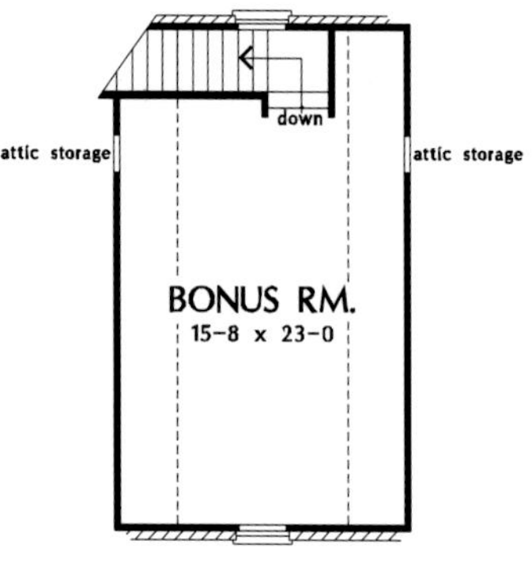
attic storage
down
attic storage
BONUS RM.
15-8 x 23-0

Yesterday we took the last of the fresh-picked strawberries to the back porch and made homemade ice cream. It was delicious.

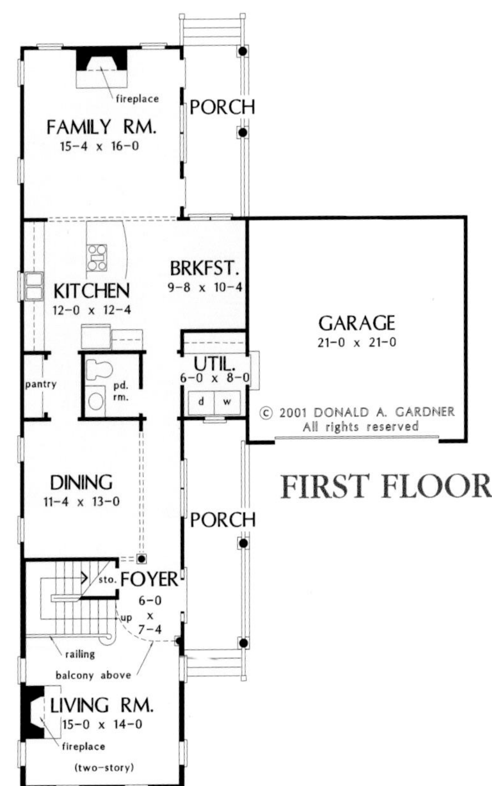

fireplace
FAMILY RM.
15-4 x 16-0
PORCH
KITCHEN
12-0 x 12-4
BRKFST.
9-8 x 10-4
GARAGE
21-0 x 21-0
pantry
pd. rm.
UTIL.
6-0 x 8-0
d
w
© 2001 DONALD A. GARDNER
All rights reserved
DINING
11-4 x 13-0
PORCH
FIRST FLOOR
sto.
FOYER
6-0 x 7-4
up
railing
balcony above
LIVING RM.
15-0 x 14-0
fireplace
(two-story)

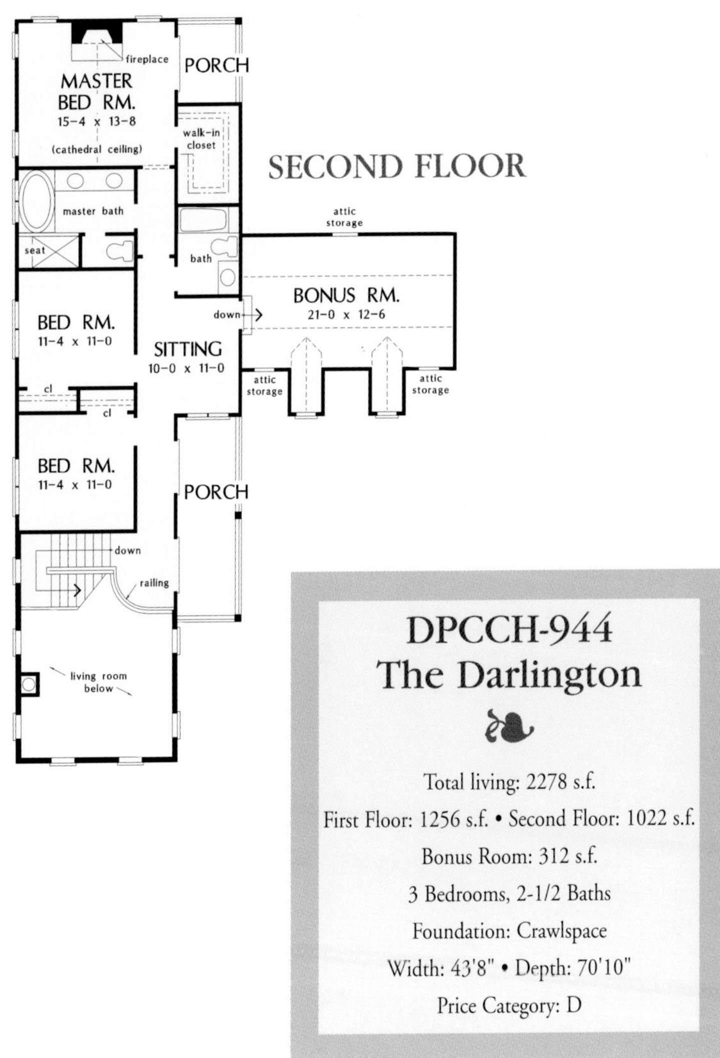

fireplace
PORCH
MASTER
BED RM.
15-4 x 13-8
(cathedral ceiling)
walk-in closet
SECOND FLOOR
master bath
seat
bath
attic storage
BONUS RM.
21-0 x 12-6
down
BED RM.
11-4 x 11-0
SITTING
10-0 x 11-0
attic storage
attic storage
cl
cl
BED RM.
11-4 x 11-0
PORCH
down
railing
living room below

DPCCH-944
The Darlington

Total living: 2278 s.f.

First Floor: 1256 s.f. • Second Floor: 1022 s.f.

Bonus Room: 312 s.f.

3 Bedrooms, 2-1/2 Baths

Foundation: Crawlspace

Width: 43'8" • Depth: 70'10"

Price Category: D

You don't entertain in the country — you fellowship. We put straw bales in the screened porch for extra seating and charm at our cookout.

DPCCH-357
The Beckett

Total living: 2563 s.f.
First Floor: 1907 s.f. • Second Floor: 656 s.f.
Bonus Room: 467 s.f.
4 Bedrooms, 2-1/2 Baths
Foundation: Crawlspace
Width: 89'10" • Depth: 53'4"
Price Category: E

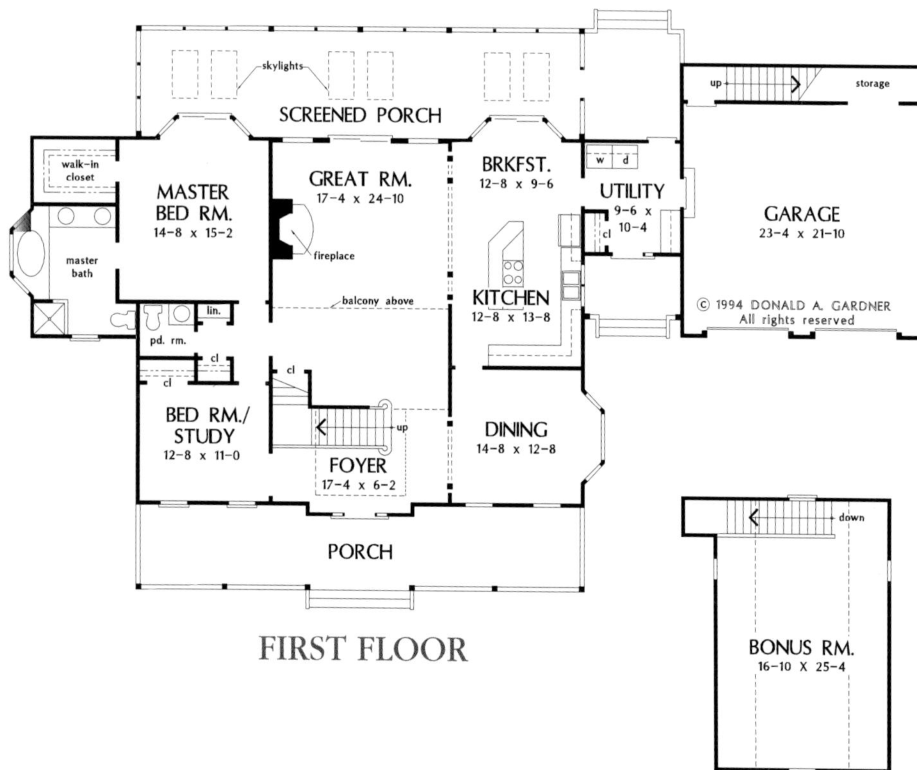
skylights
SCREENED PORCH
walk-in closet
MASTER BED RM.
14-8 x 15-2
master bath
GREAT RM.
17-4 x 24-10
fireplace
balcony above
BRKFST.
12-8 x 9-6
w
d
UTILITY
9-6 x 10-4
cl
KITCHEN
12-8 x 13-8
up
storage
GARAGE
23-4 x 21-10
© 1994 DONALD A. GARDNER
All rights reserved
lin.
pd. rm.
cl
BED RM./ STUDY
12-8 x 11-0
up
FOYER
17-4 x 6-2
DINING
14-8 x 12-8
PORCH
down
BONUS RM.
16-10 X 25-4

FIRST FLOOR

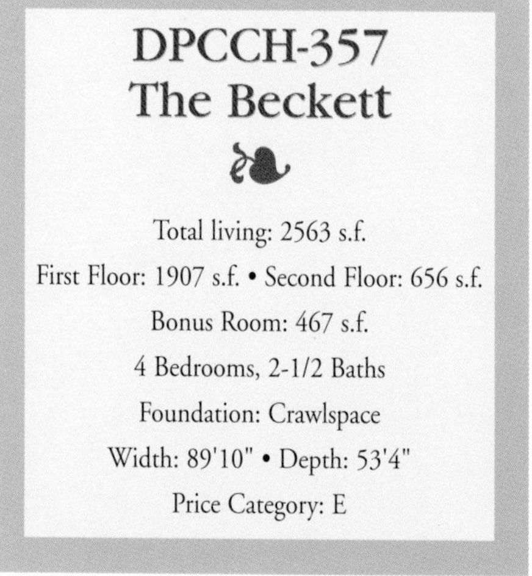

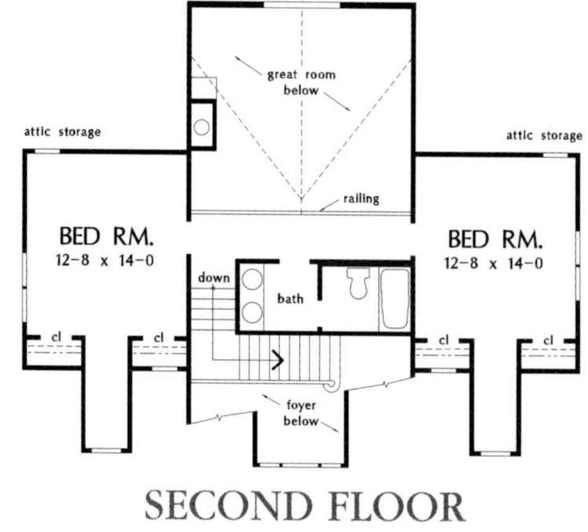
great room below
attic storage
attic storage
railing
BED RM.
12-8 x 14-0
BED RM.
12-8 x 14-0
down
bath
cl
foyer below

SECOND FLOOR

SHADY SPOTS

We have birdhouses and feeders throughout the backyard. We sit in the screened porch and watch the birds come and go.

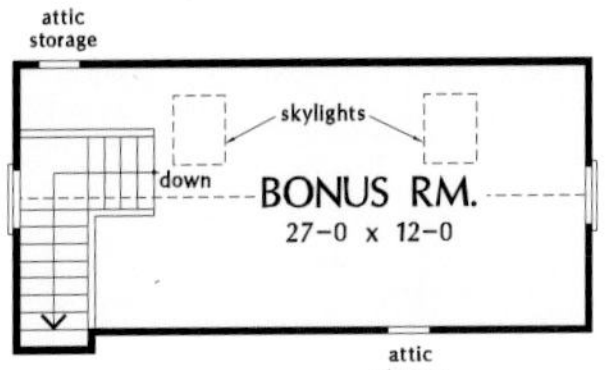

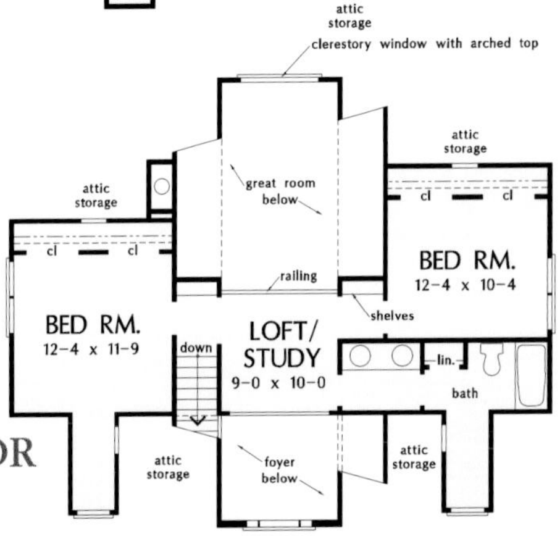

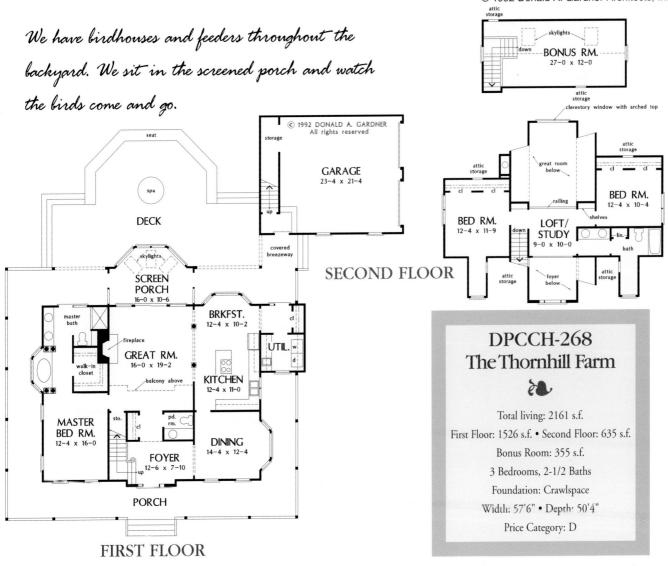

attic storage
skylights
down
BONUS RM.
27-0 x 12-0
attic storage
clerestory window with arched top
attic storage
great room below
attic storage
cl cl
cl cl
BED RM.
12-4 x 10-4
railing
BED RM.
12-4 x 11-9
shelves
LOFT/ STUDY
9-0 x 10-0
down
lin.
bath
attic storage
foyer below
attic storage

SECOND FLOOR

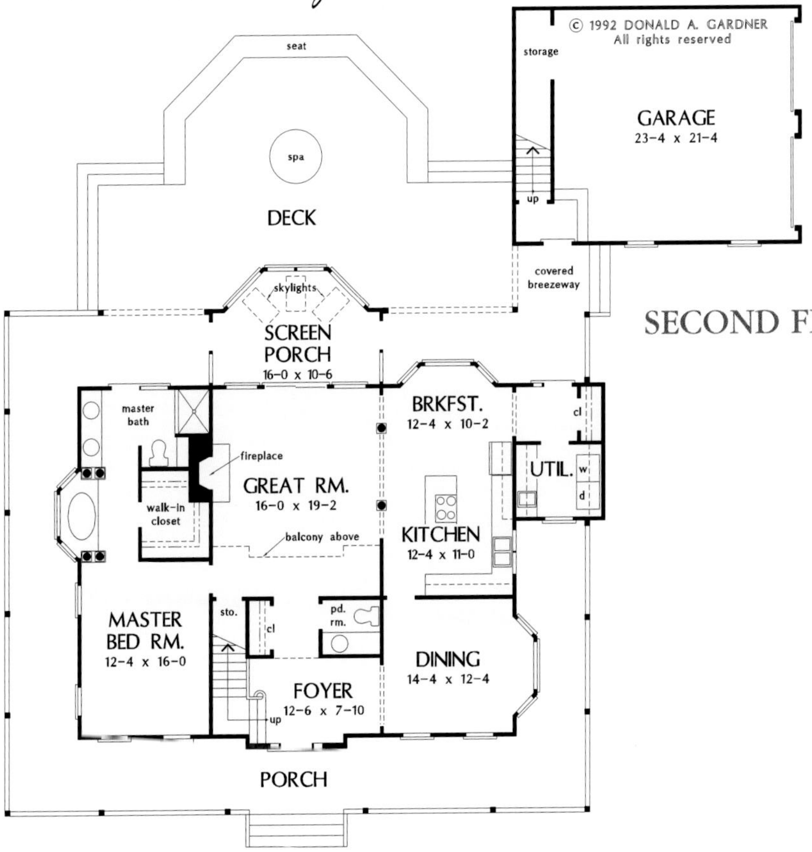

seat
spa
DECK

storage
GARAGE
23-4 x 21-4
up
covered breezeway
skylights
SCREEN PORCH
16-0 x 10-6
master bath
fireplace
GREAT RM.
16-0 x 19-2
BRKFST.
12-4 x 10-2
cl
UTIL.
w
d
walk-in closet
balcony above
KITCHEN
12-4 x 11-0
MASTER BED RM.
12-4 x 16-0
sto.
cl
pd. rm.
DINING
14-4 x 12-4
FOYER
12-6 x 7-10
up
PORCH

FIRST FLOOR

DPCCH-268
The Thornhill Farm

Total living: 2161 s.f.

First Floor: 1526 s.f. • Second Floor: 635 s.f.

Bonus Room: 355 s.f.

3 Bedrooms, 2-1/2 Baths

Foundation: Crawlspace

Width: 57'6" • Depth: 50'4"

Price Category: D

I taught the grandkids how to play checkers. They spent most of the morning playing on the porch, while I planted bulbs around the pond.

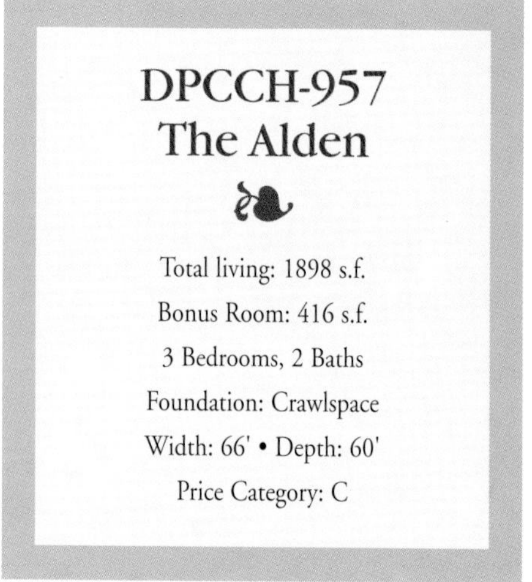

DPCCH-957
The Alden

Total living: 1898 s.f.

Bonus Room: 416 s.f.

3 Bedrooms, 2 Baths

Foundation: Crawlspace

Width: 66' • Depth: 60'

Price Category: C

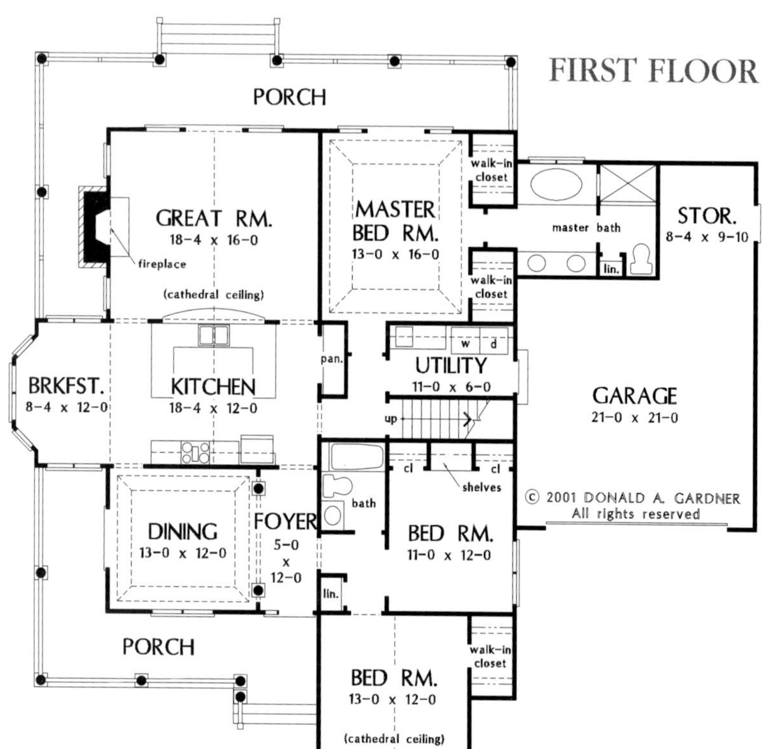
FIRST FLOOR
PORCH
GREAT RM.
18-4 x 16-0
fireplace
(cathedral ceiling)
MASTER
BED RM.
13-0 x 16-0
walk-in closet
master bath
lin.
STOR.
8-4 x 9-10
walk-in closet
BRKFST.
8-4 x 12-0
KITCHEN
18-4 x 12-0
pan.
UTILITY
11-0 x 6-0
w d
up
GARAGE
21-0 x 21-0
cl
cl
shelves
bath
© 2001 DONALD A. GARDNER
All rights reserved
DINING
13-0 x 12-0
FOYER
5-0 x 12-0
BED RM.
11-0 x 12-0
lin.
PORCH
walk-in closet
BED RM.
13-0 x 12-0
(cathedral ceiling)

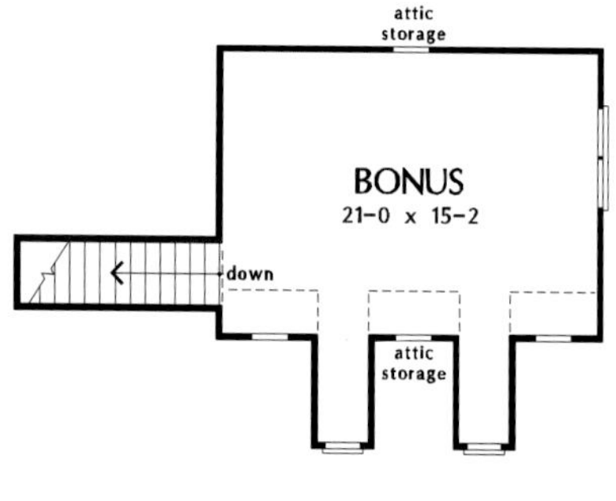
attic storage
BONUS
21-0 x 15-2
down
attic storage

SHADY SPOTS

© 1997 Donald A. Gardner Architects, Inc.

My screened porch is an outdoor workshop for my crafts. I have room to spread out, and my supplies can stay there until my project is finished.

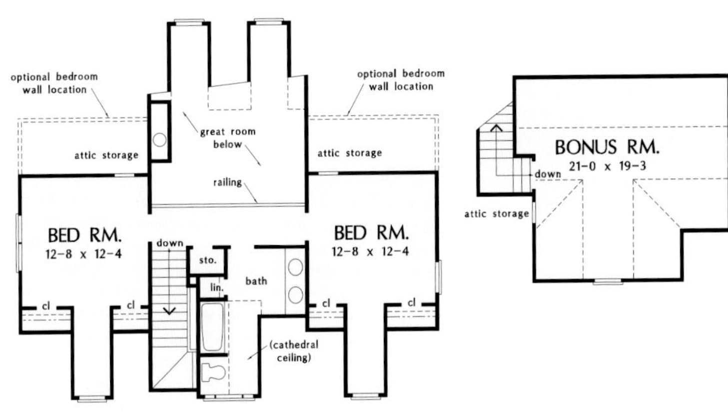

optional bedroom wall location
attic storage
great room below
railing
optional bedroom wall location
attic storage
BED RM.
12-8 x 12-4
down
sto.
lin.
bath
cl
cl
(cathedral ceiling)
BED RM.
12-8 x 12-4
cl
cl
BONUS RM.
21-0 x 19-3
down
attic storage

SECOND FLOOR

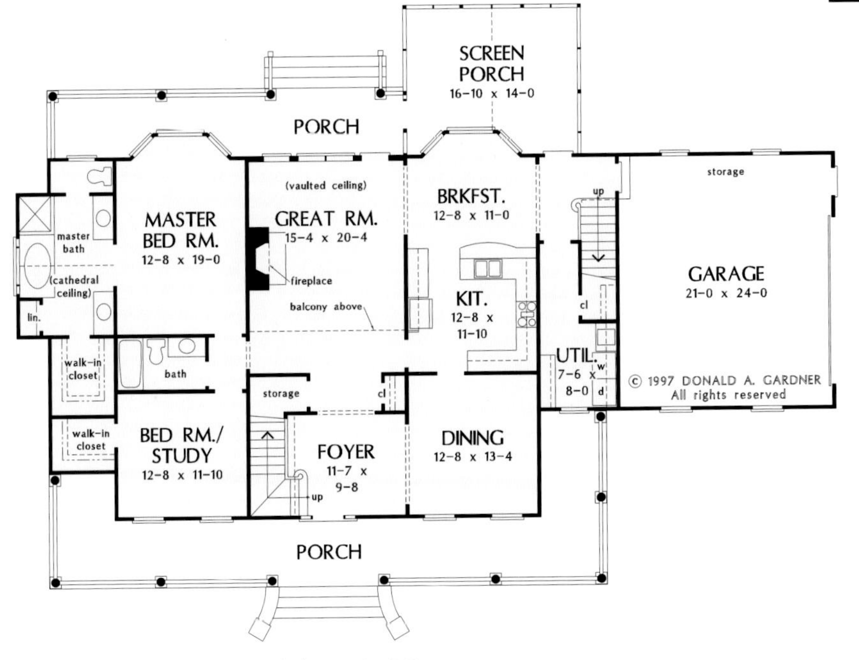

SCREEN PORCH
16-10 x 14-0
PORCH
storage
MASTER BED RM.
12-8 x 19-0
master bath
(cathedral ceiling)
lin.
(vaulted ceiling)
GREAT RM.
15-4 x 20-4
fireplace
balcony above
BRKFST.
12-8 x 11-0
KIT.
12-8 x 11-10
up
cl
GARAGE
21-0 x 24-0
UTIL.
7-6 x 8-0
w
d
© 1997 DONALD A. GARDNER
All rights reserved
walk-in closet
bath
storage
cl
walk-in closet
BED RM./ STUDY
12-8 x 11-10
FOYER
11-7 x 9-8
up
DINING
12-8 x 13-4
PORCH

FIRST FLOOR

DPCCH-484
The Sunnybrook

Total living: 2596 s.f.

First Floor: 1939 s.f. • Second Floor: 657 s.f.

Bonus Room: 386 s.f.

4 Bedrooms, 3 Baths

Foundation: Crawlspace

Width: 80'10" • Depth: 55'8"

Price Category: E

SHADY SPOTS

Wash tubs make great planters for patio gardens. An old washboard welcomes climbers like honeysuckle, ivy and jasmine.

DPCCH-737
The Palmetto

Total living: 1843 s.f.

First Floor: 1362 s.f. • Second Floor: 481 s.f.

3 Bedrooms, 2-1/2 Baths

Foundation: Post/Pier

Width: 49'4" • Depth: 44'10"

Price Category: C

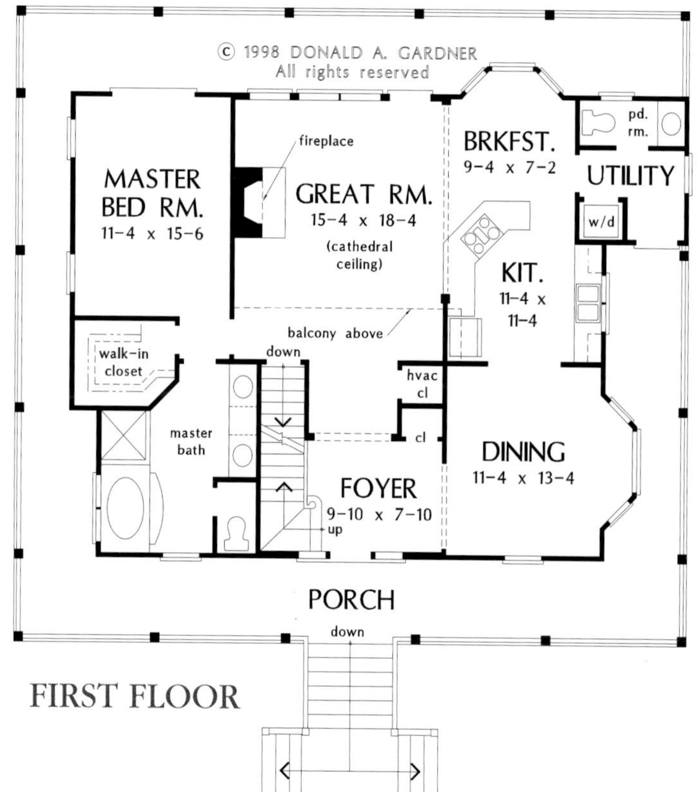
© 1998 DONALD A. GARDNER
All rights reserved
fireplace
MASTER
BED RM.
11-4 x 15-6
GREAT RM.
15-4 x 18-4
(cathedral
ceiling)
BRKFST.
9-4 x 7-2
pd.
rm.
UTILITY
w/d
KIT.
11-4 x
11-4
balcony above
walk-in
closet
down
hvac
cl
cl
master
bath
DINING
11-4 x 13-4
FOYER
9-10 x 7-10
up
PORCH
down

FIRST FLOOR

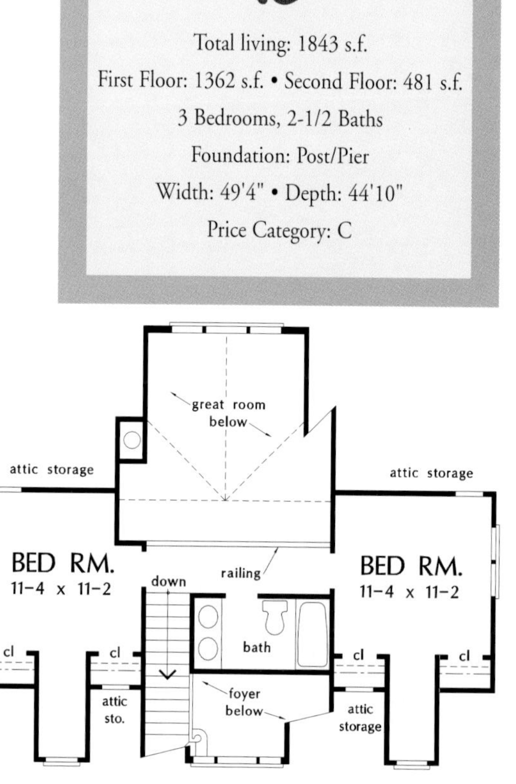
great room
below
attic storage
attic storage
BED RM.
11-4 x 11-2
BED RM.
11-4 x 11-2
down
railing
bath
cl
cl
cl
cl
foyer
below
attic
sto.
attic
storage

SECOND FLOOR

SHADY SPOTS

Bullfrogs and crickets sing a lullaby, as lightening bugs create a night light on the deck after dusk. It's like this every summer night.

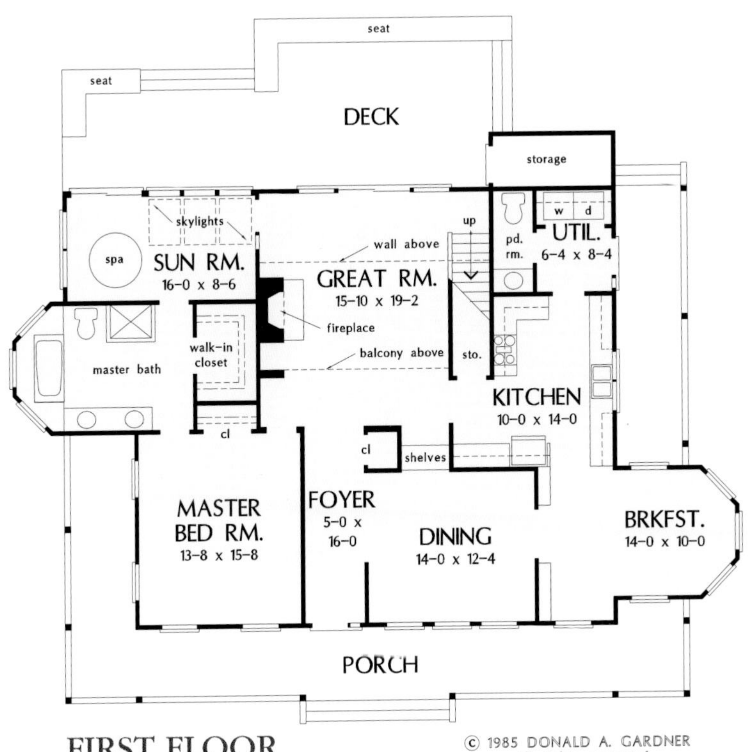
seat
seat
DECK
storage
skylights
spa
SUN RM.
16-0 x 8-6
wall above
up
pd. rm.
w d
UTIL.
6-4 x 8-4
GREAT RM.
15-10 x 19-2
fireplace
balcony above
sto.
master bath
walk-in closet
cl
KITCHEN
10-0 x 14-0
cl
shelves
MASTER BED RM.
13-8 x 15-8
FOYER
5-0 x 16-0
DINING
14-0 x 12-4
BRKFST.
14-0 x 10-0
PORCH
© 1985 DONALD A. GARDNER
All rights reserved

FIRST FLOOR

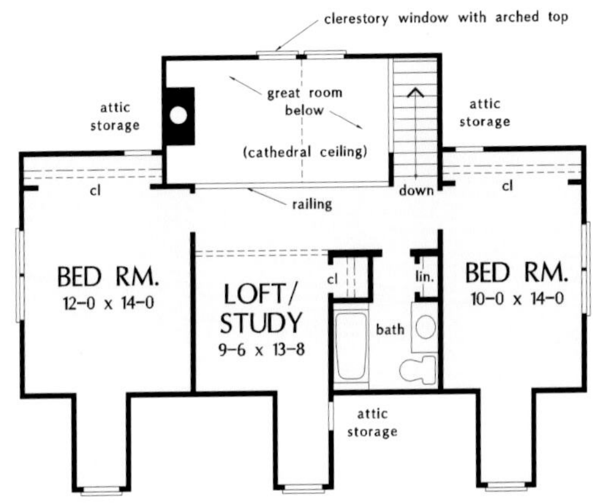
clerestory window with arched top
attic storage
great room below
(cathedral ceiling)
attic storage
cl
railing
down
cl
BED RM.
12-0 x 14-0
LOFT/ STUDY
9-6 x 13-8
cl
lin.
bath
BED RM.
10-0 x 14-0
attic storage

SECOND FLOOR

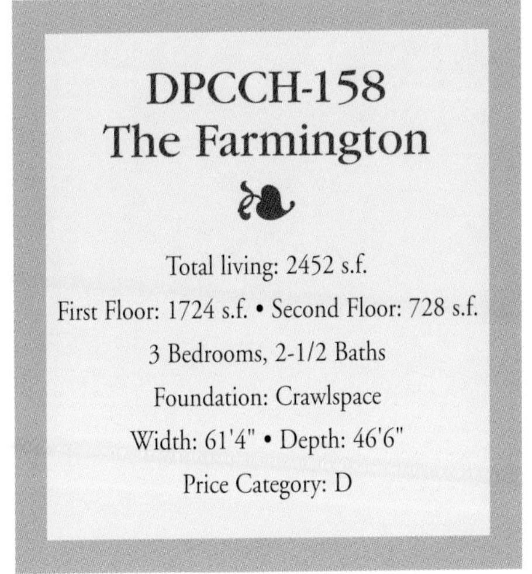

DPCCH-158
The Farmington

Total living: 2452 s.f.

First Floor: 1724 s.f. • Second Floor: 728 s.f.

3 Bedrooms, 2-1/2 Baths

Foundation: Crawlspace

Width: 61'4" • Depth: 46'6"

Price Category: D

SHADY SPOTS

It's funny how you have a fondness for certain sounds: a rooster crowing, a screened door slamming and acorns crunching under foot.

DPCCH-544
The Magnolia

Total living: 2617 s.f.

First Floor: 1878 s.f. • Second Floor: 739 s.f.

Bonus Room: 383 s.f.

4 Bedrooms, 3 Baths

Foundation: Crawlspace

Width: 79'8" • Depth: 73'4"

Price Category: E

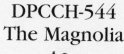

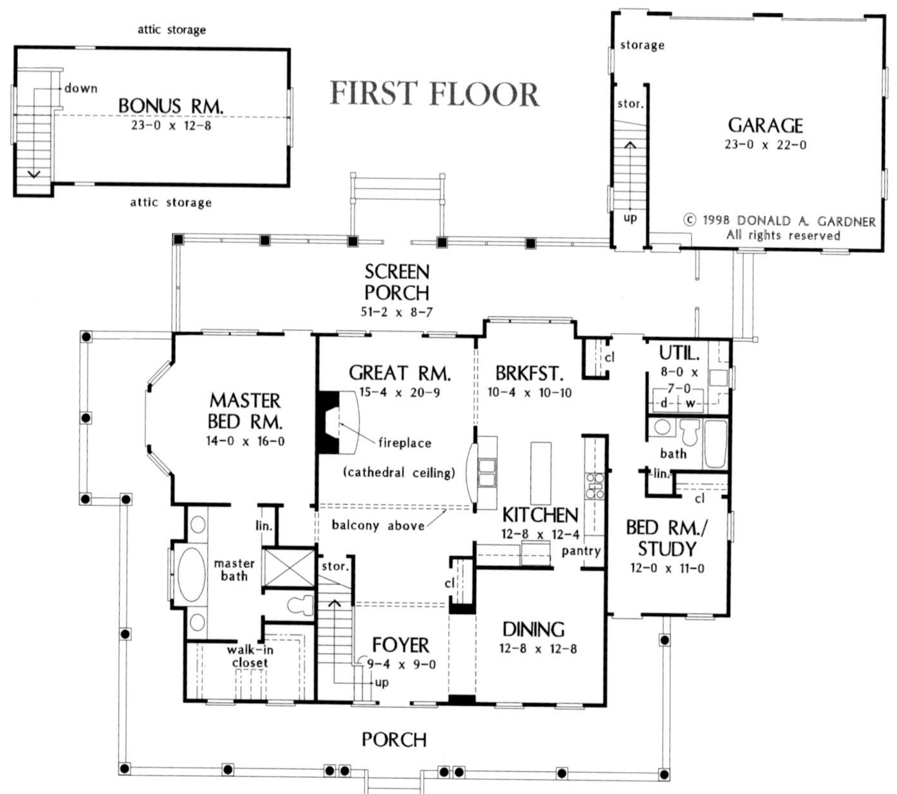
attic storage
down
BONUS RM.
23-0 x 12-8
attic storage
FIRST FLOOR
storage
stor.
up
GARAGE
23-0 x 22-0
© 1998 DONALD A. GARDNER
All rights reserved
SCREEN PORCH
51-2 x 8-7
MASTER BED RM.
14-0 x 16-0
GREAT RM.
15-4 x 20-9
fireplace
(cathedral ceiling)
BRKFST.
10-4 x 10-10
cl
UTIL.
8-0 x 7-0
d
w
bath
lin.
cl
KITCHEN
12-8 x 12-4
pantry
BED RM./ STUDY
12-0 x 11-0
balcony above
lin.
master bath
stor.
cl
walk-in closet
FOYER
9-4 x 9-0
up
DINING
12-8 x 12-8
PORCH

SECOND FLOOR

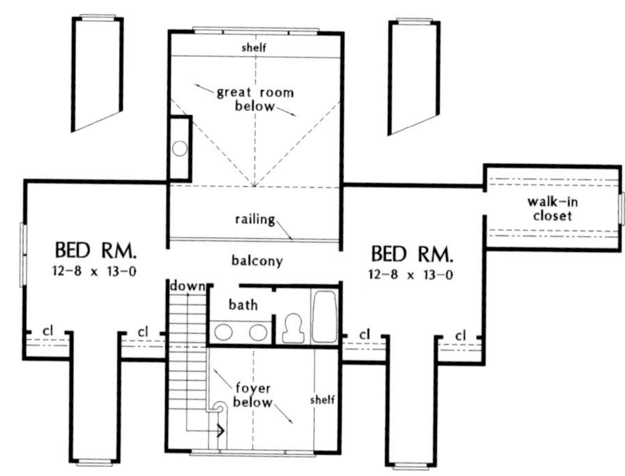
shelf
great room below
railing
walk-in closet
BED RM.
12-8 x 13-0
balcony
BED RM.
12-8 x 13-0
down
bath
cl
cl
cl
cl
foyer below
shelf

SHADY SPOTS

Burlap can create beautiful outdoor rugs. Printed sacks can be sewn together for a unique look that will add a touch of country to any porch.

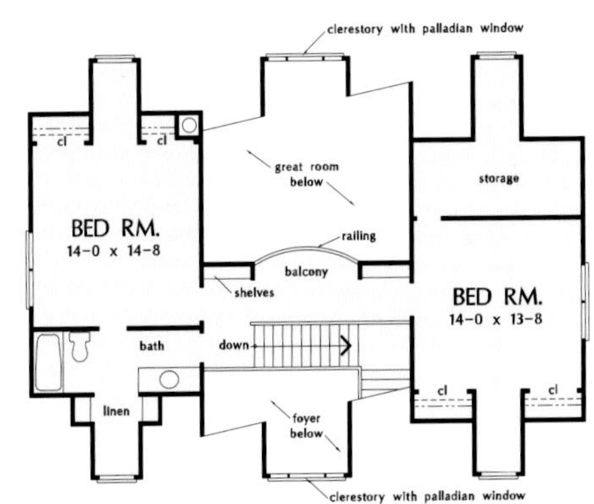

clerestory with palladian window
cl
cl
great room below
storage
BED RM.
14-0 x 14-8
railing
balcony
shelves
BED RM.
14-0 x 13-8
bath
down
linen
cl
cl
foyer below
clerestory with palladian window

SECOND FLOOR

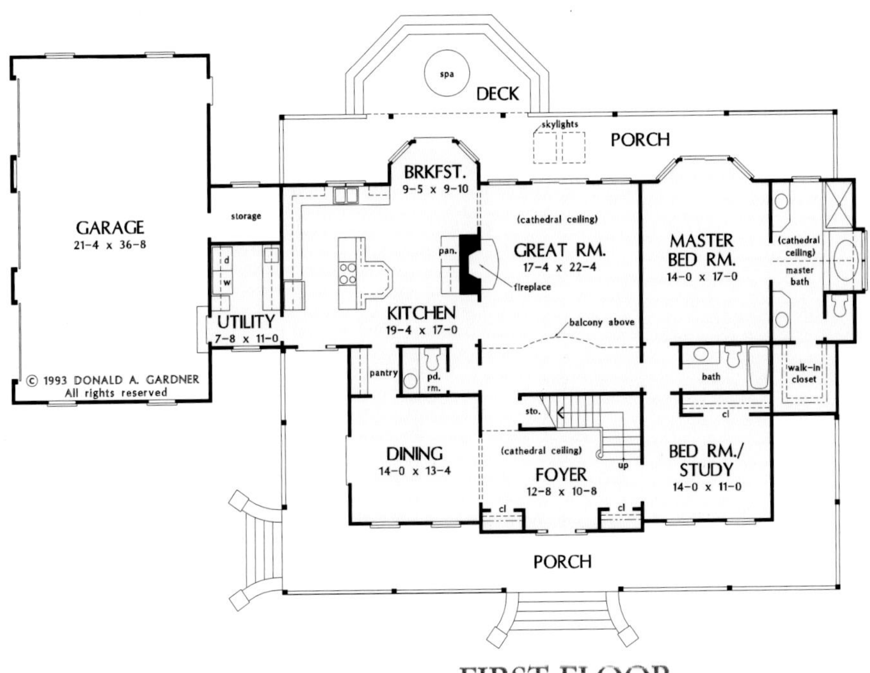

spa
DECK
skylights
PORCH
BRKFST.
9-5 x 9-10
storage
GARAGE
21-4 x 36-8
(cathedral ceiling)
GREAT RM.
17-4 x 22-4
pan.
fireplace
MASTER BED RM.
14-0 x 17-0
(cathedral ceiling)
master bath
d
w
UTILITY
7-8 x 11-0
KITCHEN
19-4 x 17-0
balcony above
bath
walk-in closet
pantry
pd. rm.
sto.
cl
© 1993 DONALD A. GARDNER
All rights reserved
DINING
14-0 x 13-4
(cathedral ceiling)
FOYER
12-8 x 10-8
up
BED RM./ STUDY
14-0 x 11-0
cl
cl
PORCH

FIRST FLOOR

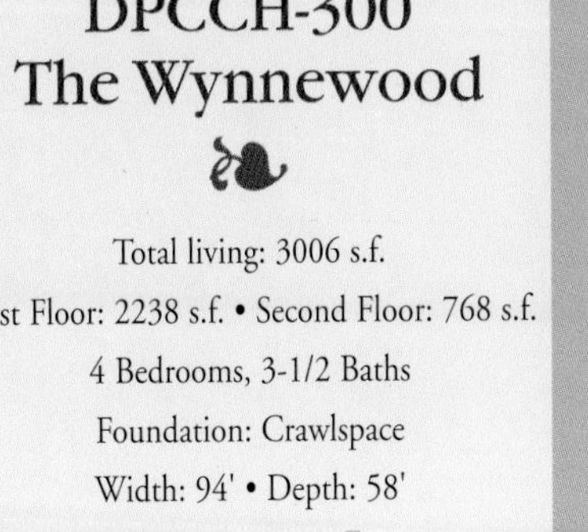

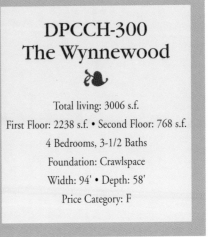

DPCCH-300
The Wynnewood

Total living: 3006 s.f.

First Floor: 2238 s.f. • Second Floor: 768 s.f.

4 Bedrooms, 3-1/2 Baths

Foundation: Crawlspace

Width: 94' • Depth: 58'

Price Category: F

SHADY SPOTS

We recreated an old-fashioned sleeping porch off the master suite by using a wrought-iron daybed and hammock. Both are great for reading or naps.

DPCCH-814
The Sassafras

Total living: 2359 s.f.

First Floor: 1339 s.f. • Second Floor: 1020 s.f.

3 Bedrooms, 2-1/2 Baths

Foundation: Crawlspace

Width: 28'4" • Depth: 79'

Price Category: D

FIRST FLOOR

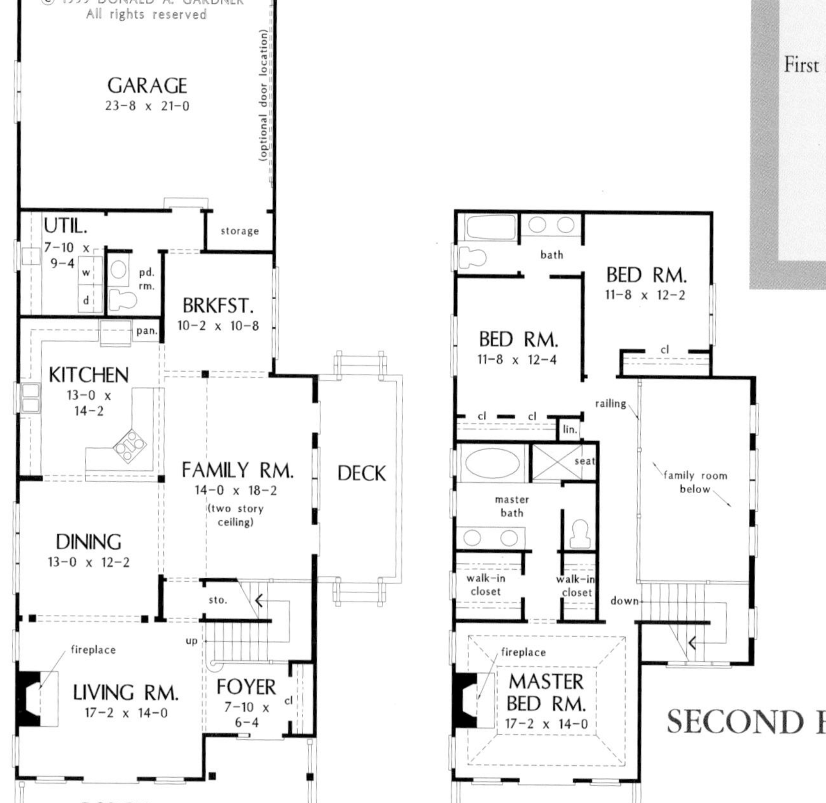
© 1999 DONALD A. GARDNER
All rights reserved
GARAGE
23-8 x 21-0
(optional door location)
UTIL.
7-10 x 9-4
w
d
pd. rm.
storage
BRKFST.
10-2 x 10-8
pan.
KITCHEN
13-0 x 14-2
FAMILY RM.
14-0 x 18-2
(two story ceiling)
DECK
DINING
13-0 x 12-2
sto.
up
fireplace
LIVING RM.
17-2 x 14-0
FOYER
7-10 x 6-4
cl
PORCH
bath
BED RM.
11-8 x 12-2
BED RM.
11-8 x 12-4
cl
cl
cl
railing
lin.
seat
family room below
master bath
walk-in closet
walk-in closet
down
fireplace
MASTER BED RM.
17-2 x 14-0
PORCH

SECOND FLOOR

SHADY SPOTS

Anyone who's lived in the country can tell you a critter is a simplified term for creature. You can sit on the deck and watch critters of all kinds: chipmunks, squirrels and rabbits.

SECOND FLOOR

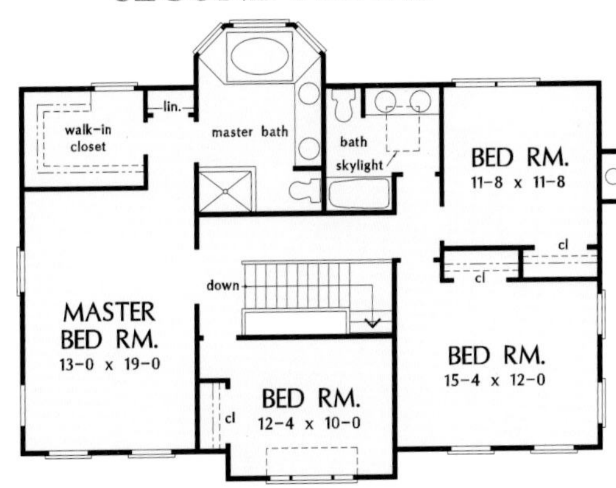
walk-in closet
lin.
master bath
bath
skylight
BED RM.
11-8 x 11-8
cl
cl
down
MASTER
BED RM.
13-0 x 19-0
BED RM.
12-4 x 10-0
cl
BED RM.
15-4 x 12-0

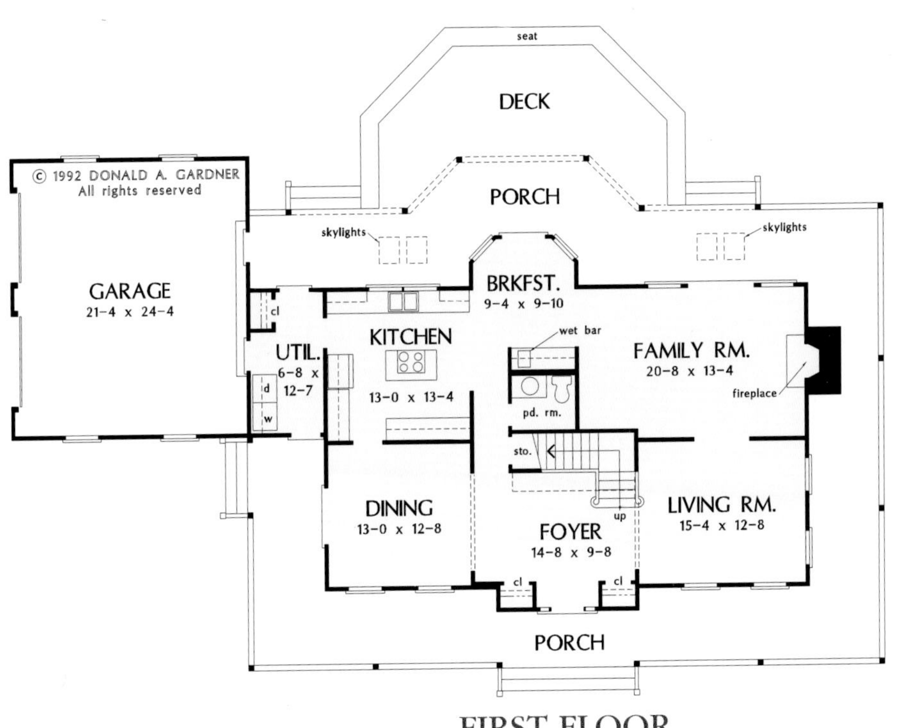
seat
DECK
© 1992 DONALD A. GARDNER
All rights reserved
PORCH
skylights
skylights
GARAGE
21-4 x 24-4
BRKFST.
9-4 x 9-10
cl
UTIL.
6-8 x
12-7
d
w
KITCHEN
13-0 x 13-4
wet bar
FAMILY RM.
20-8 x 13-4
fireplace
pd. rm.
sto.
DINING
13-0 x 12-8
up
FOYER
14-8 x 9-8
LIVING RM.
15-4 x 12-8
cl
cl
PORCH

FIRST FLOOR

DPCCH-261
The Warrenton

Total living: 2561 s.f.

First Floor: 1357 s.f. • Second Floor: 1204 s.f.

4 Bedrooms, 2-1/2 Baths

Foundation: Crawlspace

Width: 80' • Depth: 45'9"

Price Category: E

FLOOR PLANS INDEX

PLAN NAME	PLAN #	PAGE
The Alden	957	160
The Altamont	377	56
The Ammons	354	88
The Applemoor	970	30
The Arbordale	452	12
The Azalea Crossing	849	122
The Bakersfield	965	76
The Beaufort	221	96
The Beckett	357	158
The Beechwood	485	82
The Belhamy	348	117
The Braidwood	893	118
The Brentwood	998	108
The Burgess	290	70
The Calhoun	392	18
The Cedar Creek	959	74
The Cherryvale	533	40
The Colridge	1012	94
The Coltraine	966	138
The Coventry	754	89
The Darlington	944	157
The Dayton	1008	32
The Dobbins	370	66
The Edgefield	199	49
The Edgewater	1009	152
The Edisto	764	45
The Farmington	158	163
The Fayette	954	104
The Fenwicke	823	123
The Fernley	980	24
The Fitzgerald	1018	102
The Forrester	306	14
The Galveston	941	36
The Gentry	977	68
The Georgetown	393	100
The Gillespie	992	106
The Harbour Oak	467	81
The Heartland	945	62
The Heywood	991	72
The Hepplewhite	951	41
The Hickory Ridge	916	130
The Jamestowne	828	20
The Jonesboro	983	78
The Juniper	704	46
The Kyler	978	64
The Larson	360	54
The Laycrest	995	28
The Lewisville	912	43
The Liberty Hill	414	60
The Lochaven	955	90

FLOOR PLANS INDEX

Prints – What's in a Set?

Each set of Donald A. Gardner plans is a collection of drawings (including components such as floor plans, dimensions, cross sections and elevations) that show you exactly how your house is to be built. Most of our plan packages include:

COVER SHEET

An artist's rendering of the exterior of the house shows you approximately how the house will look when built and landscaped.

FOUNDATION PLAN

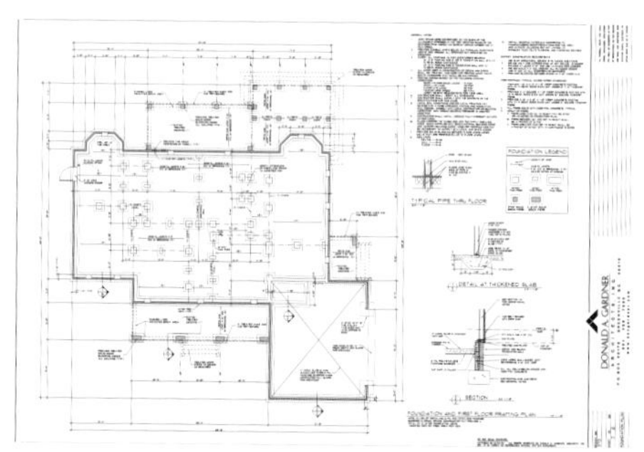

This sheet gives the foundation layout, including support walls, excavated and unexcavated areas, if any, and foundation notes. If the foundation is basement rather than monolithic, the plan shows footing and details.

DETAILED FLOOR PLANS

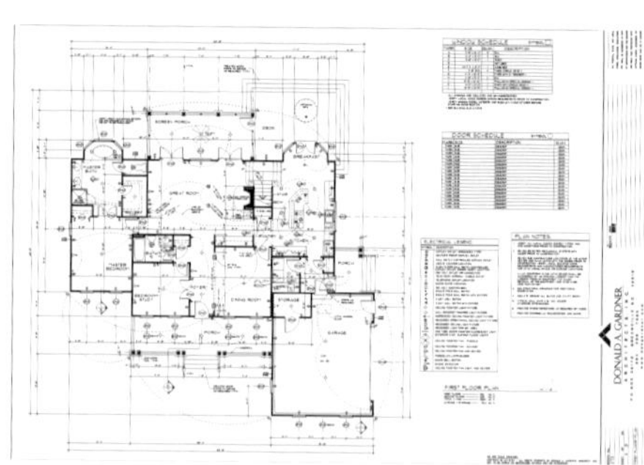

These plans show the layout of each floor of the house. Rooms and interior spaces are carefully dimensioned and keys are given for cross-section details provided later in the plans, as well as window and door size callouts. These plans also show the location of kitchen appliances and bathroom fixtures, as well as suggested locations for electrical fixtures, switches and outlets.

BLUEPRINTS

INTERIOR ELEVATIONS/ROOF PLAN

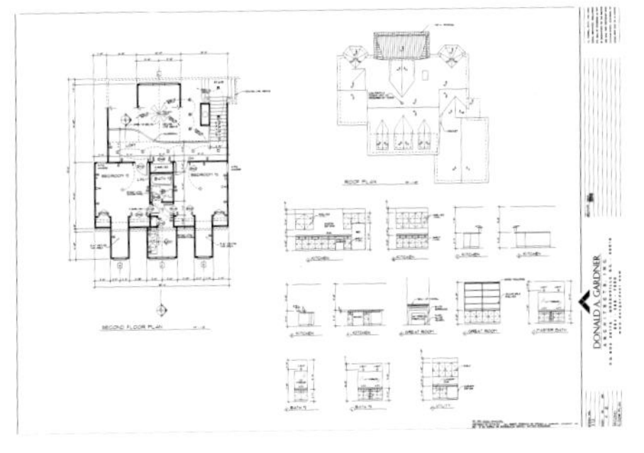

These drawings show the specific details and design of cabinets, utility rooms, fireplaces, bookcases, built-in units and other special interior features depending on the nature and complexity of the item. The roof plan shows the overall layout and necessary details for roof construction. If trusses are used, we suggest using a local truss manufacturer to design your trusses to comply with local codes and regulations.

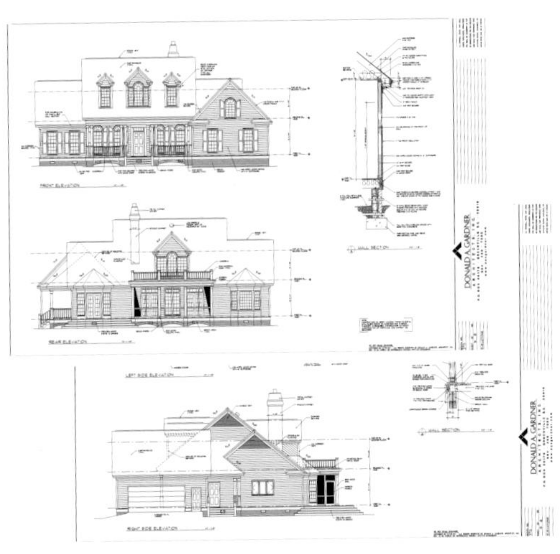

EXTERIOR ELEVATIONS/WALL SECTIONS

Included are front, rear, left and right sides of the house. Exterior materials, details and measurements are also given. This sheet also shows details of the house from the roof to the foundation. This section specifies the home's construction, insulation, flooring and roofing details.

CROSS-SECTION DETAILS

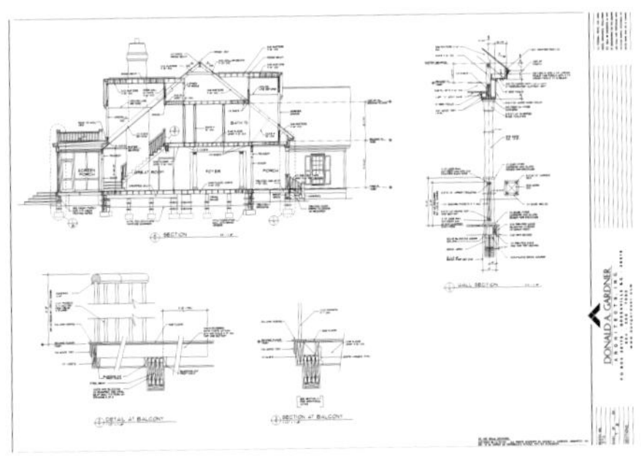

Important changes in floor, ceiling and roof heights or the relationship of one level to another are called out. Also shown, when applicable, are exterior details such as railing and banding.

STRUCTURAL PLAN

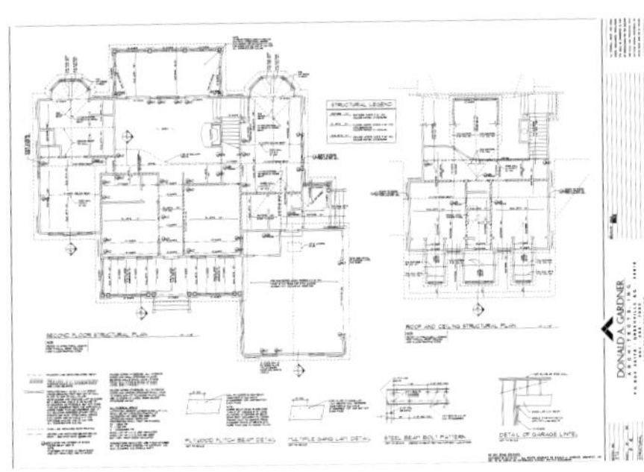

This sheet gives the overall layout and necessary details for the ceiling, second floor framing (if applicable) and roof construction.

ORDER FORM

Before You Order

QUICK TURNAROUND

Because you are placing your order directly, we can ship plans to you quickly. If your order is placed Monday through Friday before 11 a.m. EST, we can usually have your plans to you the next business day. Some restrictions may apply. **We cannot ship to a post office box**; please provide a physical street address.

OUR EXCHANGE POLICY

Since our blueprints are printed especially for you at the time you place your order, we cannot accept any returns. If, for some reason, you find that the plan that you purchased does not meet your needs, then you may exchange that plan for another plan in our collection, but all exchanges must be pre-approved by the Customer Service department. We allow you 60 days from the time of purchase to make an exchange. All sets must be returned prior to the exchange taking place. At the time of the exchange, you will be charged a processing fee of 20 percent of the total amount of the original order plus the difference in price between the plans (if applicable) and the cost to ship the new plans to you. Vellums cannot be exchanged. All sets must be approved and authorization given before the exchange can take place. Please call our Customer Service department if you have any questions.

LOCAL BUILDING CODES AND ZONING REQUIREMENTS

Our plans are designed to meet or exceed national building standards. Because of the great differences in geography and climate, each state, county and municipality has its own building codes and zoning requirements. Your plan may need to be modified to comply with local requirements regarding snow loads, energy codes, soil and seismic conditions and a wide range of other matters. Prior to using plans ordered from us, we strongly advise that you consult a local building official.

ARCHITECTURE AND ENGINEERING SEALS

Some cities and states are now requiring that a licensed architect or engineer review and approve any set of building documents prior to construction. This is due to concerns over energy costs, safety, structural integrity and other factors. Prior to applying for a building permit or the start of actual construction, we strongly advise that you consult your local building official who can tell you if such a review is required.

DISCLAIMER

We have put substantial care and effort into the creation of our plans. We authorize the use of our plans on the express condition that you strictly comply with all local building codes, zoning requirements and other applicable laws, regulations and ordinances. However, because we cannot provide on-site consultation, supervision or control over actual construction, and because of the great variance in local building requirements, building practices and soil, seismic, weather and other conditions, WE CANNOT MAKE ANY WARRANTY, EXPRESS OR IMPLIED, WITH RESPECT TO THE CONTENT OR USE OF OUR PRINTS OR VELLUMS, INCLUDING BUT NOT LIMITED TO ANY WARRANTY OF MERCHANTABILITY OR OF FITNESS FOR A PARTICULAR PURPOSE.
Please Note: Floor plans are not construction documents and are subject to change. Renderings are artists' concept only.

HOW MANY PRINTS WILL YOU NEED?

We offer a single set of prints so that you can study and plan your dream home in detail. However, you cannot build from this package. One set of blueprints is marked "NOT FOR CONSTRUCTION." If you are planning to get estimates from a contractor or subcontractor, or if you are planning to build immediately, you will need more sets. A single set or "study set" can be upgraded to a larger set package for a nominal fee.

Set packages are less expensive. Make sure you order enough to satisfy all your requirements. Sometimes changes are needed to a plan; in that case we offer vellums that are erasable and reproducible so changes can be made directly to the plans. Vellums are the only set that can be reproduced; it is illegal to copy prints. The following checklist will help determine how many sets you will need:

PLAN CHECKLIST

_____ **Owner (one set for notes, one for file)**

_____ **Builder (generally requires at least three sets; one as a legal document, one for inspections and at least one to give subcontractors)**

_____ **Local Building Department (often requires two sets)**

_____ **Mortgage Lender (usually one set for a conventional loan; three sets for FHA or VA loans)**

_____ **Total Number of Sets**

IGNORING COPYRIGHT LAWS CAN BE A

$1,000,000 Mistake!

Recent changes in the US copyright laws allow for statutory penalties of up to $150,000 per incident for copyright infringement involving any of the copyrighted plans found in this publication. The law can be confusing. So, for your own protection, take the time to understand what you cannot do when it comes to home plans.

What You Can't Do!

- **You Cannot Duplicate Home Plans.**
- **You Cannot Copy Any Part Of A Home Plan To Create Another.**
- **You Cannot Build A Home Without Buying A Blueprint Or License.**
- **You Cannot Build A Home From A Study Set. Study Sets Do Not Include Licenses.**

How To Order

Donald A. Gardner Architects, Inc.
150 Executive Center Drive, Ste. 215
Greenville, SC 29615
1-800-388-7580
www.classiccountryhomes.com

Additional Items

Blueprints (per set)...$ 60.00
Full Reverse Blueprints...$125.00

Materials List

Plan Categories A - E ....$ 65.00
Plan Category F - L...$ 75.00

Basement Plans

Plan Categories A - C $225.00
Plan Categories D - E $250.00
Plan Category F - L...$275.00

11" x 17" Color Front Perspective Rendering* $100.00
Specification Outline* ....$ 15.00
*Call for availability

Shipping & Handling

Overnight ....$ 40.00
Priority Overnight...$ 50.00
2nd Day...$ 30.00
Ground ....$ 18.00
Saturday (If available) ....$ 50.00
International Delivery (Please call for prices & availability.)

PLAN PRICE SCHEDULE

	1 Study Set	4 Sets	8 Sets	Vellum
A	$455	$505	$555	$710
B	$500	$550	$600	$775
C	$545	$595	$645	$840
D	$590	$640	$690	$905
E	$635	$685	$735	$970
F	$680	$730	$780	$1035
G	$755	$805	$855	$1115
H	$830	$880	$930	$1195
I	$930	$980	$1030	$1295
J	$1030	$1080	$1130	$1395
K	$1130	$1180	$1230	$1495
L	$1230	$1280	$1330	$1595

➤*Prices subject to change without notice.*

ORDER FORM

Order Form

Plan Number ____________

☐ 1-set (study only) ....$__________
☐ 4-set building package ....$__________
☐ 8-set building package ....$__________
☐ 1-set of reproducible vellums ....$__________

___ Additional Identical Plans @ $60 each $__________
___ Full Reverse Plans @ $125 each $__________
___ Basement Plans (See pricing above) $__________

Sub-Total $__________
Shipping and Handling $__________
Sales Tax (SC Res.) 5% $__________

Total $__________

Check one: ☐Visa ☐MasterCard ☐AmEx ☐Discover
Credit Card Number ____________________
Expiration Date ____________________
Signature ____________________

Name ____________________
Company ____________________
Street ____________________
City ______________ State____ Zip ________
Daytime Telephone Number (_____) __________
Check one:
☐ Consumer ☐Builder ☐Developer

Country means room to roam, hidden spaces, framing views and shady spots. It's rejoicing every spring with the chirping of baby birds, an icy glass of lemonade on a hot summer afternoon, being toasty warm under a thick quilt on those cool autumn days and smelling the crisp winter air mingle with a touch of smoke from a wood-burning fireplace. Country is about turning a house into a home, and you do that with things you love, especially family and friends. So thank you for visiting our homes and please come back to see us. You are welcome here anytime. ❧

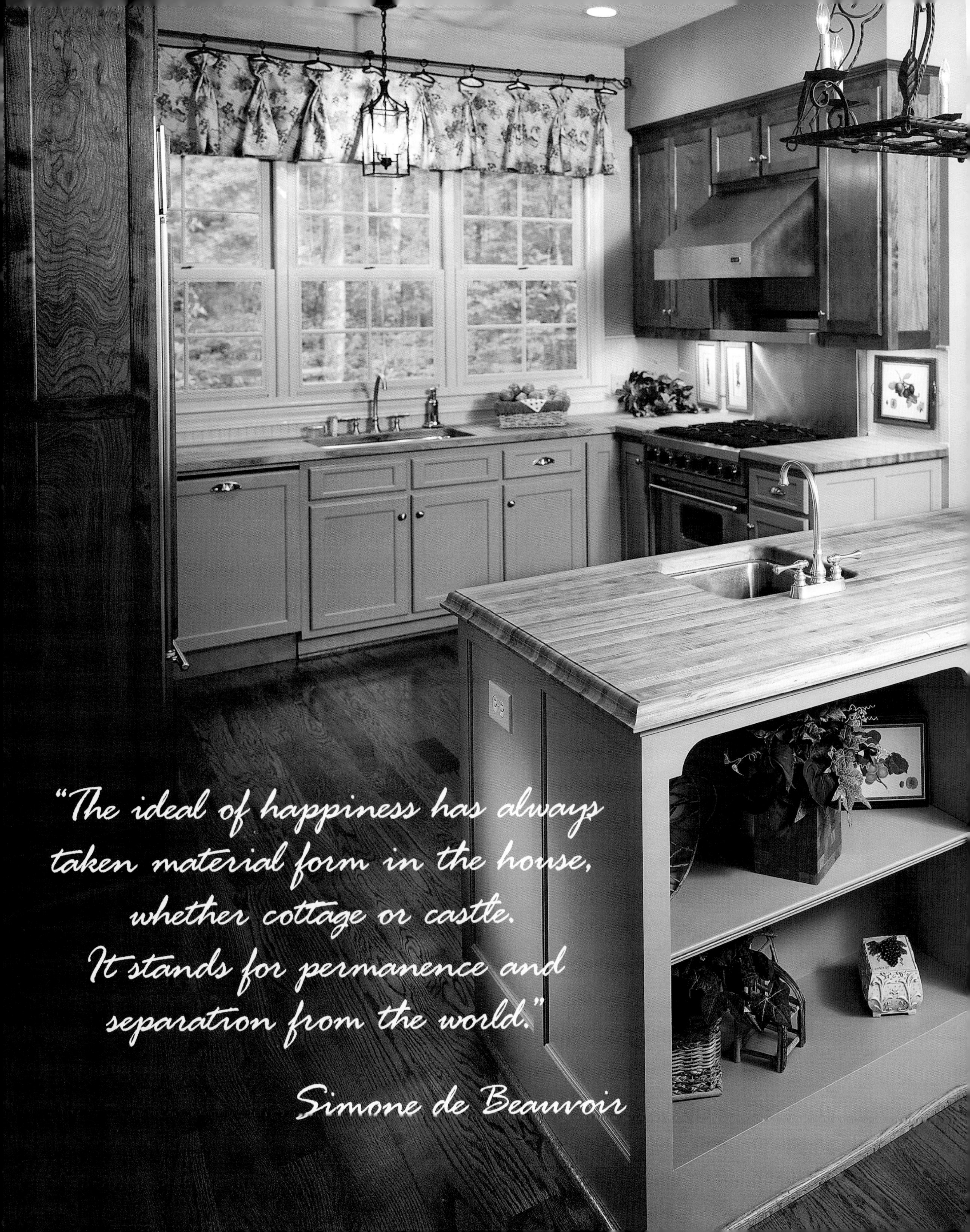
"The ideal of happiness has always
taken material form in the house,
whether cottage or castle.
It stands for permanence and
separation from the world."
Simone de Beauvoir

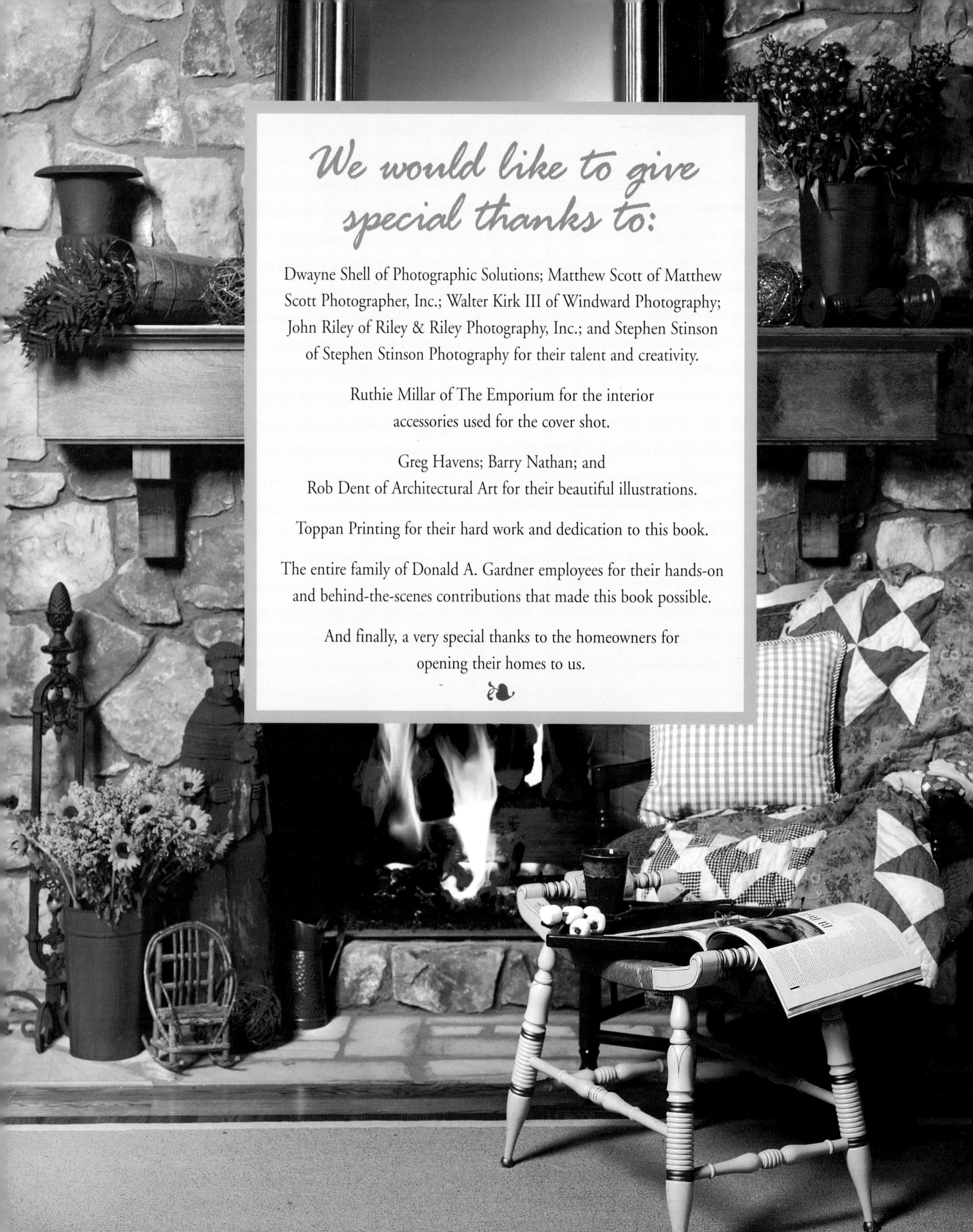

We would like to give special thanks to:

Dwayne Shell of Photographic Solutions; Matthew Scott of Matthew Scott Photographer, Inc.; Walter Kirk III of Windward Photography; John Riley of Riley & Riley Photography, Inc.; and Stephen Stinson of Stephen Stinson Photography for their talent and creativity.

Ruthie Millar of The Emporium for the interior accessories used for the cover shot.

Greg Havens; Barry Nathan; and Rob Dent of Architectural Art for their beautiful illustrations.

Toppan Printing for their hard work and dedication to this book.

The entire family of Donald A. Gardner employees for their hands-on and behind-the-scenes contributions that made this book possible.

And finally, a very special thanks to the homeowners for opening their homes to us.